1995 Edition
THE MAKING OF THE
TREK FILMS

Edited By Edward Gross

CONTRIBUTING WRITERS
Mark A. Altman
Kay Anderson
Dennis Fischer
Edward Gross
Jean-Marc Lofficier
Randy Lofficier
Ron Magid
Wendy Rathbone
Marc Shapiro
Sheldon Teitelbaum

BﬂXTREE

First Published in the UK 1995
by BOXTREE LIMITED, Broadwall House,
21 Broadwall, London SE1 9PL

The Making of the Trek Films: 1995 Edition first published by Image Publishing of New York

2 4 6 8 10 9 7 5 3 1

This publication is not licensed by, nor is Image Publishing or Boxtree Ltd affiliated with, Paramount
Pictures. This is a scholarly work intended to explore the evolution of the *Star Trek* films.

No photos appearing in this book are copyright Paramount Pictures

Book design by Paul Nicosia

Cover photo: *Star Trek: The Motion Picture* photo © copyright G. Trindl/Shooting Star
Star Trek: The Next Generation photo © copyright David Strick/Onyx

Back Cover photo © copyright Alan Levenson/Onyx

Printed in England by Redwood Books, Wiltshire

A Catalogue entry for this book is available from The British Library

ISBN: 0 7522 0973 6

Table of Contents

An Introduction

As these words are being written, the seventh *Star Trek* feature film, *Generations*, is three weeks away from reaching theatres, and it's an historic moment that brings together two generations of the late Gene Roddenberry's universe. And as this film proves, *Star Trek* has grown from a fairly obscure television series in the late '60s into something that fulfills the criteria for mythology: endurance.

From the cancellation of the TV show in 1969 to the appearance of the first movie in 1979, there was almost no input from the creators of the show. Yet the *Star Trek* universe lived on in the hearts and minds of its fans, and the phenomenon continued to grow. Now we have reached the point where there have been a total of six films featuring the original cast, nearly 200 episodes of the syndicated *Star Trek: The Next Generation*, at least three seasons of *Star Trek: Deep Space Nine* and a third spin-off, *Star Trek: Voyager* which debuted in early '95.

In the thirty years since the filming of the first pilot, "The Cage," through the release of *Generations*, *Star Trek* has arisen from its own ashes so many times as to make the Phoenix take notice. It survived a failed pilot, cancellation by NBC after three seasons, two years of an animated series, numerous aborted movie attempts throughout the '70s and the *Star Trek II* series, which was abandoned in favor of the first feature film one week before production was scheduled to commence. From there the franchise has continually metamorphosed and developed to the point where we are today.

This version of *The Making of the Trek Films* is our third edition, and has been completely revised and updated to include in-depth coverage of both *Star Trek VI: The Undiscovered Country* and *Generations*, the latter of which will undoubtedly inspire a new series of films featuring *The Next Generation*.

While *Star Trek: The Motion Picture* proclaimed that "the human adventure is just beginning," the word is that *Generations* will represent the final voyage of any members of the original starship Enterprise. A final goodbye. The adventures may have come to an end, but the memories endure.

Part of me wants to sign off with live long and prosper, but that would be a cliché.

Engage!

Edward Gross
November, 1994

Star Trek:
The Motion Picture

Paramount had never ceased to vacillate about the future of *Star Trek*, always fearful the phenomenon would abruptly end and leave them to foot the bill for an ill-advised "reunion" film or series. It wasn't until the back-to-back sucess of *Star Wars* and *Close Encounters of the Third Kind* that the studio realized there was an insatiable appetite for genre fare, thus the scuttling of the *Star Trek II* series one week before production was to commence.

When *Star Trek: The Motion Picture* was announced, Paramount Pictures envisioned it as a modestly-budgeted $15 million film. At a cost of about $5 million more than George Lucas had spent on *Star Wars*, it was imagined that the film could compete with that special effects extravaganza and win the battle hands down. Wrong! Conflicting visions, a special effects debacle that had the production begin with one F/X house then changing to others in mid-stream, and a scripting nightmare that resulted in much of the movie being shot without a completed third act, all combined to bloat the budget to $44 million, a budget only surpassed (at that time) by Twentieth Century Fox's *Cleopatra* and a Soviet screen version of *War and Peace*. Ironically, *Star Trek: The Motion Picture* reached theatre screens on December 7, 1979 — Pearl Harbor day. Based on the universal criticism it received, it appeared the film's release date was prophetic.

Star Trek: The Motion Picture was savaged by just about everyone, from reviewers to moviegoers drawn in by ten years worth of hype. The fans themselves were disappointed, though they were so desperate for *any Star Trek* that they turned the movie into a $175 million success and labored to have over an hour of truncated footage restored to a re-release in the hopes it would buoy the film. Although Paramount rejected the notion of a re-release in 70mm (the original hadn't been released in 70mm since the final answer print had only been completed several days before the release date), they did include some deleted footage in the film's video

release—another unprecedented sucess which helped launch the fledgling home video market.

David Gerrold, an integral part of the creation of the *Star Trek* spin-off *The Next Generation*, notes, "The fans had come off this two year high with *Star Wars* and the audience wanted more *Star Wars*, but there wasn't any more. So they went to see *Star Trek* and they were hungering for more, so *Star Trek* benefitted from the *Star Wars* phenomenon. They went and they saw it over and over again, but it was embarrassing to watch the fans because they were all apologists for this picture: 'Well, it's not that bad. It's a different kind of *Star Trek*.' Instead of really just acknowledging that it was a bad movie, they tried to explain that it was wonderful and you were an idiot for not understanding it. It was wonderful to watch them fuck their minds over to explain away a bad movie. The truth was that there was this movie that they wanted to love and they were so disappointed, but they wouldn't dare say that they were disappointed."

In fact, even *Star Trek*'s creator Gene Roddenberry, who had shepherded the film through production and been responsible for the endless rewrites that typified the shoot, couldn't defend the film from its detractors. Sitting next to Roddenberry on a plane heading towards the film's glamorous premiere in Washington D.C., Walter Koenig, who hadn't seen the movie, recalls querying the producer about the final product.

"Gene had just seen the cut and it was literally still wet," said Koenig. "I said 'What do you think of the picture?' He answered, 'It's a good picture.' It was a death knell, as soon as he said that I knew it wasn't going to work. He didn't put it down. He didn't denigrate it, but I heard it in his voice. I absolutely knew. Then you hope against hope that it's going to be good and you see the limousines and the red carpets and the spotlights. Then you see those first five minutes of the film with the music and you see V'ger and the destruction it causes. I got very excited but shortly thereafter I began to become aware of time; that time was passing. That I wasn't involved in the picture. I was sitting in the audience and my heart sank and sank and

sank, and I knew, ultimately, it was not a good film. I had no way of knowing what the critics would do. It was devastating, particularly *The Washington Post*, the first one that we saw the next day. It was the only time in my life that I thanked God for the relative anonymity that I had on *Star Trek*, because I was not mentioned in any way, shape or form.

"There are myriad reasons for the lack of success, including setting a release date for the picture in advance," Koenig adds. "According to Gene he fought that, because it really did back him into a corner and made the picture that much more expensive. They had to go on double time, golden time, and at one point they were shooting around the clock in post production. So I guess it was a cursed project from the start. You didn't begin it the way it should have begun."

He points out that halfway through production the film's stars, William Shatner and Leonard Nimoy, were contractually granted script approval. "We didn't have a finished screenplay and know exactly where we were going with it," says Koenig. "And then halfway through the picture the clause on Bill and Leonard's contracts kicked in that they had dialogue and story approval if the picture went beyond so many weeks. So those meetings in the morning between Gene Roddenberry, [writer] Harold Livingston, [associate producer] Jon Povill and [then Paramount executive] Jeffrey Katzenberg and Bill and Leonard and Bob Wise were seven people deciding what they were going to shoot that day and many with vested interests that it would be shot a certain way."

The auteur theory notwithstanding, the individual who was saddled with the blame for *Star Trek: The Motion Picture*'s critical savaging was not its director, but producer/writer Gene Roddenberry who, although allowed to keep an office on the Paramount lot following the film's release, was considered a pariah and the prime reason that the film had spiralled overbudget and resulted in an aesthetically abysmal enterprise.

Yet when the film was originally announced, there was a great deal of enthusiasm and belief that the filmmakers

The Human Adventure Is Just Beginning.

STAR TREK
THE MOTION PICTURE ™

The ad campaign that heralded the return of Star Trek in the form of The Motion Picture (ad slick courtesy United Artists Theatres)

would be creating a modern *2,001*.

■ The Press Conference

"The fans have supported us and consistently written us to pull our act together," announced former Paramount President Michael Eisner to the press on March 28, 1978.

Apparently the studio had, for on that day Eisner made the announcement that production would soon begin on the long-awaited *Star Trek: The Motion Picture*, featuring the entire original cast, with series creator Gene Roddenberry serving as executive producer and Robert Wise handling the directorial chores. After 10 long years, the dream was about to become reality.

Highlights of the press conference, reportedly the largest since Cecil B. DeMille announced production of *The Ten Commandments*, included:

William Shatner on returning to the role of Captain James T. Kirk: "I somehow always felt that we would be back together. Regardless of what I was doing, or where my career was taking me at the moment, I knew Captain Kirk was *not* behind me. He still would be very important in my future life—and work....I think Spencer Tracy said it best—'You take a deep breath and say the words.' Of course you have to have some years of experience to know how to say the words and suck in your breath. An actor brings to a role not only the concept of the character but his own basic personality, things that he is, and both Leonard and myself have changed over the years, to a degree at any rate, and we will bring that degree of change inadvertently to the role we recreate."

One question on the mind of the press was why Leonard Nimoy had seemed so reluctant to return to the fold.

"We've had a long and complicated relationship, Paramount and myself, for the last couple of years," Nimoy explained, "and probably the thing that took the most time was the fact that the mail service between here and Vulcan is still pretty slow. It's not really a matter of reluctance. We had a lot of details to work out. There have been

Kirk's generation meets their first supposed successors. From top left: Leonard Nimoy, DeForest Kelley, Stephen Collins, Persis Khambatta and William Shatner (sitting) (photo copyright ©1994 Globe Photos)

periods of time when the *Star Trek* project was moving forward and I was not available. For example, last summer we had come to what I felt was an understanding about doing the movie. I went off to do *Equus* on Broadway. During that period of time, the concept changed to a TV series. It was difficult then to get together because there was a question of availability. When the project turned around and I was available again, we started talking immediately. It has been complicated; it has been time consuming. But there was never a question of

reluctance to be involved in *Star Trek* on my part. I've always felt totally comfortable about being identified with *Star Trek*, and being identified with the Spock character. It has exploded my life in a very positive way. The Spock character has always been part of my life. I have never tried in any way to reject that. I'm very proud of the fact that I'm associated with the character. And I look forward to playing the character because I certainly wouldn't want either one of two things—anybody else playing it, or *Star Trek* happening without it."

One thing that Gene Roddenberry emphasized at the time was that the storyline of the film, like so many of the episodes, would bring with it a powerful message.

"It definitely will," he emphasized, "and this is one reason I was so pleased that Bob Wise joined us in the production, because he feels the same way about this motion picture. I think all good stories have something to say, and without anyone getting on a soapbox at any time in this film, we will be talking about something that we think is very important."

■ A Wise Move

"I thought it was time," explains Robert Wise in terms of his reason for accepting the directorial reins of *Star Trek: The Motion Picture*. "I have always been intrigued by science fiction, even though I have only done two other films in the genre, and I thought it was time that I did a science fiction picture that took place in space. Both my my other ones were earth-bound. In *The Day the Earth Stood Still* we had a visitor from outer space, coming in a spaceship....that really intrigued me more than anything else. So I was glad to have a chance to explore this further. I liked the idea of doing *Star Trek* from the beginning, the quality of it....It was really the fascination and the desire to do a film which dealt with the experience of being in space."

Wise admits that he was not familiar with the *Star Trek* universe before he accepted the picture. "Of course I knew of it," he clarifies, "but I had not become a Trekkie when the TV series had first come out and I had only seen one or two segments, which I thought were alright—but I didn't get hooked on it. After the President of Paramount asked me if I would be interested in considering directing the movie, I said, 'Well, I just don't know. I'll have to read the script, of course, and I would have to see several more of the TV segments.' I had to get familiar with what it was and what had caused it to become so immensely popular. So that's what happened: I read the script and I saw about a dozen episodes of the series so I could become familiar with it, and make

my own judgement."

The impression is that when Wise joined the production, he was saddled with the costumes and sets designed for the *Star Trek II* series.

"Let me be precise about a few things," he emphasizes. "Yes, the casting was practically all done because it was the characters of the series. The only person that I was involved with in casting was Stephen Collins who played Decker, because even Persis Khambatta had been set. They had the original team of special effects men [Robert Abel and Associates] already at work and a numbers of the sets were already done, but there is one area that I did have influence on: I upgraded the sets considerably from what they had originally built. What you saw in the film is not at all what I came on to. We did a lot of improvements on the bridge set, we threw away their corridors and built those you saw; we redesigned the engine room entirely—in fact, there was nothing left of the original engine room, just the super structure. So the interior of the ship was changed considerably according to my indications.

"I [also] had as much influence on the script as I possibly could," he adds. "It was one of those situations where we started with an incomplete script—we knew the story of course, but the actual final parts of the script were being worked on constantly as we were shooting. I think that when we actually started in early 1978 we only had the first act of the script written. From there on the second and third act we were changing and rewriting. I had some influence on the first act as it went. I tried to have as much as I could on the rest of the film, but it is a very sloppy way to make a film by any means."

Given his track record, it's not surprising that Robert Wise is used to autonomy on his films, yet in the case of *Star Trek* he was in the position of working closely with the concept's creator, Gene Roddenberry, which, he notes, "was comparatively easy. Of course, as much as producers and directors are separate entities, you always have little conflicts at times but, by and large, it was fine. When I came on after being asked to do the film, I said, 'What about Mr. Roddenberry? Because it's his baby,' and

Whether justified or not, Great Bird of the Galaxy took the blame for the fiasco that was Star Trek: The Motion Picture (photo copyright ©1994 Albert Ortega).

they said, 'Well, you'll have to work it up.' So Gene and I talked at some length about how we could work together, how he and I saw the whole thing. We came to reach a working agreement about halfway in our positions and I think we functioned pretty well on that level."

For his part, Roddenberry told journalist Tom Rogers that in terms of having control, he had "as much as I have the personality to take over. But more is not always more in making a movie. Making movies is quite different than making a television show. In television, I had directors that came and went, different directors every week. Naturally I had to assume a lot of control over the initial show because it was my idea, and I wanted all of the directors to be directing the same Mr. Spock next week as they directed last week. In a movie, however, which is a director's medium, I can hardly get a director of the quality and ability of a Robert Wise and then walk in and say, 'Listen, I want you to do everything exactly as I tell you.' When you bring in Robert Wise, you're bringing in his talent, his ability of wide-screen movies. There's a wonderful partnership between he and I, rather than one or the other trying to seize more control.

"There are a lot of places we disagree," he continued, "but in a friendly, professional way. My taste for costumes was a little different than his, but in the end I went with his taste because he was the man responsible for creating the whole visual image. If it had been more than just a question of taste, if I had thought the costumes violated *Star Trek* format, then we would have probably had a very serious fight. But we didn't, because it was just a question of taste. There are some places where he wanted to do some things, I can't remember an example right now, and I would say, 'Bob, the *Star Trek* format has always been this. I don't want to lock you into format, but let's not change unless we have some value that makes the change worthwhile.'"

In this respect, Robert Wise was in the unusual position of not only working in a format familiar to the audience but with a cast that had better knowledge of the characters and film than even he had.

"I should tell you a story first," laughs Wise. "After Paramount finally signed everybody, they had a big publicity party for the press and they set up a large table with Roddenberry, all the cast, etc. When my turn came to speak, I said, 'You know, I'm the alien here,' because I was the only one who hardly knew anything of *Star Trek*. They all knew more than I did. But it worked out very well. They're all very good actors, very professional. There were some very pleasant moments with all the actors on the set because I found that they really loved their characters and always looked for ways of improving their roles, like 'So and so wouldn't say it like that.' At the same time, they were never pushy or overly tempted to be demanding. I found all of them, and particularly Bill and Leonard, to be professional and very good actors."

Unlike his other genre efforts, *The Day the Earth Stood Still* and *The Andromeda Strain*, *Star Trek: The Motion Picture* represented an extremely complex shoot due to the elaborate special effects.

"Control was much simpler [back] then," sighs Wise. "In *Star Trek* all of this was very elaborate; very, very difficult because I had so much to deal with

which was not even done yet. Scenes in which my actor had to play and react to that screen and I had nothing to show them on the screen. All that came in months later. The best I ever had for them to react to was a projection of a sketch or a picture of what the effects men were planning to achieve. That's all I had for them. I had to remind them of what was going on in terms of the action, to describe the best I could from the script and from my own ideas of the sketch and what they were supposed to be looking at. It takes some very professional actors to respond to something like that, and that made it very difficult—in fact, it was perhaps the most difficult part of the film. And then we had, of course, the big problem of having to change the special effects people after a year.

"I don't like to dig too much into this," he continues. "I want simply to say that they were very creative people and they had excellent ideas, but the big concern that we had was whether they would be able to execute all of the effects in time so the film would be ready for its release of December 7th, which was absolutely imperative. That was what made us decide to change. It wasn't lack of creativeness or abilities or anything like that. They were very good, had very good ideas, but I don't think they were equipped yet to execute fast enough such a big amount of very sophisticated effects. That was a giant picture in terms of effects and work involved."

Of the F/X debacle, Roddenberry added, "It became obvious that they were not going to be able to deliver. Where that trouble was I don't care to discuss, whether it was their management or what. Enough said, they were unable to deliver, it was obviously they could not and the changes began."

One of the strongest criticisms levelled against the film was the fact that the interpersonal relationships—which were so integral to the success of the original *Star Trek*—were given a back seat to the F/X.

"It [wasn't as] if somebody say down at the beginning and said, 'Listen, we want to get a lot more special effects.' It was not a deliberate move to shift the emphasis from one area to another," Wise emphasises. "That was really because of the story. That was the script, or the story we had to tell, and we didn't

try to put more special effects in it. I didn't try. None of us tried. We had people reacting to things that were happening on the screen, so we had to show these things. If there is a valid criticism coming from those Trekkies who really love these characters with all their heart, there still wasn't anything we could do about it. We would have had to have a totally different story."

One would imagine that Wise wishes that they had.

■ The Script's The Thing

Star Trek creator Gene Roddenberry often attributed the success of the series to the fact that it showed man transcending his intolerance for his fellow man; that we as a species had moved beyond our petty differences which have, for so long, separated us, and achieved a peace amongst ourselves and the stars.

Unfortunately, what was true for a network television series and the motion picture it inspired, was not true for the real-life behind the scenes relationships which brought the magic to life. This has never been more true than in the writing of *Star Trek: The Motion Picture*.

The film began as a two-hour episode of the abandoned *Star Trek II* television series. The plot of "In Thy Image" had been derived from a Roddenberry-written premise for *Genesis II* entitled "Robot's Return," in which a NASA space probe returns to Earth seekings its creator.

Famed science fiction writer Alan Dean Foster explained, "When they were thinking of the *Star Trek II* TV series, a number of writers were called in to submit treatments for hour-long episodes. Roddenberry got in touch with me based on the *Star Trek Log* series I had done for Ballantine Books, and he said that he felt I was comfortable with the *Star Trek* universe and comfortable and familiar with the characters. So I submitted three story ideas. One of them was based on a page and a half of his notes on something called 'Robot's Return.' He thought that could be developed and wanted to see what I could do with it.

"After my treatment based on Roddenberry's page was handed in," he continued, "it was decided to open the new series with a two-hour movie for TV, which is fairly standard procedure when they can manage it for dramatic series, and it was decided that my treatment of the ones they had at hand would be the best suited to carry two hours. At least that's what I heard. I went home and developed a 32-page outline."

That outline, like "Robot's Return," dealt with an old space probe that had achieved consciousness and was now returning to Earth to join with its creator. While the story worked quite well as far as the show's production team was concerned, there was no intention of having Foster write the actual teleplay.

Harold Livingston, co-producer of the series, said, "Alan Dean Foster was a protege of Gene's and he was brought in to me to write something. So I wanted to see something he had written, and he brought me two screenplays which I thought were terrible, and I didn't want him to write. I just didn't think he was right for the job. This was obviously a very subjective judgement, but that's what they're paying me for. They either rely on my judgement or they get someone else.

"I made a deal with Alan's agent that he would write a story and agree *not* to do the script. So he wrote a story which was this business of the old machine coming back to Earth and assuming a kind of life form. I didn't know that this had also been an episode of the original *Star Trek* ['The Changeling']. By the way, at this point we're starting to come to a production date as well. I then began to look for writers to turn the story into a script. I went through two or three weeks of talking to people and I couldn't find anybody that I liked. With five weeks to go, I decided I'd write it myself.

"So I sat down and for five weeks I wrote this script of 'In Thy Image.' I finished the first draft, delivered it to Gene and Gene said, 'God, it's good. You've done your job. Now just relax and I'll write the second draft.' He writes it in a week. Then he brought it in, gave it to us proudly in a bright orange cover, and there it is, 'In Thy Image,' by Gene

Roddenberry and Harold Livingston. He took first position. We all read it and I was appalled, and so was everyone else. There was [story editor] Jon Povill, [producer] Bob Goodwin, myself and Bob Collins, who was the director."

Added Collins, "Harold and I sat there and we asked each other which one of us was going to tell him that it wasn't quite right. Finally, I said 'Hell, I'm the director,' and walked out of the room."

Harold Livingston continued the scenario, "I said, 'I'll tell him.' I went in and I said, 'Gene, this doesn't work.' Well, his face dropped to his ankles. Then I got myself wound up and I told him why it didn't work, and I said, 'Why'd you do it? When something works, you don't piss in it to make it better!' In any case, he was pretty stubborn about this. He thought it was good and said, 'We'll give it to the front office.' Well, about three days later, we have a meeting in Michael Eisner's gigantic white office. We sat around this huge table. There was Roddenberry, myself, Eisner, Jeffrey Katzenberg, the head of television, Arthur Fellows; and a couple of other guys. Michael had the two scripts. 'In Thy Image' by me was in a brown cover, and Gene's version was in an orange cover. Michael had one script in one hand and one in the other, balancing them in his palms. And he said, 'Listen, this is the problem. This,' Gene's orange script, 'is television. This,' the brown script, 'is a movie. Frankly, it's a lot better.' Well, holy shit! Everybody was clearing their throats. The great man had had his feathers ruffled. Anyway, after some heated discussion, it was decided to let Collins write a third version using the best elements of both. So Collins did this after two or three weeks, and his was a total disaster.

"Along that time, Roddenberry and I really began to get at each other's throats. December came along and my contract was coming up. Before they could fire me, I quit. We had too many problems there. I just didn't think that Gene was a good writer. He, for his part I'm sure, considered me a total interloper. Who the hell am I to come in? I understand that, in fact I understood it, but I wanted to instill some literary value into these science fiction myths. He had

his own formula which worked. He was obviously saturated with science fiction. I think he knew a lot about a lot of things, generally, and he had a great following. Here I was getting on his nerves."

One undeniable contribution to the script that came from the rewrite, however, was Roddenberry's idea of having the probe, eventually called V'Ger (short for Voyager 6) release all its data into Will Decker. Livingston's conclusion, on the other hand, merely had the probe recognizing the positive qualities of man as a species and departing the galaxy.

"Robert Goodwin theorized that I just pissed away the ending because I was so disgusted with the situation," mused Livingston. "I think the truth is that I couldn't come up with an ending. I just couldn't do it. The problem was that we had an antagonist so omnipotent that to defeat it, or even communicate with it, or have any kind of relationship with it, made the concept of the story false. How the hell do we deal with this? On what level? Everything pretty much worked in the story until we got to the ending. We tried all kinds of approaches, including aesthetic, theological and philosophical. We didn't know what to do with the ending."

Jon Povill, on the other hand, did. "We knew we had to have a big special effects ending," he said. "The problem of what was going to happen at the end and why it was going to happen, was one that plagued the script from the very start. Then Gene came up with the idea of the machine dumping its data into Decker, with a light show of all the information it had accumulated. We were going to get all this amazing, incomprehensible stuff that V'Ger had accumulated in its travels across the universe, and, of course, nobody could come up with these images, so that didn't work. It was pretty much my contribution to say that the reason for what was happening was that this thing needed to go on to the next plane of existence; that it was transcending this dimension and going on to the next. It then became logical that the machine would need that human element to combine with. It was the only thing that could have made sense."

Upon quitting *Star Trek*, Livingston went to work at Aaron Spelling Productions, believing he was leaving the 23rd Century behind him. Under the guise of wanting to infuse the production with "fresh writer blood," Dennis Clark was hired just as the TV-movie became a theatrical film. From the writer's point of view, it was *not* a happy experience.

Clark explained, "I try never to bum-rap people. The problem with Gene is that his heart was never in the right place at the right time. It's a good heart, but he puts it aside at the wrong times. I was the subject of a practical joke from him. An awful one, and it was right at the beginning of the relationship and it set things off badly. Gene's a nice man, unless you give him some power.

"In all the time I've been writing," he elaborateed, "I've got one person that I work with—and that person is now my wife. At that time, she was my assistant, my editor and everything else. Everybody had accepted that for years, and one morning I came in to find that according to Gene's dictates, she had been replaced and he had given me a gum-chewing secretary who played rock and roll music. It turned out later that it had been an actress [Grace Lee Whitney] he hired to put me on.

"It wasn't fun for me. I almost killed her," he admitted. "I have a bad temper. It would have been a great joke for anybody else, but I take my work seriously and the rest of my life with a grain of salt and some whimsy. Of course they *hadn't* fired my assistant, but they made me believe that Paramount had and there was nothing they could do. I did more damage to myself over a temper tantrum....it was bad taste, but that was Gene. I do have to say that he is the only person who made *Star Trek* work over the years, because he had the guts and the balls to hang there with it, but he makes very bad mistakes with the people that work with him. He alienates them. I was always a Trekkie. I would have been very proud to have my name on the first *Star Trek* movie.

"That practical joke was the beginning of the end. I got pissed off, Gene got pissed off and the only mediator was Bob Wise who looked at me and said, 'I'm going to have to fire you, aren't I?' And I said, 'Yes.'"

Clark's involvement with the

The Marvel Comics adaptation of the Star Trek feature.

film lasted approximately three months, two of which "I spent hiding from Nimoy and Shatner because they didn't want me to talk to them. I'd have to leave my office when they were on the lot, because actors want to tell you, 'This is how I perceive the character,' and Gene didn't want their input. He didn't want me to have their input. He didn't even like Bob Wise's input....I wish I could tell you more, but my point of view is very biased and it's a part of my life I don't even like to think about."

Paramount's Jeffrey Katzenberg,

Robert Wise and Gene Roddenberry all asked that Livingston return to the film. Reluctantly, he did so.

"I had an understanding with young Mr. Katzenberg and Mr. Wise and Gene that I would do it as long as Gene didn't write," explained Livingston. "'I don't want Gene to put pen to paper. You want me to write it, I will write it. I'll do all the rewriting you want, but *I* will do it.' I had a certain style I wanted to do the script in and I had directions I wanted the characters to explore. The first thing that happened is that I rewrote 'x' number of pages and they were to be pouched to Eisner and Katzenberg in Paris. Somehow, Roddenberry got a hold of it, rewrote it and sent that to Paris. Eisner called up from Paris and said, 'What kind of shit is this?' Then Wise and I had to explain what happened. This kind of thing continued and Gene would be very remorseful and contrite, 'I was just trying to help.' I said, 'Listen, Gene, I'm not going to do this if you're going to keep this up.' Well, I quit three times. I resigned. I'm talking about $10,000 a week."

Each time he quit, Livingston was cajoled to come back to work by either Robert Wise or Jeffrey Katzenberg. Needless to say, the same problems would begin anew.

"As we began shooting," recalls Livingston, "we would get to a point where I would send in pages and then Gene would send in different pages and Wise would get two different versions. Sometimes I would write it and put my initials on them, and Gene would put 'G.R., 4PM' under mine, as though that's what should count and my pages should be ignored. This was the way the picture was made. For the third time I quit, I said, 'Screw it, nothing is worth this.' Now we weren't talking to each other. Gene has a brilliant story mind for this kind of thing, but he's a bad writer. He's clumsy. Anyway, the third time they really went behind Gene's back. I said I wouldn't have anything to do with it, and Eisner called me himself from New York and said I had to fix the script. I said I would do it if Gene promised he wouldn't do anymore writing, which of course was broken immediately. Finally, the picture was somehow filmed."

Which is not to say that the problems were over. The writing credits proposed to the Writer's Guild by Paramount was screenplay by Harold Livingston and story by Alan Dean Foster.

"They left Roddenberry out," Livingston says, "so he protested. He's the one who launched the protest. I knew he couldn't win an arbitration, because it wasn't his script. Anything he'd done was tossed out, or most of it. In any case, I blackjacked Foster into splitting the story credit with Gene. He agreed to do it and Gene wouldn't accept it. On that basis, I said, 'Okay, Gene, screw you. We'll go

to arbitration.' When I said that, he withdrew, and he withdrew in a funk; he was mad. I said to him, 'If you felt you deserved credit, then you have a system for determining this. Why didn't you use it?' He said, 'I don't want to lower myself to that.' At that point, I guess, he decided to withdraw and assume this injured pose. But he would have lost this arbitration because he didn't write any script. All he did was rewrite, patch up, fool around and screw up everything."

At the time, Roddenberry explained, "It [the script] started off a bit simpler because it had been written as a two-hour television program. It got more and more complex as it got to be a bigger and bigger movie, and we started adding things on to make use of the wide-screen, big-vision, like the wing-walk, where they go out on top of the Enterprise saucer section. I put that in. I put the climax of the show inside V'ger, where the original script did not. I'm not taking screen credit because we had a writer who worked very hard on it. He felt he deserved the credit and my policy is to never get into a credit dispute. That was my policy all through *Star Trek*. If a writer felt he wanted it and wanted it badly enough to have a Guild action on it, I'd withdraw."

Of the situation, Alan Dean Foster recalled, "The first thing they did was try to deny me screen credit. When the credits came out to be filed with the Guild, the credits read, 'Screenplay by Gene Roddenberry and Harold Livingston, Story by Gene Roddenberry.' I'm a very low-key guy. I'm an old hand-shake-is-my-bond kind of guy. I became the non-existent man as soon as the budget increased, because it became serious money. Trying to keep my blood pressure down I called my agent and said, 'What's going on?' And she said, 'Oh, that's nothing.' 'What do you mean that's nothing?' 'Nobody's mad at you or anything, that's just the business.' I said, 'Well, it's not my business,' and we picked up and moved to Arizona.

"My agent suggested I file for solo credit. I said, 'Sure,' because I did 98% of the writing on the treatment. Then Harold Livingston called me and said, 'Just because Roddenberry is being a son of a bitch, doesn't mean that you

have to be one too.' I thought about it and I said, 'You're right.' So I called and said, 'Look, all I'm interested in here is having it read the way that it read on the script, which is 'Story by Alan Dean Foster and Gene Roddenberry,' because it was, as I freely admit, based on his one page idea. I then get this very strange letter back saying that Gene Roddenberry is off in La Costa someplace recuperating, he's very tired, very busy and he really doesn't have time for this. I just laughed. Is this real life or kindergarten? I just threw up my hands and said, 'Fine, whatever,' and that's why I have sole story credit on the movie.

"I had only worked with people like George Lucas, who is one of the nicest people in the movie business, and Ronald Shusett, who produced *Alien*. But *Star Trek* was my worst experience. Nobody had ever tried to do that to me before. That's just the way it is, apparently. They put you in the shark cage, you learn how to fight with the other sharks or you go back in the goldfish bowl. I belonged in the goldfish bowl."

Although not bitter, Foster does recall Roddenberry hugging his shoulder and saying, "You remind me of me when I was getting started. I'm going to teach you everything I know about the business."

"He *did* teach me quite a lot about the business," Foster laughed without humor, "although I don't think that's what he originally had in mind."

Considering the critical scorning that *Star Trek: The Motion Picture* received, it hardly seems to have been worth all the battles, though Harold Livingston remains philosophical.

"I was upset with the film," he stateed. "It just wasn't what I wanted. I can't honestly say this wasn't my fault, because in the end I took the rap for it anyway. But if I do a poor job, I'll tell you it's bad. I know it's bad and I'll welcome help. I'm certainly not infallible. Gene would never admit that he wrote a bad line or couldn't write. He made an industry of *Star Trek* and he's really done nothing else. Gene's values lay in his knowledge, his experience. If he had imparted that and let the professionals do their job, you'd have had a picture."

Star Trek II
The Wrath Of Khan
An introduction

Star Trek: The Motion Picture was nothing like *Star Trek*: The TV series. It was as if the powers that be decided to remake *Star Trek* by violating every principal the series' popularity was based on. Couched-in subdued, generally unpleasant hints of their former personalities, the characters wandered through an aimless and irritating plot which seemed primarily an excuse for a self-conscious special effects extravaganza. The plot was unabashedly drawn from several episodes of the series, most notably "The Changeling," and the climactic "revelation" was expounded with such numbing heavy-handedness that even the most dedicated Trekkie must have suppressed a shudder before jumping up to praise the Emperor's new clothes.

"We had no idea that the first film would be a disaster," actor William Shatner admitted in 1982. "We never knew it was falling apart while we were shooting. We didn't have an ending to the script when we started, but we had months to play around with solving it. With all the high-priced talent around, we were sure that someone would come up with a corker of a finale. Somebody would certainly create something which made *sense*. [But] we never got it together. Nobody connected with the film ever sat in a theatre and saw the movie with an audience *before* it opened. After you've spent nearly two years on a project, that's essential. By that point, you're just too close to a movie to judge it objectively. The finished *Star Trek: The Motion Picture* was really two movies: one about *Star Trek*, one about special effects. Had 15 minutes been trimmed out of the released version, I think it would have been a different, stronger film. I also felt that the characters weren't as fully realized as they could have been. We certainly were dwarfed by the special effects. It was a very confusing time for me. One felt helpless. I remember having lunch with the studio head who asked me, 'What made *Star Trek* so successful?' I couldn't tell him anything. What was I going to say? 'Character development and

BASED ON THE PARAMOUNT PICTURES FILM

STAR TREK II
THE WRATH OF KHAN

A NOVEL BY VONDA N. McINTYRE
BASED ON A SCREENPLAY BY JACK B. SOWARDS
STORY BY HARVE BENNETT AND JACK B. SOWARDS

story?' If I had told him that, he would have said, 'Yeah, but we need big effects to compete with *Star Wars*.' As a result, you wound up with a weak movie."

That "weak" movie cost $45 million "that Paramount will admit to," according to one film industry figure. But like the TV show, extensive merchandising saved the first movie. The myriad products created in conjunction with the

movie sold very well. And when the movie finally earned back its nut—a film must gross about three times its production costs to start showing a profit—it was plain that even severe maltreatment had not killed the golden goose.

Word of a Gene Roddenberry-produced sequel began making the rounds shortly after the premiere of *Star Trek: The Motion Picture*. One proposed plotline, according to *Starlog* magazine, had the Enterprise travel backwards in time to save the life of President Kennedy. As a result, all history would have been changed. Reportedly, this tired retread of "City on the Edge of Forever" would have concluded with Spock firing a deadly phaser blast at the president to set things straight. Nothing more was heard of this premise.

Then we were told that the followup would be the ultimate Klingon story. In the pages of *The Making of Star Trek: The Motion Picture*, author Susan Sackett wrote, "Gene had already been asked by the studio to begin thinking about sequel stories. One he likes involves the Klingon Empire, an inside look at their home planet, their culture and the reasons behind their love of battle. Gene states that he never really liked the TV series Klingons much, pointing out that they were invented by one of the first year television show writers in need of villains. He believes that the Klingons emerged as too simply the epitome of evil—the bad guys who always wear black—whereas one of *Star Trek*'s philosophical cornerstones was that there are many forms of truth, and other life forms (or other humans, for that matter) should not be branded *good* or *evil* solely on the basis of our own customs and values."

"We know a little bit more about how to use *Trek* in motion pictures," Roddenberry said in 1980. "The second run in anything is easier. If you've ever played golf, the second try you can always sink the putt. It's that first shot at the hole...The sequel story is much more intra-crew, intra-character. It has many more of the difficult decisions that Kirk always had in the TV episodes; decisions about morality and ideals—but I'm not going to say anything more. It's good *Star Trek*. It would have made a good three-parter on the TV show—if I'd had the money to do it."

Many of Roddenberry's views of the *Star Trek II* script would ultimately prove themselves correct, but, ironically, he would have nothing to do with the final film.

■ Project Genesis

Paramount began to think once more about bringing out the sets it had carefully stored away after the first film wrapped. This time, things would be done differently, they decided sensibly enough. This time the television arm of the studio would produce the motion picture. This time its budget would be strictly controlled and kept to about a quarter of the final cost of the first film. This time it would be *Star Trek* as it had been in the much-loved TV series: a story about people, not technology or special effects.

Gene Roddenberry, creator and executive producer of the series and producer of the first movie, became "executive consultant."

"My contract gives me the total right to produce and write all motion pictures," Roddenberry told *The Official Star Trek Fan Club Magazine*. "But I did *Star Trek* 79 times. I just can't be a creature of *Star Trek* all my life. I wanted to see bright, new people come in and put a good stamp on it and add certain differences. As the consultant, they send me everything from the first story idea to the final draft of the motion picture. I also see the dailies and rough-cuts and all of that. I make my comments to them. I have told them the only time I would say, 'no, stop, I refuse to put my name on it,' is if they should break any of the very basic things about *Star Trek*. If you're going to have good people, you've got to give good people some latitude to do it their way."

Of the first film, an associate of *Star Trek* notes that after ten years the series made the leap to the big screen, and "what does Gene do?" he asked rhetorically. "He spends their money like there's no tomorrow. He makes a $40 million epic. An awful movie. After *Star Trek: The Motion Picture*, [the executive in charge] said, 'Gene, I'm sorry, we're going to have Harve Bennett take over the pictures.' Gene did not have any clout. *Star Trek: The Motion Picture* was a critical disaster, and for a while it looked like it was going to be a financial disaster. It actually earned something like $175 million worldwide. The fans are loyal to it, because the first half of the picture is quite good, but the prob-

lem is that the cut is wrong. They left in the special effects sequences that should have been much shorter, and Robert Wise intended them to be much shorter, and they cut out the little pieces of character that said the story was about Kirk and Spock.

"[The fans] had come off this two year high with *Star Wars*, and the audience wanted more *Star Wars* but there wasn't any more. So they went to see *Star Trek*, and they were hungering for more, so *Star Trek* benefitted from the *Star Wars* phenomenon. They went and they saw it over and over again, but it was embarrassing to watch the fans because they were all apologists for this picture: 'Well, it's not that bad. It's a different kind of *Star Trek*.' Instead of really just acknowledging that it was a bad movie, they tried to explain that it was wonderful, and you were an idiot for not understanding it. It was wonderful to watch them fuck their minds over to explain away a bad movie. The truth was that here was this movie that they wanted to love and...they were so disappointed, but they wouldn't dare say that they were disappointed. They wanted to love this movie. It was only after *Star Trek II* came out that they started saying, 'This is much better than the first one. Boy, the first one was really awful.'

"If you pick up *Star Trek: The Special Edition*, that edition is actually 17 minutes longer, but it feels 17 minutes shorter because of the character material. It's a difficult picture to sit through. I don't know what the details were, but essentially at the time they looked at the box office results and said, 'Take Gene out of the saddle.' They kicked him upstairs and said, 'Gene, you will be executive consultant. We'll give you an office and we'll have you approve all of the scripts, but your creative control over *Star Trek* is over because we can't afford you.' They were probably a lot more tactful than that. The message is there: you failed."

Harve Bennett was chosen to serve as executive producer. Bennett has been respected for his intelligence, his articulateness and his fund of general knowledge since the days when, as Harvey Fischman, he was one of the original radio show "Quiz Kids" in the

'40s. Since then, he has worked for the Sun Times in Chicago, CBS-TV, ABC-TV (where he was executive producer for *The Six Million Dollar Man*) and as an executive producer/writer for Universal. Bennett was executive producer of the *Rich Man, Poor Man* and *From Here to Eternity* mini-series.

"I came to Paramount with no anticipation of doing feature pictures at all," Bennett has told journalists. "I was here to do television. But the second week I was here I got a call from [studio president] Barry Diller. Now you have to remember that running the studio at the time was Barry Diller, who used to be my assistant at ABC, Michael Eisner, who used to be a counterpart of mine at ABC New York, and running the entire operation was the great immigrant, the last of the moguls, Charlie Bludhorn, who built Gulf and Western, and bought Paramount. Barry calls me in and says, 'Will you come to a meeting in my office?'"

At that meeting were the aforementioned executives, including Charles Bludhorn, who asked Bennett what he thought of *Star Trek: The Motion Picture*. "I...decided that the truth was the only thing I could say. So I said, 'I thought it was boring.' He suddenly turned on Michael Eisner and said, 'See, by you, bald is sexy.'"

Bennett was asked if he could produce a *Star Trek* film for less than 45 million dollars, to which he responded in the affirmative, and was given the job. It was a task he felt suited for, particularly because his background had been in television, which was the approach Paramount wanted him to take.

"The real reason for this originally was that, at the time of the industry's shakes over *Heaven's Gate* and massive spending on giant pictures, someone conceived the idea of giving this kind of film to the people whose background and training was essentially in the more cost-conscious arena of television— which may be a first, as far as we know. I think they chose wisely, because they picked good storytellers and not just people who make pictures for controlled budgets. However, it was never seriously a television project. The minute the script began shaping up, it was clear to all that we had something terrific."

With the script for *Star Trek II* still to be settled upon, Bennett began gathering his production staff. He selected Robert Sallin, a director and producer of television commercials and an old college chum, to produce the movie. Bennett and Sallin both attended UCLA's Film School "in the early fifties," joked Sallin, "before it was fashionable." Sallin has made over 1600 commercials and won virtually every top national and international award, including the 1978 Clio for Most Humorous Commercial of the Year and the 1970 Grand Prix of the Venice Film Festival for outstanding commercial worldwide. It fell upon Sallin, who joined the production in February 1981, to bring in *Star Trek II* quickly and cheaply. The film's budget is officially $12 million.

Related Sallin, "Before I joined Harve on the project, I sent him a lengthy memo. I had studied *Star Trek I* and I pinpointed a lot of the fundamental weaknesses of the first film. First and foremost, I felt it was too much a special effects picture and that the humanity of STAR TREK just wasn't there. I felt that the focus of our picture should be humanity. Let the special effects support it as any effect should support basic storytelling, not be driven by the effects which so many science fiction films are. I felt that the look of the picture from a design point of view had been all wrong, the lighting was too flat and uninteresting. I made a very strong point about one thing. I said, 'Let's not attack this as though it's another film project or another television project. I want to interview every member of the crew. I want to make sure that these guys are not only mentally competent, but I want an attitude here. I want an attitude that we're all in this together. As corny as it sounds, I wanted to make sure we had a great time making this film."

Bennett also hired Michael Minor as art director and it was Minor who suggested the direction the script would eventually take. At that time the story was called *The Omega Project* and it revolved around a destructive weapon.

"Harve wanted something uplifting, something that would be as fundamental in the 23rd Century as the discovery of recombinant DNA is in our time," said the late Minor, who suggested an idea to Bennett during a casual phone call. "Then something just came to me and I said, 'Terraforming.' Harve asked, 'What's that?' and I told him it was the altering of existing planets to conditions which are compatible to human life.

"I suggested a plot, just making it up in my head while talking on the phone," he continued. "The Federation had developed a way of engineering the planetary evolution of a body in space on such a rapid scale that instead of eons you have events taking place in months or years. You pick a dead world or an inhospitable gas planet, and you change its genetic matrix or code, thereby speeding up time. This, of course, is also a terrible weapon. Suppose you trained it on a planet filled with people and speeded up its evolution. You could destroy the planet and every lifeform on it. The Federation is involved with playing God, but at the same time, trying to take barren dead planets and convert them into lovely worlds. Harve liked the idea a lot. At the story conference the next day, he came over, hugged me and said, 'You saved *Star Trek*!'"

This terraforming device was aptly named the Genesis Project and the story rapidly took shape, written by Bennett and Jack Sowards. Care was taken to keep the interplay and relationships between characters that marked the first series accurate and true. Little background details were preserved, like Kirk's interest in history and his obsessive passion for his ship.

"It was my idea for Kirk to have nautical souvenirs in his apartment and his quarters," Sallin says. "I went over to the prop house and picked out a ton of stuff. There's a diver's helmet, a model of a square-rigger sailing vessel, all sorts of things."

Other threads of personality, going back to the TV series, weave through the script. The heavy of the story comes from one of the first season episodes. Khan, the genetically-engineered tyrant who ruled a quarter of our planet in the closing years of the 20th Century, was first encountered in "Space Seed." In that episode, the Enterprise came upon him and his followers, in suspended animation, drifting along in deep

Ricardo Montalban reprises his role of Khan Noonian Singh from the original Star Trek TV series in The Wrath of Khan. Montalban is seen here on the cover of Files Magazine.

space in the aptly-named ship, the Botany Bay.

In other ways than the re-encounter with his old nemesis, Khan, the past is catching up with Kirk. The script realizes that these people are no longer the same people we met 15 years ago. They've grown older. They're surrounded by a bevy of cadets who make them feel their age. Kirk, in particular, is feeling the cold breath of mortality on the back of his neck. He has just turned another year older as the story begins,

and is starting to realize that he has not been exactly building an emotional nest.

"Throughout the story," explained Sallin, "Kirk goes through a great deal of introspection and reflection on his life. In a sense, he's having a mid-life crisis. Throughout the film we exposed and plumbed the interpersonal relationships, which were established back on the series, to a level I don't think you've seen before."

In the script, Kirk meets his son, someone he was never particularly inter-

ested in becoming involved with, and he doesn't even recognize him. David Kirk (actually David Marcus, having taken his mother's name) is not a little boy, not a teenager, but a grown man, a scientist on an advanced project, indicating years of education and experience behind him. "I stayed away because you asked me to," Kirk tells his son's mother, but staying away and staying totally out of touch are two different things, and they both know it. Kirk has always worked hard at being emotionally superficial, and it has come home to haunt him in many ways.

Stated Harve Bennett to journalist Marc Shapiro, "The main thing that rang false about the first film was that the characters had gone 20 years and hadn't aged which, to my way of thinking, was totally unbelievable. I felt a major element in future films would be to have the characters age and to focus on what they were going through as people as they did so. At one point, I even sat down with Shatner and told him point blank that there was a real danger in having a middle-aged Kirk running around like a 30-year-old."

As the script developed, Sallin began preproduction and was determined not to let the film's special effects get out of hand, a factor which drove up the budget on the first film.

"I just applied some old commercial production techniques," he detailed. "I storyboarded everything. I had a chart made which listed, by scene, every special effect and optical effect, and I timed each one. I designed and supervised all the special effects. Mike Minor, our art director, sat up here in my office and did the   storyboards. Then I held meetings with four or five optical effects companies, and some of those meetings ran over three hours.

"I gave them thorough information, so that when the movie was finished, the amount of deviation from the plan was very slight. As you recall, in the first movie there were quite a few problems with special effects. Because I knew how to handle and manage production, I was left very much alone by the studio. I think they were all a little intimidated by what had gone on previously, and the idea of of special effects escalating the way they did on *Star Trek I* was a major fear and concern. This time we came in so close to budget that you couldn't go out for a decent lunch on the difference."

The storyboarding process began in June, before the script had been finalized. As different scripts came in, art director Mike Minor redrew the boards. "I laid out four different features in storyboard," said Minor. "Literally different. Different plots, different characters, different events, different effects. I put in maybe 400 man-hours before we settled on what we used to get bids for the effects."

■ The Search For Nimoy

Harve Bennett began the process of selecting the storyline for the film by screening numerous episodes of the original television series. While quite a few of them appealed to him, the one that absolutely captured his imagination was "Space Seed," which introduced Khan Noonian Singh.

At the time, Bennett had asked himself, "'Who is the heavy? Who is the black hat? We won't make this picture unless there *is* a black-hat heavy.' You know the solution the writers and producers came with with for [STAR TREK] II: Khan. I had been watching the STAR TREK episodes, and I said, 'Okay, where's my heavy?' Montalban, especially now that he's become 'Mr. White Suit,' is the best heavy there ever was. It's great! Great reverse casting, and it works."

Initially, Bennett wrote a one-page outline entitled *Star Trek: The War of the Generations*, in which a new generation is planning on overthrowing the United Federation of Planets. Their leader, it turns out, is Khan, who sees this as a chance for revenge against Kirk and all that the Federation stands for.

Next, Bennett had to find someone to collaborate with to expand the premise into a screenplay. "After considering other writers," said Bennett, "I found out that Jack Sowards, a great 'movie of the week' writer, was a great *Star Trek* fan. We talked and he clearly knew more about *Star Trek* than I did. so I hired him. Jack and I went to work, and I say *we* went to work because the

"SNEAKY PETE" SHOT: ENTERPRISE RISES INTO FRAME BEHIND RELIANT~

TIGHTER ANGLE ON ENT. PIVOTING TO FIRE "~

C.U. AS PHOTON BANK (STARBOARD) FIRES~

Storyboards courtesy Mike Minor.

process is like this: you talk, and you rap and the responsibility is that the writer records, in whatever fashion he chooses.the fruits of the give and take of this process. His task is then to go and make it become a script. Jack made an enormous contribution to this picture."

Most notable among them was the idea of killing the Spock character as a means of enticing Leonard Nimoy to star in the film, after the star had stated he had no interest in *Star Trek II.*

"During the making of *Star Trek I,"* Nimoy has stated, "there were many days when we felt frustrated with what we were given to do as actors and how the characters were being handled. Most of the time we stood around the bridge of the Enterprise saying, 'What is it?' Then somebody would say, 'I'm not sure.' Then 10 minutes later, we would say, 'What's it gonna do next?' 'I dunno. We'll have to wait and see.' You know what I'm talking about. So I came in a number of times with suggestions of little pieces of material that I gave to Bob Wise and he said, 'Okay, let's shoot it.' And these were character touches that I felt would help the audience to have some empathy with this feature story. Thus Spock would be experiencing something as a result of V'ger that the audience could relate to, and by understanding true Spock, maybe get some emotional feelings about V'ger. We shot a lot of stuff that was cut out of the movie that was later put back in when we needed a longer version for television. I have seen in print and have gotten a lot of letters that tell me that people felt they could relate to the picture better as a result of that material.

"There have been times when I've been concerned about the future of my career, because of the identification with the character. But I never had a confrontation with the studio in which I've said I would never play the part again. My only concern with *Star Trek* has been that if we're going to do it, we do it well. I don't want to just do a rip-off *Star Trek* title just because people will pay to see it. If it's going to be good, I wanted to be there. I'd hate like hell to see a great *Star Trek* movie hit the screen and not be in it. I'd feel very jealous. [At the time] I really was adamant that I would not work

on *Star Trek II* because I had been so frustrated with the other and I was feeling very negative about the whole thing."

Jack Sowards continued the scenario: "When Harve and I had our first meeting, Harve said, 'Look, Nimoy has refused to do it.' I said, 'You want Nimoy to do it?' He said, 'Yeah,' and I told him to dial Nimoy's number. He picked up the phone, dialed the number and said, 'What do I say?' I said, 'You say, 'Leonard, how would you like to play your death scene?' Leonard came on the phone, Harve said, 'Leonard, how would you like to play your death scene?' And Leonard's comeback was, 'Where does it come in the picture?' Harve looked at me and said, 'Where does it come in the picture?' And I said, 'Right up front. Right in the very beginning.' Harve said, 'Right in the very beginning.' A minute or two later Harve hung up and said, 'Leonard will do it.' Of course when we wrote it, it came in the very beginning. But everytime we wrote a little bit more, we moved it back and we moved it back and we moved it back, until it came at the end."

In the pages of *The Making of Star Trek II,* Bennett recalled, "I said, 'Leonard, remember *Psycho* and did you see *Dressed to Kill?'* He said yeah, and his smile got bigger and bigger. I said, 'Well, that's what we're going to do with Mr. Spock. And he said, 'That's fantastic!' And right then and there we shook hands and that was it. Now, that was the beginning of an evolution that got so convoluted that its resemblance to the final film is, of course, a process."

Bennett was speaking of the moment in *Psycho* when the Janet Leigh character is killed right in the middle of the film, an unprecedented move at that. The hope was to capture the *Star Trek* audience in the same manner by killing off Spock in an unexpected way in the midst of telling the story. Unfortunately, word of this leaked out and members of fandom took to a letter writing campaign that unleashed all their fury. As Jack Sowards noted, the death continued to be pushed off until it occurred near the end of the film. Still, Nimoy was excited about the idea of playing a death scene.

"[Harve] caught me completely by surprise with that one," Nimoy related. "The more I thought about it, the more I

thought, 'Well, maybe that's the honest thing to do. Finish it properly rather than turn your back on it.' So, eventually, we agreed that Spock would die. There was a lot of controversy over whose idea it was and why. It was even said that it was the only way I would do it and that it was in my contract that Spock would die! It got to be a messy situation.

"The only thing I can tell you is that when Harve and I started to explore the idea, I thought back to the first season of *Star Trek,* when the Spock character had taken root and been widely accepted. The whole concept of his lack of emotionality, his control of emotions, was a very interesting and important part of the character. Dorothy Fontana, who was a writer on the series, came to me on the set one day and said, 'I'm going to write a love story for Spock.' I told her she couldn't do it because it would destroy the character, destroy the whole mystique about whether or not he's emotional. The whole story we'd been telling was that he was completely in control of his emotions. She said, 'I have an idea that might   work, and I'm going to try it.' She did, and wrote 'This Side of Paradise,' a beautiful episode in which Spock fell in love. At the end of it, there was a bittersweet parting and it was all over. And he had gone through this fantastic experience!

"I learned a big lesson then. That is, if you say you can't do it, it won't work. If you say let's not try it, you're mistaken. Particularly in science fiction and with characters like these, you must try interesting and daring ideas. If they're well-executed, they can work. Now there are an awful lot of people, I'm sure, who said that to kill Spock would not work. Audiences won't accept it, they won't want to see it, whatever. I think they're wrong. I think people who've said that, and who have now seen the picture, are agreeing that they were wrong, that it really does work, that they were terribly moved and excited by it.

"Suddenly you find that a whole new creative possibility comes out of that because you've taken a chance. And if I might use the word 'art' in this process, I think that's what art is all about. When you venture past the obvious, when you reach into the unknown and try something daring. If it works, it opens up all kinds of new creative possibilities. That's what I think is happening with this picture, and that's why I was willing to take a chance."

■ The Scripts Of Wrath

With the Nimoy matter settled, Jack Sowards and Harve Bennett got down to business in their approach to the screenplay for *Star Trek II.*

"For me," related Sowards, "I think the biggest problem is that I started working on the show in December. I met Harve at his house and he had a page of a story worked out. It was a good idea. In other words, somebody gives you a good idea and you say, 'Oh, hell, you do this, you do this,' and it just sets you off. Well, April 11th was the Writer's Guild strike deadline and we were always working against that deadline. When you're doing a feature, three months is not a long time, so we were always working under that pressure. As a matter of fact, on April 10th I handed in the final draft of my script. That was one of the downsides. We knew that the writers were going to go on strike and I couldn't write beyond that point. It was a pressure to get it done, rewrite it, polish it and take it as far as you could. In its conception, we all were sort of told that this was going to be a movie of the week for television, and my contract was for a movie of the week. Harve knew that if the script was right, it was going to be moved into a feature.

"We sat down and watched 'Space Seed' and the original motion picture. Actually, we sat through the original picture and talked. It was beautifully done, but the effects overwhelmed it. You can't have five minutes of dialogue and 15 minutes of effects, but that's what they did. We looked at it from the point of view that we wanted to take bits and snatches of those effects—the ships, spacedock, etc.—and use them in the picture. Of course we thought that nobody has really seen this. When you've got a character scene going and you cut outside, cut somewhere else, you don't linger on it for five minutes, it works. That's one of the reasons we

watched the original picture, to see how many of the effects we could use without making it look like we were just cannibalizing an old picture. We both knew that it had to be told in a totally different way, and that was in terms of the characters. Fortunately, the big upside is that we eventually got Nicholas Meyer to direct, who has a talent for bringing a scene to life. With him, the characters are living their lives. That's what a director is supposed to do. A director is supposed to make these scenes a part of a person's life. Some directors point the camera a certain way and shoot the scene. They don't realize that that person has to be living a life, and the scene happens within that life. If the life doesn't exist, the scenes loses its meaning."

While watching "Space Seed," Sowards found himself delighting in Ricardo Montalban's performance as Khan and knew that Bennett's instincts regarding the use of the character were correct.

"I thought 'Space Seed' was wonderful," he enthused. "Ricardo Montalban is a classically trained actor. Anybody who can deliver those lines has got to be. Most actors in town would mumble them, but the man knows just how far to go. If you've watched *Fantasy Island* or his movies, there's a smoothness. In this, he was something totally different and he knew just where to go with it without going over the edge. He *is* Khan. He brings that sort of macho arrogance to it and you believe this is a genetically engineered man who is stronger, smarter and brighter. A hero is nothing without a villain. If you overcome a slug and a snail, you haven't done anything. If you overcome something like Khan, a hero is defined.

"The one thing I've sort of gotten from Ray Bradbury is the idea of an ordinary man in an extraordinary situation. These people live in the 23rd Century. They live in an advanced time, yet there's something provincial about them. They don't know all the answers, they're not super sophisticates. They're simply bright, intelligent people doing a job. And they're constantly being faced by extraordinary situations they don't understand, which puts the audience in their pockets because the audience

doesn't understand it either."

Sowards explained that he didn't feel there was any problem in adapting the characters to changing times. "I think they're timeless," he said. "The only thing we had to do with the characters was let them age. I think they're a good set of characters you can move anywhere, and these actors are so good. They're so used to working with each other and they have such a rapport. It's almost as if they can read each other's mind. They know when the cue's coming and how to play it, and it's a pleasure to work with people like that."

The first result from the Bennett/Sowards collaboration was the December 1980 "*Star Trek* Outline," which expanded upon the elements of Bennett's one-page story idea. Added was a romantic relationship between Kirk and a bridge personnel member named O'Rourke, the death of Spock early on and a face-to-face confrontation with Khan, in which the Eugenic survivor used acquired mind control powers to try and defeat his opponent. Many of these elements, including the last one, made it to the screenplay entitled *Star Trek: The Omega Syndrome.* By the time the script was written, Khan's goals had grown considerably. He now planned on using the technology of "the Omega system" to set himself up as ultimate ruler, with the Romulans, Klingons and Federation all under his control. In between, he wanted revenge against Kirk.

Next was a screenplay called *Star Trek: The Genesis Project,* which introduced the concept of Genesis and moved the story closer to that of the finished film. Again, Khan and Kirk had a hands on confrontation.

"Kirk and Khan may not have met in the film, but they did in my script. You bet your ass," Sowards laughed. "In my script, Khan was more of a mystic than Attila the Hun. I invested Khan with certain powers. He could make you see things which didn't actually exist. It was a battle of wills, which Kirk ultimately wins when Khan realizes he cannot control his mind. Nobody wins the fight and it ends up as a fight in space with the ships. But they do have this confrontation. It was a 12-page fight that they simply took out and threw away. The fight *would* have required a lot of special effects, because it was really a mind attack by Khan on Kirk and Kirk's being able to resist it. He would take it to different places. They would be on a shore somewhere, fighting with whips. They would be in a stone room of a castle. When you got into the whole thing, it was a very expensive process, so I can understand their dropping it. But not the face to face confrontation. I could never understand that."

Shortly after this script was handed in, Harve Bennett decided to go with another writer to develop it further. Although David Gerrold and Theodore Sturgeon were in the running, he ultimately chose Samuel Peeples, who wrote, among other things, the second STAR TREK pilot (and the one which sold the series), "Where No Man Has Gone Before."

"Sam Peeples had done outstanding work in other areas when I was at ABC," related Bennett. "He had done two pilots that I had been involved with, and I thought he could write robustly. So I brought him in, he read the script and I said, 'Sam, you know more about *Star Trek* than I do. I want you to fix this.' He said, 'I know just what to do.' The result was his script."

On July 20, 1981 Peeples responded with an outline entitled *Star Trek: Worlds That Never Were*. At the time, he felt it necessary to explain his approach to the material as compared to what had already been done on the screenplay.

"My personal objection to the original version of this present screenplay was, contrary to other criticisms, simply that it was cast too much in the mold of 1967 *Star Trek* episodes," Peeples said. "When Gene Roddenberry and I first discussed his project, long before the first pilot script was written, I was much taken by Gene's imaginatively pragmatic approach. Extrapolation was the key to visual reality he sought after. But somehow, along the way, pragmatism became dogma, and only what had been used before was acceptable. This, I believe, is the major fault of the *Motion Picture* version.

"*Star Trek*," he added, "was a daring and innovative creation by Gene Roddenberry; it has become a legend, the basis of a cult of very intelligent young people. It has also, unfortunately, become something of an in-joke with still younger, brighter people, the newer generations. This is not a fair critique, using today's far more liberal and 'enlightened' attitudes to judge the creations of the past. For those of us—Gene and I—who were involved in *Star Trek* from almost its moment of conception, it is far too easy to be influenced by the traditions it has initiated. But, by the very nature of Gene's original creation, tradition and deja vu and nostalgia can not be a major influence in the *new Star Trek*. It is commonsense to use the basics that have proven so right, but it is also commonsense to stop nit-picking and open our minds to the very expansive creativity that brought *Star Trek* to us in the first place. Gene Roddenberry will, I'm positive, support me in this statement completely.

"*Star Trek*, like its creator, has grown, and expanded its horizons. Our intention is to try very, very hard to implement the past, to extrapolate not only scientific matters, but human and alien characterization, as realistically as possible. Like *Star Trek*, we are all a little older, and if not wiser, at least more experienced. But, speaking for myself, I have never lost my sense of wonder, my awareness that there are more things in existence than I can ever have knowledge of. The mission of mankind in the future cannot be one of conquest and destruction. But every type and kind of life form must be given the optimum opportunity to evolve to its highest level; and to do this, environmental control and change *must* occur. That is the purpose, the driving reason behind Operation Genesis—the recreation of barren worlds into environments suitable for the advancement of a myriad life forms. Overpopulation, like the application of brute force, has been eliminated by mankind. But, by the very nature of alien civilizations, conflict will continue; goals will conflict; personalities will clash. The nature of mankind hasn't changed in 15,000 years of civilization; why would it change completely in a few hundred more? Logic will insist it cannot.

"The 'heavies' in this newest version, are not representations of 'evil' or 'good.' They are, perhaps, the first totally alien concepts used in *Star Trek*—one more departure from traditional themes—beings from another cosmos. Their universe is not ours; their motivations are hidden from us. But within the projected limitations of their own environment, they are logical and normal. But please understand that mankind is not capable of learning or understanding everything. A case in point, exactly what is electricity? Why are some of the synaptic relays of the human brain non-functional? Why are some organisms immune to disruptive influences that destroy others of their kind? Why can energy be created but not destroyed?.....This is not intended as an apologia; it is a statement of intent."

Interestingly, the Samuel Peeples draft of *Star Trek II* incorporated many of the elements of Jack Sowards' version, with the *exception* of Khan. Added were a pair of aliens named Sojin and Moray, beings from another dimension who want to use their powers to take command of ours.

Noted Robert Sallin, "Neither the Jack Sowards or Samuel Peeples script worked. It felt like television. It felt like a long television episode, and I didn't believe that the underlying humanity and the relationships between the people were very strong. There was a lot of intergalactic weirdness in the scripts which I felt were defeating."

This script was dropped and Harve Bennett decided to rewrite the screenplay himself, at the encouragement of writer Judy Burns, author of the *Star Trek* episode "The Tholian Web" and a highly established television writer. She and Bennett had worked together in the past.

"Harve Bennett," she explained, "who had hired me several times to do *The Six Million Dollar Man*, called me in and asked if I wanted to rewrite the script. I read it, gave him all my suggestions and said, 'You're really into this and love it so much, why don't you rewrite it yourself?' He said, 'Maybe I will,' and that's what he did. I'll probably kick myself now that I didn't rewrite it, because almost everything I suggested to Harve was used in the rewrite.

"I said to Harve, 'You mustn't

kill Spock in such a fashion that he can't be brought back,'" Burns elaborated. "It was such a final idea originally that it was impossible to bring him back. He also died in such a way that there was no emotional impact on the viewer, and I said what they were missing in that script was the relationship between Spock and Kirk, which was so critical and which ultimately ended up in the scene between the two of them as Spock is dying. Originally, that scene didn't exist. Those were specifically my notes, all five pages of which had to do with character, because Harve had never done *Star Trek* before. Thank God he found Nicholas Meyer, a very good character person. Basically I went through the script and said, 'This won't fly because Kirk wouldn't do that,' or 'Spock wouldn't do that in this particular circumstance.' The greatest crux, as I said, dealt with how Spock was killed and whether or not he could be brought back."

Bennett "went right back to Jack's script and did a quick rewrite of my own, just to get everything together," he said in *The Star Trek Interview Book*. "Enter Nick Meyer. When I saw *The Seven Percent Solution*, I was so impressed with the screenplay that I went out and read the book....Nick read my rewrite of Sowards and Peeples and said, 'This has promise. What if...' He signed on and said, 'You write it, and I'll rewrite you.'..."

Robert Sallin remembered things a bit differently. "I was preparing a list of all the directors I thought might be acceptable for this film," he said. "I must have had somewhere in the area of 30 or 40 names, but I kept striking out because either they didn't want to do *Star Trek*, they didn't want to do a sequel to *Star Trek*, they didn't want to do science fiction, they didn't want to do any kind of special effects material or they weren't available. A lot of people simply didn't want to do it after what happened with the first one. Because the film was being done under the aegis of the television division, I wanted to find a director who was on his way; who hadn't hit it yet but whose heart and soul was in to it, and who would bring a certain passion to the project.

"Then," he continued, "Nick Meyer's name came up. I saw *Time After Time* and I thought it was inventive, and I very much liked the writing of the *Seven Percent Solution*. I thought that was a very fine and inventive piece of work. He seemed to come up with things with a fresh point of view. So I suggested it to Harve. We sent the script over to Nick and had a meeting with him. I remember standing in the alley, saying to Harve, 'I think the guy's dynamite. I think he has a great vision of what can be done here.' Time moved on, the studio seemed to respond to Nick and so we went with him. It is, in all candor, Nick's uncredited rewrite that is on the screen. Contrary to what the critics may say, Harve made contributions, Sowards made contributions, I made contributions, but I think it was Nick's final version that we used. Nick never took credit for it and he told me his agent said he was crazy. But he said it was just something he wanted to do."

■ The Meyer Connection

Not only had Nicholas Meyer written the book and screenplay of *The Seven Percent Solution*, but he was the director behind the sensational *Time After Time*, which transported Jack the Ripper and H.G. Wells from Victorian England to the modern world. His talents were highly respected, and the attachment of his name to *Star Trek* was a major coup.

"A friend of mine, named Karen Moore, who at the time was working for Paramount, was visiting me one night," Meyer related to journalists. "I had done nothing since *Time After Time*. I had turned down a lot of stuff, trying to get my own script for a movie called *Conjuring* made—with no success, I might add. So, I wrote the book, *Confessions of a Homing Pigeon*, which came out in October '81. This was just before that....Karen said to me, 'You know, if you want to learn how to direct movies, you should direct!' She suggested the *Star Trek II* movie and said that the two guys producing it were very nice.

"They sent me the script, which I loved. I met Harve and Bob [Sallin] and I thought they were wonderful, and I haven't changed my views since. As far as the film was concerned, I could not have been better partnered to not look like a fool because of the expertise and support I was given. The miracle of it was that we were all making the same movie. Everything really could have come unstuck if we had started going off in different directions. But there was never a substantive disagreement about the tone or the action. Details, yes."

Meyer admitted to not have ever seen an episode of the original series, noting that he didn't particularly like the science fiction genre.

"I'm interested in good stories first," he stated. "I loved *Star Wars* and *The Empire Strikes Back*, which I thought were very exciting and a lot of fun. I saw some *Star Trek* stuff after the film was offered to me, and they also ran the first movie for me. I didn't like that very much. I thought that it was spectacular in some ways, but I didn't like the way the people looked or what I considered the lamentable absence of story and human interaction. There are really two reasons to do remakes and sequels, aside from financial considerations. One is because, for whatever reason, it's been so long and people really didn't see the original, except on late-night television. The other reason is that there was something wrong with the original. It didn't fulfill what it was supposed to, or could be improved upon. I looked at the first film and thought that there was no way that we were going to make a movie as filled with ennui as that one. I also knew we could do it for a quarter of the cost, so we would probably look like heroes!

"[Adding dimension to the characters] was definitely the aim. I have always thought, to the extent that I've had any clear thoughts about *Star Trek*, that it was something that for one reason or another never quite fulfilled its promise. Either because in terms of a TV show, they couldn't afford the sets or the effects, or because in the first movie they dropped the ball somewhere. This was an opportunity to make something right that had never quite been on the nose before. The more specific you get, the better. It was not necessary for me to see

Director Nicholas Meyer, generally credited as "the man who saved Star Trek." (photo courtesy Anderson Archives).

Admiral Kirk go to the bathroom, but I said why couldn't he read a book? At which point, I grabbed the first book off my shelf, which was *A Tale of Two Cities*, and for some reason or another, I just stuck with that, which was interesting because it's the one book that everybody knows the first line and the last line to. That became the bracket of the movie and it also somehow became the theme of the movie. Leonard and Shatner got excited because they always felt in some way that they had the Sidney Carlton-Charles Darnay relationship going on between them. That's very specific, and from the book we got the glasses, which was specific too, and real! From all of that came age! Interestingly enough, *Star Trek II* is not very much about science fiction, the Genesis Planet aside. Its themes are entirely earthbound—death, aging, friendship.

"[I also wanted to] stretch the nautical analogy. I said it should be like Captain Horatio Hornblower in outer space," Meyer added. "I made everyone on the set watch the movie version of Hornblower. The young midshipman who gets killed....he's stolen right out of that movie. And it was interesting because when I first spoke to Bill Shatner about my idea, he said, 'That's interesting; that was also Gene Roddenberry's original take on it.' So far, so good. But I really wanted to pursue it. I had ship's bells, and boatswain's whistles and all that sort of stuff. And we very much stressed the idea of the ships as galleons in space. There's even that scene where they start pulling up the gratings to fire the photon torpedoes; it's followed through a lot.

"I think it's fair to say that our movie would not have been as good as it was if it hadn't been for the first picture. We definitely learned, in the broadest sense, that they had made a picture based on a technical nature with runaway production costs and we said we wouldn't do that. We tend to feel very superior to it, and I think we're right to feel superior. But at the same time, they had their own stuff to work out and they're lucky they got the movie on film!"

One of the issues Meyer was pressed with was deciding what elements of the *Star Trek* formula he should keep in the film and what should be discarded.

"Very simple," he mused. "I kept what was good and changed what was bad! I decided that I owed allegiance to what was good in either the first movie or, more importantly, the television series and that I owed no allegiance and no respect to things that were bad. What that really boiled down to was the characters. I had to keep the characters as they were but at the same time I had to redesign everything that I could—the uniforms, the sets, etc. Again, it was in the context of what they were, the overall shapes, I couldn't do anything about. But I could add twinkling lights whenever possible, I tried to get away from that grey look. Philosophically, I said that I was simply going to take these characters more seriously and more literally than anyone has ever taken them before.

"The humor in *Star Trek* is the tragicomical view of life, that of people talking, real people. It seemed very difficult for me to do the movie without including a lot of that. It's a fine line to walk. I didn't want to be camp. I wanted to be affectionate and real. By saying I was taking them seriously, I didn't mean that they had no humor. I meant that *I* took them seriously, as if they were real people. At the very beginning, I said that I'd do the picture under one condition—'Let's make it real, because everything else is either camp or bland. Let's play it up to the armpit, and if we're going to kill Spock, kill him.' Because the unforgivable thing is to take it, to rip people off that way, to manipulate them. That is tasteless."

Meyer was faced with his own share of problems regarding the cast itself. Nimoy had been convinced to come back, but there were near defections by George Takei and DeForest Kelley, who were not satisfied with the script.

Noted George Takei, "When I first got the script and saw the kind of participation Sulu had, I saw that he wasn't much more than a talking prop. There was no character there, and I decided that I just couldn't go back under those conditions. My heart just wouldn't be in it. I told this to Harve Bennett and Nick Meyer, and they understood, but the script was already written

and there wasn't much that they could do with it at that point....Harve understood the problems and had a few scenes added that bolstered my part a little, but I was still unhappy. Filming was due to begin soon and a decision had to be made. So they made me certain promises and I was on the set the first day of filming without even a contract. The first shots included me on the simulation bridge, so I was locked in. Unfortunately, when the film came out, some of the little scenes which would have added to my character ended up on the cutting room floor."

Explained DeForest Kelley, "At first I turned it down. I strongly disliked the first script handed to me. I felt it was a busy story and didn't work, so I had a big conversation with Harve Bennett. He was upset. I said I would rather *not* be in it, because the role was not meaningful, and the script just was *not* a good *Star Trek* script. He said, 'Well, what do you think we should do?' 'I think you should hire a writer who has written for *Star Trek* and rewrite it!' He looked at me funny and said, 'Well, who would you hire?' I said, 'Gee, Harve, I don't know, I'm not in that line of work." Meyer, as stated above, was brought in and did a rewrite. "I feel that Meyer brought it to life and really made it a kind of *Star Trek* script. When he sent me that draft, I said, 'That's more like it,' and I went with it."

Sharing Kelley's view of working with Meyer was William Shatner. "Nick Meyer had written a script and we were in love with the script and impressed by his creative ability," he enthused. "So even though it was only the second picture he had directed, we felt that his imagination should be given full flower. And so here he was. He had written the script but he hadn't directed very much. Whatever help we could give him was offered and he would accept it or not accept it, depending on whether he thought we were correct. But he had written the script and had therefore brought to it another unquestionable aspect."

The cast's overwhelming enthusiasm for Meyer did not prevent them from giving this newcomer a bit of a hard time during the early days of shooting.

Meyer remembered, "Leonard and Bill Shatner kidded me a lot. They used to test me in the first couple of weeks. No one ever pulled rank. No one ever said, 'Well, we used to do it differently in the old days.' They understood up front that it was going to be completely different, that's how I got them to do it, but during the first two weeks they tested me in a lot of little ways. I remember we shot a scene where Uhura had a line which I don't remember and she had to deliver it a certain way. While this was going on, they would mutter back and forth to themselves. They had me so nervous by the time they were finished, the pair of them talking about how this was wrong, that they effectively had me convinced that the whole picture had just gone down the toilet, based on this one line, which I'm not even sure is in the finished movie anyway. They ragged me a lot like that."

Ragging aside, the filming of *Star Trek II: The Wrath of Khan* was a joyous experience from the point of view of Meyer and the cast, though there were innumerable other aspects that had to be coordinated to bring the entire film together as a cohesive piece of entertainment.

F/X And Costumes

"*The Wrath of Khan* was like producing two motion pictures simultaneously," smiled Robert Sallin. "You had a live action picture and a special effects picture. Getting it to integrate was something else again."

As noted earlier, Sallin had sent out the breakdown for *Star Trek II*'s effects to various SFX houses for bids. The winning bidder was ILM, George Lucas' Industrial Light and Magic facility near San Francisco, and Sallin credits their "integrity and honesty" as well as all the preplanning for bringing in *Star Trek II* on schedule and on budget. Douglas Trumbull's Entertainment Effects Group (EEG) was one of the losing bidders. According to Trumbull, as reported in the June 1981 issue of *American Film* magazine, "EEG's bid was $1.5 million under ILM's."

Sallin refuses to discuss the effects budget, or the bid differential alleged by Trumbull, saying, "I don't

think it's appropriate to do so, or anyone's business for that matter." Sallin chalks up Trumbull's remark to "sour grapes. EEG was excluded fairly early in the bid process for a very simple reason. Trumbull made it very clear that he would not be available after a certain date, because he was going to direct *Brainstorm*."

Work began at ILM in early September, well before the start of principal photography, using the model of the Enterprise left over from the first feature. Because of the model's complexity, ILM requested advice from Trumbull, who had filmed it for *Star Trek: The Motion Picture*. Though ILM offered to pay all expenses, Trumbull refused to send any EEG technicians to ILM's San Rafael facility. Mastering the Enterprise—and master it they did—caused ILM no small amount of time and trouble.

One of the most successful effects suppliers in the business, ILM tries hard not to look like a film studio. Soundstages there don't look like soundstages and there are no fences, gates, guards or badges. The buildings have no signs pertaining to ILM, parent company Lucasfilm, or special effects moviemaking. Only when you get deeper into the non-public areas inside the building do clues appear: large framed posters of *Star Wars* in French, Italian, Japanese, German; a photo of C3PO carrying a bag of groceries down a Los Angeles street; a hand-lettered notice asking for a camera to be returned "to the monster shop."

Sitting at a big oak table in the conference room at ILM, Ken Ralston looks ruefully at a photo of the model of the USS Enterprise. The model is huge, over six feet long, and it's covered with a custom-made shroud bearing the Starfleet arrowhead.

"I hate that model," Ralston says, not without some fondness. "I think it's made out of lead. I don't know what's inside to make it so heavy; it took eight guys to mount it for a shot and a forklift to move it around."

Ralston teamed up with Jim Veilleux to supervise the visual effects ILM did for *Star Trek II*. Like many people in the effects end of the business, Ralston was a kid who was fascinated with science fiction and monster movies. It was

Ray Harryhausen's stop motion work that first got him interested. Ralston worked several years in television commercials and was freelancing when an old friend, Dennis Muren, asked him to come to work on a movie called *Star Wars*. Ralston has been with Lucasfilm ever since.

Working with the big model of the Enterprise caused many headaches for Ralston and his crew. For the first movie, the Enterprise was given a super deluxe paint job which was extremely glossy. The idea was that as you moved the ship around, it would cast off iridescent shades of color, like an abalone shell. In the movie, though, it doesn't quite work that way. Ralston decided to dull the finish down and add a little extra detailing to the surface.

"The ship won't look any different on the screen," he notes. "The iridescence effect still works, but having a little relief on the surface made things easier on us. We didn't have to horse around with the lighting to get rid of the gloss."

Ralston used the traditional blue-screen method to matte the ships in with the backgrounds. Objects are photographed against a background of a particular shade of intense blue, using a type of film which does not register that color. Anything of that shade of blue does not appear on the film, leaving a clear area into which another scene can be inserted later. Unfortunately, any reflection of the blue on a shiny surface will also disappear, resulting in a disconcerting "hole" through what should be a solid object. Such holes have to be painstakingly opaqued out of every frame.

"Any system has its problems," said Ralston. "Some people become outraged if the effect isn't just right. They don't realize that, while you want to do the best you can on each effect, you know each shot isn't the whole shoot. There are maybe 40 more to do and you've got two weeks to do them in."

In addition to its glossiness, the huge size of the Enterprise model caused other problems with the blue screen. On some of the fly-by shots, the camera had to be turned sideways and lifted up in the air to keep the blue screen behind the model. When Ralston used a wide-angle lens for close-ups, the ship would sometimes run off the edge of the blue screen and suddenly the stage or the ceiling joists were in the picture.

The same camera used in *Star Wars* was used to shoot the Enterprise and the other ships. Ralston refers to it as the "Flex," short for Dystraflex, named for effects man John Dykstra. Even using its computerized mount, Ralston and his crew were always working on tall ladders or on their backs.

When a shorted wire knocked out some of the lights in the Enterprise model, bringing filming to a halt, the person who was arm-pit deep inside the Enterprise—feeling for a loose wire—was 6-foot-5 Steve Gawley, ILM's supervising modelmaker. Gawley's soft-spoken, shy demeanor is in direct contrast to his strawberry blonde hair and flaming red beard. He got his job through Joe Johnston, the special effects art director for *Star Wars* and has been at ILM ever since.

While the Enterprise model was built for the first movie, other models seen in *Star Trek II* had to be built from scratch. The most notable was the Reliant, the ship Khan commandeers to fight the climactic space battle with the Enterprise. The Reliant was designed at Paramount, and the drawings were sent to ILM for execution. Given control of the actual construction, Gawley was able to make the model smaller, lighter and its wiring less complex than the huge Enterprise.

In addition to the Reliant, the model department made small models of both Enterprise and Reliant for distant shots, and close-up sections of each ship for use in the space battle scenes. Said Gawley, "It was very interesting and quite a challenge to construct models so that Ken Ralston and our pyrotechnics expert, Thaine Morris, could blow them to smithereens on film, without actually damaging the model."

Gawley had only a few months to build the models, which was tough even with his 10 man crew on *Star Trek II*. "We started in September and finished in late December," he said. "I've been dealing with the producer, Robert Sallin, since late August. He's been very involved."

Because of the short schedule, Gawley took some short cuts. The space-lab Regula One is actually a space sta-

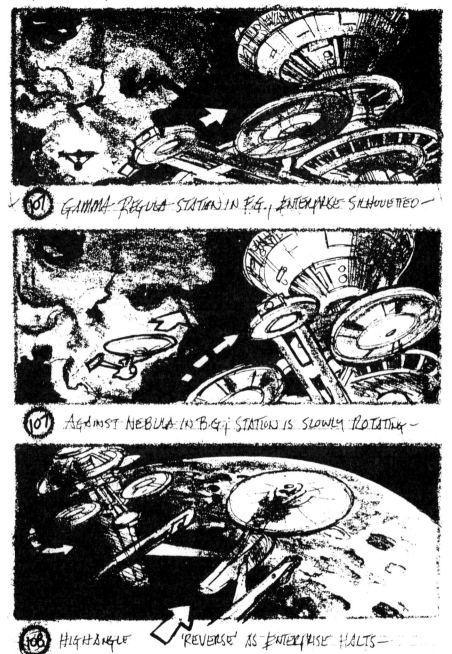

tion left over from the first movie, built by Magicam. It was the orbiting platform the crew of the Enterprise assembled on before boarding their ship in drydock. At Robert Sallin's suggestion, Gawley took the model, turned it upside down, took a few things off, added a few things and christened it a "scientific" space station.

"It was quite cost effective," he said. "It was this approach that prevailed throughout the project."

Ralston was much happier with

ILM's Reliant, than with the Enterprise. "The Reliant is a nice squat contraption that looks a lot more believable to me," he pointed out. "The ship takes the best of the Enterprise, rearranges it and adds a few goodies of its own. It's much easier to have it sit there and look right. And the model is great. It's made of vacu-formed plastic and two guys can mount it on the pipes for a shot." The wiring of the Reliant was much simpler than the Enterprise. Ralston had to painstakingly rewire an elaborate network of switches on the Enterprise to a big console every time they mounted it.

"I'll probably get attacked about this," Ralston smiled, "but I'm just not crazy about the original design of the Enterprise. It's a shape that does not lend itself easily to looking good in the frame. It's hard to come up with angles that really read like anything. There are only two good angles on it."

Another irritating problem for Ralston was the Enterprise's exterior lights, which point up surface features such as the registration number, the vessel's name and the Starfleet logo. These lights required special handling during the filming since they are really spotlights cast onto the model and don't come from inside the ship or from surface-mounted fixtures. The spotlights are made from "inky" lights. Inky as in inky-dinky. The lenses are a couple of inches in diameter, but the beam of light can be reduced to a pinpoint. For Ralston, these small lights were a huge headache, since everytime the ship rolled, all the spotlights had to roll with it. It was impossible for the whole lighting set-up to roll, so Ralston was forced to do a lot of trick shots like having the camera roll and the ship stay stationary.

"It affected the flexibility of what we could do with the models," Ralston said. "Fortunately they're not doing maneuvers like X-wing fighters anyway. They sort of lumber along, and it's what's going on all around them that creates the excitement in scenes like the grand-slam finale: the battle inside a nebula."

During the fight in the nebula, both the Enterprise and the Reliant sustain heavy damage. The Enterprise actually has a part of its hull punctured by phaser fire. To create the damage, Steve Gawley and his model-makers first sculpted a big section of the Enterprise, the diagonal main strut affair just below the saucer, out of wax. The shooting lights got the wax soft enough for Ralston to go in with sculpting tools and animate the phaser fire opening up the hull like a can opener.

On the Reliant, the rollbar—the piece that stretches across the top of the ship—blows up. Instead of destroying that piece of the model and rebuilding it

everytime, it was designed so that a lot of the structure would remain intact. Part of its skin was wax and filled with all sorts of explosives and little plastic scraps called "nernies" that would fly out.

"Audiences are going to love the finale," art director Michael Minor said of the film's aforementioned climactic battle. "The Enterprise leads the Reliant into battle in the heart of a nebula. We dispensed totally with dark space and suddenly we have the great billowing clouds of colored gasses—cobalt blue, magenta, cerise, orange, yellow, green—and new born stars, and electrical disturbances. Through them the ships are moving in vast silhouettes, the lights twinkling. It's going to be better than a cover of an old *Amazing Stories*!"

Robert Sallin pointed out that, "The whole concept of the battle in the nebula was mine. What happened was we needed that climactic confrontation. As the script was being written, I said, 'Look, guys, you can't have two spaceships of this size—the size of three football fields—pulling 9Gs. They're not going to be maneuverable. It's going to be like two rhinoceros' lumbering around in space. Visually, we've got to come up with something more exciting than that.' And that's when I got the idea. I said, 'Let's make an analogy of a World War II dogfight, where those little frail planes—although these aren't frail—battled in a game of hide and seek. Then we had to figure out where that should be and my art director, the late Mike Minor, came into my office one day and he was always toting around books about space. I saw one with a fabulous photograph on the cover and said, 'What's that?' And he said, 'That's a nebula.' I said, 'That's it. That's where the fight has to be.'"

A nebula is a vast multi-colored cloud of interstellar gases that's slowly condensing into new stars. It's full of globs of incandescent matter. Immense discharges of energy and small "baby" stars. To achieve this incredible effect, ILM special effects supervisor Ken Ralston worked with a clouded tank, which looks very much like a 4'x8' aquarium. In the cloud tank, a layer of salt water is laid down over a layer of fresh water and the two create a turbulent inversion layer.

The "clouds" are a solution of latex rubber which ILM technician Don Dow carefully injected into this layer using meat basters with long tubes on them. The latex is white, and the colors of the clouds are done with lights. A little pump moves the water very slowly and the current creates storm-cloud shapes.

The effect is difficult to control and often the best results are accidental. Sometimes shapes will last for hours and sometimes for minutes. Even the heat of the shooting lights create currents that change the shapes as they're being filmed. "If you see something starting to shape up, you run around like crazy, because your time is short," said Ralston. "Don Dow, Sel Eddy, Mike Owen, Joe Fulmer and I would race around quickly arranging lights and gels to get the maximum effect for each tank."

Ralston shot the nebula clouds at such a slow rate of exposure—about one frame per second—that he could simply take a light and walk around the tank, shining it here and there to create discharges of light and energy moving through the whole nebula, lighting up bits in huge flashes. To match the lightning in the nebula with the ship models, Ralston did "lightning passes" across the ship models with a spotlight.

After the nebula cloud photography was done, it had to be optically combined with the starships, the star field and other optical effects like phaser fire. For optical photography supervisor Bruce Nicholson, the nebula shots were the most difficult, "And the most dramatic, we hope. The ships go into a cloud-like mass of glowing gas and stars," said Nicholson. "It is almost like a hide-and-seek sequence, in which you have the Enterprise and the Reliant ducking behind clouds. You'll see one disappear behind a more solid clump of gas and dust in the background while the other ship rises up in the foreground. We tried to expose them so that you see a certain amount of nebula across them, like a veil of varying density."

"The cloud tank is an old technique," explained Ralston. "I'm pretty sure something like it was used in *The Ten Commandments* to create clouds. I'm all for old techniques when they work. You can waste an awful lot of time trying to create the same effect in some new way that you think is more high-tech and you can spend a lot of money on it. The cloud tank is a very simple technique raised to a fine art."

While ILM created its magic for *The Wrath of Khan*, Robert Fletcher, who designed the costumes for the first *Star Trek* feature, was hired to design the costumes for *Star Trek II* as well. "Nick Meyer wanted the costumes to be dashing, and a little romantic," said Fletcher, emphasizing the departure from the bland uniforms he designed for *Star Trek: The Motion Picture*. Those designs were dictated by Gene Roddenberry, who wanted a "sprayed-on" look, and director Robert Wise, who insisted the costumes be monochromatic to focus attention on the actors' faces.

In changing the Starfleet uniforms again, Robert Sallin used the rationale that uniform styles in our own present-day Navy have changed in the past 10 years. "I thought the series uniforms looked like stretch Dr. Denton's," he laughed, "and the first movie's uniforms looked like uniforms." To get a sleek, colorful, military look for the uniforms of *Star Trek II*, Fletcher went back to traditional military fabrics, natural fibers, not synthetics.

"I think the reason that clothing now seems loose and unstructured is that, for all its practicality and washability, synthetic fibers don't tailor very well," Fletcher explained. "They're terribly limited in use. You can't mold them. They don't dye, they don't drape, they don't do a goddamn thing a fabric should do. And they have very raw, hard colors. The colors I wanted for the film are what I call corrupt colors, a shade off from a pure color. The uniform jackets aren't quite red; Kirk's civilian shirt, in the scenes at his place in San Francisco, is a sort of dusty teal blue; and Spock's Vulcan robe isn't a true black—everything is an 'ish' color. Maroon*ish* red, brown*ish* green, purple*ish* black. They're not colors you see today, so in a subtle way they indicate another time."

Sallin missed the color designation of the uniforms in the series, where each department had its own color. After some experimentation with dyes, he and Fletcher came up with white tunics for Command, a soft sea-green for Medical, a bluish-grey for officers and a scarlet for cadets. Rank and station designations are carried forward on sleeve stripes and some detailing on the jacket fronts.

The wardrobe for *Star Trek II* was made at Western Costume, the huge motion picture manufacturing and rental facility just off the Paramount lot. Paramount has a very good ladies' department, but the tailoring department wasn't up to Fletcher's standards.

The biggest asset of the clothing department at Paramount were their storerooms filled with an enormous stock of old fabrics, silks and pure wools, some of them 40 years old, but kept in the dark and in good condition. "Wonderful natural fibers like those are almost impossible to find anymore," said Fletcher. "Paramount is one of the last studios that has stocks and even it is no longer acquiring for the future. When their stocks are gone, there won't be any more."

Among the few costumes which weren't made for *Star Trek II* are the spacesuits with self-contained life-support systems and propulsion backpacks, and Spock's Vulcan robes. Both are styles Fletcher designed for the first *Star Trek* movie. The spacesuits are made of Spandex.

One challenge in the costume design was to make contemporary, common-place closure devices, such as zippers and snaps, look futuristic. The method of closing the flap of the jacket, where it crosses over the chest, was a bit of a problem. Fletcher and his crew rejected zippers and buttons right off, which left them with either hooks or snaps. Fletcher decided on covered snaps, black, sewn on a black tape. Even so, when the jacket was open, they were pretty obviously snaps.

"Nobody was happy with it," Fletcher pointed out. "Then I realized that what gives them away is the little individual dots and nipples, so I took a lot of very fine silvery chain and stitched a few links between each snap. When it's open, it's kind of mysterious-looking. You don't know what it is, maybe some sort of magnetic chain."

Robert Sallin drew upon veterans of commercials production in his choices for *Star Trek II*'s cinematographer and film editor. Gayne Rescher was hired as director of photography on the strength of his work for the TV movie, *Bitter Harvest*. Editor Bill Dornisch had worked for Sallin on commercials and on Sallin's feature, *The Picasso Summer*, based on the story by Ray Bradbury.

The producer's quest for efficiency and streamlining led him to the sets Paramount had stored away after the first movie. "I discovered they had taken Joe Jennings' design for the bridge, which was made in 'wild' [moveable] pieces and locked it together. It was designed to come apart in wedge-shaped sections, and the sections were on wheels and hydraulic shock absorbers. They had bolted them together and put on a ceiling piece and hadn't made it wild. I couldn't believe it. It made heat build up, it made it hard to move the camera, it restricted your angles and coverage. The first thing I did was order that the set be broken into sections."

Sallin also disliked the bridge set's use of 8mm and 16mm film projectors for all the monitor displays. "The images dimmed unless photographed straight on," he said, "and all those chattering projectors and humming fluorescent tubes were so noisy that every line of dialogue spoken on the bridge in the first film had to be re-recorded later." He had the film elements for the monitors transferred to video-cassettes, catalogued them and put in a master control system.

■ Production Design

The designer of the bridge set, Joseph Jennings, was hired as *Star Trek II*'s production designer. Jennings began work on *Star Trek II* after Mike Minor had been hired to storyboard the script. Jennings had given Minor one of his first jobs in the business—as an illustrator on *Gunsmoke* (which Jennings art directed for seven years)—and they had worked together on the first *Star Trek* feature. "We worked together like Rogers and Hammerstein," said Minor affectionately of their collaboration on *Star Trek II*. As far as the genial, slow-talking, white-haired 60 year old production designer is concerned, there isn't much difference between an art director and a production designer. A bigger credit, perhaps, just a single card up front. "But whatever you call the job," Jennings mused, "it amounts to having responsibility for the look of the production."

Jennings was one of three art directors credited on *Star Trek: The Motion Picture*. He had been that film's original art director when it was begun as a television movie. According to Jennings, the fact that the previous *Star Trek* film had so many art directors, in addition to a production designer, is symptomatic of what went wrong with the production.

"We made a camel," he said. "It started out to be a horse, but committee got a hold of it. Everyone got into the act on that movie. There was creative pulling back and forth, fumbling around, coming and going of people ad infinitum and ad nauseam. Everyone who worked on the art direction provided too much input to be ignored, so we all got credit and Hal Michaelson, brought in as art director, ended up getting credit as production designer."

Nearly everyone on *Star Trek II* expresses some disdain for its predecessor. Few are quite as vehement as Mike Minor, who worked for Joe Jennings on the previous film as a production illustrator. "It was one of the more soiled and shabby chapters of Hollywood history, in terms of how people were treated," said Minor. "The trouble, as always, was that the wrong people were in charge. We're in a business in which the people at the top, who make the decisions, really don't know a damn thing about making pictures. I think we all knew then that we were associated with a bomb. It's too bad the movie happened at all."

Executive producer Harve Bennett and producer Robert Sallin made sure that too many cooks wouldn't spoil *Star Trek II*. Said Jennings, "I found Harve and Bob very congenial working partners. They were very receptive of ideas, yet directed the whole operation with a loose hand that didn't hover."

Minor's feeling about *Star Trek II*, which he joined in June 1981, were more sanguine. "This is sort of an unusual undertaking," he said, "a motion picture for theatres produced by the TV wing of Paramount. They have done themselves proud. I think the script is excellent. It's a real *Star Trek* script: it's fun, it's literate, it's clever and it has humor. Thank God, there's whimsy. Suddenly we could block out the memory of that first feature and we've got the energy and drive of the best of the TV series. Everybody felt good about it.

"Our technical consultant, Dr. Richard Green of the Jet Propulsion Laboratory, is also a real fan. So is Gayne Rescher, the director of photography. He really committed himself to the picture and even came in two weeks early to work with Nick Meyer, figuring out how to shoot the bridge. People are going to notice how much more interesting the photography is in this picture because the camera is always in motion."

Minor spoke of *Star Trek II* not only with the zest and enthusiasm of someone who helped create it, but with the added charge of someone doing just what he's always dreamed of doing. When *Star Trek* hit the airwaves in 1966, Minor was inspired. "I spent about four months, working all hours after my regular jobs, doing sketches and watercolors of alien landscapes, costumes, creatures, 'till I had a portfolio," he said. Minor called Desilu and asked for an appointment with series creator Gene Roddenberry. In one of many instances of Roddenberry's legendary kindness to fans, Minor was invited to bring his artwork to the studio.

"Gene liked the artwork and he had me show it to the art director, Matt Jeffries," Minor explained. "Jeffries bought about 20 pieces to use as art objects around the ship. Some of the critters were hanging in McCoy's office and cabin during the third season. A creature head I did in latex became the Melkot in 'Spectre of the Gun.' I later discovered that, in my ignorance, I had stumbled upon the only route by which I could have sold to the show...by bringing art in on spec. Union regulations prevented the production company from commissioning work from an outside contractor, but they *could* buy existing material."

Jennings, like Minor is an old hand at *Star Trek*. He worked for art director Matt Jeffries, an old friend, drawing the set designs for the original television series. In designing *Star Trek II*, Jennings kept the layout of the Enterprise consistent with the blueprint drawings of the ship (created by Franz Joseph Designs) that were merchandised after the TV series left the air.

"We were stuck with that schematic," said Jennings, "but I think we *should* be stuck with it. It's part of the *Star Trek* universe now. The fans are familiar with how the Enterprise looks and works, so it all has a sort of *de facto* existence, a bogus logic. You have to work with that, and I think a production designer has to realize it. Directors, too. Sometimes they're hard to convince and you have to do a sales job. You have to say, 'Look, that won't work, that place isn't there. You can't get there from here, and the fans know it. If you want to do your own outer space movie, then go off and do it, but don't call it *Star Trek*."

Having his production design ring true is of great concern to Jennings. "I always think of an anecdote that John Barrymore supposedly told. Someone asked him how he portrayed such a convincing limp when he played Richard III. He told them he just pointed the toes of his right foot at the instep of his left foot, and walked the best way he could. Barrymore established a frame of reference, and then was as honest as he could be within that frame. So once the writer and producer and director and the whole creative group establish the frame of reference on a production, I just try to be as honest as I can within it."

Jennings' respect for the groundwork laid by the series brought subtle character points to his sets and furnishings for *Star Trek II*. Kirk's apartment in San Francisco has a collection of antiques. In the series, Kirk's interest in history is brought up many times without being elaborated. It is Kirk who quickly realizes when and where they are in the many episodes which involve time-binding or recreations of past cultures like "City on the Edge of Forever," "A Piece of the Action," "Shore Leave," "Tomorrow is Yesterday," "Patterns of Force," and others, including the seminal episode for *Star Trek II*, "Space Seed."

"It might have been a nice touch if some of Kirk's 'antiques' had been objects from our own present," said

Jennings. "We thought about it and had the urge, but we sat down till it went away, for the sake of appealing to a broader audience. A sophisticated audience of *Star Trek* fans and science fiction buffs would love and appreciate the irony in something like that. But if I were to take a perfectly logical present-day artifact, say a toaster, and imply that this is an antique to Kirk, either I'd have to make a story point of it or your average Joe Doaks would be thinking, 'Gee Whiz, that's a toaster....what's antique about that?'"

As in the series, Spock has his quarters furnished with Vulcan art objects. Producer Robert Sallin wanted the centerpiece to be a tapestry of the Vulcan IDIC (Infinite Diversity in Infinite Combination), a revered cultural symbol of the *weltanschaung* of Vulcan, Spock's home planet.

While there wasn't time to commission the tapestry (which Jennings said, "in drawings, made Spock's cabin look like an opium den"), Jennings and Mike Minor kept Sallin's choice of the IDIC symbol and came up with a quick, cheap and colorful substitute: a wall mural composed of hundreds of tiny metals discs which has a soft iridescence, like the scales of a butterfly wing, with the convincing look of some alien artistry. To Southern Californians, however, the IDIC may look suspiciously like a "Sparkletts" sign, which shimmer intriguingly on the sides of delivery trucks for a local brand of bottled spring water and, in some respects, that is exactly what it is.

"I was dubious at first," admitted Sallin about giving the go-ahead to have it made. "It looks expensive but wasn't. The chap who makes the signs came with his little kit, which is really only a punch, some swivel wire things, and all these tiny little reflective metal discs that come in a range of hundreds of colors and tones. He worked from a big design and put it together in no time."

Jennings reused a number of sets from the first movie. In addition to the set he designed for the Enterprise bridge, which director Robert Wise had bolted together, he pulled from storage the bridge set of the Klingon cruiser, which was redressed as part of the Enterprise docking bay. Other portions of the Klingon ship became the transporter at Space Lab Regula One. The Enterprise bridge was redressed to become the bridge of the Reliant. "That's a fact of movie-making called 'The Price is Right,'" Jennings said. "The sets were already built. It would have been profligate and foolish not to use them."

Jennings modified the look of the existing Enterprise sets to get the sleeker, more utilitarian look that director Nicholas Meyer wanted. One new set built is the Enterprise torpedo room, a part of the ship that has never been shown before.

While many of *Star Trek II*'s sets came from the first movie, many of the props that dress the sets came from John Zabrucky's Modern Props. His facility, just outside Los Angeles, designs and builds both hand props and large self-contained props which form parts of sets.

The production rented many sizes and types of prop computer units which now stand in shadowy ranks amid Zabrucky's main storeroom. They are seen in the engine room of the Enterprise and in various areas of Regula One. As much as 30 feet of set can be dressed with Zabrucky's computers. Modern Props also made many of the hand props seen in the film, including the new tricorders, new wrist communicator devices, an electronic dustmop, futuristic fire extinguishers, several varieties of medical instruments, some small cargo containers which look like miniature Apollo capsules, a flange-necked liquor bottle that McCoy presents to Kirk early in the film and new hand communicators. The latter is basically a Vietnam War walkie-talkie unit, stripped of paint and plated with chrome. "It was what Paramount wanted," said Zabrucky. "We had a really great design that we wanted to build, but they were fixed on these things."

In contrast, the tricorder and medical instruments look businesslike and have an aura of technology, rather than movie prop. Lights that seem to have some purpose move within them, and they look rugged and durable. "You should see the phaser we wanted to build," Zabrucky said, "we did make one as a sample, but Paramount preferred to use the phasers that were made for the first movie."

■ Amazing Places

The surface of planet Ceti Alpha V, a desert where Khan and his followers have been marooned, was built utilizing the entirety of Paramount's Stage 8, one of the biggest soundstages on the lot. The floor was built over in scaffolding to raise a surface resembling an eroded landscape, overlaid with flooring and mats and covered with tons of sand and Fuller's earth, a fine powder. Four huge Ritter fans, which look like caged airplane propellers, were used to blow dust around. An immense cyclorama of the dust storm-swept sky was hung around the walls of the soundstage. The filmmakers wore coveralls, boots, masks and goggles, and all equipment was shrouded in plastic during filming.

Ceti Alpha V, in early scripts, was to have been an ice planet. Production designer Joseph Jennings and art director Michael Minor preferred the desert environment from a design standpoint, and changed the concept in pre-production. "We had cause to remember that change, ruefully, when we were on the set breathing Fuller's earth," said Jennings. "We were just praying for the camera not to spring a dust leak. After about three days we sort of wished we'd gone for the ice planet after all. You can always put on thermal underwear, if you actually refrigerate the stage."

The actors, as well as the crew, came to rue the set of Ceti Alpha V. Walter Koenig as Chekov and Paul Winfield as Captain Terrell had to wear spacesuits when they beamed down to the planet's surface.

"The suits were heavy," said Koenig, "as was the apparatus that went over our shoulders and back to support the helmets. But the most disquieting problem was the helmet itself. Nothing had been done about ventilating it, and once it was on, we had four or five minutes worth of air inside, and that was it. Periodically, between takes, someone would shove an air hose under the helmet and fill it up with fresh air.

"We had two mikes in our helmets," he continued, "one for recording dialogue and one which was used to talk with the director or each other. Sometimes the mikes wouldn't be switched on, so no one would hear us say we were running out of air. If we started to get light-headed from lack of oxygen, we'd go around tapping our helmets, hoping someone would understand we were in trouble. As soon as we'd stop shooting, even for four or five minutes, I'd always ask that the helmet and its support be taken off."

Koenig said he enjoyed recreating the Chekov character from the old series one more time. "I wasn't on the Enterprise in this movie, and simply by virtue of that fact I had more opportunity for my character to show a bit more color," he said. "On the Enterprise I was pretty well relegated to pushing buttons and saying things like, 'Torpedoes away!' By being first officer on the Reliant, with Captain Terrell, I wasn't compelled to speak in monosyllabic three-word sentences."

On Ceti Alpha V, Chekov and Terrell are infested by an alien parasite called the Ceti eel, an effect supplied by ILM's Ken Ralston and created by producer Robert Sallin.

Originally, the script called for an animal to attach itself to the back of the neck. But producer Robert Sallin wanted something to provide a more visceral reaction.

"I remember saying to Harve, 'Boy, is that boring and reminiscent of one of the episodes.' I'll never forget Harve saying, 'If you're so damn smart, you come up with something better.' I said, 'I will',' said Sallin. "I went away, thought about it and the next morning I went out to get my morning paper and there was a slug on the walkway. I said, 'Aha, that's interesting. What if it crept into an orifice of the body?'"

The idea is that the eel goes inside your ear and wraps itself around your cerebral cortex. They render you susceptible to suggestion. "But if they operated like that, how does that lead to anything life-threatening? Then I said, 'Wait a minute, they'll be the baby. They go inside and then they grow up and as they grow that's what kills the person.' I got all excited about it, then I went to ILM and told them the idea and they all thought it was terrific and gross. It was an

amazing device that Ken Ralston built," Sallin enthused. "When you see it on the screen you believe it. Everytime we shot that scene, everyone goes 'Urrrgh.'"

"That was one of the more enjoyable parts of the movie, for me," said Ralston. "[They] asked for eels, so I needed something that would be able to slither. But considering the desert-like environment of the planet, I thought it should have a real tough shell and look leathery."

The final design is a convincing-looking creature similar to a giant anti-lion or earwig. The "mother" is about 14" long and the "babies" come in several sizes and degrees of development. The earliest stage is a very slimy larval state that infests the ears of a host. These babies hide on the mother's back, underneath the plating. The mother puppet is designed with rods that come from underneath the tail section. The rods make the puppet move with a sort of snaky, thrashing way and there is also a mechanism for working the jaws in the head. The baby puppets are made of foam rubber and pulled along by means of a piece of monofilament fishing line. They're cut so that the front half pulls the back half, in a sort of inching motion.

Walter Koenig and Paul Winfield came to Ralston's shop for one day to shoot the effects sequence with the eels. "We had the eels crawling all over their faces for hours," said Ralston. "I'm surprised they both didn't rise up and try to kill me. We'd dip the eels in this goo, for this slime. The stuff is very unpleasant to have on your skin, especially your face, and you can't get it off. It's specially made by some guy in L.A. who makes all sorts of goos and glops and gunk for various uses in moviemaking."

Actually, Koenig didn't mind the face crawling scenes. "The only part I really hated was when they start the shot in which the eel comes out of my ear," he explained. "I fall down on the floor and we go to a close up, real close, as it emerges. They stuffed the little latex eel, with some of that sticky slime stuff, down in my ear. *That* was pretty unpleasant."

For the close up shot of a Ceti eel coming out of Chekov's ear, Ralston sculpted a huge model ear cast from Koenig's. Ralston reused the mother eel

as a baby eel with the scaled-up ear. To set up the shot, Koenig laid on a section of the floor of the Genesis Cave set brought up from Paramount. The eels were moved by Selwyn Eddy III, using monofilament line threaded up through a hole in the flooring under Koenig's body.

"It looks quite satisfyingly disgusting," said Ralston. "Something about the idea of a creature in your ear just makes everyone cringe. We did several variations of each shot, to pick the best— a dry shot, one with some blood, and the *Fangoria* shot, with a lot of gore."

Though Ceti Alpha V represented *Star Trek II*'s biggest set, production designer Joseph Jennings called the Genesis Cave his toughest assignment. The set was to show the result of the Project Genesis terraforming experiment which transforms the *interior* of a hollow, dead planetoid known as Gamma Regula. Jennings wanted to develop a geology that didn't look like Carlsbad Caverns. During discussions with art director Mike Minor, he remembered the distinctive caves in William Cameron Menzies' great little B-picture, *Invaders From Mars* (1953).

"In that film, some sort of laser weapon forms the tremendous caverns that the Martians lived in," recalled Minor, a film buff who credited George Pal's *Destination Moon* for triggering his interest in science fiction at age 10. "There was a lot of bubbling and frothing, and after the caves cooled you saw nothing but glass bubbles, eight or 10 inches across, all over the walls. I found out years later that they were condoms, inflated, stuck through holes and painted."

Jennings laughs at Minor's story, but liked the idea. The Genesis machine in the script was capable of breaking matter into its atoms and then reassembling them into a form capable of supporting life. Jennings reasoned there would be a tremendous amount of heat generated.

"We decided that the planet's surface would bubble," said Jennings. "Some of the bubbles would pop as they congealed and cooled. I've seen lava like that in the Hawaiian Islands. It was a matter of doing that on a scale so the cave could appear to be five miles long by three miles wide by two miles high."

The live action portion of the Genesis Cave is actually fairly small, a bowl shaped set representing only one of the planet's popped lava bubbles. About 300 feet across, the scale of the set in relation to the cave, is that of your thumbnail to your living room. Vegetation provides a primordial look. Tree ferns, moss and lichens make it appear as if life were starting anew. The semi-circular form of the burst bubble was made for Paramount by a company that manufactures domed swimming pool covers. Set in fiberglass, from a mold, the bubble form was carved and painted to form a section of the cave.

A camera pullback from the bubble set, showing the cave in its entirely, is a special effects tour de force. Multiple passes insert moving waterfalls, mist, changes in lighting and coloration, and sunlight sparkling on an underground lake, courtesy of ILM. Observed Jennings: "In the first movie, I felt that the special effects became the tail that wagged the dog. In this one, the effects and the story integrate very nicely, complementing each other."

The Genesis effects were executed at ILM, and featured a matte painting by Frank Ordaz and two by Chris Evans. "When something is this fantastic in the first place, it makes it doubly difficult to convince an audience that they're not looking at a painting," said Evans. "The Cave had to look incredible and like nothing anyone had ever seen before, but at the same time it had to look inviting, like a place you could enjoy living in for the rest of your life. It's a gigantic, lush underground jungle, but it couldn't look dank or claustrophobic. The closest reference to that look was found in the landscape paintings of the Amazon jungle at sunrise and sunset. They've got a golden, mystical, and tropical feeling."

An artificial sun moves through the cave. Kirk is taken out onto a promontory and looks out across a panorama including a moving waterfall, rays from the dawning sun move through the cave as he watches, and there are clouds pierced with shafts of sunlight.

To achieve these effects, Evans used a number of old and new tricks. To create the shafts of sunlight shining through the

Storyboards courtsey Mike Minor.

clouds he used a half-silvered mirror, placed between his matte painting and the camera, in front of the lens at a 45-degree angle. The mirror reflected the shafts of light into the camera lens, which also sees *through* the mirror to the painting. The light shafts are chalk lines Evans drew on black paper.

For the dawning sun effect, where the light comes across the surface of the cliffs, Evans did a set of highlight paintings which he double exposed grad-

ually into the main matte painting, revealing the light across the walls of the cave.

The idea of a moving waterfall in a matte painting may sound very difficult to accomplish. "It's simple, really," Evans insisted. "The obvious solution was to get a rotating cotton wheel kind of a device. We did a painting of a waterfall with the water motion accomplished by the cotton moving behind cut-out shapes of the water channels. We did the main painting without the waterfall, and double exposed the waterfall into it."

Though faced with what art director Mike Minor calls a "tight budget," *Star Trek II* is filled with grandiose visions, like the Genesis Cave, affordable because of design ingenuity and economy. One of Minor's money-saving tricks called for the use of a foreground miniature, seen early in the film.

Kirk and Spock have been strolling through Starfleet Academy hallways, talking, and they pause by an elevator. In a fairly wide shot, they stand underneath a large skylight, with open sky overheard, hanging plants, a stairway and a detailed concrete bas-relief wall visible. Minor built a miniature of the set because he didn't have the stage space or time to build a full vestibule or lobby set.

"I had the model shop put together this miniature on a scale of one quarter inch to one foot," he said. "I had everything installed over the weekend, and on Monday morning, our first day of shooting on the film, we did the shot. The camera was positioned one foot above the floor, shooting through this model, recording the actors 40 feet away. We had pillars set up that masked the end of our stage set, and the skylight had its own little sky scene backdrop painted, in which you can see the architecture of the elevator shaft on up through the skylight, as a cylinder.

"It's an old English technique," he added, "a foreground miniature tied to live action, but I don't think anyone watching the film is going to realize it. One day at the dailies we mentioned to the editor, 'This shot comes right after the foreground miniature shot' and *he* hadn't realized what it was."

Money was also saved by imaginative recycling. In a scene set at Kirk's San Francisco apartment, Minor used a backdrop from *The Towering Inferno* instead of painting his own San Francisco or matting it in. "We got an 80-foot portion from 20th Century Fox," he said. "It shows the city lights across the Bay, backlit. It's really very nice." The set of Kirk's apartment was constructed on Stage 8, utilizing an existing lower level accessible under the floor of the stage to form a sort of trench across the stage. Minor positioned miniature buildings, made out of spare parts from the first

movie, with lighted exterior elevators, as part of Kirk's window view.

"They were built to a scale one and one half inch to one foot," he said, "and putting them in the trench, nearer the camera than the backdrop, gives a perspective and depth to the scene. People will only see them in a quick flash as the camera pans across the room, but they add a really nice touch."

■ Spock's Ears

When *Star Trek II* began to take shape, the producers received a letter from Fred Phillips, who had done the makeup on the television series as well as *Star Trek: The Motion Picture*, that because of eye problems he would not be able to work on the project. Paramount turned to Werner Keppler, a makeup artist with considerable experience in appliance work and fantasy makeups, who got his big break working on John Chamber's makeup team for *Planet of the Apes.*

In contrast to some of the episodes of the television series, and even the first movie, makeup requirements on *Star Trek II* were not extensive. Called for were makeup to show injuries suffered by various characters, and Spock's famous ears, which are practically the hallmark—one hesitates to say the earmark—of the entire *Star Trek* mythos.

"I suppose the ears were my biggest perpetual headache," Keppler admitted. "Leonard Nimoy was in China making the *Marco Polo* mini-series right up to a few days before his part in this movie began, so I couldn't take the impressions of his ears from which to make the Spock ear-tips. Nimoy came in on a Friday afternoon, and as soon as he got in from the airport, practically, I took the impressions: I had to have a set of ears ready to use on Monday morning."

Keppler started from scratch, making the molds and then the ears, all in just a little over 48 hours. With no chance to try them on Nimoy, he had to guess the angle at which to attach the appliances. They worked fine that first day of shooting, but Keppler's headaches were just beginning.

"I was never able to have a set of ears ready in advance," he said. "They

can only be used once, because it ruins them when they're removed, so there had to be a new set made every day. I only had one mold, and every night after shooting I had to go home and make the next day's ears."

It took three to four hours for the latex ears to set in the molds. Every night Keppler had ears in the oven baking like cookies. "They'd bake till about midnight," he smiled, "then I'd check them over and smooth them off and go to bed at about one a.m. I had to be back at the studio at five a.m." If there was a failure, such as big bubbles forming in the latex, Keppler would have to cool the mold down and start all over. "A couple of nights I didn't get much sleep," he said. "And this went on for 18 days straight."

Leonard Nimoy, Keppler's uneasy subject, has never made it secret that the tedious Spock makeup is not one of his favorite pastimes. Putting on the ears, blending the edges, and doing the rest of Spock's makeup required about two and a half hours. "It started at five in the morning, when no one is at his best," said Keppler, who put Nimoy at easy by playing tapes of classical music. Keppler had heard that Nimoy liked the classics. "He just sat there and didn't move," said Keppler. "With him relaxed and still, I was able to streamline the makeup time down to less than two hours. The music benefitted us both."

A soft-spoken, gracious man—whose speech still carries a trace of his native Germany—Keppler has been a makeup artist for more than 36 years. His career began when he was a 16-year-old apprentice with opera companies in Germany. After emigrating to Canada, then to the United States, he landed a job at Perc Westmore's makeup school in Hollywood after reading about Westmore in a magazine. During an 11-year stint at Universal, Keppler worked on everything from *Jaws* to *Battlestar: Galactica.*

Keppler developed a new makeup technique for *StarTrek II*, to represent the grisly effect of thermal burns on battle victims. "Several makeup men, including myself, have been experimenting with it," he said. Instead of latex, cotton and spirit gum, Keppler used food processing gelatin, applied to actors with a spatula, sculpted, and then colored for effect. "The advantage of this material is its flexibility," he detailed. "It moves with the actor's skin and muscles." The gelatin also made the makeup easy to remove, being water soluble.

The new burn makeup was used for the first time on Ike Eisenmann, who plays Scotty's nephew, cadet Peter Preston. "It would have been very hard on him the old way," said Keppler, "since so much of his body was covered with burns. Using latex appliances would have taken three to four hours to make him up, not to mention the time spent taking impressions, and making molds and appliances. With this gelatin technique, the whole makeup job took about 45 minutes."

Keppler also used the technique on Ricardo Montalban, to represent Khan's mortal injuries as he captains the bridge of the Reliant during the film's climactic battle scenes. A spurious report in the infamous *National Enquirer* accused Keppler (as "the make-up man") of setting Montalban's wig on fire while trying to singe it with a candle.

"That's not true," said Keppler, "and Ricardo will back me up. Those wigs won't burn. They'll barely singe. I used the candle to singe the wig hair down into a wound on Khan's head, and while I was doing it Ricardo didn't move a muscle. He knew exactly what I was doing and he wasn't bothered."

Keppler also created a special makeup for Leonard Nimoy to represent the progressive effect of radiation burns which cause Spock's death, doing a bit of medical research in the process.

Despite all the hard work and the pressures of a rushed production schedule, Keppler looked forward to possible involvement in future *Star Trek* films. "I enjoyed this one a great deal," he enthused. "The only thing is, I told them that for heaven's sake if they're going to do another movie, let me know ahead of time so I can make some ear molds. My wife wants her oven back at least every other night!"

■ ILM Effects, Part II

While Ken Ralston at ILM worked on the two big space battles and the Ceti eel sequence, his effects co-supervisor, Jim Veilleux, did the rest of the space shots involving the Enterprise and supervised shooting during principle photography of the live-action effects scenes in VistaVision. The live-action photography is considered a "plate" onto which a matte artist and matte photographer combine their work into a finished shot. Everything but the plate of the actors on the set will be a painting or some ILM matte department trick.

ILM's matte artists on *Star Trek II* were Chris Evans and Frank Ordaz. Evans painted Ceti Alpha V and two mattes of the Genesis Cave, a lush and verdant landscape—after the Genesis device worked its miracles. Ordaz did seven nebula paintings, plus one of the Genesis Cave.

On some special effects, Veilleux split the plate photography into two pieces for increased control of the image. For phaser shots, he'd photograph just one actor of a group, the one who is going to be hit, against a portable blue screen. The other actors, minus the victim, are filmed separately on a set, and react as if the victim was there. The victim is inserted in the final composite via a blue screen matte, and is then made to disappear as his image is first superimposed, then dissolved out, all in conjunction with rotoscoped artwork of the phaser effect.

ILM shoots all its effects work in VistaVision, a format developed in the early 50's when motion pictures were trying to fight the inroads of television on their audiences by presenting an image fidelity and scope that TV screens couldn't match. The system runs 35mm film through the camera horizontally, instead of vertically, resulting in a frame image twice as long as normal 35mm. Since the film stock is still 35mm, it does not require the special lab processing that 70mm does, and can be handled with standard 35mm moviolas and optical printers.

"You need that large format just to account for the image degradation that occurs in the optical printer," Veilleux said. "You also need as high a quality image as possible. Since VistaVision is the same field size as 35mm, we can use high-quality Nikon lenses for all our cameras, and have dozens of lenses to give us a great deal of versatility."

Because one frame of film contains eight sprocket hole perforations, rather than the normal four of 35mm film, VistaVision is also referred to as 8-perf. The camera goes through film at twice the rate of a 35mm camera, since the film gate is twice as long. VistaVision film magazines are enormous and extremely heavy.

As is the 400 pound camera. When the camera has to be moved, pipes are run through a set of lfanges on each side of the camera body and at least four men pick it up like a sedan chair. "You have to pick the thing up and set it down again to make even the smallest change of position," Veilleux said. "Nick [Meyer] was always saying, 'Oh, let's get in a little closer on this shot' and we'd think, 'Nick, you just don't know what you're asking.'"

The enormous weight of a VistaVision camera does make it very steady. In effects work, with 1/1000 of an inch of registration a vital necessity, this is an added plus. The camera also runs the film in a steady manner.

"Where the pins lock into the film perforation, the first has to be perfect each time," explained Veilleux, "or the image will be jiggling around on the film. In a single element piece it would never be noticeable, but once you start combining one piece of film with another, such as putting the computer graphics of a space shot inside the viewscreen of the Enterprise, the slightest jiggle will show up.

"We spent a lot of effort trying to design and maintain cameras that will reliably keep the film steady. That's one of the things that makes effects work so expensive. We've built cameras from scratch, and we've taken old cameras, including some which date back to the '30s and originally ran three-strip Technicolor film, replaced the motors and turned them into very sophisticated field units which are compatible with some of our computers."

Veilleux's crew took over the enormous Cow Palace, just outside San Francisco, for the pyrotechnics work involved in the space battle and the final Genesis explosion which creates a brand new planet. "Thaine Morris, our pyrotechnics man, did that," said Veilleux. "The work is very technical, to achieve the look you want, and being inside the auditorium and not having to deal with weather factors made things much easier. You have to shoot an enormous amount of film for such shots. In a week we shot 35,000 feet. Bruce Hill provided a super high-speed camera which slowed down the action enormously. It shoots at 2400 frames a second."

All that footage eventually ends up in ILM's effect editing department, and gets catalogued by Art Repola, supervising effects editor on *Star Trek II*. A film editor ordinarily works in two dimensions. He splices pieces of film together, end to end, to construct a story. A visual effects editor works vertically, through layers of film.

"It's editing all the elements within a shot, creating the choreography and continuity of the elements," Repola said. "Effects shots are done in pieces, with each piece shot separately. If you have four spaceships and a planet and a starfield background and a laser beam, those are each separate pieces of film. The basic plan of the shot has been worked out, but as far as finessing it goes, making sure the elements are positioned right within the frame, and are the correct size in proportion to the other elements, those things are the responsibility of the visual effects editors."

Effects editing is done on a special moviola machine that can handle ILM's oversize VistaVision format, five layers of film at a time. If a shot has more than five elements, it is taken in chunks and Repola has to use his imagination to visualize the synch.

One of the most complex shots in *Star Trek II*, in terms of number of elements, involves one of the ships exploding and pieces flying off in every direction. The little pieces of debris were shot blue-screen as four elements. For each of those shots, a burning spark element and a flashing light element were filmed to match. Add to that, three explosions, the ship, the nebula in the background, and the stars in the nebula. Eighteen separate pieces of film were ultimately combined by Repola for a shot one-and-a-half or two seconds long.

The elements are edited on top of each other, to get a pre-composite look at them. Repola starts with the background and the main element because they will run the whole length of the scene while the other pieces physically start and stop somewhere within the shot. For instance, a one-second-long phaser burst might occur within a four-second-long shot.

The editor then writes it all up on an optical instruction sheet and sends it to the optical printing department. Repola tells them the timing, where to start and stop printing, where to position each element and what elements block out others in case of cross-overs (a ship moving in front of another ship or planet).

"We are essentially the last road on the process," said optical photography supervisor Bruce Nicholson. "We do the composite photography; we take all the separate elements and assemble them on an optical printer to make the final piece of film in which they all combine. We see to it that the elements are color-balanced to each other, that they're positioned correctly in the frame and are the proper relative size, and that they don't have any noticeable flaws like grain or soft focus. If there are any mistakes, we try to correct them or try to make them look less noticeable."

The optical printer used on *Star Trek II* was developed for use on *The Empire Strikes Back*. Called a quad-head printer because it has four projector heads, the electronics for it were all done at ILM and the components, such as lenses and projectors, purchased from the very best people. The machine is 10 feet long, by two feet wide, plus another five feet on a split-axis wing. It weighs roughly 2500 pounds and, since it has to be very level and stable, it rests on a laser bench.

Repola divided up the effects work with Peter Admundson. Repola edited all the effects sequences done by Ken Ralston and Admundson took Jim Veilleux's work. "*Star Trek* was supposed to have been simple work we already knew how to do," said Repola. "Once we got into it, this obviously wasn't the case. New things were needed to get the job done, half the facility was working on other films, including *E.T.* and *Poltergeist*. Paramount went over schedule down at the studio, which squeezed us. There's been quite a bit of pressure here at the end. But I love this work because every movie is different, every shot is different, and everything stretches us and pushes the state of the art."

Pushing the state of the art was also the goal behind Peter Kuran's Visual Concept Engineering, who handled the film's transporter and phaser effects, among other things.

"The way we wanted to do the transporter effect would have been more interesting than what they ended up with," Peter Kuran said. "We would have liked to show a person's body sort of building as he was beaming in...skeleton appearing first, then veins and finally clothing. Not exactly like *This Island Earth*, but more like an effect I saw once in *The Outer Limits*.

"But Paramount wanted a very high-tech electronic look, with a *moire* effect and strobes and flashes," he added. "And one of the things they emphasized was that they didn't want to use freeze-frames for the transporter process the way they had in the old series and in the first movie. They tried to make a point of having people moving while they were being transported. We did a lot of articulate mattes to follow most of the action in those sequences, which took a lot of time. Then they decided they didn't want to see that effect, so we ended up throwing most of them away."

In addition to the transporter effect, Kuran's company added animation effects to scenes involving phaser hits and dematerializations, some exterior scenes in a sandstorm on Ceti Alpha V and the radiation effect for the scene in which Spock receives his fatal burns.

Visual Concept Engineering employs a staff of from four to eight artists in a Hollywood building that once served a porno film production company. VCE received its work on *Star Trek II* through Industrial Light and Magic. "Our company has done a number of jobs either directly or indirectly through ILM," Kuran said. "The stuff they don't have time for they farm out to me. I used to work for ILM before leaving to form my own company, so they know me and what I can do."

Kuran is already a veteran of six years experience in the optical effects business. "I was 19 when I worked on *Star Wars*, and the next year I did my first freelance work, the optical animation on a piece of junk called *The Dark*." Kuran left ILM after *The Empire Strikes Back*, hoping the freedom would give him the opportunity to do new things.

"I started working with film," Kuran said, "looking into things that most people consider too basic or too boring, like how different images react to each other and what film is actually doing during the different phases of the printing process. I bought an old 16mm contact printer and started trying out different film stocks and different processes. Then I got to know some people with optical printers and used them in the middle of the night, Sunday morning, odd times like that."

It was Kuran's work on *Dragonslayer*—44 shots including the spear-forging, the glowing amulet, the resurrection and the sword fights—that established his fledgling company and proved to the industry that the money allocated for Kuran's effects would be well spent.

After *Dragonslayer*, his company worked on *Conan the Barbarian* and *The Thing*, before taking on *Star Trek II*. Kuran has never regretted leaving the shelter of a big company. "I'm having a ball," he said. "Every job is different and I'm getting to do new things, which is why I wanted to strike out with my own company in the first place. In this business, on every job you're sticking your neck out just enough that you're doing something you haven't done before. A client comes in; you decide on something; and you shake hands on it. When he leaves, you sit down and start figuring it out because often you have absolutely no idea how it's going to look or exactly how you'll do it. It's great."

■ Computer Imaging

One of ILM's innovations for *Star Trek II* involved the use of computer imaging. Jim Veilleux supervised all the various animation and special computer graphics for the film.

Above Veilleux's desk is a photo of two jet fighters taking off from a runway backed with a desert landscape and mountains on the horizon. The lighting has the shadowless quality and soft colors of dawn light. If Monet had painted F-104s, this is how they would have looked. Except, it isn't a photograph of two F-104s, but of a *computer simulation*.

Veilleux got his start doing effects work while in the military and worked at ILM as an effects cameraman for *The Empire Strikes Back, Raiders of the Lost Ark* and *Poltergeist*.

Computer simulation is one of Veilleux's specialties. When a ship moves through space in *Star Trek II*, the star fields are not the usual random pinpricks through a black back-drop. These star fields are "real," with all the stars represented in their correct colors, magnitudes and relationships. And as the ship goes along, every single star stays in its proper perspective. That's just one example of computer graphics that are changing the face of special effects. Using fast, powerful computers to produce images, one of the first applications for this type of graphics was in flight simulators. In fact, the company which produced *Star Trek II*'s computer graphics (and the photo above Veilleux's desk) is Evans & Sutherland, whose principal product is flight simulator graphics.

But it was one of Evans and Sutherland's new products that caused Veilleux to take notice. The Salt Lake City based company created Digistar, a computer system designed to display computer generated star fields and graphic images on the domes of planetariums at considerably less expense, and with a lot more versatility, than building Zeiss optical systems.

"We used Evans and Sutherland's programs after I saw simple ways of getting their work on film," said Veilleux. "We developed a very good working relationship with their main programmers on the Digistar system, Brent Watson and Steve McAllister. And our own computer division used the programs they have been working on for two years.

"The opening shot of *Star Trek II* runs about three minutes, is a special star field

with a data base of about 6,000 stars," Veilleux continued. "None of the audience may know or care about the accuracy of the field, but the overall effect is overwhelming, much more than could be achieved by multiple camera passes over a piece of artwork."

The real innovation that computer graphics bring to film is the ability to produce a wide range of motions and dynamics easily and cheaply. Special effects that would have been prohibitively expensive and involve time-consuming set-ups and tricks, even with sophisticated equipment like motion-control cameras or computerized animation stands, can be done in one piece with everything moving in perfect perspective, no matter how much detail is involved.

ILM's in-house computer division, part of Sprocket Systems (the research and development arm of Lucasfilm), has also been working on computer graphics for *Star Trek II*. Headed by Alby Ray Smith and Loren Carpenter, a team of computer graphics programmers created a demonstration of the Genesis terraforming device.

Admiral Kirk has his identity checked by means of a retina scan, and is permitted to watch a video-tape visual aid explanation of project Genesis. The tape is somewhat similar to the simulations of present-day spacecraft in planetary approaches, but at a far more advanced level.

The simulation is from the point of view of a deep space probe. As the probe approaches a dead, airless, cratered planet, it fires a projectile. The projectile hits with a flash of light and a shock wave; fire races across the surface of the planet, melting it and sending up huge clouds of gas that eventually become an atmosphere. The surface cools, then fractures and ripples as mountain ranges the height of Everest rise up, vulcanoes explode and other areas sink into vast depressions. The mist and smoke clear, snow appears on the mountain tops. The probe is so close to the planet that the curvature of the horizon is lost. At its nearest approach, the probe swoops down a long narrow canyon and out across a sea beginning to fill with water as river channels carve the continents. Green appears, creeping across the land from the water's edge, as the probe pulls away. Finally the probe flips over and looks back at the planet, now a green and blue hospitable world.

The tape lasts a little over 60 seconds and is created entirely by computer representing five months work from a 10 man computer graphics team. A total of two-man years of effort were required to get those 60 seconds, and the 20 seconds of Kirk's retina scan, also computer generated.

"The Genesis *tape* was our idea," said Veilleux. "Paramount was planning to demonstrate this Genesis effect with a live-action sequence, but nobody was happy with it. I had been trying to convince them to go for computer graphics—I used to produce educational films, and I knew that in really complex problems, computer graphics are used to simulate what you can't possible produce as a demonstration—but Paramount was concerned about whether it would be dramatic enough. I'd say they're very happy with what they got.

"But in the movie, the Genesis tape sort of goes by without being presented as remarkable," he added with a note of irony. "In the *Star Trek* universe you should expect that sort of thing."

At first, he proposed four sequences for ILM's computer imaging division: two identification processes, a retina check and a voice check, a computer programmed sequence in which Kirk sees a crystalline inorganic molecule transformed into a DNA-type organic molecule, illustrating the Genesis effect creating life, and also a demonstration of the effect on a planetary scale.

"Originally, that had been a live-action sequence in which a rock transforms into a flower, or something like that," said Alvy Ray Smith, co-leader along with Loren Carpenter of the computer graphics project. He's a big, rugged-looking man with dark brown hair well below his shoulders, and a full beard.

The molecule sequence was supplied by Dr. Robert Langridge of the University of California at San Francisco. "We tried to exploit things that people had been working on," said Veilleux. "He had worked on a computer graphic of very complex DNA mole-

cule for years."

The voice recognition bit went by the wayside. Which left just the retina scan, and the Genesis Tape. The fledgling computer division at ILM saw the work as a perfect opportunity to get the bugs out of their computer systems.

Said Moore, "The Genesis Tape fit into our already-scheduled software development plans for texture-mapping and matting, it involved a sphere, which is a simple data-base, and it was planned to be on videotape, with a monitor screen matted in, so we would only need 500- line resolution. I felt it would introduce us to the rest of Lucasfilm."

Originally, the Genesis Tape computer demonstration was supposed to be fairly simple. Veilleux wanted a zoom-in on the planet, a two-dimensional effect to indicate the explosion of the planet, a cut to live-action reaction shots, and a pull-back showing a transformed planet. The proposal, however, just grew. Given a go-ahead by Paramount, individual team-members took on different programming responsibilities and the concept was fine-tuned. As they worked on it, the demo tape became ever more complex and ambitious.

For instance, instead of just tossing the planet somewhere in the galaxy, the team wanted to keep a recognizable constellation in view. By obtaining the Yale Bright Star Catalog, they selected the names of five nearby stars which may have planets that could support life. The team selected Epsilon Indi, because it was determined that the Big Dipper would be visible in a form not too distorted from Earth's view of it. Furthermore, our sun would appear as an extra star in the constellation. Loren Carpenter named the planet Keti Bandar, the city at the mouth of the Indus River, where it empties into the Indian Ocean.

In early February, ILM matte artist Chris Evans began using ILM's in-house programming to create the final effect of the planet's metamorphosis.

Evans "painted" on a horizontal white board in front of a video monitor with a light pen. The board passes its x-y coordinate information to the computer, where the image is displayed on a video monitor facing him. Sort of like painting *with* numbers instead of *by* numbers.

"What they wanted me to paint was a three dimensional sphere of a planet in the process of weathering," Evans said. "First we made a Mercator projection of a sphere onto the work surface. Then I painted the landscape on that grid. The computer was programmed to take my flat painting and wrap it around a globe.

"It was a fantastic experience using a whole new technology like that. Painting systems for computers have been around for a while, but as far as I know no one has ever had a professional artist use one before; so I felt it was a great honor to be the first guinea pig to try their system out."

After Evans used the program for awhile, his hand-eye coordination allowed him to direct his attention to the monitor as he painted. His work was displayed on the screen continually, 30 frames a second.

Evans worked closely with computer programmer Tom Porter to actually change and refine the computer program until it could do everything Evans expected from a brush with paint on it.

"For example," Evans explained, "the way you can put a stroke down and the color will sort of fade off as you put less pressure on the brush, things like that. To make clouds, we had to tell the computer how to blend brush-strokes."

ILM's computer painting system consists of a number of programs, one for painting as well as sketch, clear, transform, fill and other program applications. An artist selects a program off the menu board with a stylus. The "Sketch" program renders whatever you do with the light pen as if it were a pencil. "Clear" allows the operator to pick a color and indicate an area, and the computer will change that area to that color. "Fill" is similar, but for arbitrarily shaped areas. "Transform" allows the operator to pick up a piece of a picture and manipulate it, rotate it, scale it up or down, move it around, a sort of cut-and-paste capability.

Once a program is selected off the menu board, a swipe of the pen to the right side puts the cursor, the point of light, on the main monitor screen. A downward swipe of the pen instructs the computer to display a color palette. Only about 200 colors are presented, but a million others are available, or a color can be selected off the painting and the computer will apply that color where indicated.

"The program is set up so that a regular artist can, with a fairly understandable set of tools, either create his own pictures or touch up the kind of pictures we can create," computer programmer Tom Porter said. "For instance, here's a fine planet surface, but we didn't provide any clouds because clouds are a difficult subject to animate. So if you want to touch it up a little with clouds, you get an artist over here from ILM."

The Genesis Tape sequence was filmed in March, by a film crew from ILM next door, using an Empireflex VistaVision camera. Computer programmer Rob Poor's retinas were photographed for the retina scan sequence. "Actually, four of us had our retinas photographed," Smith mused, "but Rob's were the most interesting."

The identification process thought up for *Star Trek II* was to move a vein template around in some interesting way until a pattern match occurred between the veins in the person's retinas and on the template, at which point some appropriate lettering and graphics would appear, indicating a positive identification.

"What we're heading for is full resolution movie theatre quality images," said Smith. "We were hired by Lucas essentially to bring the computer into filmmaking in any way we can think of. The attack points are audio, in the form of digital audio processors; in videotape editing, and in making pictures with the computer. But it's just not happening fast enough to suit us We're building tools that eventually ILM will use to make movies."

On the office walls of Rose Duignan, ILM's production supervisor for *Star Trek II*, are blankets of 6x8 photocopies of the film's storyboards. Most have "Finished" written across them in felt-tip ink.

"On this movie, we did the most number of shots in the shortest time that has been done here or elsewhere," said Duignan with a somewhat tired pride. "The original *Star Trek* had so much more time and so much more

money and so many more people involved. We basically did the entire film in less than six months. The people here work so bloody hard. And they create more work for themselves. There might be an element that's okay—the producer will buy it—but the camera people and animators and optical people will say, 'No, we can do it better.' That's just not Hollywood."

Despite his criticism of the Enterprise, Ken Ralston looks fondly at a picture of the ship composited into ILM's background nebula. "Do I fall in love with these movies as I do them?" he asks, rhetorically. "Usually I fall *out of* love with them. The planning is fun, but the doing is hard work. It tends to absorb your life. I notice I tend to date events according to what I was working on at the time. I got married during *Dragonslayer*, for instance. But when the work is done and you see it up on the screen and all that work pays off...yeah, I fall in love with the movie all over again."

On the far wall of ILM's moviola room is a large black and white photo mural of a gentlemen in a business suit, editing footage by means of scissors and a light bulb. It's Sergei Eisenstein, and it's been said you can tell, in the enlargement, that the film he's working on is from *Ivan the Terrible*. Eisenstein pioneered film aesthetics and editing techniques. If he could see what's going on at ILM under his visage, he'd be pleased.

■ The Score

The makers of *Star Trek II* wanted a rousing orchestral musical score in the best adventure film traditions of Erich Korngold and recent imitators such as John Williams. Producer Robert Sallin felt—as he had with the choice of the film's director—that they should get a composer who would be hungry, and capable of giving them something new and exciting.

To this end, composer James Horner was approached by Sallin and Joel Sill, vice-president of music for the motion picture division of Paramount, and was introduced to executive producer Harve Bennett, producer Robert Sallin and director Nicholas Meyer. Horner agreed with that approach and started

composing in mid-January.

"There is a tendency to want to compare scores of big outer space movies," said Horner, "like John Williams' music for *Star Wars* and *The Empire Strikes Back* and Jerry Goldsmith's for the first *Star Trek* film. There will be similarities, of course. For one thing, if you close your eyes and play *Star Wars* and my *Star Trek* score, the first notion that will come to your mind is that the same instruments are playing. Williams created a trend in music for space movies with *Star Wars* because that was the first big space movie to come along in quite awhile. But that style of scoring is very old-fashioned. It works well, whether you're on a train or a pirate galleon or in deep space. That kind of approach is very tactile. It's easy to use it to manipulate emotions."

Horner composed about 70 minutes of music for *Star Trek II* in five weeks. A lot of music for a film that was 129 minutes long. "The last three reels are almost wall-to-wall music," he said, "including some tremendous battle scenes." Horner utilized a 90-piece full symphony orchestra for the scoring sessions which lasted five days.

Director Nicholas Meyer, who comes from a family of professional musicians and is not bad on the battered grand piano that sits in his living room, worked closely with Horner. In fact, Horner credits Meyer with a lot of input on his composition of the score.

"He and I talked about it at great length," explained Horner. "We spent so much time together on this project that we've become rather close friends. Nick knows what he's talking about, musically. He wanted to give the film the feeling of an adventure on the high seas. It's that sort of nautical, undersail, wind-blowing spirit that I'm after, as opposed to STAR WARS' very imperial, material kind of theme."

■ He's Dead Jim

Principal photography with the main actors began on November 9, 1981 at the Paramount Studios in Hollywood. Production ended January 29, 1982, a few days over schedule and slightly over budget, a rather remarkable feat for a production of *Star Trek II*'s scope.

From the beginning, the film was marked by keen interest from fans, seemingly fed by rumors that Spock had been killed off in a script. There was considerable speculation that publicity "leaks" about Spock's death were deliberately planted to stir up Trekkies and media attention for the film. Such suspicions were exacerbated when the TV news magazine *Entertainment Tonight* (also produced by Paramount) ran a call-in viewer poll on the subject of whether Spock should perish or be spared, and then it conducted three-days worth of interviews on the bridge set of the Enterprise.

"The studio did not generate any of the rumors about Spock's death," said producer Robert Sallin. "People have assumed that when this movie was conceived the first thing the studio did was to run out and create the rumors that Spock was going to die, to get the Trekkies excited and generate publicity. That is contrary to my knowledge. I know that the position of the studio brass is that they would just as soon nobody said anything. Early drafts of the script were stolen and made their way into the hands of fans, and that fueled the furor."

However the rumors were promulgated, in the final analysis Spock *did* die, so at least the concern on the part of the fans was not completely wasted on cynical manipulation. What constitutes Death is a matter of semantics and debate even now, let alone in the 23rd Century. "In science fiction there are many kinds of life, and many kinds of death," Sallin pointed out.

Ironically, this was one death that Leonard Nimoy himself had tried to avoid as filming of that scene grew closer. "I found myself being moved by the scene early, very early, at about the point where Kirk says to Scott something about you have to get us out of here in three minutes or we're all dead," related Nimoy to *Starlog* magazine. "You see Spock hear that and react. I'm already feeling emotional about what's coming. [I] really came within a hair's breath of walking off the lot rather than playing the scene. The day we were going to shoot it, I was very edgy about it and scared of it—scared of playing it, almost looking

for an excuse not to, finding something to pick an argument about. It was a very tense time. And I *still* feel that way seeing it. It's a moving scene and I'm pleased with it in the context of the film. I'm glad we did it. I think we did it well. I think we did it honestly and sincerely."

According to Nicholas Meyer, it was the filming of that scene which finally made him comprehend the true power of *Star Trek*.

"The scenes which were the most difficult, or at least the most wrenching to do, were the death of Spock [sequences]," he said. "Everybody stood around on the stage in tears, which was very surprising to me because I'm not that experienced as a movie director and I was amazed at how moved they were. The next day at the dailies, same thing. Everybody cried. I come from the 'less is more' school of thinking. You can have somebody point to something and say, 'Look at that' and you don't have to cut to what he is pointing to. In fact, you can raise considerable tension by not showing the audience what the character sees. For example, once Spock enters the reactor room I deliberately didn't cut back to him for a long time. After hearing, 'You can't go in there, you can't go...', you gotta be wondering, 'What's happening to him?' You want to see what's going on there. It's a matter of choice, of taste. I would rather underplay and let the audience imagination rise to meet something halfway. From what I've seen of the series, I tend to think they overacted or showed too much.

"My attitude has changed perceptively. I don't know whether it was the actors themselves or the characters, but I finally thought, when I was watching the death scene and I realized that *I* was choked up, I thought, well, we have now transcended the subject matter. This is no longer simply about a man with pointy ears, which is how I felt because I didn't know it that well."

One aspect of Spock's demise remains in William Shatner's mind; a moment which paved the way for a film followup and a tale of resurrection.

"It was never anticipated," Shatner said. "An accident happened. Maybe it wasn't an accident if you don't believe in accidents. But it was really

very strange. We were getting ready to do the death scene of Spock. This wasn't scripted, but Leonard put his hand on DeForest's head and he was looking for something mysterious to do. For some reason, in this last scene, Leonard said 'Remember.' It was very mysterious. It was meaningful to somebody in *Star Trek* but we didn't know what it meant. And that was the end. Spock was dead and the question was, will there be a *Star Trek III* and how could you do it without Spock? But that was a whole other question. As far as everyone was concerned at that time, Spock was dead."

At the time of *The Wrath of Khan*'s release, Nimoy gave an interview in which he discussed just what significance the "remember" scene might hold for a subsequent sequel. He mused, "I feel that the next *Star Trek* offers a great opportunity for exploration of science fiction involved with Vulcan mysticism, Vulcan metaphysics, if you will. There's a world of ideas to be explored in terms of the Vulcan beliefs about life, death and life—Vulcan beliefs about reincarnation of transmigration of the spirit. What was it that Spock planted in McCoy's mind when he said, 'Remember?' ....Remember what?

"It's obvious there's some kind of ticking clock going on in there that might be explored later. We can open that up and say, 'What is McCoy carrying around in his head that he may not even know about consciously yet that may spring to life later and be a factor in the next movie? Can you imagine what would happen if Kirk had any reason whatsoever, if he were given reason to believe or hope that there might be a way to get Spock back? To save him or help him? He would be obsessed, wouldn't he? And if McCoy were dragged into that mix as the medical officer and as the person who has that thing in his head, whatever it is...boy, you've got a pretty driving kind of motivation going on immediately. I certainly would love to be involved in the very early stages of discussion."

And Nimoy ultimately would be, with Paramount Pictures giving him the opportunity to direct the next film.

While ILM finished the special effects work on *The Wrath of Khan*,

Paramount began to lift the film's veil of secrecy in an effort to publicize the forthcoming release. Public statements by director Nicholas Meyer led to some friction on the production, however. Robert Sallin took exception to off-hand remarks made by Meyer which characterized the ongoing effects work as being disorganized.

"I don't believe in taking credit for other people's work and I don't believe in making myself seem more important at other people's expense," said Sallin. "Nick did not supervise the creation of the effects storyboards, and Nick did not supervise the execution of the shots. He attended one meeting with me at ILM, at which time I ran through every frame of every shot, and that was it. He was overwhelmed with the special effects and just backed away from them."

During final editing, just prior to release, two human-interest subplots were dropped to pick up the film's pace. One dropped scene involved Scotty's young nephew, Peter Preston, who dies while working in the engine room. The scene establishing Preston as Scotty's nephew also went by the wayside, leaving the exact basis of Scotty's affectionate attachment to the young man rather open to interpretation (although this scene was restored to the version that eventually aired on ABC). Another excised scene involved a somewhat unlikely romance between Kirk's hot-tempered son, David Marcus, and the supercilious Lt. Saavik.

Director Nicholas Meyer was pleased with his cut of *Star Trek II*. Traditionally, the first editing of a film is done at the director's order, but may be amended or recut later, at the discretion of producers or studio. Meyer's cut was tightened somewhat, according to Robert Sallin. "We had too much plot, essentially," he explained. "Nick's background is that of a writer, and in his version there was an extraordinary amount of exposition that we didn't feel was totally necessary; so Harve Bennett and I made some changes, in response to notes from the studio. It had to do with the tempo of the film. What we have is essentially the same picture as the director's cut."

Meyer reportedly hated the subtitle *The Wrath of Khan*, saying it is trashy and foolish sounding. He had

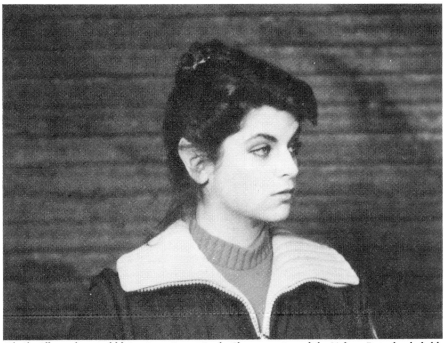

Kirstie Alley, who would later go on to co-star in Cheers, portrayed the Vulcan-Romulan hybrid, Lieutenant Saavik (photo copyright ©1994 G. Trindl/Shooting Star)

always preferred the original subtitle, *The Undiscovered Country*, but had been aware for months that the studio didn't care for it and planned to change it before the movie was released. Ironically, as Meyer has returned to the *Star Trek* fold with *STAR TREK VI*, he is finally being granted his wish as the film's subtitle is indeed *The Undiscovered Country*.

Meyer has also disputed the idea that fans had any influence on the ultimate ending of the film. After a screening at a science fiction convention in Kansas on May 8, a high-placed Paramount official indicated that other endings had been considered, perhaps filmed, and that the one used would depend on fan reaction. Meyer has firmly denied this.

"My job," Meyer told journalist Dennis Fischer, "is not to find out what the public wants and give it to them; my job is to make the public want what I want. If you take a vote on things before the fact, you will never do anything. Nobody wanted Spock to die. There were threatening letters [from fans]: 'If Spock dies, you die.'

"The question in my mind was not whether he died, but whether he died well. His death needed some organic

relationship to the rest of the movie, and a plausible connection to whatever else was going on. If we did that, I don't think anyone would question it. On the other hand, if the movie suddenly turned around a corner on two wheels and we 'fulfill Leonard Nimoy's contract by bumping off his character which he has grown tired of playing,' if indeed that was the scenario, which I have never heard, that wouldn't be so good. That stuff that we were going to have more than one ending, that we were going to let the audience decide...that was all bullshit. Art is not made by committee and it's not made by voting.

"I don't think it was ever seriously considered," he continued. "I never had any pressure about it. The closest thing that happened was that we were under great pains to keep the whole movie under wraps. We succeeded until a month before it opened, when Paramount insisted on previewing the movie in Kansas City. The next night, Johnny Carson was on TV. He said, 'Well, it's out; he dies.' And I thought, they must be crazy. Here we tried so hard to keep this under wraps and then they insist on doing this. And *then* the Paramount publicity department started cranking out this stuff about whether there was actually more than one ending or not. They were trying to convince people that there was more than one ending to keep the suspense going. I said, 'I'm not going along with this.' I'd just look stupid. I have enough trouble not doing that anyway. So that was the only time there was any attempt to convey the illusion that the thing wasn't locked up. They were just trying to backpedal."

As far as can be determined, Spock always died, in every version of the script and every cut of the film. Additional scenes involving Spock's death were shot by an ILM crew, with Robert Sallin, at San Francisco's Golden Gate Park in late April, more than two months after principal photography wrapped, when the movie was, for all intents and purposes, complete. The scenes show Spock's casket, a photon torpedo casing, drifting after his burial in space, finally coming to rest on the planet created by the explosion of the Genesis device aboard Khan's ship. Originally, Spock's casket was simply set adrift in space. These extra scenes were filmed after the results of opinion screenings before carefully-selected, demographically-balanced audiences.

"One of the major conflicts Nick and I had in the making of the picture was the whole idea of reminding people, of planting the seed that Spock might come back," explained Robert Sallin. "It was not in the original script, that idea of going back to the planet. Nick hated the idea, but I think the studio wanted it because they were getting so much flack about killing Spock."

■ Commenting On Khan

Star Trek II: The Wrath of Khan was a critical success, with the majority of reviewers noting that this is the way the first film should have been done.

The cast, as related to various journalists, had nothing but unanimous praise regarding the film, believing it to be far superior to *Star Trek: The Motion Picture* and a much more satisfying experience.

William Shatner: "I was nervous about it. Especially after the first film. The

success of your performance, essentially, rests in the words. Everything rises and falls on the script. When a script is good, it takes a heroic effort to ruin it. As this script developed, I swung wildly from awful lows to exalted highs. I began to realize that the movie might be good. By the time we were ready to shoot, I knew *Wrath of Khan* would be great. I knew we had ILM for the effects, so the movie couldn't *look* bad. We also had a very human, *Star Trek*ian script. It was a wonderful working experience. It was as if the years between this film and the old show never existed."

Leonard Nimoy: "In doing [*Star Trek: The Motion Picture*], somebody, somewhere, decided that if we're going to do a motion picture, it must be different than what we did on TV, so we must now start to work out the differences. We'll change the color of the bridge, the wardrobe, the attitudes of the characters. It seemed to me that somebody was watching *2001* a lot, and getting into a cerebral, futuristic trip rather than an adventure romp, which is what *Star Trek* is built on. Maybe it's because they felt that people would not pay to see in the theatre what they had seen on TV, that they would want something different. My opinion is that if we can do the best *Star Trek* episode ever done, well-produced and well-acted, and put it on the big screen, it will work. I think that's what we've got this time. It's great! There's nothing wrong with success. It's terrific and I'm relieved because Bill, Dee, myself and other people who have talked about this picture before its release, felt strongly that it would be successful and that we were on the right track. What has happened here is that our perspective of what *Star Trek* is really supposed to be has been verified. The audience has said, 'Yes, that's right.'"

DeForest Kelley: "In my mind, there's no comparison [between the first two films]. This is the kind of film that in fact we had all hoped for the first time. It's not easy to convince the studio that, as successful as *Star Trek* was, the fans nevertheless have a deep feeling about the characters, and that you can't ignore it. In my opinion, that was the mistake that was made with the first film, ignoring the relationships that were so popular in

the TV series.

"You have two different schools of thought in a motion picture studio. They're thinking in terms of motion pictures, and it's hard for them to conceive the success of *Star Trek* was in its people. It's the story of a group of very qualified people, moving about centuries beyond, doing a job and doing it well. They have passion and warmth, and they care for each other. They're trying to seek out new worlds without blowing each other apart. The series was certainly all of that. I feel a lot better about this movie than I did about the other one, because I feel that those relationships are there again. The first picture relied on hardware and special effects."

James Doohan: "To me, this movie is *Star Trek* the way it should be. The first one was just some grandiose idea that somebody had. There is gorgeous action going on at all times. The characters all have some great things to say. It's just a beautiful blend of all of the good things that were in all of the good shows that we had in the series."

George Takei: "I think in *The Wrath of Khan* we have genuine drama because of the confrontation of two strong, cunning, inventive adversaries that are driven to an inevitable collision. You know that they are not going to avoid each other, that there is going to be some dramatic confrontation. Ricardo Montalban is an awesomely well-suited adversary for Kirk."

Nichelle Nichols: "I was both pleased and surprised [with *Star Trek II*]. I felt that, this time, they did it right. I think this is the definitive *Star Trek*. They've captured the essence of what made the show wonderful."

Walter Koenig: "I think that if you can point to one single element that makes this film successful, it is the presence of a formidable, worthy antagonist. You can't have conflict unless you have something to butt up against. V'ger was more like something you were in awe of. I think Ricardo Montalban, on the other hand, has done a wonderful job with the character of Khan. Not only is he a presence in terms of villainy, but he's also a character of depth. Even when you hate him, you feel a certain sympathy toward him. That, to me, is extraordinary. Nick

Meyer was quoted as saying that he would like to direct Montalban in KING LEAR, and I can believe it. I think that is what makes this story work—-the fact that he's not only against Kirk but against the whole crew. We're all heroes to varying degrees, and our opponent has to not only be the equal of Kirk but also, in effect, the equal of all of us. I think Montalban embodies that very well."

One person not overly impressed with the film was *Star Trek* creator Gene Roddenberry. "I think it was an exciting picture," he explained. "I had many problems with it, though. I thought they were very lucky they had the actor they did in Ricardo Montalban to play Khan, since it was not a well-written part. 'I will chase you through the moons of Jupiter' and so on, in the hands of almost any other actor would have gotten snickers from the audience, Montalban saved their ass. Khan was not written as that exciting a character, he was rather flimsy. The Khan in the TV episode was a much deeper and better character than the movie Khan, except that Montalban pulled it off.

"I also objected to other little things. Remember when the eel came out of Chekov's ear? What did Kirk do? He had a look of disgust on his face and grabbed his phaser and went 'zap.' Now, how dare he destroy a life form that had never been seen before! It needs studying. They had him act like an old woman trampling on a tarantula. Now that's not the Kirk we built up for three years. So many of those fine little things in the episodes, hundreds of them, are what gave *Star Trek* its quality. Unfortunately, they began doing those things incorrectly in that movie. There was also a great deal of violence. But yet, it was exciting— exciting photographically. I'm grateful that it did what it did."

At this juncture in time, the results of "what it did" are obvious. *Star Trek II: The Wrath of Khan* was quite successful, grossing a little more than half of *Star Trek: The Motion Picture*'s take, but proving itself to be considerably more profitable due to its much lower budget.

PARAMOUNT PICTURES presents
STAR TREK II: THE WRATH OF KHAN Starring WILLIAM SHATNER LEONARD NIMOY
also Starring BIBI BESCH and PAUL WINFIELD as TERRELL Introducing KIRSTIE ALLEY as SAAVIK
and Starring RICARDO MONTALBAN as KHAN Executive Consultant GENE RODDENBERRY
Based on STAR TREK Created by GENE RODDENBERRY Executive Producer HARVE BENNETT
Screenplay by JACK B. SOWARDS Story by HARVE BENNETT and JACK B. SOWARDS
Produced by ROBERT SALLIN Directed by NICHOLAS MEYER   A PARAMOUNT
DOLBY STEREO ™   PANAVISION ®   PICTURE
IN SELECTED THEATRES
PG PARENTAL GUIDANCE SUGGESTED
SOME MATERIAL MAY NOT BE SUITABLE FOR CHILDREN
Copyright © MCMLXXXII by
Paramount Pictures Corporation All Rights Reserved
STAR TREK is a registered trademark of Paramount Pictures Corporation

Additionally, the hoopla surrounding Spock's death ultimately became little more than a moot point, as evidenced by the next film in the series, *Star Trek III: The Search for Spock.*

The saga of *Star Trek* would most definitely continue..

A sample of the advertising campaign used to sell the second Trek film, The Wrath of Khan (ad slick courtesy United Artists Theatres).

Star Trek III
The Search For Spock
Beginning The Search

Leonard Nimoy's desire to involve himself with aspects of filmmaking other than acting seems to be one of the major forces which have ultimately propelled the direction of the *Star Trek* films, particularly concerning the death and resurrection of Spock.

Though he will, to this day, deny that he had anything to do with the creative decision to kill Spock in *The Wrath of Khan*, it is well-known that Nimoy pined for an end to, or at least a vacation from, living in the Vulcan's shadow. When he heard about the plans to kill Spock, he was not at all against it. Hoping it might lead to a career in other directions, he played the death scene in *The Wrath of Khan* with some regret, then actively pursued other work, including his Emmy-nominated role in *A Woman Called Golda*.

He had to know, however, that *The Wrath of Khan* would only spur on the *Star Trek* fever. He had to know that the fans would demand his return. He had to know that some way would be found to bring Spock back and that he would be the one to reprise the role.

What he never expected, and what made his career move to temporarily get away from Spock all the more successful, was that he would end up being the director of *Star Trek III: The Search for Spock*.

Getting the job was, to some degree, an accident. Prior to *Trek III*, Nimoy still wanted his contract with Paramount to include projects other than *Star Trek*, but they did not have anything specific for him to do in the future. "For many years," Nimoy explained, "my concern has been to try to build a career outside of *Star Trek* so that it wasn't that single straight line of only *Trek*-oriented work. So there was nothing for us to discuss. I said to Gary Nardino—I was being arrogant—with all due respect to Bob Wise, who directed the first picture, a top notch filmmaker; and all due respect to Nick Meyer, an extremely talented writer/director who directed *Trek II*; I

know more about *Star Trek* than either of them and I said I could direct *Star Trek III* successfully. When I first presented the idea of my directing to Paramount, the response was very good—but there were certain trepidations. We had to talk them through. My position during those discussions was 'I don't want you to perceive me as a problem. I don't want you to think I'm an actor trying to build a directing career on the strength of my leverage. I want you to see me as the *solution* to your problem. You need a director, and I know this material. I will bring you a movie that will satisfy the *Star Trek* audience.' I didn't want to take the posture with the studio of, 'You want me to act in *Star Trek III?* Then *I'm* the director, period.' Instead, we worked out what I felt was a constructive approach. Basically, I told them, 'Promote from within.'

"Michael Eisner [then Paramount president] got very excited about it and said, 'Great idea! Leonard Nimoy directs *The Search for Spock*!' It went downhill from there. At one point they said, 'No, we're not going to do it.' Harve [Bennett] and I kept operating on the assumption that it was going to work out and kept talking story ideas. In April of '83, I started my prep on the picture, reported on the lot and immediately went to work with Harve."

It may be hard to believe, coming from someone who has been a part of the industry since the 1950's, but Leonard Nimoy insists he honestly felt that moving out of the cast and taking over the film would not be a major concern to his fellow cast members. It was only a matter of time before he discovered that he was wrong.

Said Nimoy, "I must be really naive about this. I really must. I was surprised that there was so much interest and so much concern about that. The interests and concerns are valid. I just didn't perceive the potential problems or friction that other people perceive. My fellow actors were concerned about it before we started doing the picture. I simply took it as fact that I had their best interests at heart. That I would know their characters well, and I certainly knew their potential well and would try to explore it. That was one of the things I argued in that period of time when I was

asking for the job.

"I said, 'I know these people. I know these characters. I know what can be done with them.' So it was ironic for me and kind of startling that the very thing I thought would have the greatest success with was the cast, and that was the major question that people were more concerned about. I didn't have anybody say, 'What do know about shooting a $16 million movie with spaceships and planets exploding, fire scenes and fights and people falling off cliffs and stuff like that?' Nobody asked me about that. They said, 'What about the actors?'

"I discussed it later, after the fact, with some of the cast, and they admitted to me that they had been concerned. I think the concern grew out of a potential competitiveness. I discovered that there was more of a sense of competition between actors than I have ever been aware of. That's a strange thing to say. I'm an actor, have been in television and films since 1950. This was the first time that I had it really enunciated to me that some of the actors in the cast were concerned that my competitiveness would....I think we got over that very quickly. Generally they saw that I was well prepared, that I was well intended where they were concerned, and that they were given the opportunity to develop and have some fun in their performances. I see each of the cast as individuals. I don't see them as simply 'the chorus.' I understand their potential as actors, and I understand the potential of their characters. I wanted to have their contribution in the movie. It wasn't something I reluctantly felt obligated to do. It was something I *intended* to do from the start."

One interesting thing that happened, possibly as a test to Nimoy's intentions and loyalty, was when he and producer Harve Bennett first discussed the script with friend and co-worker William Shatner. Naturally, since Nimoy was now in the position of authority, Shatner might feel a bit threatened, if not downright insecure about the situation. Before, he and Nimoy were a team. What if that changed?

"Leonard and I are the dearest of old friends," Shatner told writer James Van Hise. "We had shared a mutual struggle

This artwork, featured on the cover of Files Magazine, was used in promoting Star Trek III.

with the management in various stages, whether it was a script, a thought, a concept or a dressing room and ask each other what we thought. We'd have a plan! Whenever we were to deal with management, we'd plan it out together. Now, suddenly, my 'brother' was saying, 'Well, you should do this and I think you should do that.' There was an awkward period of time for me, although I don't think for Leonard, where I felt alone in anything I might have objected to. From my point of view, it was more awkward in the beginning than with either of the other two directors [Robert Wise and Nicholas Meyer]. But that slowly erased itself."

Harve Bennett recalled, "When the draft of the piece was finished and Leonard and I were both very happy with it, we sent it to Bill. He called and said, 'I'd like to have a meeting.' So we came over on a Sunday morning to Bill's house and there was Bill's lawyer, his agent and one guy who kept his hands over his chest. I thought maybe he was from *T.J. Hooker*, the stunt guy or something. Very intimidating. And he said, 'Are you happy with this script?' I said, 'Yeah, we like it a lot.' Leonard said, 'Promising. Very promising.' Bill said, 'Well, I just can't do that.' The complaint was that there wasn't enough of him in the material. That he was standing by, that he wasn't leading. We said, 'Let's talk about it.' There was merit in much of what he said. He said, 'Oh, good. You other guys can leave now.' And the lawyer and the agent left and the gunsel left. And we had five hours of intense conversation.

"You have to understand," Bennett added, "that is not quite as selfish as it seems. This is their career. It's like a quarterback saying, 'Who's going to be blocking for me?' The actor says, 'How am I going to come off? Are they going to like me? Are they going to love me so that I can make the next picture?' Being a star over a long period of time is a nerve-wracking affair. So that's where his thrust was and we had neglected to protect our star.

"The compromises that came out of that—some of them were funny. Bill said, 'I think I should be in the scene where Bones talks to Spock.' We said no. 'You see, that's a very lovely scene and I should be there. Why am I not there?'

We said, 'Well, Bill, it feels like one of those moments when two guys are joined together and Bones has not really had his moment.' On that one he said, 'Why don't we shoot it both ways?' Then he said, 'Now Bones gets to go up there with the priestess, don't you think I should be up there and do something that makes it all happen?' We said no. He said, 'Well, maybe that's too much.' I said, 'Bill, I'll tell you what you are. You are a quarterback who wants to call the play, run back, throw the pass, catch the pass, score the touchdown and lead the cheers.' He hugged me and said, 'You're right. I can't help it.'

"Bill is a Shakespearean actor. It shows in everything, even on *Hooker*. He has to wind up to draw a gun. And Bill has, in candor, a great talent and a great ego. Did you notice the last scene as the cast is surrounding Spock? Who remembers where Kirk is? By himself. He knew where his light is. This is not a fault. It's the way he is. He's a matinee idol in the traditional, historical sense of that word."

In writing the script, Bennett did 12 outlines in all. It took six months. He says the last scene in the movie is the first one he wrote. "Somewhere along the line I read a fan poem in one of the hundreds of fan magazines about *Star Trek*. It was first person Kirk. It said, 'I left you there. Why did I do that? I must come back to you, my friend.' I thought, 'That's it!' I suddenly had a thrust. It got a lot easier from that point. A great motion picture has a very similar last scene. It was almost, beat for beat, the last scene in *The Miracle Worker* by William Gibson. It is the moment in which, after the entire play, little Helen Keller is at the well with her teacher and she begins to get some understanding, and finally with her hand on his face she says, 'Water.' And the teacher says, 'Yes!'"

Contrary to popular belief, the third movie was not in mind when *The Wrath of Khan* was filmed. Bennet explained, "It would have been very easy to say that at the conclusion of *Star Trek II* that all the things we have done to modify that film's ending to be ambiguous about the death of Spock were carefully designed and that the plot for *Star Trek III* was already in my mind. Not true. All of that, like most decisions I

have ever made, are done in a flurry of intuition and sometimes pressure of time. The last weeks of *Star Trek II* were frenetic because of an organized campaign: *Don't Kill Spock!* And the studio panicked that this would affect the box office. Nick Meyer was steadfastly going to walk on the picture. He said that we said we would kill him, so we're going to kill him.

"Leonard was getting threatening letters. This was a serious thing and I felt that the compromise we had to make, with Nick's blessing (reluctant though that was) was that we made an ambiguity out of the ending by saying, 'There are always possibilities.' We said, 'Who knows with Vulcans?'

"I have said once or twice at a few *Star Trek* gatherings I have gone to that I have always tried to be fair. I have a great affection for these people, even when they're so proprietary that they come over and tell you that you can't do it your way, you have to do it my way. But these people keep that franchise. It is a business. They keep it healthy and strong. They are its lifeblood. So you do not disregard that. To be fair, you've got to give clues and those were the clues we dropped.

"On *Star Trek III*, I said, 'Look, it's got to be faster and more efficient [than the writing of *The Wrath of Khan*]. So I was the sole writer on *Star Trek III*, [which] was the easiest writing job I ever had. The reason for that it, since it was so direct a continuation of *Star Trek II*, the outline was already in place. I knew exactly what I had to do and I did it in six weeks.

"I had to make a story out of the following 'givens': One, there is a casket on a planet that has been created by the reformation of life forces and life has been created from death. Two, 'There are always possibilities.' Three, before he died, Spock said, 'Remember.' Remember what? The puzzle was solved so easily that I think 17 other people could have written the script to *Star Trek III*. If you end a film with a Genesis device that can, in one 'poof,' create life where there was lifelessness, you have created an enormous story device that can not be ignored. Now the fans would be justified in saying, 'Well, why not just

Leonard Nimoy, General Scott, William Shatner, the late Gene Roddenberry and Harve Bennett during production of Star Trek III (photo courtesy the Anderson Archives).

create a planet as a plot solution?' Or, 'What would happen if the Klingons got hold of this? They wouldn't use it to make a planet, they would destroy a planet.' Therefore, the final puzzle solving was the denial of the validity of the Genesis device. That was—as 'The Lord giveth, the Lord taketh away—necessary, or we would have expanded the borders of *Star Trek*, even subliminally, that it would have had the same impact the A-bomb had on the 20th Century, so as to make conventional things no longer viable. That's fine, but who needs to restructure STAR TREK on that basis?"

Writing the script, Bennett ran into other problems that were set up in *The Wrath of Khan*. First, there was Saavik. The original character, played by Kirstie Alley, did not want to come back to do the movie. "We didn't want to cut [her] scenes," Bennett said, "so we decided to recast the character and keep the part. How did we fare putting Robin Curtis in where Kirstie Alley had gone before? About even."

Kirstie Alley, who has achieved incredible fame since *Star Trek II* thanks to her varied movie roles as well as her stint on *Cheers*, told *Starlog* magazine,

"They offered me less money than they did for *Star Trek II*, so I figured they weren't very interested in me for Saavik. I thought [Robin Curtis] was at a real disadvantage playing a role someone else established, especially with *Star Trek*, which has an enormous following. I think she did a fine job. I have no problem with what she was doing except that, when I saw the film, I said, 'She isn't Saavik, I am.'"

Said Robin Curtis, "I did want to keep things fairly separate between myself and Kirstie Alley and as it turned out, each and every one of the people

Robin Curtis replaced Kirstie Alley in the role of Saavik for the third and fourth Star Trek films (photo copyright ©1994 Karen Witkowski).

involved in *Star Trek III* were wonderful. I think Leonard set an example that everyone followed and that is to say I was never made to feel like I had to fill someone else's shoes. Never for a moment was I made to feel like that and I think that was really Leonard's kind of healthy approach to the whole thing."

Another character not written into *The Search for Spock*, and quite obviously missing, was Carol Marcus. Bennett detailed, "She was the fifth member of a four-man relay team. She was the extraneous character. She was in the story outline. I thought it might be fun to have her relating to David and have something going with Saavik. But then protomatter came up. Then something happened: Did Carol know? If Carol knows about protomatter, everything about David making a mistake—cheating, being responsible—doesn't wash. Then it's not David's ambition, it's mother and son in some kind of oedipal whim to cheat the world together. And they don't tell Kirk, which is very out of character. Also, then I would have had to kill them both.

"Writer's problem. Answer: Don't get Carol involved. Get her out of this issue. David doing it without his mother's knowledge enriches it for me. And his father certainly doesn't know. If you think it's tough answering that, think of how it was when I tried to explain it to Bibi Besch. She was deeply upset. She cried. She thought it was a rejection of her talent. Bibi's a very adult actress, so

you can understand that may sound strange to you, but it's not. She thought she must have done something wrong. But I got a lovely letter from Bibi after the picture opened. It said, 'I've seen the picture. Now I understand. You were right. I hope you can find a place for me in one of the other films.'

Another writer's problem was in deciding to use Sarek as a character, but not Amanda, Spock's mother.

"We couldn't find a way to do it," Bennett states. "All she would have contributed was sympathy. The economy of the story was that Kirk and crew get Spock back. Family is secondary. That would have depreciated the moment Spock says, 'Your name is Jim.' Then we'd have to cut to mother and she would say, 'Oh my God, he speaks!'"

Two other major script decisions, killing David and destroying the Enterprise, were rather easy for Bennett. He believes in a balance. If you get something, you have to pay for it. Kirk gets Spock back, but at what cost? He loses two very major things along the way. Is it worth it? That makes for a good script, and lots of emotion and tension.

"I confess to being old fashioned," Bennett continued. "There is in my vision such a thing as ultimate retribution. The reason David dies, structurally, is because he's messed with mother nature. He allowed himself to bend the rules at the wrong time, in the wrong place. He's there on that planet for only that reason. The whole story dates back to David putting protomatter in the matrix. The death of Spock, everything rests on his shoulders if you want to blame him for it.

"Also," Bennett said in the pages of *The Star Trek Interview Book*, "we did not feel that the character of David was a viable character upon which to build further stories. We didn't set out to kill him. We didn't even set out to use him, but when I got to the crisis and came up with the idea, 'I'm going to kill one of them,' then, with an eye to plot it, [it] became obvious which one I would have to kill, because it was the one I didn't need. I had no idea what the future of Saavik might be. Clearly, I couldn't kill Spock a second time or the picture would be over, and David was

extraneous then. It wasn't the actor's fault so much as [that] the character just didn't make it. It was like the [Decker] character in the first movie: it was a good try, and it is very interesting to see the number of tries to bring 'new blood' into 'the family.' It's hard, and I don't know the answer to that. I've given up trying. I have no desire to bring in new commanders and all that stuff. I don't think the fans want it, particularly."

One of the secondary themes of *Trek III* is don't mess with mother nature. The concept fo the Genesis device was too massive to deal with in the *Trek* universe for future stories. It had to be destroyed. "Gene Roddenberry said, 'Let's try protomatter.' It became a tool for me to solve the problem,' " Bennett explained, "which is the interjection of a human value system in an otherwise antiseptic, impossible box—the perfect scientist. The value system is ambition. That interested me. It all snapped together. Kirk changed the computer on the Kobayashi Maru scenario before *Star Trek II*. His son says to him, 'You've cheated.' His father says, 'I changed the rules.' Well, it turns out that the kettle was calling the pot black. David says it at a time when he knows he's changed the rules."

The loss of the Enterprise was the big risk in the script, the big surprise, though word of it leaked to the fans and campaigns, not unlike the ones to save Spock, were begun to save the Enterprise from its demise.

Said Leonard Nimoy, "I understand how they feel, I sympathize com-

Merritt Butrick reprised his role of Kirk's son, David Marcus, in The Search for Spock (photo copyright ©1994 Karen Witkowski).

pletely. But my feeling was that it was not arbitrary. It was well-built into the story. I've had people say, 'Gee, why did you do that?' My response is, 'What else would have had Kirk do under those circumstances?' It seems to me that the script laid itself out that it was the only thing to do. I can understand the emotion connected with it, but nevertheless, it was a dramatic event. I think it was played very successfully as a dramatic event. Frankly, I thought it was well executed. We didn't destroy the Enterprise for cheap or inflammatory reasons but because therein lay drama. It was a certain kind of drama which you can do in motion pictures, but you can't do on television. It was drama that I think we're mandated to do, because we're not doing television anymore. As Nicholas Meyer said about killing Spock in *Star Trek II*, 'We're not playing games here. This isn't a red herring, like they do on TV. Spock is *really* dead.' Destroying the Enterprise was the same. It was a valid dramatic choice, not a transparent TV plot."

Bennett admitted, "The death of the Enterprise caused serious ripples. The death of David did not. That's.backwards for me. How could you destroy the Enterprise is a burden I take full responsibility for. I will justify it to the end and once again I think I have been playing fair. My choice was a humanistic choice. It began as a writer's problem. Usually it happens when you reach a sticky point. I had a whole justification for it. Oliver Hazard Perry of the U.S. Navy scuttled the Niagara at the battle of Lake Erie and won the battle as a result. He was rowed on a rowboat to another ship and took command. Perry happens to be one of James T. Kirk's great heroes. Actually, there is a model of the Niagara in Kirk's quarters for those who love *Star Trek* trivia. So, the scuttling of the ship to achieve the greater good is a tactic. Also, with the death of his son and the hopelessness of the situation, it seemed like the right solution, and also because in the series there had been one notable, false countdown."

Star Trek creator Gene Roddenberry made no secret of the fact that he disliked the idea of the Enterprise being destroyed.

"I'm upset about it," he said at

Leonard Nimoy and William Shatner have a confrontation of a different kind on the set of Shatner's T.J. Hooker (photo copyright ©1994 Columbia Pictures).

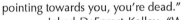

the time. "I felt it wasn't really that necessary. I would rather have seen the saucer blow up. As all the old-time fans will know, our ship is supposed to come apart. The star-drive part is the nacelles and the underneath, and the saucer is not star-driven. If the saucer had been blown up, at the end of the picture we couldn't had a new saucer come down and reunite the two. Symbolic of the end of the story. They preferred to do it the other way."

Actor William Shatner saw the death of both David Marcus and the Enterprise in a different light. "I thought the loss of the Enterprise and David's death were very clever devices used to create drama in a situation. The problem is that, in a continuing series of movies where the characters appear through all the films, we have to raise some jeopardy. But everybody knows the characters are not going to die. So, two elements that were expendable, David and the Enterprise, were killed off because nothing else could be killed off. In fact, the real problem is, what else can we kill? We're looking around for people to die! It's like the court-martials where you come into the room and if the knife is

pointing towards you, you're dead."

Joked DeForest Kelley, "When I read that in the script, I couldn't believe it! You know, I thought, 'My God, the Enterprise is a bigger star than any of us! If they're shooting this guy out of the script, they can shoot anybody out!'"

"There are two elements in the making of a story whether it's on film or not," Bennett stated. "Suspense and surprise. You're either hoping a character will do something or he does something that you didn't expect. The sure knowledge of the audience saying, 'Oh, no, they're not going to do that,' and the sheer surprise of saying, 'Oh, yes we are.' There are many other moments in the film which were intended to be one or the other. The death of David is one clear example of surprise, because you're playing off the cliches of the expected. One of the joys of motion picture writing as opposed to television is that you have full use of those two ranges. In television the surprise is limited, and suspense is limited to the fact that the episode must end with the hero surviving."

One obvious aspect of the film was that Kirk and company would ultimately locate Spock, alive and, relatively speaking, well. The return of Spock at the climax, which is something Leonard Nimoy was not at all nervous about.

"I had confidence in the way the story was structured that it would work," he told *The Official Star Trek Fan Club*. "I certainly didn't want to do a ghostly Spock like Alec Guiness in *Star Wars*. I felt there was obviously a tremendous amount of interest from the fans as to whether or not he was coming back. By the time the picture opened, I think the feeling really was, 'OK, he's probably coming back, but let's find out how.' And if it's done interestingly, then it works."

Since Leonard Nimoy's directorial credits were limited to such episodic television fare as *The Powers of Matthew Star, Night Gallery* and *T.J. Hooker*, the challenge of getting Bennett's script on film was a difficult yet exhilarating experience, from the filming of scenes to the actual editing of the movie. His love for *Star Trek* and his obsession for perfection is what made the movie work. However, that kind of dedication has a price.

"The shooting began on August 15, 1983," Nimoy stated, revealing what his workload as director was like. "It was 49 days of shooting during which the biggest problem I had was lack of sleep. I went to bed at 9:00 or 9:30, set the alarm for 5:00 or 5:30 and would be up at 3:00, the head going with ideas. I was just so super-charged and wired. It was a constant tiredness of the best kind."

There were many things he learned, too, on this project, such as how frustrating it can be to direct oneself.

"There is no question in directing yourself that you need help," Nimoy explained. He relied quite heavily on Harve Bennett, William Shatner, director of photography Charles Correll and others for that help. They are "People off camera I've come to trust. I cannot emphasize enough that you don't make these pictures alone. You sure need an awful lot of talented support. In some cases, there is simply the fact that there are things going on behind you that you cannot see as an actor. The biggest problem I had, and this is really silly, but it happens that it was the scene in the sick bay of the Bird of Prey. Spock is unconscious and McCoy is talking to him. Now, not only am I in the scene, but I have to play the scene with my eyes closed. So I can't even look to see if the actor I am playing the scene with is looking anything like I think he should look. It drove De Kelley crazy. He swears that I was trying to direct him with the movement and flutter of my eyelids. It was very difficult. In a sense, I was very pleased and relieved that the design of the story allowed me to do a minimal amount of performing."

As a stylistic director, Nimoy has given himself time and room to grow, noting, "I'm probably somewhere in between Bob Wise and Nicholas Meyer. Not as precise as Bob, not as imaginative or rough-edged as Nick. I think the major difference, and for me the most important difference, is my attitude toward the story and the actors. [Wise and Meyer] are looking for a different kind of final product than I am."

Said Bennett about one moment of Nimoy's directing, "I'll tell you what was a great directorial achievement by Leonard was getting emotion over David's death out of Shatner because he wanted to play it more stylistically. It's the only scene I remember where Leonard said, 'Clear the bridge.' Literally, he said, 'Will everyone please leave. I want to talk to Bill.' I never asked him what he said to Bill. It was very personal. It was director talk to actors."

That scene was a very crucial part of the script. It was the moment where Kirk realizes he has lost a good portion of the fight with the Klingons because they have in their hands everything he loves or cares about. It called for a riveting, emotional and yet not overdone performance. Nimoy explained:

"On the day of the shooting of that scene, he and I got ourselves off into a corner and discussed it slowly in a relaxed atmosphere, and privately. What I said to him was this: 'You have to decide how far you want to go with this. How far you want to take this reaction. My opinion is that you can go pretty far and get away with it, maybe strip off some of the veneer of the admiral, the hero, always in charge, always on top of the situation, and show us a vulnerable person.' He took it further, frankly than I expected him to. And it was scary. I mean, how many space epics do you see where your hero, on receiving personal news, stumbles back and falls on the person's own ship? You don't see that a lot. It was a scary thing for all of us hoping that it would be perceived as a very touching moment. Some little kid breaks in laughter in the audience and you're dead. We did several takes and used the one where we really thought Bill lost control and stumbled and fell. It looked accidental, not a performance. I'm very moved by it. In my opinion, it is some of the best work he has ever done. It looked as though he had received a physical jolt, as if somebody had hit him with the information. He looks deeply hurt. Some of the most personal and vulnerable work I've ever seen done in the role of Kirk."

An intriguing part of the directing for Nimoy involved editing. "In the editing process, specifically, the most interesting challenge was how to tell the story and in what sequence. Having seen it on the screen in its rough cut form, we all came to the conclusion that there was something about the juxtaposition, scene to scene, idea to idea, character to character; it wasn't quite in its proper order. The jigsaw puzzle hadn't quite fallen into place. Gradually we worked our way towards it and discovered what the picture turned out to be.

"The flow just didn't want to come to life until we repositioned certain of the opening scenes. For example, what we came to call the caper, which was the gathering of the Samurai to steal the Enterprise. In its original form, it was scattered in pieces throughout the first third of the film and they were all wonderful, fun pieces. But somehow, when you cut away from each of the happenings, it was always as though the fun was being interrupted. When you came back to it, you had to get geared up to have fun again. And suddenly that little piece would be over and you were being interrupted and taken away from the story again.

"The one major reconstruction that took place in editing was to put much, if not all, that caper together as a piece so that once we start with the idea of Bill Shatner walking up and saying, 'The answer is no, I am therefore going anyway,' it starts. So that piece became a trump within itself whereas it had been originally constructed as several pieces. I think 14 minutes from the time we first started looking at cuts of the film were cut down to its present condition. Perhaps two or three minutes were cut after the picture went to preview audiences. So we were pretty close to what we had planned to put on the screen. I think that's due in great part to very successful writing and producing for the film."

Another part of directing is dealing with authority. Just because you are the director or even the producer, never means you have the final word.

The pon farr scene, according to Bennett, was Gene Roddenberry's idea. "I didn't care for the idea, but I do now. Leonard refined the concept with great skill. It really is an idea that works or it doesn't work on stage. That's not something you can write. The best you can do on that is say it is a sweet, gentle moment in hopes that the intention is understood by the front office. So the front office said, 'Take out that silly scene with the girl and the Vulcan,' and when they saw it on the screen they were even more convinced. They said, 'Take out the pon farr sequence.' Leonard and I said, 'Why?' They said, 'You'll get very bad laughs.' We said, 'We haven't had any laughs in the previews.' They said, 'Well, those people love *Star Trek*. When you get to the real people, they'll laugh.' We made a bet. Leonard and I each put up 50 cents. We had another preview and came to the pon farr scene and we got down in our seats and said, please, don't laugh. So there's a framed dollar bill in my office."

The studio also did not like or understand that fact that there was so much smoke on the bridge of the Bird of Prey. Bennett had a challenging time trying to explain it to them and convince them that it was stylistically necessary.

"Finally," Bennett said, "I set a piece of film in the executive screening room and I said, 'Before we talk, would you please come with me. I want to show you five minutes of film.' I had racked up the last five minutes dance number of their smash hit *Flashdance* where a girl dances in smoke and there is only one judge in the room who is smoking a cigarette. You could hardly see the girl against the windows. It was so beau-

This DC Comics adaptation of Star Trek III featured a sequence filmed but ultimately cut from the final film, which first demonstrated the influence Spock was having on McCoy's mind. Nimoy felt that it tipped their hat to the audience earlier than necessary.

tiful. After that, they stopped bothering me about smoke."

Occasionally, studio heads would be able to see things and comment on them in a way that the cast and crew were unable to due to their closeness to the project. One such item involved a bit of costuming which appeared to be in somewhat poor taste for the character.

Noted Bennett, "Next time you see the film, there is a scene during the first stealing the Enterprise sequences when civilian clothes are seen for the first time. The first time you see Chekov, well, we didn't see his costume objectively next to Kirk's macho jacket and Bones' marvelous pants. But all of a sudden, we see Chekov on stage and he has this great Little Lord Fauntleroy white collar. The phone started ringing. We got by it without re-shooting the day with a series of clever cheats. We got a new collar and picked up close-ups on the black turtleneck for the rest of the picture. But he still has it in the master shot. Bob, our costume designer, did Bones from his Georgia background, Kirk from his admiration of naval flyers and stuff like that. This was supposed to be Chekov's admiration, get this, of the poet Pushkin. Now, that's a fine hobby for a Russian space person to have, but Pushkin is always drawn in his great Byronic collar from that period and it looks darn silly. So that one shot with the collar still exists."

Star Trek III: The Search for Spock completed production on schedule and under budget. For both Nimoy and Bennett, it was a job well done.

"For me," Bennett said, "this movie is about honor and friendship and decency and values higher than the complex value system we have inherited since the atomic age. It's a return to innocence."

Noted Nimoy, "I wasn't making a personal statement. The major theme in this film is about friendship. What should a person do to help a friend? How deeply should a friendship commitment go? What price should people be willing to pay? And what sacrifices, what obstacles, will these people endure? That's the emotion line of the film. For me, that's its reason for existence."

■ Starship Security

Few of the production people who had worked on *Star Trek: The Motion Picture* or *Star Trek II* were invited back to work on the third film of the series. The reason for this, said art director John E. Chilberg II, was that both productions had leaked like sieves.

"On *Star Trek II* it got so bad," he recalled, "that when the art director sent a plan out to the crew on the stage, it wouldn't last for three hours before someone had stolen it."

Both features had, in fact, come to resemble nothing so much as a Hollywood analogue to the Soviet economy. While both productions officially dedicated themselves to implementing Paramount's "five-year plan" for getting *Star Trek* to boost its share value, some middle-echelon personnel tapped into the lucrative Trekkie black market for *Star Trek* paraphernalia. A single page from an official *Star Trek* script was found to command $50 at a convention.

Cameron Birnie, a set designer on *Star Trek III*, noted that security on the production had been the most unusual thing he could recall. It got so out of hand, he noted, that he and his colleagues would taunt their leak-conscious superiors, saying that they had accidentally procured the plot of the picture and intended to auction it off to the Trekkies.

This would have been no mean feat. The people who constructed the sets for *Star Trek III* had not been shown complete copies of the script. The sets were created out of sequence and the production crew was given only as many pages as they needed to design a particular set. "I guess they didn't want to burden us," observed Birnie.

And that wasn't all. Personnel working on the production were given temporary badges allowing them access to the sets and production offices. A few weeks into the project, they were given picture ID badges which were checked scrupulously by security guards. Scripts were chemically treated so that copies could be traced back to their source. These were reputedly tamper-proof. Stationary and documents used by the production were notably bereft of any insignia or mention of the production.

The code-word "Trois" reportedly figured on these instead.

Offices and workshops on the Paramount lot were not equipped with identifying shingles. "I didn't have a sign on my office," noted Chilberg. "It was there, and if you knew where it was, you knew where we were working."

Personnel were also given strict instructions to lock up all offices and sets when they left them, even if only for a moment. Double-locks were installed on single-lock doors.

Security at Industrial Light and Magic, which contracted to undertake special visual effects for the picture, was even more painstaking. Chilberg said that he had visited their plant several times, while ILM was concurrently working on *Indiana Jones and the Temple of Doom*. While the storyboards for *Star Trek III* would line one wall, the boards for the sequel to *Raiders of the Lost Ark* lined the opposite wall. "And they'd say to you, 'When you come into the room, look only at the storyboards on the left.'"

What worked extraordinarily well at ILM, however, achieved only partial success at Paramount, despite the fact that most of the production had been restricted to five of its sound stages. Birnie remembers that, at one point during the production, it was discovered that drawings began to disappear during the process of running prints to the print room.

"So they told us that, from then on, we would have to stay in the print room to make sure that they copied only the number of copies we had ordered," said Chilberg. "But security on the locked stages didn't work as well as people hoped. They never took anything that was expensive, though. Mostly, they ripped off a lot of electronic stuff—little transistors and things like that. Junk, for the most part. These things were inexpensive, but they cost a lot in labor to reinstall."

Star Trek costumery, it was learned, carried a particularly high premium among fans. Costume designer Robert Fletcher, who had worked on *Star Trek II: The Wrath of Khan* as well, recalled that items he had counted on using, things which had reportedly been locked up, were, he discovered, either lost or stolen.

A close check was maintained on costumes throughout the production of the third *Trek* film. But the clothing budgets, Fletcher said, had to be kept elastic, both because of thefts and because, as the production progressed, William Shatner tended to grow out of his clothing.

"We had 12 shirts made for him," he said. "He diets before a movie and shows up looking terrific. But he would slip as it went along."

■ Costuming The Search Party

Robert Fletcher has designed costumes for *Star Trek* through each of its feature film manifestations. He's also a tad older than most of the people who worked on the film and even the great actor from Montreal's St. Urbain St. Jewish ghetto would have felt sheepish giving him grief for his remarks.

As costume designer for the production, Fletcher was basically responsible for sketching the outfits, choosing the fabrics and completing the fittings of the principal characters. He worked with costumer Jim Linn, who had to fit the extras, match shots and handle the enormous logistics of laundering, mending and transporting all clothing used in the film.

Fletcher noted that the production relied in the main upon the uniforms and engineering suits that had already been used to good effect in the second *Trek* movie, although he did design one new uniform for it. Some of the white uniforms from the first film were renovated as well.

For this particular production, though, he said that he had wanted to avoid featuring the principals in uniforms, and to dress them in civies instead. He felt that the idea worked particularly well for George Takei, who he said had been pleased with his cape because it gave him the look of a swashbuckler. "He kept trying to wear it in many different ways, some of which I didn't really approve of," said Fletcher.

Fletcher clearly did not have it easy on this production—there were

enough new characters and aliens to keep him properly busy. This was just as well, because his knowledge of the history and uses of clothing and material were legend. And nothing he designed for this film was arbitrary.

Take the stone-like ornament on Mark Lenard's robe, worn by Sarek, Spock's father. "In my mind," he explained, "they were like the stones on the breastplates of the high priests of the Jews. There's a description in the Bible of each one, in fact. Each stone has some kind of philosophical significance, rather like a birthstone. The concept I generated was that Vulcan is a planet of precious minerals. And every citizen has a stone that symbolizes his position and mental state and level of consciousness. And Vulcans would also have stones in their hats as well as their costumes, each bearing matching pictographs in the Vulcan language, depicting their social and mys-

tic accomplishments."

The stones shown in the film were each separately modeled, cast and polished, using a resinous material.

Fletcher added that, in accordance with his concept, Spock has a stone in his drawer which has great personal significance. "I used the pictograph on his costume in the first movie," he explained, "but I haven't had the opportunity to use the stone yet."

The costume crew on *The Search for Spock* had hoped to reuse the Klingon costumes featured in the first film. "Everyone had decided that they liked them," Fletcher recounted. A dozen had been made for the movie, but only six were found, for the most part in tatters. What happened, he explained, was that an executive at Paramount had given his OK for the costumes to be used on an episode of *Mork & Mindy*. If you look closely at the episode of that show in

Christopher Lloyd, seen here as Doc Brown in the original Back to the Future, portrayed the Klingon, Kruge (photo copyright ©1985 MCA Universal).

which Jonathan Winters plays Mork's son, you may see, under silver paper and assorted junky embellishments—thousands of dollars in damaged Klingon outfits. The ones you don't see had been destroyed, he said, on publicity tours.

Fletcher pieced together what remained, though that alone took three months to do. And he did so while bearing in mind the exobiological exigencies of being a Klingon: "They are a race of reptiles," he said. "But I envisioned them as having descended from a race of crustaceans, who wore their skeletons on the outside. As they evolved, however, they retained their distinctive spines."

They also retained their bony-plated foreheads, which were first revealed in *Star Trek: The Motion Picture*. "But we tried to make them somewhat less brutal, less prominent, so that you get a better sense of the Klingons' individual faces. I always liked to think of them as authoritarian, almost feudal, like Japan had been. There's some of that in their clothing."

In fact, Fletcher was asked to design the Klingon and Vulcan makeup for the show as well. He said he was delighted at being given the chance. "So often your concept is evaded or warped or destroyed by the makeup department. This way I was able to maintain a unified look for the film. I suppose Leonard asked me to do that part of the makeup because he trusts me. He asked me to do many things he perhaps wouldn't have otherwise."

Another reason Fletcher may have been asked to pitch in with the makeup was that the studio had procrastinated in contracting the work out. At least, so said Tom Burman, who landed the contract a scant three weeks before the film began shooting.

Burman said that Paramount had initially wanted makeup artist Werner Keppler to take on the job, but a bid of some $134,000 was thought to be considerably beyond the $50,000 makeup budget that the studio had first envisioned. Burman's bid was for $160,000, but he was hired because his competitor had dropped out of the running and Paramount found itself running fairly close to the line. "It didn't come down to money in the end but to who could do it

quickly. Werner was getting nervous and, anyway, lacked interest. And we had a rep for working fast and doing quality work."

Burman worked closely with Fletcher, who supplied him with designs he then tried to flesh out. And he shared, among other things, Fletcher's opinion that the original Klingon forehead would have to go. "It was just too cartoonish, and I didn't want a *Star Wars* look in this movie. There had never been a good marriage between the forehead appliance and the actors' faces. We tried to keep them in character rather than have these obtrusive things on their heads."

Doing the Klingons right, he said, took a good two hours each. Although the Vulcan ears had given the makeup men a rough ride during the TV show, the technology had developed appreciably since. Fitting them individually for each actor, Burman ultimately produced about 150 sets of close-up ears as well as 300 pairs of background ears. Completing Nimoy's Spock makeup required just an hour of work. "And we got his color looking healthier than it had on television."

Probably the hardest thing for Burman was making one of the younger versions of Spock featured in the movie look like Nimoy as he was transforming into an older version of the actor/director. This was accomplished by creating a duplicate of Nimoy's head and face, and creating appliances from soft polyurethane.

While Burman struggled to do several months of work in as many weeks, Fletcher, faced other, equally daunting tasks. There were, for instance, some 250 Vulcans to be outfitted for the religious scene at the end of the movie. Fletcher had worked on costumery for the Ice Capades, and had designed and dealt in some 500 costumes for a Chicago opera rendition of Don Carlos. But with 350 costumes in all to assemble for the *Trek* film, he found himself pressed. He did have good luck, however, in finding much of the brocades and metallics he required in store rooms on Paramount that held material dating back to the DeMille days. Fabrics that would have cost some $200 a yard were available, he said, by the ton.

His greatest challenge in this production had been fitting out the Vulcan guards on the film with appropriate armor. "There were the most splendid variations of the clothes worn by Spock's father, Sarek. We gave them these gaudy armor and helmet sets with jewelled motifs and tried to make the stones seem to float on top of the armor."

These outfits, however, were by no means as gaudy as the outfits worn by the cocktail waitresses in the film's bar scene. These came equipped with tracking lights. "I thought of these girls as 'electric bunnies,'" chuckled Fletcher.

Decking out Dame Judith Anderson, as the Vulcan high priestess, in a somewhat more stately manner proved almost as complicated. "She claims to be 5' 2"," said Fletcher, "but she's really closer to 4' 8". And she asked me to do what I could to make her appear taller. Of course, I would have suggested it anyway."

Fletcher gave her the needed height by recalling a trick actress Lynne Fontaine used to pull. She would wear special built-up shoes and wear her dresses some six inches to a foot longer around the hem. "She used to kick the dress away from herself as she walked." But Anderson proved to have difficult feet, and fitting four-inch wedges into her red-leather shoes was problem-laden.

The job was handled by "Willie the Shoemaker" with his reputedly usual aplomb. Anderson didn't even complain that they looked terrible and had open toes. She was lifted onto a four-inch box and gained another few inches from her crown.

"They liked her on the set," Fletcher recounted. "When she first came on, Shatner led the cast in a rendition of 'There is Nothing Like a Dame.'"

■ Designing The Search

Principle photography of *Star Trek III: The Search for Spock* began on August 15, 1983. Special visual effects were provided by ILM, working under the supervision of Ken Ralston. The on-set special effects supervisor for the film was Bob Dawson.

ILM contributed some 120 shots to the movie. Nimoy involved George Lucas' special effects company in most pertinent aspects of the production. He did this from a very early stage, saying that he did not want to get into a situation where he was essentially walking into ILM with a "laundry list" of work required by the production.

To help ILM produce the kinds of opticals, miniatures, models and props he wanted for the film, Nimoy insisted that the entire production be storyboarded from start to finish. One of the production illustrators charged with working with ILM was Tom Lay, who had, in fact, worked on the previous two pictures as well.

Lay brought a varied background in landscape architecture and environmental design to these productions that began in television commercials. He later acquired feature credits at Disney and at Universal. On the first _Star Trek_ film, Lay worked as "a utilities man for Paramount."

In the main, Lay did story sketches for _Star Trek III._ But he also produced set sketches, sculpture and prop designs. "A lot of loose ends came my way," he said. Lay worked closely with ILM on such sequences as the Bird of Prey landing on Vulcan that was featured at the conclusion of the film. He reported that work with the effects house proceeded smoothly and efficiently. Indeed, Lay claimed that the collaborative spirit that dominated the production enabled him to exceed the responsibilities normally attributed to production illustrators. One particularly distinctive bit of design contributed by Lay was the examination table in the Klingon Bird of Prey sickbay.

Lay's initial concept for the diagnostic table was, he admitted, "about as wild as I could get." The table was fashioned in the manner of a snake lying on its back with its head coiled above the prone body of a patient. The instrument panel of this examination bed utilized assorted warm hues of red to suggest the opening of the snake's mouth. The sides of the diagnostic bed were equipped with fangs.

He explained that he had come up with the design by thinking about threatening objects. "I found that it's hard to come up with an original threat. Most of the things that scare us originate with objects we identify as dangerous. It comes down to a variation of fangs and horns and vertical pupils—they almost always have animal origins."

This particular design, unfortunately, never made it through the production. It was brilliant, but also costly. More painful, however, was the cutting from the final print of another of Lay's designs—the Vulcan Hall of Ancient Thoughts. The Hall, obviously one of the hotter tourist spots on Spock's homeworld, reportedly featured large heads set atop columns and illuminated by large balls of flame. The sculpture featured in the Hall towered some 20 feet high.

According to set decorator Tom Pedigo, the heads perched atop these columns were actually photographic cutouts possessed of considerable depth. The scene showcasing the Hall was cut because the Vulcan episode, which included a procession also not seen in its entirety in the final cut, seemed to drag on interminably.

ILM took more than the usual cue from sketches in _STAR TREK III._ According to Ralston, much of the model work in the production originated from sketches instead of blueprints. Ultimately, Ralston has indicated, ILM came up with a handful of prototypes, based upon these sketches, for the space dock. The Klingon spacecraft required two, the Merchant ship and Grissom, several.

Reportedly, the space dock underwent several bouts of redesigning in the course of one day, while Nimoy, Bennett and Ralph Winter, the film's associate producer, threw out suggestions. Ralston was said to have been especially enamored by the shooting angles presented by the Klingon Bird of Prey model. The Enterprise, on the other hand, had been making the people charged with shooting it crazy for years.

"There was never truly a good angle on the damned thing," complained production designer John Chilberg, who added that the Klingon Bird of Prey had originally been intended to be a Romulan spacecraft commandeered by Klingons. "That exposition got lost in the editing. By the time they decided on that, we were already building the thing."

Set designer Cameron Birnie

recounted having worked the bottom of a spacecraft set on Vulcan which had extended landing gear. ILM was charged with putting the rest of the shot together. "They'd be there looking over our shoulders," he recalled. "There would be times that we didn't know which way to go. They'd say, 'You can design this thing any way you want to. But it has to be in the right shape so we can fit our stuff into it.'"

Other noteworthy ILM contributions to the film included the design of Klingon props and hand weapons as well as the Klingon "dog," which was intended to resemble a cross between a wolf and a lizard.

Graphics for the film were subcontracted out to a Northridge artificial intelligence company as well as to firms in Washington and Toronto. These not only provided the rough-hewn triangular lettering on the Klingon vessel, but the primitive graphics visible on the merchant ship and Federation graphics as well. These companies also fed graphics into the computer screens so ubiquitous on the film's various sets.

According to associate producer Ralph Winter, these firms undertook the work at cost for the credit. For the most part, electronics for the production were procured from an outlet in the San Fernando Valley. The first two _Star Trek_ films had back-projected monitors visible on the sets. But according to Chilberg, the noise generated by the projectors forced the producers to loop in every bit of dialogue used in those scenes. He also noted that on _Star Trek II_ the monitors had been rebuilt to lessen the ruckus. "But on this show, we couldn't afford to do that. Basically we adapted the sets to the monitors we had."

Winter added that there had been talk of replacing standard _Trek_ issue communicators in the production for watch-televisions such as Sony has put on the market. "But it proved too expensive," he said.

ILM shot the picture in tandem with the production's director of photography, Charles Correll, using a massive VistaVision camera. Correll and ILM used the same stock in order to avoid obvious jumps from one camera to the other.

Ralph Winter had been heard bragging during the production that,

"There wasn't a single thing in the movie that you could buy in a store." Well, almost. There was a drinking glass with a swirl straw featured in the bar scene that had been purchased at Bullock's.

"Most everything else had to be custom-made," explained set decorator Tom Pedigo. Take the officer's lounge, for instance. Pedigo got hold of some stereo chairs and recut them. They were then upholstered on the lot.

The main trick, said production designer John Chilberg, "was staying within the parameters of the original show. You can't stray too far without risking audience rejection."

Chilberg regarded these parameters with pronounced ambivalence, finding them alternately "a great pain" and "a relief." Chilberg also worked on *Battlestar: Galactica*, where he had not been "saddled with an entire liturgy. He had come to that series lacking any experience in science fiction filmmaking assuring a dubious Glen Larson that this would enable him to approach the show from an unbiased angle. "And we worked hard to give it the feel of a completely different time. We were careful not to look like any of the other SF shows." Nevertheless, the production was sued by George Lucas for copying *Star Wars*.

StarTrek, however, had its own rules. It was Nimoy's encyclopedic grasp of the *Star Trek* liturgy that made him a shoo-in for the job of director. In the main, however, Chilberg and crew pursued functional forms. "You can't get very far beyond the state of knowledge today," he noted. "You realize, at some point, that a drinking glass is going to look like a glass 500 years from now. The thing still has to hold water. You really can't go too far out of your own time frame."

"For *Star Trek*," added Pedigo, "we had to find a style that exists now but which could also exist in the future. We opted for art deco because geometric forms will always be around."

Even settling on a color scheme for the movie meant consulting the *Star Trek Compendium*. "*Star Trek*'s characters are very human," said Pedigo. "So we had to stay away from cold colors because we'd get a cold effect that would undermine the characters."

Chilberg noted that the color scheme had been more or less settled on in accordance with the preceding film. The Enterprise color scheme would remain a series of blue-gray tones, indicative of a cool, military look. He found himself forced to repaint the Enterprise bridge floor, however, after discovering that it was too black to photograph well. Because the initial black did not reflect light, the bridge stations, as they had appeared on *Star Trek II*, had looked like "holes in the wall." Chilberg instructed his crew to lighten the floor by a factor of 30%, making it gray.

Kirk's San Francisco apartment was done in the same, earthy tones that had distinguished it during the second film in the series, and came replete with nautical antiques from Paramount's prop stores and rentals from Modern Props.

The only distinctive area on the Enterprise that underwent a drastic color-change was Spock's private quarters. They had always been gray, but Nimoy did not feel that this expressed the Vulcan look he was aiming for. His quarters were brightened with deep reds, orange and amber. The unusual mural on Spock's wall was based upon the design of the Sparklett's water company logo. It was comprised of thousands of sequins hung from pins.

Other examples of Vulcan symbology in the film were somewhat less haphazard. The large symbol viewed in the Vulcan temple, for examine, had been designed as a stylized version of the Vulcan split-fingered salute. Chilberg said that he had done the original sketches for the symbol, a 12' high construct which was fashioned from plaster and styrofoam and afforded the appearance of floating.

"The edifice," Pedigo elaborated, "was designed to have a utilitarian sculptural effect. It was intended to look as if it was sculpted out of stone."

Another set that provided its designers with a great deal of fun was the bar. Set designer Cameron Birnie noted that it had been fashioned from a revamped Enterprise sick bay.

According to actor DeForest Kelley, there had been talk during the storyboarding stage of walking McCoy down the street leading into the bar, so that a greater variety of aliens could be glimpsed. "We were going to locate the Star Wars bar across the street," he declared.

Although the set designer is generally responsible for translating the art director's vision of a set into a blueprint that the carpenters can work with, Birnie said that he had been given input into the designs of the bar and other sets by Chilberg.

Less amusing was the process of painting a backing for the Vulcan temple area where Spock was to be reacquainted with his body. The backing was intended to convey that the temple was located high atop a mountain, in a mountainous area. The illustrator responsible for the painting had researched the problem thoroughly and determined that if one were really atop a mountain and if mountains were only scattered in the foreground, the only thing that would be visible in the background would be sky.

"The argument we had," recalled Birnie, "was that if all you could see was sky, how'd you know you were high up?" The solution that presented itself was to play with the horizon line. And so, a very expensive backing was painted on the stage, extending some 250 degrees along the set. But the horizon-line was placed too high and it looked, said Birnie, "like the temple was situated in a crater." Needless to say, it was repainted.

■ The Search For Genisis

Creating the Genesis planet set was probably the most complex task facing Chilberg and his crews. The set occupied the whole of Paramount's Stage 15, otherwise known as the DeMille stage, in recollection of his parting of the Red Sea on its premises. It is one of the largest stages in Hollywood.

The set, which eventually measured in at 300' x 100', was built to encompass a number of particularly varied settings, where a desert scene and a lush tropical scene could be set up alongside a snow-swept area and another to stage the volcanic confrontation between Kirk and his Klingon nemesis, Kruge.

Two Genesis sets were constructed, in fact—one for live action and one for miniatures. The Genesis set was first rendered in a series of sketches, but because of its vast size, models of the set were eventually constructed and then cut up into sections three to four feet in scale, and from four inches to a foot in height. These sections, replete with miniature versions of the truss systems required to create the earthquake fissures, were then turned over to the carpenters. According to Cameron Birnie, this made it easier for the carpenters working under his direction to visualize exactly how the set designers wanted it to look. "It basically eliminated the errors you would otherwise expect in transferring a drawing into a finished product," added Chilberg.

"It's fairly common to build this kind of set this way," said Birnie. "Of course, you don't build too many sets like this one in the course of a career."

The earthquake section of the Genesis set, said special effects supervisor Bob Dawson, was rigged in much the way that he had rigged a similar set for the production of *Shogun*. The surface of the set reached some 20-25 feet at its highest point. The fissures had to range from 20 to 50 feet in length, two to four feet deep. Dawson posted four by four wooden beams, six feet apart from each other, in two opposing rows. He would connect these with a long piece of timber extending in a V-fashion downward, about two feet below where the surface was envisioned.

The way to bring about their collapse lies in their preparation. Each of the posts is cut through from the middle section down, and is equipped with a hinge. A cable is then wrapped through and around these "weak knees." These lines, each holding perhaps as many as 10 posts together, are then attached to a drumless air hoist. The gap between the posts is filled with sawdust and dirt. And when the lines are yanked, all hell breaks loose. The surface of this fissure-ridden set was fashioned from plywood instead of the usual dirt mats. An old steel mine in Fontana provided truckloads of gray slag which was used as soil and, when not ground up, as rocks and boulders. Decomposed granite was also mixed in

with it. The hydraulic platforms were then covered with topsoil and trees.

One area on the Genesis stage which was intended to portray the planet in an advanced stage of decomposition was filled with the entire stock of a nearby company that specialized in renting out gnarled tree roots and limbs.

The waterfall which figured in the more idealistic segment of the Genesis set was basically an old recycling pump of the garden variety which had been uncovered in an old store of props. It was placed among huge fiberglass boulders that, Dawson said, may have dated back to an old episode of *Bonanza*. Dry ice and food coloring were added to the water to give it a strange hue. Somewhat less mundanely, Dawson rigged a portion of the Genesis stage for explosions. Flames generated by nap-gas bottles (containing napthalene and propane) were timed to shoot out the fissures as the bombs went off.

Concurrently, Dawson had to coordinate the creation of smoke generated from standard issue smoke canisters and fog from mineral oil. "The set became extremely noisy," he recalled. With all that happening at once, Dawson had only one chance to bring it off, and to make sure that no one got hurt in the process.

Dawson said that half the battle had been won from the start because the cast, which had worked with him on *Star Trek II*, had learned to trust him with their safety. "That the name of the game there. You have to prove yourself to them first. Why, on the second film I blew Leonard [Nimoy] right out of his chair!"

To bring off the final destruction scene, however, Dawson orchestrated a 14-man special effects crew. Because of the noise created by the equipment, he could not rely on radios to communicate with his men. Hand signals were used when the radios could not be trusted. The scene went off without a hitch, which was probably a surprise to Dawson's colleagues, who had by then concluded that stage 15 was jinxed.

■ Exit: Stage 15

Stage 15 had been built during the 1930's as a temporary structure

that would eventually be replaced. It never was.

It was, in a sense, three distinct stages separated by massive sound-proof doors supported by an ancient truss system. To get the doors to lower, you had to pull a chain. One day, the chain for the door separating stages 14 and 15 got caught on something and no one was able to see it. So the person who was trying to close the door kept pulling on the chain until the roof trusses collapsed.

"We heard this big snap," recounted Birnie, "and both the door and the roof fell three feet and then just hung there, suspended."

All personnel were ushered out of the area. The lot sent out for some sturdy 12-foot-long wooden beams which were used to prop up the fallen door and the archway.

Art director John Chilberg was under intense pressure when this mishap occurred to work some time-lapse changes into the Genesis surface. But because the door separating the sets could no longer be closed, Chilberg's crews found themselves able to work only at night, when their noise couldn't disturb anyone.

Two weeks before the shooting began on the stage, Cameron Birnie found himself in the art department on the Paramount lot, around the bend from the stage. He heard sirens, which was not an uncommon occurrence around movie studios. The film's construction coordinator quipped that the fire trucks would probably he heading for Stage 15.

"He said it as a joke because we'd had such bad luck with that stage already."

But as they poked their heads out the door, they saw that fire trucks were indeed careening toward the luckless stage, the western wall of which, it became evident, was very much ablaze. What happened was that the New York Street on the Paramount lot had caught fire. The exterior of Stage 15, it turned out, was made of celotex, an intensely flammable porous material compressed with fiber.

"When the flames hit it," Chilberg remembered, "the walls just coughed."

Fortunately, some special

DC Comics shows us yet another sequence filmed then cut from Star Trek III.

effects technicians had been working on the Genesis sets when the wall caught fire. The three of them were reportedly joined by William Shatner. They ejected all other personnel from the stage while laying out hoses.

Birnie, who had dashed out to the stage, claimed that he had never seen anything burn as fast and as fiercely as that wall. "It was like kindling!" But the effects crew and the actor climbed atop a lift and began to hose down the burning wall from above the stage. They cut a hole through the roof to let some of the heat out and the water in. As it happened, the flames burned completely through the wall, exposing the flooded set inside to sunlight. Had cool heads not prevailed, the stage would likely have burned to the ground. Luckily, the building only had to be resided and about a foot of water drained.

But the fact that Stage 15 was the only one on the lot damaged by the fire spooked a lot of people. Their overall sense of security was not improved by numerous electrical mishaps which would cause the huge 10k movie lights suspended over the set to explode peri-

odically. This event would generally trigger a general electricity shutdown on Stage 15, forcing shooting to be delayed as electricians hastened to rewire the set.

And then there was the business of Bob Dawson nearly losing his face while blowing up the Enterprise. It had never been a secret that the makers of the *Star Trek* films had never cared much for the Enterprise. The model had always proved unwieldily and nearly unshootable. The bridge proved almost as problematic. ILM's Ken Ralston has, in fact, indicated that he may have been personally responsible for the Enterprise's glorious exit. He had pitched the idea to Harve Bennett during production of the second *Star Trek* movie.

"We figured it was high time for the crew to move into something a little bigger and more elaborate," said Dawson. "After all, the thing was 20 years old. It was kind of like moving out of the family station wagon and into something a little sleeker."

"It freed us," added Chilberg, "to put together a more state-of-the-art spaceship for the next film. A lot has happened in electronics, for instance, that

has just never been reflected in the series."

Ralston has reported that he had been tempted to blow up the $150,000 Enterprise model that Douglas Trumbull had assembled for the first *Trek* movie. Or, as he was quoted saying, "to take a mallet to it." He settled, however, for blowing up the smaller, six-foot model that had been left over from the last film.

While ILM gleefully dispatched the aging starship to the great beyond, special effects supervisor Bob Dawson saw to the destruction of its interiors. Wrecking the bridge proved difficult because the elevator doors had been constructed from fiberglass. "And you don't blow up fiberglass with people nearby," he noted.

He solved this one by remaking the elevator doors with balsawood. Dawson fitted nine inch in diameter steel tubes behind the doors, which served, in essence, as mortars. He equipped each with 2oz. and 4oz. bombs triggered by detonator wires and packed down with a special packing agent dampened with gasoline. Detonating these explosives was as elaborate a bit of business as rigging the Genesis set for an earthquake. There were numerous tertiary explosions to overlook as well and there would be no second chance to get it right.

Dawson ran his pyro crew through dozens of drills, his own hands triggering the main blasts. But he found that both he and his people had talked the bridge destruction scene past the point of diminishing returns. "Problem is that you talk it up until it gets ridiculous," he explained. "It was getting everyone nervous so I said let's just do it."

The bridge went up in fine fashion and no one got hurt. "I was glad to see the end of the bridge," Dawson said. "You could never do anything with it. Everyone cheered when that sucker went up—although it was probably more of a cheer of relief than delight."

Dawson pushed his own luck, however, when he rigged a nondistinct Enterprise corridor to blow up as well for a shot that would cut into the destruction scene. According to Birnie, Dawson had rigged stock charges toward one end of the corridor, stationing himself at the other end. But the charges apparently contained too much gunpowder. When they exploded, a huge fireball was sucked through the ensuing vacuum, down the corridor and into Dawson.

"The explosion burned his arms and face quite badly," said Birnie of Dawson's accident. "Of course we rushed him to the hospital and he took a couple of days off to rest. He came back and did the rest of the movie in bandages. But that was just part of the excitement of the show."

■ Shooting Spock

Of all the color schemes ever employed by *Star Trek*, Charles Correll, the film's director of photography, preferred those used in the original TV series.

"The intense, exaggerated colors of the television program lent itself to the mystique of *Star Trek*," explained the self-avowed non-Trekkie. "And we took those colors into consideration."

Correll noted that Nimoy had also been an enthusiast of the old color schemes. Both had viewed the experimentation with color on the first feature to have been as misguided as most of the

other efforts to alter the *Star Trek* product too considerably.

Star Trek II had been a step in the right direction, he indicated. But as a predominantly interior picture, in which some 65 percent of the shots were culled from two spaceship sets, there had been definite limits on how far color schemes could be pushed.

Correll had anticipated that the third *Star Trek* feature would lend itself to greater experimentation with color and lighting, especially in exterior shots. Perhaps oddly, he had not been pleased to learn that with few exceptions, exterior scenes would be shot on Paramount's sound stages. He had, in fact, argued in favor of shooting Genesis on the island of Kauai, and Vulcan in Red Rock Canyon, to avoid what he called a "phony" look. But Correll apparently realized quite quickly that with craft and imagination, the line between phony and truly alien could be stretched. The D.P. was therefore able to give Genesis planet's sky a cold bluer-than-blue look that surpassed anything that could be accomplished with the actual sky. On Vulcan, Correll aimed for deep oranges. "We wanted the planet to look like it was always sunrise."

He accomplished this by smearing gels on the lights. Correll generally avoided filtration or diffusion because, he said, the ILM shots he received were letter-sharp, and he thought it best to go for the sharpest image possible. He said that the Kodak stock used on the film enabled him to achieve unusual depths of field as well.

The red alerts photographed on the Enterprise and some of the other ships were accomplished by actually rigging the sets with red lights. He noted that he had also been pleased with the pastel and magenta hues he was able to achieve for the bar scene at the start of the movie.

"Leonard [Nimoy] was the person who suggested that each ship, each planet and each set should have an original color scheme," Correll recalled. He did, however, observe that for all of Nimoy's understanding of the intricacies of the *Star Trek* universe, and despite his pronouncedly calm and reasoned approach to filmmaking, "Nimoy doesn't have what you can call a camera or a

directing style. Basically, Nimoy didn't want this to be a camera picture. He thought that this would detract from the plot and from the characters. We treated some scenes with movement and others very classically, almost statically. Whatever seemed to work best."

The hardest thing for Correll on the picture, however, was shooting the Genesis planet apocalypse. It took three weeks to complete, he said, because of the complex nature of the scene. "There was a lot of optical work in that scene, which meant that we had to match lighting to it. We had to do two or three angles of everything. And there had been the story-boarding and the discussions about color schemes."

The movie, in fact, had been a one-camera show. Two cameras were used primarily during the Vulcan parade which ultimately had to be cut from the film.

Shooting convincing day exteriors also proved problematic. ILM matte paintings, however, afforded some perspective which Correll believed helped him immensely. "And we always tried to incorporate elements of weather to give it reality and life. There'd always be something going on in the air—wind, leaves, atmospheric smoke, ground fog, haze. I wasn't crazy about the plastic snow, though. The stuff doesn't react like snow. It falls differently and if the camera focuses on it for a few seconds, you realize it's phony. But we combined it with smoke, which indicated coldness. It does give a texture to the picture."

■ A Fruitful Search

The "texture" of *Star Trek III: The Search for Spock* came together beautifully as far as fans were concerned. The film was released in June 1984 to generally positive reviews, though the critics weren't quite as enthusiastic as they had been about *The Wrath of Khan*. As *The New York Daily News* noted, "Installment three falls somewhere ahead of the first feature and way behind the highwater mark of [*Star Trek*] *II*. Enough exciting sparks are struck— rest assured—and now that the gang's all here, 'the adventure continues.'"

Despite the fact that the climax

of the film was a foregone conclusion (there was simply no way that they weren't going to find Spock), *Star Trek III* does make a terrific episode, giving each of the characters a moment to shine and examines the depth of the Kirk-Spock-McCoy triangle.

Additionally, Nimoy's co-stars had nothing but raves for him as well.

William Shatner: "Leonard had a point of view and knew what he was doing. [He's] very organized and methodical. He's very creative. I'm looking forward to working with him on *Star Trek IV*. I thought *Star Trek III* was very good. I think it could have been a little more complicated in storyline, but very good."

DeForest Kelley: "I enjoyed watching *Star Trek III* more than I did *Star Trek II*. This one comes closer to the TV series than the others. I, for years, have had full confidence that Leonard could direct *Star Trek*, or for that matter, anything he wanted to had he been given the opportunity. Leonard is the kind of director who will accept input from you because he knows that we know and feel certain things about our characters."

George Takei: "Leonard brings with him an intrinsic understanding of the show, the characters and the relationships. That was a great advantage. He also is a guy that is very intelligent and a fine artist, so he brought those qualities."

Walter Koenig: "*Star Trek III* is obviously a very successful film. I think it, perhaps more than either of the first two features, promotes a sense of family and congeniality and warmth. I think there's a feeling of affection generated by the members of the Enterprise crew, much more a sense of simpatico."

On his feature directorial debut, Leonard Nimoy hit the proverbial home run both critically and financially, as *Star Trek III* matched the gross of its predecessor. Things were, however, amiss in the *Star Trek* universe itself, given the death of David Marcus, the destruction of the Enterprise and the fact that her former crew were now renegades who had disobeyed Federation orders to go after Spock.

The groundwork had been laid for a fourth film, which would ultimately prove to be the most popular of all.

■ Star Trek IV
The Voyage Home
The Voyage Begins

Considering the resounding success of *Star Trek III: The Search for Spock*, it came as no surprise to anyone that Paramount Pictures was interested in dipping back into the well at least one more time with a fourth film. The trek got off to a less than smooth start when William Shatner made it plainly clear to the studio that he would not return as James T. Kirk unless the good admiral was given a considerable pay increase.

Six months passed while returning director Leonard Nimoy and executive producer Harve Bennett awaited word. As negotiations continued, a variation of the *Star Trek* formula was developed.

"A proposal was made by me that we didn't have to have Bill," said Bennett, "that we could do *Star Trek* in the beginning, which was Ralph Winter's idea. Let's do them at the academy. That picture seems to have worked in a variety of incarnations including *Top Gun*. It's a very workable picture. But the franchise wasn't the same without the stars and there is merit in that argument."

Interestingly, the story, entitled *Starfleet Academy*, would come up again shortly after the production of *Star Trek V*, a fact which will be discussed in depth further on in this volume.

Finally, after a total of eight months had passed (and this delay would ultimately have repercussions on Shatner himself when he took the helm of the fifth film adventure), Shatner signed on the dotted line for $2 million and *Star Trek IV* was back on track. By this time, however, quite a bit had happened behind the scenes, the least of which was the development of the film's tone and storyline, as well as the idea that this would be the concluding chapter of a trilogy; a trilogy which had not been intended when Bennett took over the series' production reigns.

"In moving through the trilogy," Bennett has stated, "I confess that every one of the major tricks I learned in television, I used. I'm out of tricks now....I've gotta find another one because we have

THE FATE OF THE FUTURE LIES HIDDEN IN THE PAST, SOMEWHERE ON EARTH...1986.

STAR TREK
IV
THE VOYAGE HOME

One version of the ad campaign utilized by Paramount (ad slick courtesy United Artists Theatres).

now completed a trilogy and we have to go where no man has gone before. When you go where no man has gone before, you have to build things and then it starts getting expensive. Here are the three tricks of the trilogy: *Star Trek II*, in television we call that the 'bottle show.' The 'bottle show' in television takes place in an elevator that's hopefully trapped between two floors. Or it takes place in a mine shaft where people are desperately coming to try to save you and you have to stay down there and talk a lot. Sixty-five percent of the film was on the Enterprise bridge in one incarnation or another. It was also the Reliant bridge. And it was also part of the science station. We used that set for 65 percent of the movie and that is an incomparable savings in terms of time, dollars and moves. We'd shoot a scene, move the people out, repaint it and it would now be the Reliant.

"*Star Trek III*," he continued, "was the classic television 'the leading actor loses his memory' show. I did that on *Mod Squad, Six Million Dollar Man, Bionic Woman*, and you usually do it when your leading actor is exhausted or needs a rest. He's in a coma-like state. In *Star Trek III*, we had a man who was directing the movie, and who had never directed a feature before, and we felt that to act and so forth would kill him. We had our choice of how to utilize that asset, and what we did was we spent most of our money building one great set, the Genesis planet, and the story became let's find him while he directs. [For *Star Trek IV* we decided to use] local location. We've gotta add some size to this picture, so what do we do? We go out. How do you go out in the 23rd Century? You come to the *20th Century*."

Said Leonard Nimoy, "We decided early on that we wanted to do a time travel story. When I say we, I'm talking about Harve Bennett and I. We were asked by the studio to come up with a story, and our very first conversation was about doing time travel, which we both agreed was a good idea. We also felt that we should lighten up. The picture should be fun in comparison to the previous three. The first movie had no comedy at all. That was intentional. It was intended to be a serious study of a problem. The second film had a little. The third film had a little. But there we were dealing with a lot of serious drama. There was a lot of life and death going on. In [*Star Trek*] *II* Spock died. In [*StarTrek*] *III* Kirk's son died, the

William Shatner (Admiral James T. Kirk) and Leonard Nimoy (Mr. Spock), on location in San Francisco for The Voyage Home (photo copyright ©1994 Bruce Birmelin/Onyx).

Enterprise was blown up and people were being killed and planets were disintegrating. I just felt it was time to lighten up and have some fun. That meant that if we were going to do time travel, the best thing we could do was come back to contemporary Earth, where we could have some fun with our people. They would more or less be a fish out of water on the streets.

"Now the next question becomes, why are they coming back in time? Is it accidental? We knew we wanted them to come home and face trial for all that had happened in *Star Trek III*, rules being broken, the Enterprise destroyed and all that. It would have been out of character for them not to at least try to come home and deal with their obligations. So we figured we would start them on their way home in this Klingon Bird of Prey. Does something go wrong? Do they find themselves going through a time travel accidentally, or was it intentional? For a number of reasons, we chose that it would be intentional. If they're coming back to the 20th Century, what are they coming back for? Is it something they need, something they want? That led us to the idea that there's a problem in the 23rd Century, which can only be solved by something that's now gone, extinct. I have had a lot of good conversations with scientists. Some of the things I have learned from them have been technical, some philosophical.

I think the most pertinent to what is happening in this film is that there are scientists who are deeply concerned, because of the prevalent attitude, that we don't have to worry about what we do on this planet. The attitude is whatever problems we create, science will fix. They are afraid that something will go terribly wrong and someone will turn around and say, 'Fix it,' and they will have to say, 'We can't. It's gone too far and it's something we can't control.'

"We experimented with a lot of different ideas on that subject, including the idea that certain crafts and techniques might be lost by the 23rd Century. Maybe there's nobody who knows how to make a violin anymore. Probably by that time we won't have anybody who knows how to crack oil anymore, because it won't be necessary. Cracking oil will be an extinct process by then. Suppose we needed to start an oil refinery in the 23rd Century, it might be useful to find someone in the 20th Century who would know how to do it."

Shortly thereafter, Nimoy had numerous conversations with members of M.I.T. regarding communication with other species.

"We were talking about the idea that if alien intelligence was trying to contact us, it would probably take quite a long time for us to know what it is saying, and for us to communicate with it," Nimoy stated. "I became intrigued with the idea that there was some lack of communication that was causing the problem. [I was] aware that humpback whales sing this unusual kind of song, which we don't understand but which obviously means something to them. They communicate it to each other, they pass it on one to the other, they repeat it. It has a form, lasting anywhere from six to 30 minutes in cycles, and they sing it again and again. Then they cease periodically, and they change the song. It's quite a complex structure, and that's very interesting. We don't know, and we may never know, what the communication is all about, so supposing that something in the 23rd Century is trying to communicate with them and they're gone. That's how it all happened, and it's a hell of a lot more interesting and challenging, cinematically, to come back to the 20th Century to pick up a pair of whales than it is to pick up a plant or insect."

In the pages of *The Official Star Trek Fan Club Magazine* [#56, June/July 1987], Nimoy added, "I did some homework and researched different scientific concerns of modern day. I started looking into the problem of endangered species. I had read a book by a Harvard biologist named Edward O. Wilson called *Biophilia*. In the book, it said that by the 1990's we'll be losing 10,000 species per year off the Earth at the rate we're going now. A lot of those species we may not even know exist, but, nevertheless, they'll be gone before scientists and biologists even have a chance to research them and understand them. So there's many different forms of life facing extinction and one of the most well-known are the whales. Wilson states in his book that there are certain 'keystone species.' That means, for example, if you build a house of cards, you can pull out so many cards without the house falling down. But there are particular 'keystone' cards, that if you pull them out, the whole house crumbles. So we may not even know which species on this planet are the 'keystone' cards, so to speak, for our ecological system. If we were to wipe out one species, it could start the whole thing crumbling."

Concept in hand, Nimoy and Bennett gathered with screenwriter Daniel Petrie, Jr. to develop a story and a subsequent script. What would have been

Officially Licensed By Paramount Pictures Corporation

$2.50

STAR TREK
THE OFFICIAL FAN CLUB

HARVE BENNETT
Behind-The-Scenes on Star Trek IV!

a fruitful collaboration did not pan out.

"[Dan Petrie] left the studio," related Harve Bennett. "He was a *Star Trek* lover and loved the story when he read it, but the administration changed and he went to Disney where he still is. But he would have been perfect!"

The search for a new writer began, while the film was struck with an interesting....dilemma. Eddie Murphy, a golden boy at Paramount at the time, had been pretty vocal in the fact that he loved *Star Trek* and would be very interested in co-starring in the new film.

"Now the meeting with Eddie Murphy was a little bizarre," said Bennett. "He had a separate meeting with Leonard. Leonard said, 'He's a little strange in a room.' So he came in with two thugs, good looking thugs, and they were all in black leather. [We] told Eddie this story and the thought about it for awhile and he said, 'It's good. Let me see a script,' and he walked out. We sat there and thought, 'Wouldn't it be terrific to have Eddie in this movie?' Later, the studio started getting very anxious for a very good reason. Here you have a franchise called *Star Trek* and it performs in a certain wonderful way. Here you have a franchise called Eddie Murphy and it performs in an even bigger way. Why not take them together and form one franchise? Bad economics because you are probably diminishing by compositing. So the studio was resistant to it, but Eddie has a certain amount of clout and he said that he hadn't decided whether he wanted to do it or not and so much of the development of the story was with the very distinct possibility that Eddie Murphy was in it."

As is the norm for *Star Trek* films, word of this little news item reached fandom, and memories of Richard Pryor's guest starring in *Superman III* sent a shudder through them. Naturally, a letter writing campaign was quickly initiated.

Said Harve Bennett, "The *Star Trek* fans who are our greatest asset, are also gigantic pains-in-the-ass. They know I love them and they know I can say that. They do have a propriety interest and to some extent they do pay for it. The fans found out about this and they got the word out."

"*Star Trek* is a lot of different things to a lot of different people," related Leonard Nimoy. "Some people watch it because they love the Enterprise, some people because they love the space battles, others because of the characters or the aliens. There are a lot of different reasons that you enjoy *Star Trek*. There have been people who have said to me, 'How could you destroy the Enterprise? What's *Star Trek* without the Enterprise?' We're doing drama. We're doing entertainment. We're doing fiction. If there's an individual who can't handle that and who steps over into a personal fantasy, that's his personal problem. I think the handling of the death and resurrection of Spock was tastefully done, dramatically done and

was good science fiction. We're doing an entertainment piece. It shouldn't be taken too seriously."

■ Penning The Voyage Home

Based on their screenplay *The Long Way Home*, a black comedy about the plight of the Indian in America today, Steve Meerson and Peter Krikes were chosen to write the screenplay for *Star Trek IV*.

Said Meerson, "We sat in a room with Leonard and Harve, and Leonard told us that he wanted to do a departure, although they weren't sure what they wanted to do."

Added Krikes, "They wanted to do a film sort of based on 'The City on the Edge of Forever'...."

"Leonard started talking about plankton, cells, that cells become plankton, that things eat plankton and then whales entered the conversation."

"And we said, 'Why not make it as simple as the whale and the whale song?' That was our idea, though that's not to say that Leonard hadn't done research on whales, because he had."

"Leonard has mountains of information on various things," pointed out Meerson. "I guess we were hired in February of 1985 and between that time and May or June, Peter and I did several outlines of what eventually became the story. Before we could start writing the script, we had to get the studio to approve the outline. We registered all the outlines with the Writer's Guild, and after we came up with the story for the movie, Harve and Leonard took our outline and went through it step by step with the studio executives, and we got the go-ahead to start writing."

The duo were given two instructions: keep Eddie Murphy in mind for the guest star, and make sure that the character of Admiral Kirk is the driving force behind every aspect of the story.

"The approach we were told to take is that Kirk really had to be the one to lead everyone," explained Meerson. "Not necessarily that he had to actually have the idea to do something, but it had to appear as if he has the idea. I think the

perfect example in the movie is when Spock goes into the belly of the Bird of Prey to use the computers and learns that the sound is whale songs. It's Kirk who has the idea to go back through time, although Spock is the one who plants the suggestion in Kirk's mind. Kirk verbalizes it, and that's the way it had to be played. We were told Bill had to be the leader at all times. In that scene, if you're reading it, you say, 'It's Spock's idea,' but on film Spock's discovery that it's humpback whales is not as important as Kirk's idea of going to get them."

"Visually," added Krikes, "the scene between Spock and his father at the end is another example. You kind of ask, 'Why is Captain Kirk standing there listening to this?' He has to be a part of *everything*."

Naturally word reached them of the controversy surrounding Murphy's possible appearance, and the fact that the cast was not happy about the idea.

"I think all of those guys became terrified that Eddie would blow them off the screen," mused Meerson. "They also got a lot of negative mail from the fans."

All of the "noise" ultimately came to nothing, as Murphy decided to bow out.

"I'm a Trekkie," claimed Murphy. "I've always loved *Star Trek* and *have* wanted to do one of the films. I wanted to be in *Star Trek* and that's where they got the idea of coming back in time to Earth in 1987. The script was developed, but we eventually dropped the idea. *Golden Child* came along and I decided to do that film instead, because I thought it would be better for my career. In retrospect, I might have been better off doing *Star Trek IV*."

Explained Harve Bennett, "We went through every writer we could think of. We finally found Steve Meerson and Peter Krikes, whose work was highly regarded. Nothing came of it. Some of that, in fairness to them, was because we had saddled them with what appeared to be a male character that we thought was going to be Eddie Murphy at one time. Then when Eddie Murphy fell out, we had to readjust the script. But, by then, it had turned to paste, it just didn't work. Frankly, there are two scenes in the picture that they wrote that stayed pretty much the same. One of them is outstanding, which is the hospital scene that had minor modifications by Nick Meyer and me. They had also laid down the outline for the plexiglass factory scene. But, essentially, we didn't have a script we felt good about or even submittable to the studio."

As one would suspect, Meerson and Krikes *did not* take kindly to such comments.

"Actually," stated Meerson, "every beat of the film's first, second and third acts is *exactly the same* as our script. The *only* thing that changed slightly was that our Eddie Murphy character and the marine biologist were combined. Eddie Murphy was going to play a college professor who taught English, but a professor who we probably all had in the '60s or '70s, who's a little bit wacky and believes in extraterrestrials. Every Wednesday, he would open up his class to a discussion and the room would light up with conversation."

Krikes said, "He would play whale songs, and it was the whale songs he played in the classroom that the ship locked on to."

"That was in the first draft we wrote, but the second draft was different. After you write a first draft of anything, once the director, the cast and the producers come aboard, *everything* changes, and not necessarily for the better. But the tone was pretty much a reflection of what was in the movie. For example, there was a scene where the Eddie Murphy character was trying to convince the Catherine Hicks character that aliens do exist on Earth. In the first draft, Hicks was a newswoman and there was a marine biologist as well. Gillian Taylor was ultimately a marriage of about three characters."

"Murphy believed in aliens and saw them beam into the classroom."

"It was the boy who cried wolf," Meerson noted. "No one would ever believe him, so he took it upon himself to follow the crew, and in one scene, he lifted a phaser from Kirk, took it back to the newswoman and said, 'See, they really *do* exist.' And she says, 'What's this?' and casts the gun aside, accidentally activating it. The phaser lands on the floor and her cat jumps off the couch.

Catherine Hicks, seen here in Child's Play, portrayed marine biologist Gillian Taylor in The Voyage Home (photo copyright ©1988 United Artists Pictures).

We follow her to her bedroom and she goes to sleep. The cat keeps phasing things out of the apartment by hitting the phaser, and when she wakes up, she sees that all the furniture is gone."

"That's just the side stuff," Krikes remarked. "If you look at our script and the movie you saw, basically everything is still there, like Eddie Murphy going to meet the aliens in the park to bring them gifts, and he runs into the invisible ship...."

"....Which is what Catherine Hicks did when she ran into the park to find Kirk. The structure really is exactly the same. Also, she grabbed Kirk's waist, Eddie Murphy grabbed his ankles. Murphy says goodbye to Kirk who starts to beam out, then he grabs him by the ankles and is transported aboard. He goes back to the 23rd Century, and he salutes Kirk when they get the Enterprise II. You know when Spock nerve pinches the guy on the bus? In our draft that took place in an underground subway system....You can't imagine the frustration of watching them take all the credit for something that was completely blocked out for them."

"Plus they removed a lot of the emotional qualities that we thought it would have," Krikes mused. "It's interesting how they downplayed certain things. We spent months trying to figure out how you could get dilithium on Earth, since there was none. We had put in a sequence with a linear accelerator, where they break into the linear accelerator at Stamford University and have to take whatever element we have and charge it. And Spock had to work on rearranging the elements."

"They simplified the sequence, essentially, and said, 'Let's just stick this little machine on top and it'll change it into something.' I think it was actually a good idea, because it wouldn't have fit into the movie."

That's not to say that there weren't some significant differences as well, including the idea that Lieutenant Saavik was pregnant due to her *pon farr* sequence with young Spock in *Star Trek III.*

"There was a scene with Kirk on the Bridge of the Bird of Prey," recalled Krikes. "They cut out five lines where Kirk says to Saavik, 'Have you told him yet?' And she says, 'No. I'm taking a maternity leave.'"

"That's why she's standing with Amanda when the Bird of Prey leaves," Meerson revealed. "Because Amanda *knows* Saavik is carrying Spock's kid."

"All they did was cut out five lines of dialogue, and you lost that whole thing, which, I believe, will turn up in a Harve Bennett script in a couple of years."

Stated Meerson, "You'll have a story meeting with Harve Bennett for about eight hours and you'll say something in the first hour, and in the eighth hour he'll say, 'What does everybody think of this?' And it's exactly what you said eight hours ago. But that's really what Saavik's involvement was."

Krikes recalled another change. "One of the things we had in our earlier drafts that they took out was what happened when they first went through time. Instead of that horrible time sequence that looks like Russian science fiction, we had them using the sling-shot effect around Jupiter and Mars. Also, when they first appeared in the 20th Century, they were in a fog, and as they lowered, the monitors picked up all of this cheering and applause. As they come out of the fog, they find themselves over a Super Bowl game and everyone thinks it's a halftime show. Then, they cloak and disappear."

Meerson explained, "That's how we introduced the Eddie Murphy character, because he's at the Super Bowl and he's the only one who believes he just saw what he saw. I thought that would have been a wonderful moment. Also, I love our ending better. Our sequence of events were similar. After the shuttle has picked them up and Earth is saved, we cut to this little chamber where they're waiting to stand trial."

"They discuss whether or not they would do everything the same if they could...."

"....And they say they would. We cut away to Spock and Sarek, who have that same chat that they had in the movie. It was originally much more bonding, but they removed about half-a-page of dialogue, which changed things quite a bit."

Commented Krikes, "Basically, Sarek was saying, 'You're half-human and I'll never understand that, but I accept you.'"

"So we cut from that to someone knocking on the door and saying, 'It's time to go on trial,' and they put them in a pool. They go through this endless black tunnel and come out into the docking area for the trial...."

"....And everyone is gathered by the windows of the dock, cheering them on."

Meerson smiled at the memory. "Everyone is confused, saying to the pilot, 'Where are you taking us?' That's when the pod rises and you see the new Enterprise II. It would have been much more emotional, instead of saying, 'You've been exonerated for this, this and this,' you could have done it in three sentences, and with everyone cheering, screaming and yelling, it would have been an emotional high. Harve likes bookends, which is why the film begins with a trial and ends with a trial. That was always a point of contention between the three of us, that you didn't need to do that sequence again because it would be understood why. You could just take them to the ship so that everyone would be on a high, rather than waiting for it to happen. Structurally, I think they made a mistake."

Meerson and Krikes emphasize that they were excited when they were

contacted about the film, but found that the road to the screen wasn't exactly easy. Part of it was the difficulty in giving *all* of the characters something to do, as well as what happened to their script after they handed it in.

"We were told to *only* worry about Kirk, Spock and Bones," said Meerson. "In their minds, those are the only people that matter."

Added Krikes, "They also took out a scene we wrote which dealt with the people's mortality and age."

"My favorite scene we wrote was between Bones and Scotty, where they talk about the fact that they're getting too old to be doing this. I personally they they [DeForest Kelley and James Doohan] would have loved to play it. It was two guys sitting on a park bench in Union Square, completely out of time and space, saying, 'We're really getting too old. If we ever do make it back, maybe we ought to give it all up and retire.' Then, they both decided that they'll *never* retire, because there's more to life than sitting on your duff."

As stated earlier, once Eddie Murphy left the project, Bennett turned his attention to other writers. One of his first creative decisions was to alter the Murphy character into a female marine biologist, who would also serve as Kirk's love interest.

Recalled Bennett, "I remember saying, 'Well, I know it's corny, but it would be better if it was a woman. Kirk hasn't had a woman to play to, which he does so wonderfully. The whole series is the woman of the week. Remember that whale special we saw where the girl was bidding adieu to the whales who had to leave Marineland because the female was pregnant and they could not keep them and they had to send them back to the sea and she was bereft? Remember that character? That's the lady,' and Leonard thought that was great.

"So, now we're getting down to where we've got a movie to make and a whole new script to write. That's when we were fortunate enough to find that Nicholas Meyer was available."

In the pages of *Cinefantastique*, Meyer told journalist Dennis Fischer, "I got involved in number IV because they had another script they were not happy with. Dawn Steele, who [was] the head of Paramount and has been a friend of mine for many years, called me and said, 'Would you do us an enormous favor?' And I said, 'For Harve and Leonard? Yeah, absolutely.' They had a script written. The script, I guess, was for Eddie Murphy as a guest star. I never read it, so I don't know. But they weren't happy with it. They wanted to go back to their original story and write another script. Harve said, 'This is what I want to do. I write the first 20-25% of it, and when they get to Earth or when they're about to get to Earth, then you take it, finish the Earth stuff, and I'll do the ending.' We went over each other's stuff. My contribution begins with Spock's crack about 'Judging by the pollution content of the atmosphere, I believe we have arrived at the late 20th Century,' and goes from there to someplace after they get the whales and leave. I didn't read the other script because I just thought it would confuse me and since they didn't like it, why bother?"

Reflected Bennett, "Nick and I had written the final script of *Star Trek II* in 10 days. This one we wrote in about 20, and it was very simple to do it that way because I took act one and act three and Nick took act two. Now if you think about that in structural terms, I got us into the dilemma and into time travel, he carried us through San Francisco, and I got us back. That was like breathing for me because it's pure *Star Trek* and it was like breathing for him because his irreverence is what really makes the fun. Then we swapped pages and I rewrote him a little bit and he rewrote me a little bit and we put it all together and had a script. Nick always said, 'You know the problem with this script is you've got five endings.' And he was right, we did have five endings. He said, 'Why don't you have the whales save the Earth? That's the end of the picture!' No, I said, that's the end of the picture for the hoped for extended audience who's never seen *Star Trek* before. But for people who have seen *Star Trek* before, we have a trilogy to complete. So we've gotta get them back, get them off the hook and give them the Enterprise back. We've got to do that, so that when we finish this picture, we have brought the franchise back

to square one and it can go anywhere it wants to go. That's only fair. Besides, that's what the fans want. So that's what we did. We kept every ending."

As finally rewritten, *Star Trek IV: The Voyage Home* opens with an alien probe that is threatening to destroy planet Earth. Kirk, Spock, McCoy and the rest, on board the Bird of Prey and head-ing home to turn themselves over to the proper authorities, discover that the alien signal is actually being transmitted in the language of humpback whales, a species extinct in the 23rd Century. They take the Klingon vessel back to Earth circa 1987, get involved with marine biologist Gillian Taylor, who plays an integral role in their obtaining the necessary whales and then joins them on the return to the future. There, and once Earth has been saved by the whales singing to the probe, she joins the crew of a science vessel, and our people have the charges against them dismissed, with their being sent aboard a brand new starship Enterprise.

As vehemently as Meyer opposed the suggestion at the close of *Star Trek II* that Spock would come back, he was against Gillian's sojourn through time.

"In my version of the script," he said, "originally, when they all leave to go back, she didn't leave. She said if anyone's going to make sure this kind of disaster doesn't happen, somebody's going to have to stay behind, which I still think is the 'righter' ending. The end in the movie detracts from the importance of people in the present taking responsibility for the ecology and preventing problems of the future by doing something about them today, rather than catering to the fantasy desires of being able to be transported ahead in time to the near-utopian future society of the *Star Trek* era."

While it's common knowledge that rewrites are a part of every produced screenplay, writers Steve Meerson and Peter Krikes were nevertheless shocked to discover that Harve Bennett and Nicholas Meyer had been nominated for lead writing credits on *Trek IV*. This led to Writer's Guild arbitration.

Steve Meerson said, "Harve wanted to sort of roll up his sleeves and, as he called it, *Trek* it up, claiming that we weren't that familiar with *Star Trek*, which was a lie. Unbeknownst to us, he was telling the studio things like, 'They're going to deliver the first act today,' which he never told us and of course the studio got upset with us and said, 'Where's the first act?' and then Harve would say, 'I didn't say that.' Basically, you're talking to two people who did not leave this office for seven months. I'm talking we were working seven days a week, with food being slipped under the door. Our arbitration statement on the movie said, 'If a story had previously existed, what were we doing between February and May and June coming up with like seven outlines to write the script from?'"

Noted Krikes, "I don't know if you're aware how arbitration works, but

within three days from the end of filming, the producer entities must turn in all the written materials to the Writer's Guild. In this case, it took two months to turn them in. They were trying to get our names off the script."

"There's actually a rule you can go by," stated Meerson. "When a script goes to arbitration at the Guild, the people that get first position—it goes to follow—did the lion's share of the work. We got first position on the script. I don't really want to get into the arbitration, *per se*, only to say that it was very political. Peter and I were lucky that we ended up with any credit at all. They have a very high-powered machine which is not very kind to outsiders, and we aren't the first people to experience that. It was a difficult pill to swallow. The reason it hasn't affected us that much is that everyone in town *knows* we did the story. They know our work, and it's such a departure from the other movies. *Star Trek IV* was so different, and we were the only new element."

Both men found their experience to be enlightening and—despite everything—something to be proud of.

"We can sum it up by saying we learned to sit with our backs to the wall, and to make sure what's on the other side of the wall first," said Peter Krikes. "It was a real roller coaster experience and, so far, it's the most successful in the series. *That's* a wonderful feeling."

Noted Steve Meerson, "When you go into story meetings with people who are constantly claiming that your ideas are theirs, what you need to do is take notes, write memos, confirm memos about what transpired, make sure all materials are registered and make sure you're aware of the arbitration process, which is supposed to function on your behalf, but doesn't. It's very political. You learn the avenues that are open to you, and basically you grow up. You learn that you can't trust anyone.

"By the same token, I think we were both delighted that we were a part of something that will go on forever, and I also think it said some things that needed to be said. There are some important messages there, and being allowed to have that forum was very exciting. It's hard for me to say this, but it was worth

all the aggravation."

■ Blue Skies & Star Fields

Of all the bizarre landscapes and alien worlds, some beautiful, some terrifying, that have filled the first three cinematic adventures of the crew of the Federation starship U.S.S. Enterprise, none is more extraordinary than the one Captain Kirk, Mr. Spock et al. must brave in *Star Trek IV: The Voyage Home*. The task of making the unbelievable believable in the *Star Trek* universe had, for the third time, fallen to the highly skilled effects conjurers of Industrial Light and Magic. In the case of *Star Trek IV*, however, some of the parameters had been changed. Drastically.

While taking the *Star Trek* crew and placing them in present day surroundings may not sound like it fills the tenets of a film that should go "where no man has gone before," in actuality, seeing a Klingon Bird of Prey swooping under the Golden Gate Bridge has got to be one of the most exciting images in the entire series—not to mention one of the most difficult to achieve. As any of ILM's *Star Trek IV* team will tell you, in space, no one can see your matte lines; but against our own blue sky—that's another matter entirely.

"That really gave us an opportunity to push ourselves," said Ken Ralston, the film's visual effects supervisor. "Believe me, those backgrounds, especially for the shot where the Klingon ship goes under the bridge, took forever to shoot and had endless problems, but they're really outstanding shots." Ralston has been designated "ILM's *Star Trek* brain trust," having worked on more of the film in the series than anyone else at the effects facility. Ralston characterizes his association with *Trek IV* as little more than "giving my two cents worth at dailies," but in reality, his input was considered invaluable, particularly due to the unusual demands of this film versus others in the series. For his part, Ralston sees *Trek IV*'s earthbound action as a shot in the arm both from a creative effects point of view and as a fan of the series.

"*Star Trek* has been in space so

long," he explained, "that to go back there again would be pretty dreary in a lot of ways. You've seen it all before, many times. But, to see those ships that you've become accustomed to suddenly put into a more terrestrial environment is a refreshing way to view them, and we can do a lot more. When I have a ship in front of a starfield, I have no opportunity to be very creative. Sure, I could put another nebula out there, but we're really locked into things. When we come down to a more interesting environment, boy, the possibilities are endless!"

There are, of course, a few sequences that take place in space, as well as a tearful farewell when Kirk and company must leave the planet Vulcan and head back to Earth; and then San Francisco had to be "updated" to the 23rd Century. All of these varied locations were enhanced and, in some cases, entirely supplied by, the ILM matte department: specifically painters Chris Evans, Sean Joyce and Frank Ordaz, and cameramen Craig Barron, Wade Childress and Randy Johnson. The finished film features somewhere around an even dozen matte shots, some of which are among the most complex they ever attempted.

One of the more difficult shots involves a panoramic vista of Vulcan, and incorporates a cluster of miniature rocks in the foreground, a blue screen plate featuring Spock's mother and Officer Saavik, the departing Klingon Bird of Prey miniature, and a motion-controlled sun. The problem with this shot as it was originally planned was that it was very reminiscent of a similar vista from *Enemy Mine*. "We looked at our work in *Enemy Mine*," recalled Barron, who photographed the alien landscape at sunset matte painting for the Wolfgang Peterson film, as well as the one in question on *Star Trek IV*, "and we said, 'That's fairly impressive, now how can we make this one better?' We decided the way to make it better was to be able to pan off the live action as the Bird of Prey flies by and then zoom into the sun."

The problem with adding the pan at this point stemmed from the fact that the live-action blue screen element of Saavik and Amanda had been shot with a static camera. "Don Dow and I figured out that the element could be projected onto a white card, and then we could add the pan using the Automat camera," Barron said. "The move would then be recorded, so that we could also use the Automat to shoot the painting, the foreground rocky ledge miniature and the sun element—all with the same move. The different elements would then be composited on the optical printer."

However, more problems developed from the addition of a light source, representing the sun, that now had to be motion-controlled in order to create the proper effect, as Wade Childress explains. "We had a problem here because the Automat camera has a linear pan, not a radial pan. We wanted to pan onto the sun and then zoom in to follow the ship, and we wanted the sun to remain in the shot. With this system, if the sun was stationary, we'd lose it as we continued our pan, because it was just a focused point of light aimed through a separate lens at the camera lens. We had to motion control that focusing lens to compensate for the parallax in the shot, so that as we pan across, the sun stays focused on the camera lens to give the impression of a radial-type pan rather than a linear one."

Both the matte shot just described and one depicting the exterior of Starfleet Command in 23rd century San Francisco were actually planned down to the most minute detail by ILM's matte department, including the choice of camera angle. Chris Evans, the department supervisor, regards these shots as a new direction in matte painting, where the painter essentially "art directs" the shot from the beginning. "Usually, matte shots start with a plate and then we continue the perspective and design the shot around the plate," he said. "In this case, we started with a production illustration that was worked out in detail to the correct perspective, and then we actually shot the plate to conform exactly to this illustration. We found that in order to get the shot of Starfleet Command, the lens had to be exactly 15 feet above ground level—the only thing that would make it possible to do the shot the way we wanted to do it."

The matte shot of the exterior of Starfleet Command is one of the most complicated ever attempted at ILM, and reveals just how far the effects crew is willing to go to achieve as realistic an effect as possible. In this case, the matte department made something out of literally nothing. The final shot features the exterior of Starfleet Command and a waiting space shuttle—neither of which ever existed except on Chris Evans' glass painting—and a latent image element of people interacting with *both* the building and the shuttle. The "set" actually consisted of a group of actors in Starfleet costumes standing on a strip of runway at Oakland Airport. In order to allow the actors to appear to interact with the matte painting shuttle, Evans created a diagram of his painting on the same sheet of glass where he would ultimately render it.

"We lined up the camera to the diagram and then painted in the hard edge of the matte where we wanted the space shuttle and the various buildings to be," Evans explained. "We even painted in hard-edged shadows on the ground. When we were out on the set, we directed the actors to act as if the objects we were going to paint in were actually there. We put tape marks on the ground so they would walk where they were supposed to and not through our matte lines, so the whole thing was choreographed down to the inch. This was the most planning we've ever done on a matte shot."

To a lesser degree, the creation of San Francisco's futuristic skyline provided some unique challenges for Evans and Barron, who discovered it's often easier to start from scratch than to build on something that already exists. "It's hard to make a real city look futuristic," Barron said, "because if you add taller buildings to it, it just alters the scale of the city and you feel like you're closer to it. It was a struggle to come up with a futuristic San Francisco skyline that still looks like San Francisco."

In the end, Evans decided to modify the existing skyline only slightly: "There's a building moratorium in San Francisco, so people of the future are probably going to be more into green plants than concrete and steel, so we just added a few towers to the skyline, space needles and things like that. Most of it's existing architecture, otherwise it wouldn't be recognizable as San Francisco."

Eye Of The F/X Storm

One of the most exciting aspects of any *Star Trek* film are the wonderfully complex creations of the ILM model shop; beautifully detailed, motion-controlled ships that seem undeniably real. While *Star Trek IV* has its share of elaborate miniatures, including an unusual space probe from another galaxy, the most difficult one of all was a 16 foot long section of the Golden Gate Bridge.

An avowed goal of the ILM staff was to bring this *Star Trek*'s effects in for less money than the previous effort, which meant that the model crew had to find ways to do many of their shots live, to cut down on the number of optical composites required at the end of the show. Among the main series of effects the model crew was expected to create were several "world in peril" sequences, all of which involved water, which is extremely difficult to work with in a miniature environment. Most of these sequences revolve around the Golden Gate Bridge, which can be seen easily from a large picture window in Starfleet Command overlooking the bay.

"In order to create a storm / havoc situation," said Jeff Mann, ILM's model shop supervisor, "we had to build a scaled down version of the Golden Gate Bridge and create a miniature environment in which we could control the atmosphere and the clouds—in fact, the whole weather pattern—and it had to be consistent so it could be intercut throughout the film."

The Golden Gate Bridge miniature was complicated not only because of its immense size, but due to the fact that it was designed with a forced perceptive.

"We only built half of the bridge so it had only one tower. Because the perspective on it was forced, the foreground roadway measured about 16 inches wide, while at the very end, on the other side of the tower, it was two inches wide. We had to scale all the girders and everything else to taper. We

picked a point of view that was similar to that of the council chamber of the Federation headquarters in Sausalito, so that at different points in the movie, people could look out the window and see the bridge, the raging storm and the huge waves."

Originally, Mann and his crew had hoped that by photographing some terrific storms that occurred in the San Francisco area where they were just beginning to plan *Trek IV* in December of 1985, they would be able to save themselves the headache of creating one artificially. No such luck. "There were some great storms happening then, so we took some plate cameras out to the Golden Gate Bridge and tried to get something we could use—but, even though it was storming in reality, on film it looked pretty tame. We wanted the storm in the film to be just *wild*, so after we completed construction of the bridge, we built an enclosure for it in one of our parking lots that was about 20 feet high and about 100 feet square. Within that enclosure, we built a tank that was about 18 inches deep, and then we tried everything to create rain and wind and smoke levels and clouds: smoke and wind machines and water sprayers."

For a sequence near the end of the film where Kirk's Bird of Prey crash lands under the Golden Gate Bridge, Mann and his crew actually built a wire rig so the Klingon ship could be flown "live" in the enclosure, which helped immeasurably to keep *Trek IV* on its low optical program.

"It was quite a thing to see," Mann reflected. "We had the Golden Gate Bridge sitting in the water tank, wind machines, foggers and sprayers, and the wire rig with the Bird of Prey flying past as it crashed into the water. That was fun. We tried a number of different things, including literally taking the model over our heads and throwing it in the water. The beauty of that was that we could do 20 or 30 takes and do it 20 or 30 different ways, see it in dailies the next day and then we'd have a really good idea of how it was going to look and we could move much faster. By incorporating the Bird of Prey on one set, live, we could get it all in the camera in one shot. When you put a lot of

different elements together optically it takes time and everything stacks up at the end of the show and we sometimes have to make compromises. This way, we were able to achieve what we wanted in a single shot."

While the "live action" approach to filming the Bird of Prey's crash landing made things easier for the optical department, it was very wearing on the models themselves. The shots necessitated the creation of several additional Bird of Prey miniatures that were subjected to being tossed, burned and otherwise brutalized during the filming.

"The original Bird of Prey model, built for *Star Trek III*, is motion controlled, very expensive, and only for use on stage," Mann reminded. "When the Bird of Prey flies around the sun during the time travel sequence, it catches on fire, and when it crashed underneath the Golden Gate Bridge, we couldn't just take our motion control model out there and fling it around, so we built four additional Birds of Prey. We took our original model apart and took molds of everything, and then cast the duplicates out of really high-density furniture foam. Some of them were made of styrene plastic with aluminum armatures so we could fly them and not worry about wrecking them, and others were coated first with epoxy and then with a pyro solution so we could set them afire, throw them and film them."

Because most of *Star Trek IV* takes place on modern day Earth, the demands on the model shop to create various Federation spacecraft, were slight. Most of the work consisted of refurbishing old models from the earlier *Trek* films, modifying them slightly and changing their names so they could pass as other ships in Starfleet.

"We had an incident in the beginning of the film," said Mann, "where we needed a Reliant-class ship [the Federation ship Khan stole in *Star Trek II*], so we put a new paint job on the old Reliant model, changed a small shuttle called the Grissom to the Copernicus and we added a back half to the shuttlecraft that Scotty flew around the Enterprise in *Star Trek: The Motion Picture*. We also ended up putting the space dock back together, which was a major undertaking. It's huge! It's 20 feet in diameter, and it has thousands of feet of fiber optics in it. We had wanted to use stock footage of the interior of the space dock from *Star Trek III*. We hoped that we could take some of the old effects elements from that scene and composite them with some new movement, but nothing worked quite right, so we had to refurbish and rebuild it. It was an expensive undertaking."

Devising a probe from outer space that looked like it might communicate with whales was one of the more difficult aspects of *Star Trek IV*, and required some experimentation and refining before it seemed right.

"Basically, it's a cylinder that started off to look like a section of a whale," Mann said. "We used a barnacled type of texture for it, and it was originally painted with a crusty-textured white on a blue background. It was sort of organic looking, and that was the design we originally settled on. We built several versions of this monolithic probe that threatens the Earth. The main model that we used was an eight foot long cylinder about two feet in diameter, and it had a hole at one end through which an antenna ball emerges on a shaft of light and sort of searches around. We built a smaller version to scale for the distance shots, and then we built a large section of the ship—just a third of a side of it—and it was tapered for a shot where the ship is heading towards the camera and then flies overhead. Like a takeoff on that first shot in *Star Wars*. We also built some large antennas for close-ups."

After shooting a few sequences with the various probe models, the general consensus was in favor of altering the ship's color to make it appear more dramatic, and a few changes were made to the antenna as well. "We worked for quite a while on these models with a specific color and texture in mind," Mann added, "but then we reached a point where they just didn't look right. It wasn't exciting, because it was blue, like a whale. Also, the antenna originally didn't move and it didn't have a light source in it, so we made the antenna move and added an interior light to the ball. For the antenna's beam of light, we added a hot shaft of light in the center and put a

much milder glow around that. I think it was Ken Ralston who came up with the idea to paint the probe black and eliminate all the color from it so we could use light and reflections on it to create interest and mystery."

One of Mann's more unusual assignments was to detail a full-sized, operational boat to turn it into something audiences would believe was a modern-day whaling vessel. "ILM handled the second unit whale sequence," noted Mann, "so we had the task of finding a whaling ship. The one we found was named the Golden Gate, and it was a 140-foot minesweeper from World War II, and I had to put it together to make it look like the real thing. It had a lot of rigging on it, it was the right size, so all we had to do was build a flying bridge and some props on it. We built a big harpoon deck, and then the model stage pyro guys built a big harpoon cannon and some harpoons and gear."

Some of the more unusual models Mann was responsible for were two separate elements which, when optically dissolved together, created a beautiful miniature of our own sun.

"To create the center of the sun," Mann explains, "we first took some lead pellets a little smaller than marbles, spread them out over our vacuform machine and vacuformed two round pieces of clear plastic about two feet across, so they had a look somewhat like a shower door, only more bumpy. We then built a device that had two stepper motors that were synced with our motion control camera, and we had one disc going one way and the other going the opposite direction. To make the rounded outer surface of the sun, we took a large, clear plexiglassdome, lit it and gelled it from the inside, and put vasaline on its surface in globs so that when we photographed it, it appeared to have solar flares erupting on it. They did several passes on that, each registered off just a little bit. As the Bird of Prey moved behind the sun, they dissolved from the plexiglass dome to the flat discs as they did their pan across the sun. The two discs going opposite ways created an effect, like hot spots. Then when the ship came around the other side of the sun, we dissolved back to the clear plexiglass dome. I think it worked out really well."

There Be Whales Here!

It's rare that the success or failure of a film like *Star Trek IV* hinges on only one element, but due to the fact that the critical story points revolves around the Enterprise crew's ability to literally save the whales, Paramount was understandably concerned that the mammals appear as believable as possible. As it turned out, they had nothing to worry about. Thanks to ILM's whale supervisor, Walt Conti, things went swimmingly. Conti and his crew devised two of the most lifelike mechanicals ever—and, undoubtedly, the audience will never notice.

The beauty of Conti's mechanical whales is the fact that they are not only self-contained, they are self-propelled. Conti's miniatures can actually swim, freeing them—and the production—from any possible problems that might result from dealing with cable controls and other paraphernalia usually associated with special effects creatures.

"It was actually Nilo Rodis, *Star Trek IV*'s art director, who pushed the concept of having this self-contained free swimming whale that we could actually move anywhere to get any kind of angle we needed," Conti revealed. "In some ways, doing something like this, trying to replicate a real mammal, is actually tougher than trying to do a fictitious creature because the audience already has a preconceived idea of how it should look. To insure that it would look and move exactly like a real whale, Conti made sure the sculpture was done under the careful guidance of Pieter Folkens of the Oceanic Society. Richard Miller was responsible for the finely wrought sculpture itself, which, with slightly different paint schemes, became both the male and female whale. After the sculpture was completed and molded, what followed was a lengthy period of research and development in which Conti, assisted by Sean Casey and Tony Hudson, experimented with different materials until he found the one that gave the whales a proper blubbery quality. Most difficult of all, even after finding the right material, further research was required to determine the perfect thickness of the whale's skin to insure that the tail movement would appear fluid and natural.

"The problem was that when the tail would bend, you'd see all this buckling," Conti said. "We ended up using a Smooth-On urethane, and when we put a lot of plasticizer in it, it ended up feeling like blubber. The tail mechanism was really just a simple universal pivot joint that was capable of moving the tail up, down and sideways, but all of that fluid motion just comes from the material itself and the way it interacts with water."

Conti had built a water pump into the whale mechanism to provide forward movement, and was shocked to learn that his whales so perfectly mimicked the motions of the real thing that the action of their flippers and tails actually made the mechanical swim!

"The only time we used the water pump was to turn the whale, we didn't need it at all for forward movement," he said proudly. "The jet of the pump is hidden in the black of the tail, so when we move the tail into position and use the pump, it'll drive the whale up or down, or, if the tail's off to one side, it'll turn the whale. Inside the front half of the whale there's a fiberglass shell, so it's very rigid and inside that are all the servo motors. There's actually seven servos inside, and it takes two people to operate the whale by radio-control. One person controls the tail and the direction of the whale is moving, and the other person controls the flippers, which can move up and down, fore and aft, and rotate—independently of each other. Rick Anderson and Paul Harris did the fiberglass undershell and worked with me on the mechanics."

Watching the graceful movements of Conti's creations as they majestically glide through the water, only inches from the camera lens, it is almost impossible to accept that the actual miniatures are barely four feet long! Surprisingly, Conti's background is not in special effects, though he has helped out on other such projects. "I was really brought in because of my background in mechanical engineering and robotics," Conti explained. "I had collaborated with Nilo Rodis on some other projects and it was he who actually hired me, because he knew we would be pushing the state of the art."

When pushing the state of the art, problems will inevitably arise, although Conti encountered relatively few during the course of perfecting his mechanical whales. Aside from the fact that, initially, the servo mechanics tended to shatter under the pressure of the water when the whales were operated below 16 feet, the only other trouble Conti encountered had nothing to do with the whales, but with the ability of the operators to see them.

"We used diatomaceous earth to cloud the water in order to make the whales look much more realistic. When you look at a whale in the ocean, although you might see the head clearly, the tail, which is 40 feet back, tends to be somewhat obscured. To get that effect with our four foot miniature, we really had to cloud the water up, which created a problem for us when we were trying to control the whales. Even though they operated perfectly, we couldn't see the whale! That was somewhat unexpected."

■ Beam Ups & Warp Drives

Some of the most difficult effects in any *Star Trek* film go unnoticed, if not unappreciated, because they are so much a part of the *Star Trek* vocabulary that they get virtually the same amount of attention as someone driving a car down the street in an ordinary film. Beam ups and downs, warp drives and phaser beams can drive the ILM animation department to distraction, but, according to consulting effects supervisor Ralston, "People block them out because they're like transition shots. It's amazing how much effort goes into these shots that are generally something no one thinks about anymore because they just accept it as if it's real!"

It's precisely because people do respond to these sequences involving transporter beams and such as if they're real that makes the animation department's burden so heavy on a *Star Trek* film: one false move and the fans will spot it. Also, because these effects have come so accepted, so commonplace in the *Star Trek* universe, the animators spend a lot of time trying to figure out ways to make the effect this time around more interesting, and generally more complex, than in the last film. In order to do this, the animation department has had to expand beyond its usual frame-by-frame and rotoscope animation techniques to include motion-control abilities as well, all of which the department supervisor, Ellen Lichtwardt, finds tremendously exciting: "This time through one *Trek*, we did a lot of things on the motion control stand, including the Enterprise and Bird of Prey warp drive and a beam-up shot on a moving person."

Using the motion control stand to shoot the Klingon Bird of Prey warp-drive resulted in one of the most elaborate and beautiful effects in the entire film. "Jay Riddle established the look of the Bird of Prey's warp drive," Lichtwardt said. "There's one shot Jay did that appears almost as if you're looking into the engines of the Klingon ship out in space, and the artwork just comes streaking past your field of vision. There are red and green engine streaks with white light that comes from the sides and a little outline of the ship that's streaked back, so it's a really dynamic looking warp drive, much more complex and dimensional looking than in the other *Trek* shows."

The same can be said about the

new and improved Enterprise warp drive, which we are treated to in two shots at the end of the film, also executed by Riddle. In order to achieve the effect of the Enterprise beginning as a white dot in space and then suddenly filling the entire screen in seconds as it goes into warp drive, Riddle had to modify the existing motion control equipment in order to get the required extreme zoom ratio.

"The motion control stand has a set-up where the mounting base with the lens in it can only get so close to the table, where the artwork is," Lichtwardt explained. "What we had to do was get a relay lens, which extended the lens about a foot below the mounting base. Because of the nature of these shots, the Enterprise will go from a tiny point to something really large on the screen. If we used the old lens, we could only get so close to the artwork and then we'd cut off, we couldn't get the perspective we need. The relay lens gave us a zoom ration of 200:1 instead of the motion control stand's usual 20:1, which is dramatically different."

While the results that can be achieved with the motion control stand are indeed remarkable, the equipment is much more tedious and time consuming to work with than other animation tools. "For the Enterprise warp drive effects," Lichtwardt related, "it took Jay two minutes to shoot every frame. Since there's 120 frames or so, and four passes on every frame, he's been spending an incredible amount of time on this camera, up to eight hour shoots for one pass of artwork! It's very similar to stop-motion animation, and very elaborate."

The Enterprise was first photographed on stage, where it could only achieve a narrow range of motion. "Jay then got some transparencies of the Enterprise," Lichtwardt added, "and, using them, he took the ship from the point it had left off on stage down to a speck. Then he set up the motion control camera with the relay lens and shot slit scan artwork for the warp drive effect, something we've never done before—we've always used straight artwork. This time, the warp drive has a really nice look, the artwork is fancier, and the whole effect is very dramatic because the Enterprise goes from being just a dot to

extreme close-up."

The sequence involving the crash landing of the Bird of Prey into San Francisco Bay at the end of the film, which had been shot live by the model department, needed an extra bit of drama, so the animation department arranged for Sean Turner to enhance the scene with interactive light and lightning, as Lichtwardt explained: "Sean got together with Tobe Heindel and they shot Polaroids of the ship on stage in dramatic lighting set-ups so that Sean could see the way light interacted on it. Then optical went through and gave us a print of the sequence with flashes on it to time our lightning to. Sean did beautiful lightning animation and then airbrushed interactive light that glows on the bridge and dapples on the water as the Bird of Prey crashes down, and that made the sequence work nicely."

One of the film's most emotional moments occurs when Kirk, Spock and company leave the "cloaked," invisible Bird of Prey for the first time, a sequence that was literally saved by the animation department. Imagine looking at Golden Gate Park when shards of light suddenly burst through what appears to be a geometric hole in the fabric of reality—and then the Enterprise crew disembarks on a ramp that has apparently come from nowhere. If it sounds difficult to explain, it was even more difficult to devise!

"A lot of the ramp that was shot live action against blue screen was just a mess because the blue screen was contaminated with seams and they couldn't pull a matte off it," Lichtwardt said. "Jack Mongovan did a spectacular roto-matte on the whole ramp area as it was descending, which was incredibly difficult because it was all drafted, straight edges done frame by frame, and the ramp was moving very slowly, so it required a lot of control. It was a nice piece of work, and I was really impressed with it."

Another impressive effect is a "standard" beam-up shot with a twist— Mr. Spock is walking towards camera as he is being transported back to the ship. The effect was one of motion control executed by Bruce Walters, who also created an unusual transporter beam patter for the whales.

"The whales needed to have sort of an interesting transporter look, because they're so big," Lichtwardt related. "It's very similar to the other look, but there are more panels of beams which expand across the screen, over which we added a nice white element. The shot with the most interesting problems to solve was the transporter effect on Mr. Spock, because it's the first time we've ever seen someone walking who gets beamed up. We had to do the transporter beams and match the move to Spock's movement, and the dots that appear as he's being transported fade out in perspective as he's coming toward camera."

To add a little more life to the model shop's miniature of the sun, some animated flares and coronas were shot by Jack Knoll. "Just by shooting some backlit artwork, Jack was able to match-move a really nice hazy yellow glow, to create a sort of warpy corona around the sun," recalled Lichtwardt. "After he shot that, he added a set of solar flares that lick up and fly off the sun, using slit scan animation and then pin blocking them onto the sun, which means he shot a set of generic flares and then match-moved them onto the sun wherever he felt they should go. They have a great fiery look to them, different from what you'd expect from a camera-generated effect—they almost look like real flames."

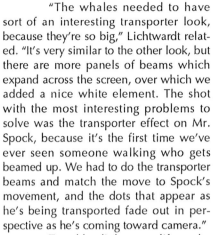

■ Splitting The Red Sea... Almost

The effects which reveal the Earth in grave peril after the alien probe has launched its attack wrought more havoc off-screen than on. One particularly difficult effect, involving a giant pillar of water that goes shooting heavenward from out of the ocean began as a purely mechanical effect (the "water" was actually small glass beads traveling across a black formica surface), and was then enhanced by virtually every department. The main problem stemmed from the inability to match the mechanical effect to a live action water plate.

"We were having trouble joining the wall of water onto our water background plate," said Lichtwardt. "There was this funky junction line, so we did all this nice bubbling animation to hide it, and preceded it with an animated wake along the front. We also added big blasts of water that go flying up into the clouds, which will have articulate mattes on them to help blend them into the sky."

Deciding exactly how to pull off some of the other "world in peril" sequences was the main problem plaguing the optical department right up through the film's release.

"We're all but parting the Red Sea here!" laughs department supervisor Ralph Gordon. "The biggest difficulty was doing it without going for tons of miniatures and matte paintings. We wanted to stay away from cutting to stock shots of storm clouds and other acts of nature. We're using cloud tank photography to create a huge storm cloud with a kind of an eerie look to it, but blending the cloud tank into the scene [was] difficult. When you work with a cloud tank, there's a certain look to it when the chemical disperses within the water. If it's lit properly, it can blend well, otherwise it can look like dishwashing liquid in water! Also, working with water and miniatures is a losing battle many times, because water droplets will congeal at a certain size regardless of what you do, so the challenging stuff for us is to take effects elements and, by adding in lightning flashes and things like that, make it look very impressive."

Writing about the job of the optical department is always nearly impossible to do, because their work is everywhere in a film such as *Star Trek IV*, but generally, it consists of composing the elements created by the other departments into a seamless whole—the most critical part of the entire process.

"The job of optical is blending everything together," Gordon stated, "and there were an immense amount of opticals in *Star Trek IV*, even though it is a basic, straightforward picture in the *Star Trek* realm. We have to take the large number of separate elements and put them onto one piece of film, and we have to do it in such a way that everything doesn't end up looking like a paper cut-out. An optical supervisor is only as

good as the people who work for him: John Ellis, Jim Hagadorn and Dave McCune have been running cameras, and Don Clark and John Alexander—our master element makers—have been generating elements. Our optical line-up team includes Peg Hunter, Bruce Vecchitto, Brad Kuhn and Tom Rosseter—those are the people who figure out how the shot goes together once we give them the elements. Ken Smith who is the head of the optical department, has been a great mentor, watching over us to make sure we don't slip up."

For the sequence where the hatch of the invisible Bird of Prey opens up in Golden Gate Park, Ken Ralston suggested that the scale of the shot be reduced, to make it more impressive.

"We had to take an actual blue screen element of the people walking down the ramp," said Gordon, "reduce that in size to make it fit into our plate, and then we had to have the proper mattes made to isolate that image. But when that great door opens, it's like time and space are suddenly being ripped open!"

For all the various effects teams that worked on *Star Trek IV*, it seems the greatest burden was not the innovation of new effects, but making sure these innovations were consistent with the *Star Trek* universe.

"I hope I have lent a certain boldness to the shots," Ralston added regarding his position as consulting effects supervisor, "but a lot of times the *Trek* approach goes *against* what I might actually want to do. There's a certain world that the *Trek* films encompass, and a certain reality that we have to follow, because it's amazing how picky the fans are, how we are scrutinized by them. I don't think Leonard Nimoy or Bill Shatner know as much as some of the fans do about TREK, and if I do something that doesn't go quite right with what's come before, I always hear about it."

■ Bringing The Voyage Home

Although the set of *Star Trek IV* was generally very upbeat, there was a severe falling out between Leonard

Nimoy and Harve Bennett, reportedly resulting in Bennett's actually being thrown off the set.

In the pages of *Capain's Log*, Bennett explained, "I had been emotionally beat up by Leonard Nimoy. I respect him for what he has done, but in the transition between *III* and *IV*, Leonard had come to regard me as in his way, with regards to the auteurship of the film. I was not only the man who said 'No,' but the man who was conspiring to....you know. So that on one occasion, it got really mean on the stage—mean from him to me. I was smarting—'Who needs this shit?'—was foremost on my mind."

A production source wishing to remain anonymous added, "Harve, actually, was barred from the set. He and Leonard weren't speaking on literally half of the filming. They had a major argument on the set and Harve was thrown off."

While Nimoy did not discuss this issue with the press, he did detail the challenge of not only directing the film, but co-starring in it as well.

"It was hard physically," he said. "But I had a good time doing it because I really enjoyed playing the Spock character in this picture. He's a very different Spock. A Spock who's evolving, who's confused. He's trying to figure out who he's supposed to be and how he's supposed to function. It was great fun to play, but, physically, very tough because it's a long day. If you just direct the picture, it's a tough job. If you act in it as well, it's tougher. Then you have to add on a two hour make-up job every day, which means that you have to be in at 5:00 every morning. [But] this is a funny Spock. He's also very touching. I think it's a very touching moment when Spock discovers his identity. It happens at the moment when Kirk and McCoy are talking about what to do about Chekov in the hospital, and Spock says, 'We must help Chekov.' Kirk says, 'Is that the logical thing to do, Spock?' Spock replies, 'No, but it is the human thing to do.' I hope audiences [were] touched by that. It's the kind of moment when you say, 'Ah, Spock is there. He found his way.'"

As a director, Nimoy felt that *Star Trek IV* was much more ambitious and exciting than the previous films.

"We were off the soundstages for the first time," he enthused. "The first three pictures were almost exclusively on the soundstages. In *Star Trek I*, we were off the soundstage for a couple of days; on *STar Trek III* we were off for a couple of nights for the Vulcan exterior scenes. To get off the soundstages on this one was very invigorating. It gave a lot more energy to me and the cast of the picture, and I had a little bit more time. I shot *Star Trek III* in 49 days and on this one I had 53. Actually, I had 57, and I came in four days early."

Interestingly, the majority of the on-location material was achieved via a hidden camera on the streets of San Francisco.

Explained Harve Bennett, "You'll notice that [Uhura and Chekov] walk across the street and the lady who comes up and says, 'Oh, it's in Alameda,' is a real person. Leonard wisely said, 'Let's do it like *Candid Camera*. That's one of my favorite sequences in the picture. You can't write that. The written line is, 'Can you tell me where to find the nuclear wessels?' But what Leonard and the actors made out of it is what's called movie-making."

Added Nimoy, "I covered the scene exactly as it was written, but once I had that, then I began to improvise and explore to see if there was more to be had. The scene as written was, he finishes looking at the phone book and she says to him, 'Did you find it?' and he says, 'Yes, now all we need is directions,' and he turns to a passerby and says, 'Excuse me, can you tell me the way to Alameda where they keep the nuclear wessels?' Cut. So we got that. Then there was a police officer with a motorcycle who was part of our unit helping to control traffic, and I had him moved into that spot and said to him, 'You just stand here and stare at the guy,' and we dropped the camera a ways back so that people would not be self-conscious about the fact that they were being photographed. We were about 30 or 40 feet back, almost like a hidden camera kind of feeling, and we just sat and watched the people come through and said react to whatever happens here. And the two of them, Walter and Nichelle, did this wonderful thing about these people going by.

William Shatner and Leonard Nimoy at the Academy Awards, where Star Trek IV's effects were honored.

And sometimes you get really lucky. A lady who was not even on the job with us that day, asked to be hired as an extra to walk through the scene. I said thank God they did because she walked through and they stopped her and she said, 'I don't know, I think it's across the bay in Alameda.' And I said, 'We've got it! We've brought the whole thing full circle.' Then I got a close-up of the cop just to have something to cut off to; to have a reaction cut away to, and we walked away from it. But I knew I had the scene at least as written before I started experimenting."

To put it mildly, *Star Trek IV: The Voyage Home* was a great success, pulling in some $126 million and quickly establishing itself as the favorite of the series among many people, including the vast majority of film critics and some of the cast members.

William Shatner: "We discovered something in *Star Trek IV* that we hadn't pinpointed in any of the other movies—and it just shows how the obvious can escape you—that there is a texture to the best *Star Trek* hours that verges on tongue-in-cheek but isn't. There's a line that we all have to walk that is reality. It's as though the characters within the play have a great deal of joy about themselves, a joy of living. That energy, that 'joie de vivre' about the characters seems to be tongue-in-cheek but isn't, because you play it with the reality [that] you would in a kitchen-sink drama written for today's life."

DeForest Kelley: "I have always felt from the very beginning that the core of *Star Trek* was the family. It was always this group of people that were working in this bizarre-type world together. That's what made the show successful. One of the greatest mistakes in the first motion picture was that they neglected the people and went around us. It's taken some time but now it's back to normal thaniks to Leonard Nimoy."

James Doohan: "*Star Trek IV*

was absolutely delightful. It was a delight to do, and a delight to watch. Our best, dramatically speaking, mostly on account of Ricardo Montalban, was *Star Trek II: The Wrath of Khan*. But *Star Trek IV* was cute and funny, and everybody loved it just for that. Also, there was the great comraderie between the characters. The fans just absolutely love the banter that goes back and forth."

George Takei: "I thought *Star Trek IV* was perhaps the most successful *Star Trek* movie we've done. It brought together the various elements that made *Star Trek* as a television series so sucessful. It certainly had the interrelationships of all the characters that the series such an accessible show....In terms of commentary on a pertinent contemporary issue, we explored the fact that there is a price to be paid when we play with our ecology."

Nichelle Nichols: "The first film was good science fiction if you don't think of it as being *Star Trek*. Unfortunately, that's what everybody thought they were getting which is why it seems to be people's least favorite film. The second film was centered around Spock dying and the third, around bringing Spock back to life so there wasn't enough time to introduce the things that made *Star Trek* on TV so great. Those elements finally came together with *Star Trek IV*. The humor and action were there. The idea of the whales was wonderful. It was definitely a step in the direction of what the old series was all about."

Walter Koenig: "I thought *Star Trek IV* was a delightful picture. The biggest surprise was seeing Leonard's performance, because I'd never seen him work in the picture, except for the scenes in which he was behind us on the bridge, but those individual scenes....those scenes with Bill, I'd never actually seen. That was the most effective performance he'd given as Spock because he maintained the sense of emotional distance and at the same time there was a wonderful underpinning of compassion to the character. I'm pleased for him, for his success, for the picture's success, and I'm very pleased to have been part of that."

Leonard Nimoy summarized his own feelings regarding the film, by noting,

"[The feeling on the first film] was that we had to do a 'motion picture.' Nick Meyer brought a jauntiness back to it. I tried in *Star Trek III* to do a dignified job of resurrection, and do it with a sense of mysticism, a sense of wonder and, above all, to really capture the loyalty of these people for each other; their willingness to sacrifice themselves and their careers for the purpose of helping Spock. Having done that, I really wanted to have a good time on this one. Somebody had been constantly dying in the films, and this time I said, 'Nobody's going to die. I don't want anybody hitting anybody, I don't want anybody shooting anybody,' or any of that stuff. If anybody was going to be injured, it was going to be accidental.

"I insisted that there be no bad guy," Nimoy closed. "We had done two pictures in a row with black-hat heavies, and I didn't want a bad guy anywhere. Circumstances would be the problem. Lack of awareness, lack of concern. Ignorance would be the problem. Not a person. I hope with this one we've really gone full circle and come home, which is why, in a sense, we're calling it *The Voyage Home*. We're saying, 'Enjoy yourself, have a good time, and don't mind us as we drop off a few ideas along the way.'"

As this ad emphasizes, the critics for the most part raved about the fourth installment in the series (ad slick courtesy United Artists Theatres).

Star Trek V:
The Final Frontier
Captain's Log

Star Trek IV: The Voyage Home was both a critical and commercial success that achieved its goal of being the much sought after "crossover film;" a *Trek* film that appealed to the mainstream audience. As such, it was a hard act to follow, a fact that no one could deny, let alone William Shatner. The actor had, as stated previously, made a point in his contract for the fourth film in the series of being given the opportunity to direct number five. After all, Leonard Nimoy had twice been given that chance and Shatner knew that he was contractually entitled to the same thing.

In the pages of *Captain's Log*, Shatner stated, "Somewhere along the line, Leonard's lawyers and my lawyers had gotten together and drawn up a favored nations clause, which meant everything he got, I got and vice versa. Well, in the beginning, I was commanding more money, so that any raises I was getting, Leonard would get also. So I made Leonard a great deal of money on my lawyers by bringing him up to the salary I was getting. We used to joke about that, how that clause had benefitted him so much. But in the end, the fact that Leonard directed a picture, which meant that I would get to direct one, was by far the most important consequence of that clause."

"Directing has been a lifelong dream," Shatner enthused elsewhere. "My business is to entertain people, and to communicate my feelings to them, so I find the best way is to direct. Directing is the pinnacle of our business. A really good director has a point of view on his film and all his other skills emanate from that spine. I've always wanted to entertain, and I think I can do that with my point of view, so I'm under the impression that I can gather all my skills around me to make people laugh and cry. I wanted to do more. I haven't done it to the extent that I wanted to. I think the movies have matured beyond the series and we have to give our audience that maturity. I'd like to think that's what I've done."

No sooner had production been

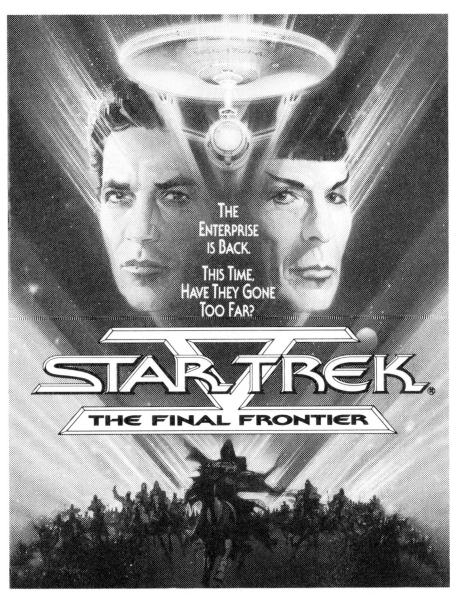

Ad campaign put into effect for William Shatner's directorial debut, *Star Trek V: The Final Frontier* (ad slick courtesy United Artists Theatres).

completed on *Star Trek IV*, then Shatner began thinking of the next chapter in the ongoing saga.

In terms of his goals, he stated, "I have two things that I'd like to see. They're contrasted and yet unified. One is that I'd like to see romance in the stories again. The second is that I would like to see gritty realism. You know, with hand-held cameras, dirt under the fingernails and real steel clanging doors. I hope that the end result will reflect certain life experiences that I am going through, because as we take the characters through the aging process, there are cer-

tain inevitable questions one asks oneself through each passage, each decade that we pass through, roughly. We ask ourselves questions which are universal that don't occur when you're younger [and] so I hope that the end result will reflect some of these questions that I want the characters to ask. It is our hope that this film, like *Star Trek IV*, will appeal to a larger audience than just the aficionados of *Star Trek*. With the humor and action/adventure the film has, it is my fervent wish that that will come true."

Shatner definitely had his storyline in mind, beginning with the fascina-

tion he had always held for television evangelists who claim that God is speaking through them, rather than someone else. "I took the TV evangelist persona and created a holy man who thought God had spoken to him," said Shatner. "He believed God had told him, 'I need many followers, and I need a vehicle to spread my word throughout the universe.' That vehicle he needed became a starship [the Enterprise] which the holy man would capture when it came to rescuing some hostages he had taken....Finally the Enterprise arrives at the planet where God supposedly resides, in the center of the universe....Kirk, Spock, McCoy and the holy man are beamed down to the planet. It's like the drawings of Dante's *Inferno*, like a flaming hell. When God appears, he seems like God....but gradually, in a conversation between God and the holy man, Kirk perceives that something is wrong and begins to challenge God. God gets angrier and angrier, and begins to show his true colors, which are those of the devil....So essentially that was my story: that man conceives of God in his own image, but those images change from generation to generation, therefore he appears in all these different guises as man-made Gods. But in essence, if the devil exists, God exists by inference. This is the lesson that the *Star Trek* group learns. The lesson being that God is within our hearts, not something we conjure up, invent and then worship."

To turn his story into a screenplay, Shatner went to *Ninja* author Eric Von Lustbader, whose work he felt had the right touches of mood and mystery that would be perfectly suited to the premise of *Star Trek V*. Unfortunately, Lustbader reportedly wanted a cool million for his services, which Paramount Pictures refused to pay. While Shatner threatened—albeit briefly—to quit the project, he ultimately came to his senses. Both he and the studio decided that they wanted Harve Bennett to serve as producer, but Bennett, who, as previously discussed, felt that he had been abused on *Star Trek IV*, was not too taken with the idea. However, he and Shatner had an extremely long and intense meeting and ultimately decided to work together. Upon coming aboard, Bennett's major problem was that he didn't like the basic

thrust of the story.

"The real problem with *V*," Bennett told *Cinefantastique*, "was that the premise was faulty. You pick up a *TV Guide* and you read the log line which says, 'Tonight on *Trek*, the crew goes to find God.' Automatically, and unconsciously, you know we're not going to find God because no one has and no one will, and no one would be so arrogant to say what they're depicting on screen is actually God, because others will say, 'No it's not.' So we know we're going to face an anticlimax, a trick. The nature of the trick is the only suspense in the story. But you'd say this to Bill and he's say, 'No, no, it's the greatest adventure of all time,' and I'd say, 'No, it's not an adventure because everyone is ahead of you. So what we have to do is make getting there as interesting as possible.'"

■ The Final Screenpaly...?

"I would say that the trilogy probably stands because of its centering on the life, death, resurrection of Spock and his refulfillment," stated Harve Bennett to *The Official Star Trek Fan Club Magazine* (#64). "This film is continuous only in the sense of time. What we are trying to do in each picture is explore other angles and other undiscovered depths of these very legendary and familiar characters. And that's not too easy because you reach a point where you say, 'How much more can we explore these people?' But remember, these people are also aging, which they did not do in the series. So as they age, they are revealing more and more of their back and foreground stories. That's where the challenge is for me: to try to keep mining these relationships. [*Star Trek V* also] has with it an imperative of going back to deep space. *Star Trek II, III* and *IV* were all, to some extent, manageable in terms of budget, shooting time and scope. With *Star Trek V*, we have now come to the space imperative and we have some very, very difficult appetites: planetary and construction appetites—things you have to show and places you have to go, and an alien here and there. All these things make the cost and complexity of the film

more difficult."

To make things a bit easier, both Bennett and Shatner began an intensive search for the proper screenwriter to bring this vision to the screen. Who they found was David Loughery, the writer behind *Dreamscape*.

"I sold an original screenplay to Paramount called *Flashback*," said Loughery. "Based on the merits of that script, Paramount offered me an overall deal, which I accepted, and one of the executives at that time asked me if I had any interest in working on *Star Trek V*. I said, 'Sure,' thinking that would be the last I ever heard of it. A couple of weeks later, they put me together with Harve Bennett. We talked and got along real well, and then we met Bill Shatner, who had already written an outline which he had turned into Paramount."

That outline, subtitled "An Act of Love," dealt with the Enterprise being commandeered by a rogue Vulcan named Sybok (as is the case in the final film), and being led to a world beyond the Great Barrier where they encounter God, who turns out to be the Devil.

"Paramount liked Bill's outline," said Loughery, "but they thought that it was a little too dark. After the success of *Star Trek IV*, they wanted to make sure that we retained as much humor and fun as possible, because they felt that was one of the reasons for the big success of that film. They wanted us to inject a spirit of fun and adventure into the story. I think they just wanted a balance between the darker elements and some of the lighter stuff. That was never really a specific edict. It was something we'd always wanted to do from the beginning. But when you're writing an outline, it's kind of hard to work in elements of humor. Those are the things that come out in the screenplay or the execution and the style of how you do it. There was an effort, but not one to make the film as funny as *Star Trek IV*. I think everybody felt they'd sort of had their romp and now they were getting a little more serious again, but let's keep that spark alive. So it really became one of those skull session three weeks, where Harve, Bill and I sat in a room and came up with a storyline that Paramount approved, and then I went ahead and wrote the screenplay which went through many, many rewrites before it was finished, as these things often do.

"One particular change was in the character of Sybok. Originally, he was a very messianic, possessed kind of figure who was willing to trample anyone who got in his way, but he began to remind us too much of Khan and we had to take him in a different direction. It would have been easy to write Sybok as a black-hat or a crazed Mohammed, but that was too much Khan.

"The idea of God and the Devil was reflected in the script's earlier drafts. Those drafts were much cleaner and more comprehensible in terms of the idea that you think you're going to Heaven, but you turn out to have found Hell. We weren't literally saying Heaven and Hell, but we were suggesting the idea that it was like, 'Wait a minute, is this God or the Devil?', without saying specifically that it's either, but instead is an alien entity that has tapped into our perceptions about where they're going. We did, however, run into some problems, one with Gene Roddenberry."

Roddenberry rejected the notion of the Enterprise encountering God, believing that *Star Trek* should avoid such specific religious themes.

"I didn't object to it being an alien claiming to be God," Roddenberry said in *Captain's Log*, "but there was too much in it that an audience could have thought was really God or really the devil, and I very strongly resist believing in either. I do not perceive this as a universe that's divided between good and evil. I see it as a universe that is divided between many ideas of what is."

This stance seemed particularly ironic, since in 1975, Roddenberry himself penned a proposed *Star Trek* movie script entitled *The God Thing*, which dealt with similar themes.

"Maybe Gene turned around and figured that it didn't work, and wouldn't work the way we were doing it either," Loughery mused. "I just don't know. I think we managed to pull off something that is able to tread the line. I don't think it was too controversial and I don't think anyone was too radically upset by what we did, although it seems to me that *Star Trek* was always

STAR TREK THE OFFICIAL FAN CLUB

STAR TREK V INTERVIEW:
LAURENCE LUCKINBILL

meeting God in some way or another. That idea permeated many of the old episodes, and it certainly played a part in the first movie."

The writer quickly added that as fascinating as the theme of "meeting God" may be, it was the exploration of the relationship between Kirk, Spock and McCoy that appealed to him the most.

"To me, God was never the most important part of the script," he explained. "Yes, it was part of the story, but my focus and concentration was on the relationships. The whole God idea was almost a subplot. We had to tread a fine line, because we could really become very pretentious and pretend that we're saying something infinitely important. What I think we're really saying is something that's very simple, which is that if there is a God, he's not a place you go to in terms of outer space. He's a place you go to inside yourself. We also wanted to challenge the audience's imagination and expectations when they realized that this is what Sybok's divine mission was. We really wanted the audience to stir around, look at each other and say, 'Are they serious? Can they possibly mean that we're going to see God?' Because, for me, *Star Trek* is probably the only arena in which you might actually try to do that. *Star Trek* has always been big enough to encompass almost any kind of concept, so we thought

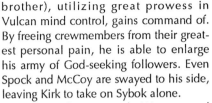

when we dropped the bomb and said, 'Oh, by the way, we're going to see God,' it would be something the audience would be excited about and say, 'Gee, maybe they will....who knows?'

"In terms of the Kirk, Spock and McCoy relationship, one of the things that occurred to me," he stated, "is that if you look at *Star Trek*, you see these three men who are in middle age, and their lives have been spent in space. They're not married, they don't have families, so their relationship is with each other. They represent a family to each other, maybe without always acknowledging it. That, to me, was the most attractive thing, saying, 'What is family?' If it's not three people who care about each other, I don't know what it is."

Interestingly, Loughery wasn't much of a *Star Trek* fan as he was growing up.

"Like any kid who grew up in the sixties," he smiled, "I watched *Star Trek*, but to me it was just another show and it probably wasn't until years later, when I was in college and caught the episodes in syndication, that I kind of began to see that there might be something special there. I guess I was never a Trekkie or Trekker."

Nonetheless, his screenplay does seem to capture the true essence of the characters. "I was really familiar with the show," explained Loughery. "It's just one of those things that whether or not you studied *Star Trek*, it doesn't really matter. It's kind of something you've accumulated without really knowing it. I think you could say the same thing about other shows you saw when you were younger that were popular at the same time. If somebody told me they wanted me to write a movie version of *The Man From U.N.C.L.E.* or *The Wild Wild West*, or something like that, I could probably sit down and do it based on a kind of collective memory from watching those programs. So the characters were fairly clear to me, and also, to prepare, I watched the previous movies and some of the episodes. I write at night a lot, and usually at 11p.m. they would run *Star Trek*, so if I wanted to take a break, sometimes I'd go over and turn on the TV and that would sort of give me a feeling of the characters. But, really, there comes a point where you

have to throw away that continuity and knowledge, and kind of sit down and make it your own. The continuity of *Star Trek* is that there are 78 episodes, 22 animated episodes, now there are five motion pictures, and I don't know how many paperbacks, comic books and all that stuff. The trick is to find something fresh."

■ Nobody Said It Was Gonna Be Easy

There was a point in the development of *Star Trek V* in which William Shatner had to go off to act in Ted Turner's *Voice of the Planet*, while David Loughery and Harve Bennett wrote yet another draft of the screenplay. This version was *so* different from the original concept, that Shatner felt betrayed upon his return.

"In truth," explained David Loughery, "we had gone too far, but sometimes you need to go too far in order to really see where you need to be. We found a median that was satisfying to all of us. We had some interesting ups and downs. I did lots of drafts over two years, and each one was a little different from the one before. What Harve and I had written—where we had really gone off from the original concept—was where we began to deal more with the idea of this legendary planet, this mythic place called Sha Ka Ree, being Sybok's goal and thinking of it more in terms of Shangri-La. It's a kind of Eden that existed, and a place one could reach by passing through this ordeal called the Barrier. We were leaning in the direction of it being more a mythic and heaven-like place, and dealing less with the idea that a physical God existed there. We were shying away from the idea of going to see God, and thinking more in terms of achieving Heaven. What we ended up with, as you can see in the film, is a balance between those two things."

The resulting screenplay chronicled Sybok's abduction of representatives from the Federation, Klingon and Romulan Empires, and using them as bait to lure a starship in. Naturally that starship is the Enterprise, which Sybok (who improbably turns out to be Spock's half-

brother), utilizing great prowess in Vulcan mind control, gains command of. By freeing crewmembers from their greatest personal pain, he is able to enlarge his army of God-seeking followers. Even Spock and McCoy are swayed to his side, leaving Kirk to take on Sybok alone.

Both Leonard Nimoy and DeForest Kelley were unhappy with the way their characters were portrayed. In Kelley's case, it was a flashback sequence where Dr. McCoy performs euthanasia on his father. For Nimoy, Spock had been written in such a way that Sybok revealed to him his greatest pain, which was coming to grips with his human half, resulting in his betraying Kirk and the Enterprise to partake in Sybok's divine mission.

William Shatner explained, "After De read the script, he didn't want to do the scene. So I took him to lunch and tried to convince him it would work. I said, 'De, this is the best scene you've had to play in a long time.' He's such a wonderful actor, and I really felt he hadn't had a chance recently to show what he was capable of doing. Finally, after much talking, I convinced him to do it. His one stipulation was that we add an explanation of why McCoy committed the euthanasia. We added a short bit of dialogue where Sybok asks, 'Why did you do it?' and McCoy answers, 'To preserve his dignity.' With these new lines, De felt that McCoy's motivations were clearer and more understandable. Once we solved De's objections, we were then closer to getting the scene I had envisioned."

In #71 of *The Official Star Trek Fan Club Magazine*, Kelley explained, "When the scene was first presented to me, it was a little harsher. Once we smoothed it out, I still knew it was going to be a difficult scene to do and I felt if that scene didn't come off absolutely right, we would be in trouble....I don't know whether the public realizes it or not, but a character that people have watched for over 20 years was being stripped in front of them of a very private and secretive situation that took place in his life....That moment of McCoy's privacy in *Star Trek V* would have been divulged to Kirk before anyone. His opening line in the scene was, 'Oh my God, don't do this to me!' And that meant many things: he knew that it was happening to him there, in front of these people, plus the fact he had to relive it again was tough.....The more I looked at it and studied the scene, the more important it became to me because it's a topic that goes on today. I thought it would be interesting to lay it out in the presence of a motion picture audience and let them decide within themselves what is right or wrong."

To digress for a moment, this sequence, which marked the passing of Bones' father, was highly significant to many of the crewmembers, including William Shatner and Andrew Laszlo.

"It's the strangest thing," said Shatner of that moment's relation to the death of his own father, "but I have played that scene over and over in my head for months. It came out almost exactly the way I had imagined it. What an incredible feeling for me...my father, the dialogue, the performances—it was all there."

This unique flashback effect was achieved live on set with startling results, using standard theatrical technology. "We had two walls with identical texture and similar lighting for that particular section of the observation deck—a solid wall and a scrim," Laszlo revealed. "As we approached this sequence, we replaced the solid wall with a transparent scrim of similar texture used on the legitimate stage by theatrical companies. When the lights came on the hospital set behind the wall, the set became visible, and conversely, when we shot the reverse angle on Bones, we can see the observation deck behind him."

As stated above, Leonard Nimoy wasn't at all happy with the flashback Sybok takes Spock on, nor his betrayal of Kirk.

Explained David Loughery, "Leonard had some problems with the earlier drafts, feeling that there *were* things that Spock would not do. His suggestions were very helpful, and along those lines we made the change that Spock had *previously* come to understand his human self, and does *not* betray Kirk. The way it turned out, I think is interesting because it really shows that the bond between these guys is strong and can't be broken. Rather than have Sybok walk off in a snit, he kind of

admires this. His reaction is not really one of disappointment when it turns out that Spock won't go with him. He really kind of understands that Spock *couldn't* go with him. I think he sort of admires that in a way. I was surprised, actually, when I eventually watched it with an audience. When Spock told Sybok he couldn't go with him, the audience let out a cheer. I wasn't anticipating that. And when McCoy sheepishly says, 'I guess you better count me out too,' they went for that. Then you go to Bill, who has this look on his face that says, 'Eat it, Sybok!' And they loved that too.

"One of the smart things we did early one was bring Leonard and De in to go over the script, because we wanted their input. These guys have lived with these characters for more than 20 years, and have very strong opinions on what their characters would and wouldn't do. There were problems with this too, however. As originally conceived, only Kirk held out against Sybok, which gives you more of a one man stands alone kind of thing, betrayed by his best friends. Leonard and De objected and it was changed. Suddenly there were three guys against Sybok. When you start doing that kind of stuff, bit by bit you remove and dilute the real strength of the original vision and finally you end up with a bit of a mish-mash. It would have been great for Kirk to have squared off against Spock in some way. But you find the script beginning to accommodate the needs of the actors who know their characters and say, 'Spock wouldn't do that.' It's kind of indefensible. You don't really have an argument that can turn them around on something like that."

The script—which had been finished shortly before the 1988 Writer's Guild strike that lasted some six months—was only part of William Shatner's problems. During its long development, Leonard Nimoy accepted the assignment of helming THE GOOD MOTHER, thus delaying production by several months. Rumor had it that Shatner threatened to shoot the film without Nimoy, but everyone knew that this was a threat without meaning. One can't help but wonder if, in some way, Shatner was being paid back for prolonging negotiations on *Star Trek IV*, thus delay-

ing production on that film.

To make matters worse, Paramount announced that *Star Trek V* was overbudget and that cuts would have to be made. The natural place to cut was special effects, the majority of which occurred toward the end of the film. A frustrated Shatner related, "My original concept for the movie had the characters descending into the equivalent of hell. The angels surrounding 'God' turned into horrible gargoyle-type figures and chase Kirk, Spock and McCoy into a burning chasm. I was quickly told that my idea was much too expensive. So we changed the gargoyles into Rockmen. That is, as Kirk, Spock and McCoy are running away, these huge, twisted shapes break free from the rocks surrounding them and pursue the characters. I had in mind six Rockmen, six hulking, strange creatures—terrifying! But each of those Rockmen were incredibly expensive....so the first thing I was told was that I could only have one Rockman. So here I had gone from this fantastic image of floating cherubim turned into flying gargoyles, then to six hulking Rockmen, now down to one Rockman. It was one of the first lessons I had in the realization that the movie in my head was going to be different from the one in reality."

Ultimately production snafus would cost the actor-director even his one Rockman, and much of his original vision. There were times when the production was in chaos, and it was all that everyone could do to stay as close to schedule and budget as possible.

Noticing what was happening, Leonard Nimoy on *The Tonight Show* said, "I gave him one piece of advice the first couple of days of shooting. I said stop talking so fast. It's the sign of a first-time director. You come on a stage the first day on the set and you're excited and you've got the adrenaline going and you're nervous and if you want to spot a first-time director, you look for the guy with the sweaty palms and he's hyperventilating and he's talking too fast. He thought that by talking fast it would speed up the schedule but you couldn't understand a word he was saying."

In the pages of *Cinefantastique*, Harve Bennett was a little more succinct in what he thought the problems with

Shatner were.

"I was offered a lot of money to control Bill's appetites," he said. "They were extravagant because he didn't know anything. He had spent all those years in front of the camera, and believed because he had directed *T.J. Hooker* and Leonard had done it, he could too.

"Bill'd come in and present a concept and he thought he was discovering the wheel. And you couldn't say, 'No, that shot was used in *Lawrence of Arabia*, it's not worth $100,000 to get that shot in, and anyway, it won't prove you are a great director.' It is funny how first-time directors try to be pioneers in craft. Nimoy, on the other hand, is three yards and a cloud of dust. Fundamental. Here's the camera—shoot a movie. Billy Wilder shot like that. It works when the actors are working well, and the *Trek* family adored Leonard."

■ F/X InThe Final Frontier

The visuals of *Star Trek V: The Final Frontier* span the gamut of special effects, employing the diverse talents of effects supervisor Bran Ferren, makeup artist Kenny Myers, mechanical effects supervisor Mike Wood, motion control expert Peter Wallach, modelmaker Greg Jein and cinematographer Andrew Laszlo to create images no man has seen before. It's difficult to imagine that a film like *Trek V* could experience a budget crunch, but from the outset it was plagued by shortages of funds in nearly every department that would have shocked even the most hardened of low budget filmmakers.

In an effort to save time and money, producer Ralph Winter and executive producer Harve Bennett decided to leave the safe harbor of Industrial Light and Magic and venture into a different effects facility—breaking the tradition established with *Star Trek II*. It seemed the best way to handle the effects on their limited budget was to do as much live on-stage as possible. As a test, they challenged ILM and four other effects houses to design the film's climactic "Undisclosed Wonder" without resorting to opticals.

July 1989 $3.25
Canada $3.50

American Cinematographer

100-Year Start on Tomorrow

The Final Frontier Unfolds in *Star Trek V*

One Century of Film— It's Only the Beginning

According to Winter, "Bran Ferren's company, Associates and Ferren, produced the most creative result....I wanted the problem solved in-camera, on-stage. That was the challenge. We were on a fast train to get the picture in the theatre, so we felt it would be wonderful if we could shoot most of our effects in-camera, and have half of them finished by the time we completed shooting. That was our intention. Bran came out by far on top, but I still wanted to let ILM handle all the motion control stuff, because they're so good at it. Unfortunately, they were not available because they were doing *Ghostbusters II*.

Visual effects supervisor Bran Ferren is an unusual blend of mad scien-

tist, inventor and eccentric, and has produced some of the most memorable and exciting imagery of the eighties, from the psychedelic brainstorms of *Altered States* to the cartoonish madness of *Little Shop of Horrors*. A round man with an offbeat sense of humor, capable of rattling off fantastic sounding scientific jargon at a furious clip, Ferren was the ideal fellow to implement Harve Bennett and Ralph Winters' live on-stage approach.

"My general dislike of blue screen results in a lot of process projection wherever possible," Ferren explained. "There were many scenes where blue screen, computer generated mattes or rotoscoping were appropriate and useful, but whenever we had people walking in front of effects or wild camera movements, I felt we did ourselves a favor by avoiding blue screen."

Unfortunately, the preponderance of Ferren's rear process projection screens and accompanying hardware severely curtailed the type of shots director William Shatner and cinematographer Andrew Laszlo could achieve in those scenes.

"I had planned these beautiful shots," Shatner had shaken his head, "but I was forced to shoot close-ups not too close, and master shots because of the demands of the D.P. I mean, you couldn't breathe or you'd end up with matte lines! It was frustrating because I had imagined this film and planned it as a series of flowing images and I ended up with some very choppy scenes instead."

Ferren went to some unusual lengths to avoid using blue screen: to create the effect of the galaxy hanging outside the starship Enterprise's large observation deck window, he implemented a 44-foot-wide rear projection screen. "Doing images 40 feet wide is difficult," he admitted. "Using ultra-wide angle projection, we sometimes had only a 30 foot throw to project an image 45 feet wide, which required particularly good distortion control to maintain flatness of field, which was a bit of a challenge.

"We build all our own process projection equipment, basically in frustration that there hasn't been any new equipment made in 40 years, even though a lot has been learned since then. It's like having to shoot a contemporary feature on uncoated Baltars—and that's recent compared to a lot of the lenses used for process work. You need a lot of light and well geometrically and chromatically corrected lenses, because if you have significant chromatic aberration at the edge of the field on a star—which is basically a white dot on a black background—it becomes a color test pattern, so you will see little red, blue and green dots all separately positioned."

Mechanical stage effects supervisor Mike Wood was in charge of creating myriad live effects to help keep Ferren's optical workload down at the end of principal photography. Wood previously contributed first rate services to *Innerspace*, which was shot by *Star Trek V*'s Andrew

Laszlo. Though not a violent man, Wood set fire to the Enterprise and Klingon bridge sets whenever the script demanded it. "We supplied the sparks and fire and smoke when the ships took a hit," he clarified, "and we also provided all the dials, gauges and polar motion graphics—the things that give life to the set."

One of the more difficult sequences Mike Wood handled involved flying William Shatner, Leonard Nimoy and DeForest Kelley up a vertical shaft on board the Enterprise as the trio flee from Sybok's people via Spock's jet-boots.

Shatner stated, "I'm not exactly acrophobic, but I don't like heights. In the shaft, there was no getting around the fact that DeForest Kelley, Leonard Nimoy and I had to be flown on this levitation rig. This was very dangerous, because the shaft was about 60 feet high, so our stunt coordinator worked very hard testing and retesting the levitation rig. It was scary being on the rig, but its velocity and the comedic velocity of the scene helped cover any nervousness I felt. For the close-ups, of course, I felt calmer because I was floating 60 feet in the air. Under the circumstances, I was anxious to shoot this scene as quickly as possible, so Andrew and I would come down to the set at the end of the day's shooting and look at it. I'm happy and relieved to say we finished the scene on schedule."

Getting there was half the fun. "We had to come up with a rig that would fly three of our principals 55 feet in the air safely at great speed," Mike Wood said, "and we only have five or six weeks to research and build the mechanism that flew them. We contacted some engineers, but they didn't want to touch this. They needed time to engineer it and, of course, we don't have time. One of the things that made this job really tough was that we were handling human lives in dangerous situations. We shot it many different ways, from 24 fps to 12 or less fps, but even though we undercranked the shots, we had the actors moving quite fast on set. People think, 'Oh, you're just flying the guy'—but what happens if you drop them 50 or 60 feet?

"We finally settled on a variation of the old magic levitation gag magicians have been using for years," Wood

continued. "Instead of wires, we used a levitation bar on rollers that ran up a track behind the set. In essence, we built an elevator to carry three people—without an elevator car. We put all three actors on one bar which branched off to three receivers, and it was hidden from camera by the actors' bodies where it came through the wall of the set. The rigging factor was quite involved because we were working on a three-story vertical set with neon lighting.

"We had special sets of fiberglass flyingpants made for the actors which extended from mid-thigh to waist height and supported them like sitting on a bicycle seat. Our costumers built slightly oversized pants designed to slide over the fiberglass harnesses. The fiberglass pants offered more comfortable support when they were hanging on the levitation bar. Once we put them on this thing, they were stuck there for quite a while until we could get that shot."

From the outset of production, it had been Ferren & Associates' hope that both a normal landing and a crash-landing of the Enterprise shuttlecraft would be effected live on set using full-scale mock-ups on wire rigs. Sadly, the mock-ups ended up weighing some four tons and could not be flown. "All of a sudden, we were presented with this 8,000 pound shuttlecraft—when it's empty—then they stuffed 10 or 12 people in it and expected us to make it fly," Wood laughed. "It was too heavy to use wires, but we were able to hook it up to an airwinch to pull it through the shuttlebay about 50 feet. It was on castors so we could slide it in and out, but the darn thing was very difficult to manipulate. For shots where we just see its nose, we had people pushing it from behind. It was all shot forward motion as the craft skidded and crashed, knocking the pylons off on either side. We had a cargo net hung at one end to keep the shuttlecraft from crashing into the set."

Andrew Laszlo distinctly remembered the use of the shuttlecraft on location in the desert. "We actually landed the craft by suspending it from a huge construction crane," he explained. "Not only does it land on the sand dunes, but a second later the rear hatch opens and out pop a bunch of marines, who leap over the camera, followed by the crew of the Enterprise. We did that in a single shot! Everything becomes very difficult when you work in the sand—vehicles can't move, especially those that can transport and then lift a very large 8,000 pound object. Although this difficulty was foreseen, even with the greatest foresight, certain things can and will go wrong, especially in the course of a motion picture being photographed on sand dunes. Just turning the shuttlecraft around to accommodate another camera angle meant bringing the crane in, picking the craft up, turning it and having the crane clear out of the shot—it took about an hour and a half."

In terms of the crash-landing of the shuttle in the Enterprise shuttlebay, Ferren reluctantly accepted the fact that it had to be accomplished using a combination of miniature, optical and physical effects.

"No matter how much we didn't want to intercut between models and live action, we ended up having to do it here," Ferren said, chagrined. "It's the typical effects film nightmare. Intercutting between a 150-foot long real set and a miniature can be the kiss of death. The trouble was to just maintain a match so that the flow of the scene looked credible. Fortunately, none of these intercuts had to stand up to microscopic scrutiny, they just had to work within the context of a quickly cut sequence.

Building the miniature sets was relatively easy since Ferren assigned modelmaker extraordinaire Greg Jein, whose previous credits include the creation of the stunning mothership of *Close Encounters of the Third Kind* as well as the new Enterprise of *Star Trek: The Next Generation*. Besides being among the very best modelbuilders in the business, Jein is also devoted to *Star Trek*, and Ferren made sure he would be available by tying him up through production and having him build all the handprops for the show. Once the props were out of the way, Ferren knew he could rest assured Jein's miniatures would be exact in every detail.

Working from the blueprints for the full sized shuttlecraft mock-up, Jein made a 1/12 scale, 2 1/2 foot model, and supervised David Sharp, who fabricated the larger 1/6 scale, 5-foot miniatures.

"We built the 2 1/2 foot shuttle using plexiglass slab construction," recalled Jein. "After filling it with foam and turning out a finished piece, we then molded it, even though we ended up only making one of this size. We needed three of the five foot models—one for the crash sequence which required pyrotechnics and breakaway pods, one for motion control and one for a shot of the craft parked in the shuttle bay of the Enterprise. It was only after the fact that they decided they wanted the engine pylons to break off—which wasn't originally budgeted—so we made a mold of that part and cast them out of rigid polyfoam so the pyrotechnics guys in New York could pack them with whatever they wanted. We used magnets to attach the pylons to the body so they would fly off from the impact of the explosion, which seemed like a quick, foolproof way to do it. The shuttles weren't hard to paint—they were basically one color."

Jein also recreated the Enterprise shuttlebay in two scales to match the 5 foot and 2 1/2 foot shuttlecraft models. "The actual hangar interiors we made were only background pieces, so the camera will not dwell on them for too long—it's just something you see the shuttle crash against," Jein insisted, modestly omitting that his miniatures were beautifully detailed and painted to match the full-scale set exactly. "The most demanding part of the job was the space problem in my little shop! The 1/2 scale set was so big, we had to take the door apart to get it out of there! The 1/6 scale shuttlebay was over 20 feet wide, but we built it in sections like stage flats that bolted together, so it fit through the door easily once it was dismantled. Both sets were constructed of plywood, like big dollhouses."

Once the miniatures were constructed, Jein shipped them to Ferren's motion control expert, Peter Wallach, of Peter Wallach Enterprises. Wallach's solution to the shuttle crash problem was very much in keeping with Ferren's in-camera philosophy—he decided to do as much of its live as possible by actually launching the shuttlecraft model into the set. "Though we did some 75 shots using motion control, it was my belief you can't do a crash convincingly using motion control, so we built a giant slingshot made from two 22' rails and a sled with roller-skate wheels on it," Wallach smiled as he explained his unorthodox approach. "One has to be flexible with motion control and realize that there's a time to use it and a time not to. One should never lose sight of the fact that a simple rubber band can be a life saver."

In this case, the "rubber band" was a couple of two ton garage door springs cocked back by a three and a half ton winch. "We pulled this slingshot back varying distances," Wallach remembered. "Prior to launching, this $10,000 shuttle at a $100,000 shuttlebay, we built the 'Guido II'—a plywood mock-up we had made of the shuttlecraft—which we fired a number of times to determine the best velocity and camera speed for the pyro as well as the scale."

The Guido II tests assured the more nervous members of the production team that the shuttlecraft miniature and shuttlebay would survive Wallach's live action approach. "One of the main reasons some wanted me to shoot the crash motion control was they were concerned we'd break the model doing it our way," he explained. "My attitude was just to put a little more fiberglass in it, and catch it so it wouldn't break. We were having so much fun doing it, we wound up doing six takes in all, and in six takes there was no damage to the model. It was just a paint job away from being ready for the next take. We only needed about 45 minutes between takes."

Two highspeed cameras encased in plexiglass booths within the shuttlebay model itself recorded the action from the front and side, as the shuttlecraft plunged at breakneck speed.

"The shuttle sled was cocked back six and a half feet, then released, launching the model at about 300 miles per hour-on fire," Wallach revealed. "Inside the shuttle was a control box which triggered a series of explosions on the ship at half-second intervals. We shot the shuttle head on at 72 frames per second, which is low-end high speed. Usually, high speed miniature photography means something like 300 frames per second, but if we had shot this much beyond 7x2 frames, it would've made the

William Shatner and Leonard Nimoy scale El Capitan while in character for early sequences in the fifth Trek film (photo copyright ©1994 Globe Photos).

sparks look a little phony. The side shot went by rather quickly, so we cranked that up to 90 frames per second. We also got creative for one shot, where we cut a hole in the set and mounted a front silvered mirror at a 45 degree angle, which enabled us to shoot the shuttlecraft coming directly into camera almost as if it was shot right between your eyes.

"After it whizzed by the camera, the shuttle wedged itself into an ice cream cone shaped funnel of foam rubber which we designed to stop it, and my pyro crew stood by with fire extinguishers to put it out. It was a very exciting shot. By launching it for real, we added a much greater sense of realism to the effect than it would've had if we used motion control. It also enabled us to meet a very difficult production schedule in that the show was composited all as one."

In addition to contributing the shuttlecraft and shuttlebay miniatures, Greg Jein built a copy of the Pioneer 5 satellite and an oversized miniature wing section of the Klingon Bird of Prey.

"The satellite was supposed to be floating junk in space which ends up being used for target practice," Jein explained, "so certain sections had to be rigged to break away. We worked from photos of the real Pioneer 5, which was surprisingly small—our model is very nearly 1:1 scale, about six feet across. The dish turned out to be the exact size and shape of a home satellite dish, so we used a real one, and Mike Joyce machined a lot of parts for its rotational axis. He also rigged out a three foot Bird of Prey wing section so the gun was stop-motionable. We made the oversized section so the gun, which you never saw rotate in previous films, could actually take aim at something. We couldn't take too many liberties because it had to match up with their stock footage of the Bird of Prey, but there are some obvious differences we had to have to allow it to pivot. The gun was built of brass."

■ "Hi, Bones. Mind If We Drop In?"

At one point, the *Star Trek V* crew moved to Yosemite National Park to shoot a sequence in which Captain Kirk climbs El Capitan, appropriately enough. The immense flat-faced mountain overlooking the park is a favorite amongst alpinists, who regularly scale it using ropes and other safety devices that Captain Kirk, being who he is, dispenses with in favor of climbing it hand over hand.

"These scenes loomed ominously ahead of me through the whole schedule," Shatner laughed. "We actually shot on top of El Cap, where I was literally hanging on a wire hidden up one of my sleeves overhanging Yosemite valley, which was very scary."

Since William Shatner is less foolhardy than the character he plays, a stuntman dressed as Kirk was photographed as he scaled the rock by a mountain climbing team, and this footage was to be matched to footage of Shatner climbing a mock-up of the mountain set up in the parking lot atop El Capitan.

"Believe it or not, we took a rock to Yosemite," smiled D.P. Andrew Laszlo. "We recreated the mountain's face and set it up in the parking lot so the scenery in the background would match the shots of the stuntman climbing the real El Capitan. That presented all kinds of crazy challenges. The parking lot turned out to be one of the most famous lookout points, and the flood of tourists never stopped. At one point, I suggested that by way of explanation we put up a sign saying, 'Sorry for the inconvenience while we're repairing the rock.'"

To sell the illusion that Shatner was actually climbing El Capitan, it was decided to place a camera above the actor as he climbed the mountain set, showing the valley spread out thousands of feet below him. "We went all over Yosemite to see if we could find a safe position to do this. There were no solutions to be had until we got to one of the lookout points and I suggested we build a fiberglass rock face over the railing," said Laszlo. "Though we were able to assemble the set on location in the better part of the day, designing the thing so it could be set up in that particular spot took weeks and weeks and several visits to the location. Because of the size and the position of this rock, it became obvious that certain precautions had to be taken, so a number of safety devices were built into the set and cleverly hidden.

"Once the set was in position, we even went to the extreme of putting camouflage nets over the swimming pools below because we didn't want to see any features that would say 20th Century. We constructed a large platform on parallels to the set on which we would put a tulip crane. The crane was equipped with a cam-remote, which is linked to a video monitor so that although the operator is nowhere near the camera, it can make all the normal motions of a camera, including looking straight down."

Although Laszlo realized this

was one of the more difficult and demanding shots of the picture, he had no inkling that after all the planning, anything could seriously go wrong with the shot.

"Everything was set up," he detailed, "we only had to set our exposure by adjusting the aperture of the cam-remote and we were ready to shoot. Suddenly we were informed by the cam-remote technicians that this was not possible because they didn't have the proper gear. The initial impulse was to kill. We attempted to deal with a situation that was completely unexpected and should never have happened. Meanwhile, despite all the safety devices, William Shatner was practically hanging by his fingernails from this artificial rock thousands of feet above the valley floor! It was terribly frustrating. We made the shot, but with all this elaborate preparation, expense and planning, it just did not work the way we hoped. It was a very big disappointment. When something like this happens, it gives one very little solace to find out why it didn't work."

Once shooting shifted from the Yosemite location to the Paramount lot, Captain Kirk took a tumble off El Capitan, only to be saved in the nick of time by Mr. Spock, who floats by in a pair of levitation boots.

"We had to create a method that permitted Spock to appear to levitate," said Laszlo, "so he could save Kirk inches before he splattered all over the valley. In order to accomplish this, our special effects department had to build yet another piece of the rock on the backlot of the studio. This one was designed as a horizontal set so Spock could be flown without any overhead wires being seen. By laying the camera on its side as well, the wires supporting Spock come out of the side of the shot instead of the top, which makes them far less noticeable."

The execution of this sequence is something that bothered screenwriter David Loughery. "What was strange about *Star Trek V* is that we had this guy named Nicos Rodis who was the art designer. He had worked on *IV* and he went on to work on *VI*. He designed spaceships, uniforms...just a wonderful, brilliant conceptual artist. He had done

these full-color storyboards and the designs were fantastic in terms of what people would wear on a camping trip in the 23rd Century, and he'd come up with these amazing designs. When they actually went to make the costumes, Bill just kind of stepped back into almost making them look very contemporary. If you look at him, he's wearing almost a pair of jeans and a denim jacket. I felt that was really kind of a mistake. Many of the designs were changed and made more 20th Century. Even things like Spock's gravitation boots looked like ski boots. I remember sitting around a table and getting into a discussion with Harve and Bill about these boots, and they're talking about, 'There should be these jets on the back, you work them with your toes or a belt.' They were being very, very 20th century about it. I like, how would we do this if we were really making one of these? My concept was put Spock on a flat disk with no explanation as to how this thing works, because by the 23rd Century we would have the technology. Throughout this movie they seemed to always be trying to explain the technology in present terms rather than saying, 'Let's do some amazing shit and let the kids figure it out.' That's just the personality of the people you get involved with. There are certain things that they will fixate on, and that's just their way of doing it. That was definitely what happened with this movie. Costumes and devices started looking more contemporary. Suddenly we're riding horses, fighting Arabs in the desert with popguns....all kinds of different things. I thought it was a mistake."

■ Props & Makeup

William Shatner's hoped-for revolutionary approach to *Star Trek V* extended to such things as the crew's hand-held weaponry, the phasers, which are a far cry from the small plastic weapons of the earlier films and TV series: big, black and very dangerous looking, they may well change the look of *STAR TREK* hardware to come.

"I didn't want them to be squirtguns," said Shatner. "I wanted them to be .45s. We load them on camera and you can run out of power—you can run out

STAR TREK V
THE FINAL FRONTIER

KLINGON / ENGLISH PHRASEBOOK

This Klingon/English phrasebook was handed out as part of the press kit for Star Trek V.

they slap the magazine into the corrugated steel butt of the pistol and pull the cocking lever back to expose the mechanism to see if its charge is activated, just like the Green Hornet checked his Hornet's Sting on the '60s TV show. Since the phaser firefight was shot at night, we put red LEDs in the barrels to give the animators a cue mark for their phaser blasts."

Jein also also created "pipeguns" for the mining planet pioneers. The crude pipeguns came in a wide variety of styles, including rifles, bazookas and Gatling guns. "The basic premise was that no weapons were allowed on the planet, so all the inworlders had to make their own from scavenged parts—like futuristic zip guns," he recalled. "We came up with the idea that they're run off a methane gas that is buried under the planet's surface. Evident in all these weapons are the storage areas for the gas cannisters. The guns were designed with valves so they'd look like gas-sucking devices that run off these cannisters. The 'bullets' were rocks found on the planet's surface.

"The guns were relatively simple to put together, and were relatively indestructible because they were made of metal, which also gave them a nice heavy feel," Jein added. "We went to a lot of war surplus places to find things the government paid thousands of dollars for, then never used and sold for scrap. The bazookas were made from plastic navy sonar buoy tanks. The Gatling guns had bigger air cylinders in the back and a hand crank so they could alternate blasts from their eight barrels. Once we got the basic feel of how the pipeguns would look, we just swung into that mode. The guns were supposed to be in a very toxic atmosphere, so we painted them to look rotten. Our mechanical floor effects supervisor, Mike Wood, selectively rigged a number of the guns to shoot out a bit of flame."

The strange humanoids wielding these unusual weapons are the product of make-up effects artist Kenny Myers' vivid imagination. Myers has been responsible for creating memorable effects for numerous low budget films, including the phenomenally successful *Return of the Living Dead* series, but *Star*

of bullets, in other words. It makes sense. So we could have a gun, and then not have a gun. Also, I wanted the phasers to sound differently, too. Instead of tinkling, I wanted them to crackle."

Laughed Greg Jein, "There were a lot of things we wanted to build into the new phasers, to make them more believable as a weapon than a squirtgun. In one scene, a Federation SWAT team is preparing an assault, and the new phasers give the feeling if an old war movie. The team members actually check their equipment—they pull the phaser magazine off their bandoliers and if it lights up it's in working order. Then

Trek V was his biggest credit at the time and it led him to *Back to the Future Part II* and *Part III*.

Myers' priority was the design of the inhabitants of the boomtown planet gone bad. "The aliens had to look lost," he explained. "We wound up with a combination of no eyebrows and no hair. The description in the script read, 'Humanoid—but not quite,' and to convey that we made the teeth double the width of a normal human tooth, extending only an eighth of an inch above the gumline. Rex Holman, a wonderful actor, played the first of these aliens we see—J'onn, a prospector who's out in the middle of the huge desert drilling holes for water. Jim Cale made a brow piece to cover Holman's eyebrows, and I made him a set of really stunted teeth that almost looked like they'd been gnawed down to the gum, which made him look really pathetic. I designed the character but it was Wes and Jeff Dawn who applied the make-up on the set each day."

In addition to the large number of close ups and multi-piece prospector makeups, Meyer also had maskmaker Joe Reader sculpt and cast full over-the-head prosthetics that could be worn like masks by actors in the background, and glued down only around their eyes and mouths. "I started doing that with Joe Reader on *Return of the Living Dead II*," Meyer said, "and it was also used effectively on a movie I assisted with called *Alien Nation*. The *Star Trek* people had never seen this before, and our production designer, Nilo Rotas, was quite surprised how well these prosthetic masks worked. However, these pieces can be quite difficult to make, because tolerances are extremely close. If you screw up, molds lock and you end up cursing a lot and wanting to sell ice cream for a living!"

While the Catwoman makeup bears no relation to the villainess of Batman comics fame—she's a feline, alien dancer in the bar on the boomtown planet, Nimbus III—she is sure to set male pulses pounding from Earth to Arcturus. Making a "sexy alien" is one of the most difficult tasks you can set for a makeup artist, but Myers and Ron Wilde pull it off, aided by the fact that Catwoman is played by the beautiful stuntwoman Linda Fetters. Myers decid-

ed to retain the full body prosthetic made by Makeup Effects Lab, which featured three breasts, and they added a huge mane of blonde hair and some very exotic body tattoos. The problem was that she had to be dumped into the water without losing her tattoos. "We used Fred Bau's tattoo makeups—which are cellulose based and alcohol soluble—to airbrush Catwoman's stripes directly onto the actress' body. No one had ever done that, and Bau was excited and anxious to see if it would work.

"We practiced for a number of weeks on different women, to get the right look to the stripes, and to see if the makeup would hold up overnight. I wanted to make sure this would work in case it was necessary. We actually sent our model home one night and told her to talc her bed and sleep normally. We allowed her to shower using only certain soaps. When she came back the next day, there was only a 30% loss of pigment in 24 hours. However, when it came time to shoot, we sprayed Linda Fetters' body down with base and a number of different colored stripes, and it stayed on all day. I don't know how many times she had to come up here until we got the right coloration down. She had a magnificent look to her, as the catcalls she got on the lot would attest."

■ Singin' The F/X Blues

When principal photography wrapped, supervisor Bran Ferren was faced with a three month deadline to deliver all the visual effects for the effects-laden film, forcing him to fight his way through what he refers to as "a typical nightmare panic post production." One of the problems this rapidfire schedule created for Ferren was the fact that there simply wasn't enough time for his crew to experiment with each effect before shooting it. As a result, every shot had to be treated as if it was going to be an element of the final composite—because it usually was. To make matters worse, even the things Ferren thought would make his job a little easier became major bothers during his precious post-production period—like the original

models Paramount sent out. "There was a lot of time wasted on the film," he flatly stated. "Ultimately, every model we received from Paramount had to be completely refurbished prior to shooting. We had to have Greg Jein build some new ones, while we created five planet landscapes and moons as well.

"One entire side of the Enterprise model was spray painted matte gray, destroying the meticulous original paint job. We had to go in and fix it before we could shoot it, which took two painters and an assistant about six weeks to do. Also, the Enterprise turned out to be an electrical challenge that only continued to work because there were sufficient short circuits within it to keep it arcing into operation—so we had to rewire it. As much as we wished we could just walk into something that was ready to go, that's seldom the case."

Ferren was also frustrated by the fact that he majority of the modelwork amounted to continuing *Star Trek* tradition instead of blazing new trails—which can be a bit boring for even the most enthusiastic effects artist. "It's not exactly like *Star Trek* is a new concept," Ferren observed. "We knew what it was supposed to look like, so our job was really to be faithful to that look rather than try to reinvent the wheel. *Star Trek* usually means models with soft light. I wouldn't light them that way if I were going from scratch—though there's nothing wrong with it. I would've preferred a stark, cutting, contrasty, less filled look. Unfortunately, we couldn't just randomly introduce that, since the look of the Enterprise and of the other models is something that has been created and maintained for four films. We just accepted the fact that most of our model shots had to match what had been done before. Whenever we had the opportunity to do new things, we really had fun.

"For example, we were able to integrate laserdisc video preview equipment for the first time on this film, so that instead of doing film tests, every motion control shot was digital video slopetested, where each element was recorded onto laserdisc and comped 100% on video so we could do movement checks before shooting any film."

As one might expect, *Star Trek*

V's model photography was quite straightforward, supervised by Peter Wallach at the special Hoboken facility set up specifically to handle the film's 80+ model shots. While ILM recomped about five existing shots, Wallach used two motion control systems in conjunction with one another to do the rest: a hybrid of the new IMC system with an 80 foot track and an old Disney system built for *The Black Hole*, which was rebuilt for use in overhead model rigging. On occasion, Wallach rigged blue screens to this overhead cross track so they could be moved via computer to keep them in-shot for big moves on models. The combined system has 80 feet of running track with 30 feet of floor mounted cross track and a mobile 40 feet of overhead cross track.

One of Wallach's more complex effects was creating the streak on the Enterprise when it goes into warp drive. Ferren had instructed Wallach to follow the work that had been done previously.

"Of course, if we could improve on it, because the technology had gotten better, we were certainly going to try that," Wallach said. "ILM's solution was to use artwork on an animation stand, which didn't look real inspiring because the effect was not believable; the Enterprise moved on its trajectory through space while the art work moved in a flat plane. We wondered why they didn't do it as a motion control shot. We soon found out why. When you shoot something in a streak mode, you uncap the shutter and move the camera a certain distance. Then you go back to the starting point and redo the shot. After shooting about 30 frames of the Enterprise's streak, we had already filled the IMC computer beyond its capabilities."

Wallach concluded that ILM had abandoned the use of the motion control system to produce the streak effect when they ran out of memory space in their computer, as he had. Undaunted, he was determined to do the shot using the IMC—with or without computer assistance.

"My belief has always been that it's the people who make the shots magic, not the equipment," he said. "Here we had this wonderful motion control system with its computer filled beyond capacity. I decided to bypass the

computer and use a little of our own ingenuity and logic. Using some yellow glow in the dark tape, we taped the 80 foot motion control rail every six inches. We calculated the stop and start points of the streak moves, then numbered them so when we reached that number we'd yell, 'Capper on!' and cover the shutter, then drive to the next position, 'Capper off!' and uncover the shutter.

"We had to do as many as six passes by hand, but because we shot them at the same time in the same place on the same set of rails, it worked perfectly. By running the whole motion control system manually, minus the computer, we were able to create a very beautiful streak that almost had the look of neon light, using the actual lights of the Enterprise to give us that look rather than using some artwork shot on a stand. I don't mean to downplay the importance of the IMC, but computer art is a contradiction in terms, just as military intelligence is. It's always the artists that make it work, and when the computer didn't allow us to do what we wanted, we turned it off and did it by hand."

Mike Sullivan served double duty as Wallach's director of photography and art director, dictating the look of every shot. Another helpful innovation Wallach contributed to the production was the creation of what he calls "animatics" of every effects sequence, which amounted to little more than his crew flying various models by hand, which were shot on film and inserted into the workprint. "We all dressed up in black ninja costumes and acted each effect shot out, which they actually cut into the film prior to its completion," Wallach proudly explained. "It was kind of amusing to see the first print of the film with the actors reacting very seriously to shots of little store-bought Enterprise models being marched along by people in black costumes, but it really helped the editor and those watching the rough cut—instead of blank leader and the words, 'omit scene,' they actually had a piece of film to look at. Not only did it enable them to have something to cut in and work with prior to the actual shot being completed, it proved very beneficial to the composer and the sound effects editor because they were able to score the

film and get the sound effects locked in place, for the most part, by working from our crude animatics."

"A lot of people talk like there's some great secret to all of this, and the fact is there isn't," Ferren boldly conceded. "Just be competent and try within the general scheme of things not to screw too many things up! That's why I don't like to call attention to specific composites. The number of elements doesn't make it more difficult, just more tedious. The really difficult composites are the ones you have to re-do 30 times before they're right. Hopefully that's an exaggeration, but we do have simple composites in the film that for some reason just won't die—there's one dumb shot in every film. It could be a Bird of Prey flying by, and one time the motion control system goes down, so we shoot it again and the internal lighting in the model blows up halfway through, so we do it again and everything's good except there's a scratch on the beauty pass! That, to me, is a difficult composite."

Ferren opted to use experimental cloud tank photography and microphotography to create believable, understated effects for a long-awaited approach to the Supreme Being's planet.

"We weren't trying for a 'Can you top this?' approach to the visuals," he explains. "Instead, it was a matter of of what was appropriate, tasteful and fit within the *Star Trek* genre. I'm not interested in effects calling attention to themselves. Fortunately, half of our company is involved in serious scientific research, and that resource of people and hardware is available to our effects calling attention to themselves. Fortunately, half of our company is involved in serious scientific research, and that resource of people and hardware is available to our effects unit as they need be. Consequently, we decided to design the Supreme Being's planet using unconventional watertank photography, incorporating high intensity ultraviolet strobe lighting. By bombarding various chemical interactions in the tank with the high intensity UV lighting, we were able to create a unique, luminous look to the atmosphere of the planet.

"It's hard to describe," Ferren conceded, "but then the idea was to make something that would not be describable. More often than not, the atmospheres surrounding effects planets look awful, and I really wanted to make one that was believable, and that had a sense of turbulence and vortex. This is why we ended up doing fluid dynamic modelling with dye, rather than using animation elements or cottonball passes. The tough part was getting the fluids in the cloud tank to envelope a sphere. We wanted the stuff to look unusual but organic, and at the same time, have it swirl and wrap about the planet in three dimensions.

"The whole affair came to be referred to as the 'Soggy Planet Project,'" Ferren laughs, "because our solution was to place a spinning planet model with pressurized chambers, nested one inside the other, in the tank. This effectively 'held out' the area where the planet would be. Within this 'Soggy Planet' model we created pressure gradients, into which we injected ultra-violet dyes that physically encircled the core with a luminescent 'atmosphere.' It was shot with in-tank motion control photography using computerized heads and snorkel lenses, which produced a nice effect of fluid-looking clouds."

One of the more standard effects in a picture like this is the obligatory skim of the surface of a planet, usually achieved by passing a camera across a large mock-up of a planet surface. Ferren maintains this effect always looks fake, and decided to use a breakthrough technology his company designed, involving scanning electron microscope cinematography to create a convincing "skim" of the Supreme Being's planet surface.

"We wanted to make images that were reminiscent of the very first U2 photographs looking across the surface of the Earth from outer space," he reveals, "rather than something that looked like an [effects] alien planet. I guess this marks the first time the approach to a planet's surface was generated by micro-cinematography, but we reviewed all the other ways of doing this type of work, and the trouble was models generally look like models, and matte paintings and computer generated imagery using fractiles have the same basic problems. Since the whole point of any effects is to look

real, we felt if we started with something that *was* real, we'd be halfway there.

"The Supreme Being's planet is supposed to have craggy, crystalline, desert-like terrain," he continued, "so many of our micro models were just Pyrite and other found objects measuring 1/10 of an inch or 1/100 of an inch across, which we sometimes acid etched and spattered with gold palladium. We actually constructed some of our bigger models—measuring an inch across—with microsurgical instruments and epoxy, whose surfaces were then gold plated and carbon shadowed. [Note: The final five second long footage selected for the film is a gold plated lobster claw discovered at lunch]

Since most effects artists prefer to start with as big a miniature as possible, Ferren's micro-cinematography of very tiny things might seem suspect if it wasn't so logical. "Because we're photographing real things, it looks real," he said. "It's quite an interesting look—it's intended to be almost a throwaway, so it doesn't call attention to itself, but we wanted it to look definitely organic and like a planet, but different from what you're used to seeing.

"It was a little ambitious to design scanning electron micro-cinematography for this one effect," Ferren agreed, "but we needed it and it didn't exist. We couldn't go out and buy a scanning electron microscope with high resolution VistaVision imaging and motion control—but we were lucky enough to get Zeiss, PGT, Denton and a few others to help us get it together, then we integrated it and wrote all the special software for it. We started with a Zeiss digital electron microscope and added digital multi-axis motion control, literally scaled down to microns rather than inches, to move our micro-models.

"We also designed a digital image processing and output scanning system with help from companies like Gamma Tech, who specialize in high-resolution image processing. The images in the film were shot at 2500 line resolution, though we had the ability to go to 4096. We also were able to generate RGB or CMY color separations right off the digital data scanner instead of shooting onto color negatives and then doing

our separations, which saved a generation. It's a whole different way of seeing than people are used to, and we look forward, now that the system is integrated, to see what else can be achieved with VistaVision or 65mm ultra-high resolution movies of very, very tiny things."

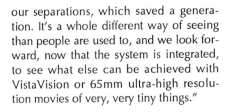

Oh, God!

When it came time to shoot the "God sequences," executive producer Harve Bennett and producer Ralph Winter realized the futility of trying to handle a mammoth effects sequence live on-set in the midst of their breakneck production schedule—especially when Ferren made it clear that in-camera effects were near impossible to alter in post-production. Since people were still undecided as to just what God should look like, everyone agreed the only alternative was to handle the effects using "traditional" opticals.

"When our heroes confront the Supreme Being," Ferren revealed, "he metamorphoses from one form of Savior to another, which ultimately leads into the 'Godshow'—a combination of on-set reactive lighting, optical and make-up effects."

Prior to the "Godshow" proper, the alien being probes the minds of those members of the Enterprise crew who are watching, and shows each of these spectators their own vision of the Supreme Being, as interpreted by Kenny Myers and his makeup effects crew. Myers began experimenting with various terrestrial and extraterrestrial depictions, and ultimately designed some 10 or 12 characters he refers to as "Godheads," which would optically meld and metamorphose into one another, in what Ferren cryptically calls the "Godpole" effect, which spearheads the final "Godshow." As with any complex makeup, Myer's Godheads began as a series of sketches.

"Although I didn't do it consciously, I began working a halo effect, either in hairstyle or in lighting, in each of the Supreme Being sketches," he recalled. "I knew they were going to be strongly backlit and bleached out, which would give them something of a half effect, and I think that was probably what I was thinking subliminally when I drew them."

Laurence Luckinbill who joined the Trek family as Spock's half brother, Sybok, who led the Enterprise on their journey to meet with God.

from lightweight urethane because I wanted something that wouldn't have a tendency to shift on his head. I did a real translucent paint job on them, to make them really look like bone.

"The Andorian 'Christ' also had little horns, which I simply attached to his wig. We stuck with the classic blue look and long, bone white hair. Not being a Trekkie, I was a little taken aback when someone asked, 'How are you going to hide his ears?' I didn't know what they meant, so they explained that Andorians didn't have ears. I thought, 'Oh, *really!*', because that wasn't the kind of stuff they hand out to you when you're about to do a *Star Trek*, and I never paid attention when I watched the show. I'm still not sure if the Andorians have ears or not, but I played it safe by covering the actor's ears with the wig!

"The Klingon Supreme Being was the only Klingon I made for the film, but I knew I wanted something that would imply a little more history to their race, so I slightly redesigned the forehead so it was a little higher, in order to give a sense of evolution. We put jet black hair on him along with white, *Bride of Frankenstein* streaks at the temples—and bright blue eyes. Most of the actors we chose to portray these Supreme Beings had light eyes—or if they didn't, I gave them light eyes using special contact lenses Richard Snell makes in conjunction with a doctor to create a certain classical impression."

The final vision of God drove Myers, Shatner and nearly everyone else to distraction in an effort to make something unique. Figuring out that look was, according to Shatner, "a tough one. That was the big nut to crack. What does God look like? I saw God while talking to our production designer, Nilo Rodis, while we were sketching out ideas of a face in a column of light. As I looked at that face, I said, 'It seems to be He'd be closer than that,' so Nilo drew it closer. Then I said, 'Wait a minute, God is in the eyes!' and then we closed in on the eyes, filling the column of light with the eyes, the nose and the mouth of the actor that played God—a wonderful stage actor named George Murdock. We pre-filmed George. In fact, his stuff was the first thing we shot. Then we trans-

All of Myers' Supreme Beings were created using prosthetics except for the one drawn from classical Greek and Roman mythology, Juno/Hera basically the flipside of the same coin. "To illustrate this concept, Bill had the wonderful idea of making half of her Roman, which meant a surrealistically beautiful flesh and blood approach—and the other side Greek, which was stone," Myers says. "I took a young lady and split her face right down the middle and gave her a stone wig and matching makeup on the Greek side, while applying a more normal classic beauty makeup on the Roman side. Then we put her on a turntable, so first you see the beautiful Roman side, then

the split look, and finally, the Greek look. That was an interesting experiment.

"We had an African chief, the Zulu Supreme Being, which was really fun. He was a full prosthetic job, including a bone through the nose, and I lifted his headdress design from a book on the Zulu. Whenever the Supreme Beings came from Earth, I tried to copy the look as exactly as possible from our own history. There was enough fantasy with characters like the Bullman and the Andorian.

"Our Bullman Supreme Being was played by bodybuilder Danny Fisher, who wore full facial prosthetics and horns attached to a skullcap. I made the horns

ferred the footage to videotape which we ran on a television mounted in the place we thought God's head would be on the set—so in the raw film, before the special effects split screen stuff was put in, there was the crew of the Enterprise bowing and scraping before a television set, which got an occasional laugh in the previews before the special effects were put in."

"How do you make God?" Myers asked rhetorically. "When they said we had to make God, I went crazy! Our first question was whether to go for that classic Jesus look, or for an alien look. The first thing he suggested was to think of the audience—a lot of baby boomers—and their ideas of God. We decided we needed something people could immediately identify with, so we chose Charlton Heston's Moses combined with God as depicted in the Sistine Chapel ceiling as the look that would sell most people. It's that long flowing white haired look combined with that very fatherly, smooth talker that just makes you feel comfortable."

As difficult as coming up with a look for God that a modern day audience wouldn't hoot off the screen was casting the role. Wisely, as stated above, Shatner chose the fine character actor George Murdock to play the supreme Supreme Being. Equally wisely, Myers decided to use as little prosthetic makeup as possible on Murdock. Instead, Myers chose to create the God look with a beautiful set of hairpieces and a long, flowing wig crafted by Karen Asano Myers—Myers' long-time girlfriend, whom he married in the midst of shooting—who handled all the elaborate hair work on *Star Trek V.*

"I didn't want to tamper with the wisdom in that face," Myers said of Murdock. "We put a false nose on him to lengthen the bridge of his nose and added all that hair, and that was it. It must've been hotter than hell in there because they filmed him in extremely bright light to overexpose the image. I remember trying to touch his make-up up under those lights, and I was sweating bullets just trying to do that! I'll never understand how he could hold up so well. After the first dailies were screened, I got a call from Nilo Rotas, the film's production designer, who said Murdock

looked like God come to life off the Sistine Chapel's ceiling."

Ferren combined his on-set reactive lighting effects with Myers' make-up effects with opticals to create the Godshow—which he and the makers of *Star Trek V* banked on as a unique but acceptable depiction of the Supreme Being, who speaks to the crew of the Enterprise from within a brilliant shaft of light.

"When it breaks out of the ground," Ferren explained, "that shaft of light was done using animation elements. Once it was just sitting there, we used a four foot diameter, 15 foot tall cylinder of Scotchlight spinning at about 1000 rpm, which scared the hell out of you! We built a very well balanced big cylinder, and shot that to create the brilliant glow element which was then optically inserted into the scene, along with the images seen within it.

"The more complicated issue was building up the other side of this effect, a series of supreme beings followed by the Supreme Being, which was basically a big guy's face talking to the crew of the Enterprise from within this super-brilliant shaft of light. One of our biggest problems was finding a way to make these interesting faces appear on basically clear film. Our optical cameraman, Bob Rowholt, who's in charge of all our compositing, developed a series of complex overlays and mattes with glows and high contrast elements. Most shots have fifteen or twenty elements stacked up together, some of which hold back the shaft glows and some of which enhance them by creating an almost bronzed look to the original photography. It looks like the old solarization or posterization look, but done as elegant gradations of color in the midst of all this brilliant light and energy.

"You're not supposed to see the various Supreme Being heads clearly—a lot of our energy is directed towards making sure they don't look like make-ups," Ferren cautioned. "Instead, the 'Godheads' form from images generated from tank photography, then come zooming out of the 'Godshaft.' The Gods' faces appear within this primeval super-intense shaft of energy, literally coming towards you amidst explosive elements

of lightning with fluid tank elements behind them to create turbulence."

Ultimately the daring decision to hire Associates and Ferren by *Star Trek V*'s producers represents far more than a mere switch from one effects house to another. It represents the unusual situation of an East Coast effects house offering a challenge to what is generally regarded as a West Coast industry.

"Most New York effects houses are not particularly set up for VistaVision effects photography," Ferren explained. "We are. We're a VistaVision house, so everything is organized towards Vista photography, including all of our motion control systems and optical benches. We've designed and built a significant portion of our own optical printers as part of an ongoing self-improvement process over the past few years. A project like *Star Trek* allowed us to fuse a lot of different technologies together simultaneously—integration of transportable data files from computer graphic systems to electron microscopes to optical printers—that actually worked rather well on a project like this. It's the only way we could have done it all in three months. Still, it was a fun project to do.":

After considering for a moment, Ferren spoke for his entire team in concluding: "But, it would've been nice to have had a year."

■ The Lost Ending

A major complaint lodged against *Star Trek V* is that once the Enterprise broaches the final frontier, everything else seems anti-climactic. Ironically, earlier drafts of the script had a much more extensive conclusion, which was cut due to budget over-runs.

Originally, the ending was far more exciting. Everything plays out exactly as it does in the film, until the discovery is made that this being is most certainly *not* God, and the rest falls into place.

"It would appear that the entity is trapped here," notes Spock. "This volcanic crater is the power source that contains him."

Kirk responds, "And if he gets his hands on the ship, he'll be able to spread himself across the galaxy."

"Precisely his intention!"

Sybok leaps into the crater, and both he and the demon disappear within it as fire fills the sky. Kirk, Spock and McCoy make a run for it after hearing a horrible shrieking sound, that turns out to be numerous living gargoyles spewing from the crater. Running for their lives, the group is slowed down by McCoy, who falls off a ledge and breaks his leg. Kirk carries the doctor as they make their way to the shuttle.

Once inside the shuttle, they are unable to take off as the gargoyles have arrived, and torn apart the thruster units. Kirk contacts Scotty and is told that he can beam them up one at a time. Bones is first to go, then Spock. Cut to the Enterprise, Scotty activates the transporter beam for Kirk, and actually beams aboard a gargoyle who has grabbed the captain's communicator. Freaking out, Scotty picks up a hand phaser and destroys the creature, but in so doing he also accidentally destroys the transporter. *There's no way to bring Kirk back up!!*

As the Klingon Bird of Prey approaches, Spock is struck by an idea and goes to Klingon General Korrd, now on board Enterprise. The man is resistant to help, but Spock responds, "Damn you, sir, you will try!"

Back on the planet, Kirk is being pursued by the gargoyles. He freeclimbs a small mountain (much as he did at the film's beginning) and reaches the top. Armed with two hand phasers, he kills as many of the creatures as he can, but their numbers are legion. It looks like curtains for James T. Kirk. But then, the Bird of Prey decloaks, the machine gun phaser weapon lowers into frame and starts firing, blowing the gargoyles apart, and sending the rest scurrying back to the pit from which they came. Kirk stares at the ship.

"You want me, you Klingon bastards? Come and get me!" he screams, firing the hand phasers at the vessel. As in the film, he is brought to the bridge, where he finds that Spock is the gunner. Much of the remainder of the script plays out as it did in the final version, although more mention is made of the fact that the rescuing of Klingon, Romulan and human hostages will result in a better understanding between their races, and a

path toward the future—actually toward *The Next Generation.*

Spock notes that Sybok has turned out to be a false prophet, but Kirk isn't sure.

"He may have been misguided," notes the captain, "but perhaps his cause has served a higher purpose. The Federation, the Romulans, the Klingons—none of us—will ever be able to see each other again in quite the same light. We have Sybok to thank for that."

Certainly a more exciting finale to such an intense build-up.

Explained screenwriter David Loughery, "When the torpedo came down and explodes the hole, it's like the bottle is uncapped and all the imps spill out, free, and chase our characters back to the shuttle. That was our original concept. A movie, especially a movie like this one, goes through so many transformations from original story to final film. Because of all the hands involved in the making of these movies, it sometimes starts to take on a committee atmosphere to moviemaking. Things don't turn out *exactly* the way you originally wanted them to, but there are reasons for that.

"We certainly wish we could have hung on to some of that concept. The area of the movie that has always been in flux is *how* we represent the God-being. That sequence got lost when it became financially impossible for us to create the gargoyle creatures. That was really more of a budgetary concession than anything else. You're always sorry to see those things go, because your imagination is one thing and the budget is something else. In various places, we had to make certain cuts and rearrangements based on how much we could afford. In the best of all worlds, you usually throw everything in the first draft and it gets pared down. Frankly, there is a point where Paramount will *not* finance these movies. They have a line that they draw, and that's just the way it is. Everyone else says, 'Oh, for crying out loud, it's going to make money,' but they have their line.

"As a writer," he elaborated, "you're always saying, 'I wish they had stuck to the earlier draft, it was better during draft three,' or something like that. You always have your rationalization,

and a dream-picture in your mind of what it *should* look like. But, a picture takes on its own reality once it starts being shot. After a certain period, you really don't have very much influence over how they turn out. You have to take the good with the bad. I don't feel badly about it, but I just wish some things had been better, because it would have given us more of a chance."

■ Summing Up The Final Frontier

When the word was first given that William Shatner would be directing the fifth *Star Trek* film, more than a few eyebrows were raised. For some, he just didn't seem to have the same level of creative expertise that Leonard Nimoy had, for others there was the fear that his ego would run rampant; that, essentially, if Kirk had run the show before, he would *really* be the captain this time.

Those critics were correct on the one hand, but wrong on the other. It's true that he did not not have the directorial smoothness or sureness of Nimoy and that the proceedings seem somewhat choppy. But, to give him the benefit of the doubt, he had a great deal working against him in terms of budget, schedule and so on.

On the other hand, each of the characters were given enjoyable bits of business to play, while he, Nimoy and DeForest Kelley actually managed to expand the horizons of their characterizations, as evidenced in the Sybok-induced flashback sequences as well as the film's opening campfire scene.

"The only scene that I can think of that almost never changed at all," mused David Loughery, "and it was one of the first scenes I wrote, was that campfire sequence. I know there are a lot of people who are kind of upset by that scene, but I love it. It was pure character and I think that's why I wanted to do *Star Trek* anyway."

Enthused Leonard Nimoy to STARLOG's Marc Shapiro, "I felt the idea of having Kirk, Spock and McCoy sitting down and being with each other with no adventure involved and nothing to deal with was wonderful. It put the whole *Star Trek* experience on a very human scale and, in a very positive way, recognized the validity of the relationship these three have had over the years." Of acting without directing, he stated, "Believe me, just acting was a wonderful break for me. I had just finished four films in a row with almost no break in between and I really enjoyed the idea that Bill would be carrying the load and that I could sit in my trailer and take it easy. [Though] Bill's such a physical guy to begin with and I immediately found that was going to spill over into this film. There was much more running and jumping than I normally like to do. I was constantly going up the elevator, down the stairs, across the cliff, down the rocks. We shot in the heat of the day and the cold of the night. It was a fun film to do, but it was also a very difficult one."

Shatner's colleagues offered a variety of opinions on his directorial debut.

Gene Roddenberry: "No one person made it terrible, and no one wanted it to be terrible."

DeForest Kelley: "I feel that regardless of what is said about this film, that Bill is a very energetic kind of man and a good director. I knew going in that he was gong to bring energy to the film. I think he did. This was a tough film for him. It was a nightmare in more ways than one. He handled it very well and when he looked around and got his feet on the ground, he went forward in a thoroughly professional manner and I felt Bill did an excellent job. I think if there's anything wrong with the film, it would be the story content itself but certainly not in his direction."

James Doohan: "There is really only one person on the show that nobody can stand. He tried to do too much for *Star Trek V*, and look what happened—it wasn't a good story and it wasn't a good movie. He can't even act. He doesn't act: He makes faces. He'll wrinkle his nose like a rabbit and that's supposed to mean, 'Oh look, I'm about to cry.' *Star Trek V* doesn't have enough of all the characters. We all have what are called 'cheap shots.' When they start thinking of STAR TREK now, they should start thinking in terms of the whole group of seven rather than just the group of three."

George Takei: "*Star Trek V* will please the fans, unquestionably. It's an exciting film. It's really the Kirk-Spock-McCoy troika. They make up the dramatic triangle, that's where the focus is. The rest of us are kind of incidental. Bill says we all have wonderful things to do, but we're really just there."

Nichelle Nichols: "Bill was a wonderful director. I was not so much surprised at his ability as his demeanor. He was warm, exciting and creative. He was far more patient than I've ever known him to be. He knew what he wanted, and it was fun to watch him get it."

Walter Koenig: "I thought it was an okay film. It was entertaining. I think you could write a thesis paper comparing the problems of *Star Trek: The Motion Picture* and *Star Trek V*. In some ways, they're very similar. I think we had in each case an antagonist that we couldn't make up our minds about—is he going to be a good guy or a bad guy? How much peril was this guy going to generate for the crew? It started out one way and then became something else. And instead of the conflict that was so necessary for good story structure, it kind of went off in another direction. In *Star Trek V*, we really ended up with jokes. In *Star Trek: The Motion Picture* we ended up with awe. The biggest laugh in *Star Trek V* is when Kirk says, 'Just a minute. Why does God need a starship?' And I thought that was indicative of the problem of the film—the biggest laugh of the picture comes when it's supposed to be evoking the most tension and the most drama. I think the problems with the film were in terms of structure. I also think you need good guys and bad guys and we got a little muddy on that point in *Star Trek V*."

Star Trek V: The Final Frontier was released in June of 1989 to generally negative reviews (which focused on the storyline, direction and special effects) and mediocre box-office. With just over $50 million in the coffers, the film was considered a major disappointment and the odds were fairly slim that there would be a sixth film. In fact, if not for the fact that 1991 marks the original show's 25th Anniversary, it isn't likely that there would be one at all.

David Loughery has his own theories as to why the film warped out of theatres almost as quickly as it warped in.

"That was the summer of *Batman*," he reflected. "I don't know how many movie-spending bucks there are out there, but I think that everybody had a weekend that summer. We had an opening weekend where we made $17 million, and everybody thought we were all right, but it just didn't continue that way. Frankly, it was the kind of summer where the money was divided among a handful of films, and *Star Trek V* didn't turn out to be one of them. We were all taken by surprise.

"Had we released *Trek V* at a different time, maybe it would have been a different situation," mused Loughery. "I wondered what the factors were that reduced our impact. One of them, I think, may be the fact that *The Next Generation* has been on TV the last few years. It made a *Star Trek* movie seem like a less special event. I think it was Harve Bennett who said that if you eat turkey sandwiches every day, Thanksgiving doesn't look like such a big deal. I look at *Trek V* with very mixed emotions. The FX turned out to be very disappointing, and this is a movie where we really *needed* them to put us over the top storywise, especially at the end. You don't ever like to say that, because you don't want to think that a movie is dependent on special FX. Certainly *Star Trek* is the kind of thing where the FX play less of a role than the characters and the story but I think the story we were telling this time, at least at the movie's end, very much needed unique and convincing special FX to make those story points work. Those FX don't quite deliver, and in some cases, it looked a little shoddy and ludicrous.

"In retrospect, you look back from the distance of a couple of years, and I've always felt—it was always in the back of my head—that one of the problems is that it's a reactive story rather than an active one. What I mean by that is that our guys are kind of required to stand by and be dragged along on somebody else's quest. In this case, Sybok's. It's sort of his quest and his passion, and Kirk, Spock, McCoy and the rest of the crew are dragged along almost as though they were a supporting cast to this guy. If it had been Kirk who suddenly had this vision of God and hijacked his own ship and turned against the Federation, *then* you've got this much more active, passionate kind of story.

"In *Star Trek V*, one of the things that was sort of cut out of the movie is that the reason Captain Klaa was so passionate about chasing down Kirk was that he not only wanted that feather in his cap, but because there was still a bounty on Kirk's head. That was sort of the thematic thing that would have joined into the next movie as well. Then, they had this ridiculous sort of reshoot that was done without me in which Kirk comes aboard the Bird of Prey at the end. The original script is that he walks in, the chair turns and here's Spock. They have this big embrace, 'Please, Captain, not in front of the Klingons,' and there's this big laugh. But they went back and shot this bit where Klaa is forced to step out and say, 'I apologize.' Their thinking there, I guess, is that he had gone off on his own after Kirk, rather than because Kirk was a wanted guy. That was something that bugged me. The only thing I do get out of it that's really pleasurable is that during the reshoot, which was two or three months afterward, in the close-up of Bill, his face looks about 10 pounds fatter than in the previous shot. So there's a little bit of revenge there, although I don't blame Bill for that....or anybody, really. It's just one of those situations where they felt they had to plug a hole.

"I have to say that Bill is the greatest guy to be with, because he is just so enthusiastic. His energy is so great and he's a lot of fun to go on location with. I really enjoyed being with him, getting to know him and it was very nice of him to always involve me in all facets of production. He's a great guy and the best things that he does in these *Star Trek* movies are kind of those moments where he plays his age a little bit. To me, the greatest moment in any of these movies is in *Star Trek II* where Kirk pulls out those granny glasses and put them on in order to see the console. He just has this moment where he looks around a little bit embarrassed and puts them on. He was right on the mark in that movie.

"Something I've noticed in all sequels is that each time you make another movie, they get more and more abstract. The situation gets kind of broader and stranger, and out of control a little bit because, basically, you've done the thing so many times that you've always got to try and do something a little bit more the next time. I think this is a problem with sequels in that they get bigger and the themes increase and get larger too, and you get farther and farther away from the truly basic appeal of these films, which are the characters that we've fallen in love with. If you can do a great drama that just takes place between these characters in one room, the audience wouldn't give a shit. They'd love it. They're not really that interested in the space ship effects, but we keep trying to get bigger and bigger, let's go meet God and do all these gigantic things."

Director, co-writer and star William Shatner looks at *Star Trek V* rather philosophically.

"There are some wonderful scenes in *Star Trek V*," he noted, "wonderful acting scenes, wonderful kinetic scenes. In those moments, it's just as good as any non-science fiction movie. If entertaining, communicating and making people laugh is what we do in our business, I think *Star Trek V* accomplishes that. Still, the differences between what I dreamed and what's on the screen is considerable. From the first story thought I had to the way the film has resulted was achieved by many compromises, most of which I assume were correct because the film looks good to me. I hope the audience [agrees] with me, but I stand by what I've done. Overall, considering.... overall, I'm happy with the film."

Down time on Star Trek V provided William Shatner with the opportunity to write the novel TekWar, which in turn has inspired a weekly series that airs on the USA cable network. Shatner is seen here with actor Greg Evigan (photo copyright ©1994 MCA Universal).

Recently, in the pages of his biography *Star Trek Movie Memories*, he adjusted his opinion as follows: "And While I didn't by any stretch of the imagination consider *Star Trek V* a bad film, and indeed I was tremendously pleased with much of what we'd accomplished, I ultimately came away feeling like the big brass ring had somehow eluded my grasp. I was truly convinced that this was going to be a terrific film, but by the time it all came together, it was not. We'd come close, but since we were dealing with neither horseshoes nor hand grenades, close simply didn't cut it, and I was sure I had marked the end of the *Star Trek* films once and for all."

Favored nations clause not withstanding, the subject of Shatner's possibly directing *Star Trek VI* never came up.

Star Trek VI:
The Undiscovered Country

"Starfleet Academy"

After the chilly box-office reception of *Star Trek V* and the continuing chorus of naysayers criticizing the cast as being too old to continue, many suspected the silver screen voyages of the starship Enterprise had truly passed into the final frontier. But Producer Harve Bennett, in conjunction with *Star Trek V* screenwriter David Loughery, was hard at work creating a new vehicle to continue the *Star Trek* movie missions.

"Every time they go to make one of these *Star Trek* movies," noted Loughery, "the producers and the studio always run into the same problem in getting the original cast together. The reasons for that are money, power, creative differences, ego, health, unavailability....all of those things. Harve always had this ace up his sleeve, which was if we can't get everybody together for one of these *Star Trek* movies, we should do a prequel."

Called *Starfleet Academy*, the proposed film would have chronicled a young Kirk, Spock and McCoy's days at the Academy, as part of *Trek*'s 25th anniversary celebration. Instead, a sixth and final film featuring the original "classic" cast was put into production by Paramount, resulting in Harve Bennett's departure from the series.

"We had a better movie and we had a film that would have allowed them to make the same *Star Trek VI* eighteen months later," said Bennett of *Starfleet Academy*, which was aborted after objections from fans made the project untenable.

"I think there was a fat chance of that happening," commented Walter Koenig. "I can't read Harve's mind, but if *Starfleet Academy* had done well, they would have gone on with that group. If it hadn't, they probably would have abandoned the whole project."

"Because of the way *Star Trek VI* is being sold, don't miss your chance to say good-bye, it's unlikely that *Starfleet Academy*, which asks 'Would you like to know how it all happened?'

will be made," continued Bennett, whose previous producing chores included work on *The Mod Squad, The Six Million Dollar Man,* the Emmy Award winning miniseries *A Woman Called Golda* and *The Jesse Owens Story.*

Starfleet Academy chronicled the story of a young James T. Kirk, a Spock who is estranged from his parents and becomes the first Vulcan to attend Starfleet Academy, and Leonard McCoy, a 30 year old doctor who attends the Academy after having pulled the plug on his terminally ill father and is searching for meaning in his life. Michael Curtiz's

1940 film, *The Santa Fe Trail,* served as an inspiration for what Bennett envisioned as the classic triumvirate's first trek. The film which could have been made, according to Bennett, for $27 million would also have avoided the hefty multi-million dollar salaries of its leads—Shatner and Nimoy—as well as Kelley's take-home of nearly a half a million dollars and the $125,000 paychecks the supporting players pocketed.

"I pitched the idea to Harve at his daughter's Bat Mitzvah," recalled *Trek VI* producer Ralph Winter. "We had already locked in the *Star Trek IV* story-

The novel, Enterprise, bore some resemblance to Harve Bennett and David Loughery's proposed Starfleet Academy.

ing, but from the point of view of storytelling, because I worked so closely with these characters on *Star Trek V*, that the idea of doing an origin story—where you show them as young cadets and kids—was tremendously exciting. What it was, was a real coming of age story. In outline form, it was the story of Kirk and Spock meeting for the first time as cadets here on Earth. We've got a young Jim Kirk, who's kind of cocky and wild. He's not exactly what you might think starship captain material might be. He's like one of these kids who would rather fly hot planes and chase girls. Spock is this brilliant, arrogant, aloof to the point of obnoxiousness, genius. It's this mask he's hiding behind to cover his own conflicting human emotions. He's an outcast, he left Vulcan in shame against his father's wishes and, like all adolescents, he's trying to find a place to fit in, but he keeps screwing it up.

"Over the course of this story," he continued, "which is one year at Starfleet Academy, Kirk and Spock are sort of put to the test and they begin as rivals and end up as friends and comrades who learn that they have to combine their talents for the first time to defeat a deadly enemy. In the final scene, where they say goodbye at graduation and go their separate ways, we're able to see the legends that these two boys are going to grow up to become."

But for Bennett, who had spent a decade living with *Star Trek, Starfleet Academy* was not to be. The rejection of the project was a big disappointment for the veteran producer who planned the film as his freshman directorial effort.

"It meant a lot to me because I came out of UCLA film school wanting to be a director and other winds blew me to to other ports," said Bennett. "It was a desire of mine to direct and it was accepted by the studio and, the fact is, part of the deal was for us to do a *Star Trek VI*, with the original cast after *Starfleet Academy*."

But once word leaked out about the project, support was marshalled against the film and vociferously denounced on the convention circuit by members of the supporting cast, as well as *Star Trek* creator Gene Roddenberry.

Said Roddenberry in the pages

line with the whales and I said, 'You know, I have a great idea, let's do a prequel' in the middle of this reception for his daughter. I suggested we develop a series of films to be another franchise, another tent pole that we could open. We could do a prequel and find out how Kirk and Spock met at the Starfleet Academy. When we were doing *Star Trek V,* we got the studio to approve work on the script. It is an excellent

story, but it has been misperceived. It's a great story finding out about this young cocky character on a farm who goes to flight school and meets up with the first alien that comes from Vulcan and how they meet the other characters. It would have been a gift for the fans on the 25th anniversary."

David Loughery noted, "When I heard about the idea, I thought it was terrific. Not from the point of view of recast-

of *Cinefantastique*, "I didn't like it. Who was going to cast the new Kirk and Spock? No one has ever cast a *Trek* character besides me that's worked. Braggadocio or whatever, that is the history of *Trek*. It wasn't good. Some of it was like *Police Academy*. You could hardly do this without the magic of a group of characters tailored for *Star Trek*, which this was not."

Letters began to pour into Paramount decrying the planned feature as heresy.

"We were really caught off guard and surprised by the fans who reacted so negatively to the idea of this movie," admitted David Loughery. "Somehow they conceived it as sort of a spoof or a takeoff. That's where we got off on the wrong foot. The fans had misinformation, which may have been put out there by people for their own reasons. Certainly if we were going to make a movie like that, it meant that Walter and whoever wouldn't get that job a year or two down the line that they had come to expect. I don't know if that's the case, but I do know that the misinformation released had people convinced that we were going to do a cross between *Police Academy* and *The Jetsons*. It was never that kind of story. I think it's traditional that the fans have objected to different things. Harve's always been smart enough to double-cross them; give them what they've objected to, but surprise them with something that makes it good and worthwhile. We felt that there was a powerful story there, one that the audience would be interested in. We're always interested in young Indiana Jones and young Sherlock Holmes, and how they started and came to be who they are. This was sort of the way to explain Kirk and Spock and where they came from."

"There *was* pressure from a lot of people not to do this," Bennett emphasized. "I don't think there was any question that the self-interest of the supporting cast was not served by it and if I was George Takei, I would do exactly what he did and if I were Jimmy Doohan, I would be a really unhappy man. The only one I'm really furious at though is Jimmy Doohan. He said I was fired and I can't abide lies. My term was up and I was offered $1.5 million to do *Star Trek*

Star Trek VI represented the last time that Leonard Nimoy, William Shatner and DeForest Kelley would appear together on film (photo copyright © 1994 Albert Ortega)

VI and I said, 'Thanks, I don't wish to do that. I want to do the Academy.'"

Responded Doohan, "I was impressed with Harve when he first came in and did *Star Trek II* and *III*, but I think he got a little greedy. He wanted things his own way. He wanted to take over *Star Trek* for himself. What the heck, you don't do that sort of thing, trying to destroy instead of building. He obviously did not realize the strength of the old

cast. The whole thing would have been starting out as if from scratch. I think it was [Frank] Mancuso who didn't realize we were not going to be in it. When he found out, [he] said good-bye Harve."

"My last words to Mancuso before he was asked to leave [by the then recently installed head of Paramount, Stanley Jaffe] was if it was a question of anyone's concerns about my directing, I'd back off on that," said Bennett. "They

CINEFANTASTIQUE

April 1992

$5.50
CAN $6.60
UK £3.40

STAR TREK VI

FILMING THE LAST HURRAH

EVIL DEAD III
Filming Sam Raimi's
wild and wacky horror

NAKED LUNCH
Cronenberg on drugs,
sex and special effects

STEPHEN KING'S SLEEPWALKERS
Columbia wades into the blood and gore

then offered me *Star Trek VI* and gave me a pay or play commitment to direct and produce *Starfleet Academy* afterwards. My position was, and I think it was correct, that they would pay me to do *VI* and make the movie which would have been a real big, fat check for me and never made *Starfleet Academy*. To be paid off because the movie I might have done, which is being done by others, would close the franchise was not my intention. I had a life, it's not like I hadn't done anything else before *Star Trek*. The *Star Trek* curse is something that the poor supporting cast has to live with, but I don't."

Opined William Shatner, "Harve was striving to find an answer for the studio's question 'Are these guys too old to continue?' So he tried to find a solution as a storywriter and he must of said here's a way of going. Apparently everybody agreed, but at some point they shut him down after preparing this production for a year and he got very upset about it and left. I wasn't too clued in on the politics of what was happening. I had heard about the prequel and was considering my options, but it was never approved and we didn't know whether or not there would be another *Star Trek* until the last second."

Bennett holds the supporting cast entirely accountable for the film's demise. "Their jobs and livelihoods were jeopardized," he said. "You have to understand there's good news and bad news for these people. They are the principal bearers of the *Star Trek* curse. The good news is everybody loves them and the bad news is they can't work anywhere else. They have managed to generate handsome incomes, some more than others, by tapping the convention and lecture circuit. That's fine, they're entitled to do that because no one is casting Uhura and George Takei because they're so identifiable and they become liabilities in other material. *Starfleet Academy*, like *Star Trek IV*, would have reached beyond the cult. It would have interested people who had never seen a *Star Trek* film which did not exclude the regulars, but it simply said, if you don't understand what it's all about, come see how it all began."

For Ralph Winter, *Starfleet Academy* would have ushered in a new approach to the *Star Trek* franchise for the studio in which a coherent plan would be created for producing the *Trek* films on a semi-regular basis as opposed to the sporadic, fitful stop and go start-up on a new film every three years with the arduous contract negotiations that initiating each new chapter entailed.

"*Starfleet Academy* may have looked like a mistake," said Winter, "but look at the franchise as a whole. We have a successful series of feature films, then a new television series and with the film series ending it made sense to start a new series of films. You could have opened a whole new frontier. When *Star Trek: The Next Generation* came out, the people said this will never work, how can we have a new Captain? It will never equal Kirk and Spock. But they've achieved their own success. It could have been the same with a prequel cast, now you would have three different fronts. Make the successful features with the original cast, features with a prequel cast and the television series with the new cast. That's what could have happened. You look at the long term and you develop two or three scripts at a time and you maximize production. The unfortunate part about today's economy and the thinking of these big companies is let's see how this one does and then we'll decide on the next one. There was never a plan after any of these films to do another one. *Star Trek II* was the last picture, Spock was dead. That was it. It's just getting too expensive to drag out all the wardrobe, sets, models. With a long term plan you could milk this forever and the fans would be thrilled, but if you go one step at a time and don't know where you're going, then the films are expensive and maybe it does make sense to the do the sixth film with the original cast."

As for the *Star Trek VI* that did materialize on the screen, Bennett has mixed feelings. "I'm sure glad that it's not my movie," he mused. "I was presented with the choice of doing *Star Trek VI* in 11 months and I didn't want to do a conventional film and I didn't believe I could do it in that time. The fact that they did it is a tribute to all my buddies, and they are good buddies. Nicholas Meyer is the fastest writer in the world, Ralph Winter is the most ethical and perfect producer of special effects movies anywhere and one of the nicest men I've ever know. It wasn't easy to walk away from that, but if your heart is not in something and you've earned the right not to have do things that cause you pain, then you don't do them."

In terms of the future of *Starfleet Academy*, as the saying goes in the *Star Trek* universe: "There are always possibilities."

■ "On the Beach"

During the Christmas 1991 movie season, while Oliver Stone was pinning the murder of President John F. Kennedy on the CIA and the military-industrial complex, simultaneously grabbing the covers of every major magazine from *Esquire* to *Life* to *GQ* to *Newsweek*, *Star Trek* was not only attributing the assassination of its architect of the new frontier to these familiar and conveniently nebulous 20th century arms merchants, but perhaps the very fabric of galactic peace to their nefarious machinations.

But, of course, no cover stories here. It's only sci-fi, right?

The genesis of *Star Trek VI* began when Leonard Nimoy, at the behest of then Paramount studio chief

Frank Mancuso, set about to revive the floundering film series for its 25th anniversary. In essence, he became the newest in a long line of perennial great birds of the *Star Trek* galaxy.

"Frank Mancuso had called Leonard into his office and said, 'Leonard, help me make this film,'" recalled *Trek VI* co-writer and novelist Dennis Martin Flinn, author of a number of well regarded detective novels including *San Francisco Kills, Killer Finish* and *Lady Killer.* "At that point, Leonard was the producer, writer, the director, the star and it was up to him to discharge those duties or pass them onto other people. Mancuso apparently knew he could trust him to get the whole thing going and to get it going quickly, and I think that had something to do with *Star Trek V.* Let's face it, nobody wanted to have anything to do with anybody who had anything to do with *V,* except as necessary. I don't think *Star Trek V* was entirely Shatner's fault by any means. Moviemaking is a very collaborative business, but no one was happy with it."

In total agreement with Flinn is screenwriter Mark Rosenthal, who, along with partner Lawrence Konner came up with the original storyline for the film, a fact that did not become apparent to the public until about a week prior to the film's opening when newspapers heralded, "Story by Leonard Nimoy, Lawrence Konner and Mark Rosenthal." Even the paperback adaptation does not feature their names amongst the credits.

"We were under contract at Paramount and the feeling was that they were not going to do another *Star Trek* movie," reflected Rosenthal, whose credits include *Jewel of the Nile* and *Superman IV.* "The guys were getting old and *Star Trek V* was a disappointment. Everybody was disenchanted with Shatner's direction. There was a bad taste in everyone's mouth and no one wanted to go out like that. They knew the 25th anniversary was coming up, and we were approached by the vice president of production, Teddy Zee, who's now at Columbia. Teddy called us up and said, 'Frank Mancuso has spoken to Leonard, Leonard was still upset because of the last one and he was floating out the idea of one last adventure.' He asked us what

Star Trek VI co-writer Dennis Martin Flinn seen in San Francisco, home base of Starfleet Command (photo courtesy Dennis Martin Flinn).

we thought about it. The reality was that I am a Trekkie and my partner is incredibly non-science fiction oriented. We were kind of a Yin-Yang but we liked that idea, because Larry would provide a good balance.

"Our initial response," he added, "was that we should do something where *The Next Generation* has to come back in time and work with the classic cast. The poster would be Patrick Stewart, William Shatner, Leonard Nimoy and Brent Spiner. That would have easily been a $100 million film. Feelers were put out on that and there were some very strong negative responses. The TV department was totally against it. The TV series was doing extremely well, and everyone was afraid that the old guys' egos would get involved and they would say that it was a sign of a lack of confidence that they could carry a film. So that was the end of that. When that idea got squashed, we had a meeting and there we said, 'What's going on in the world?' The wonderful thing about *Star Trek* was that it was always sort of an allegory of the United States and the Soviet Union. We had two meetings with Leonard and Teddy, where we said the film should be about a peace with the Klingons, and that it would be a nice parallel to reality."

Stated actor-writer-executive producer Leonard Nimoy, "The Berlin

Wall had come down. The Russian government was in severe distress. Communism was falling apart. These changes were creating a new order in our world. I thought there would be a new kind of dialogue, a new thinking of these relationships. And a whole new military vision and a whole new vision of hardware. Realizing that over the 25 year history of *Star Trek*, the Klingons have been the constant foe of the Federation, much like the Russians and Communists were to democracy, I wondered how we could translate these contemporary world affairs into an adventure with the Klingons. I thought it was an ideal way for us to have our closure too, because the Klingons for us have always been the Communist Block, the Evil Empire. It just made sense to do that story."

"The main thing we were concerned with," Rosenthal said, "was that we had never really gotten details about the Klingon Empire. There was a whole question of whether we should go to the actual home planet. What happened was that they felt in terms of budget, recreating the entire planet would be impossible, so it became this prison concept. The original idea was to go to the actual capital city. I still think it was a better idea, but you can see how this process happens. The first *Star Trek* had a horrendous budget and it was a bad movie. Paramount began to realize that the Europeans did not grow up with *Star Trek*, so there's a very small market for it. The studio always feels that they have to make their money in a domestic situation, which for a big-budget special effects movie is tough. When you write, you try to come up with stories that take place in one ship, because that's pretty cheap to do. When you start talking about sets and locations, the budget gets very high.

"At one point we had a discussion about using Chernobyl, and that really opened the floodgates," he enthused. "Then we began to look at specific events and, of course, recent Soviet history serves as some kind of basis for the movie. Once you get on that track of thinking, we said, 'What's really going on?' Everyone is paranoid that someone is going to try and sabotage peace between the Soviet Union and the United

States. Why not have the same thing occur between the Klingons and the Federation? It all kind of led to the idea of assassination. What if Gorbachev was assassinated and the blame fell on Kirk? That was really the key. We were also trying to see what else had happened in *Star Trek IV*, what kind of threads could be picked up. Everybody remembered that a Bird of Prey had crashed into San Francisco Bay at the end of the movie, and the Bird of Prey was equipped with a cloaking device. That led us to thinking. One of the rules about the Bird of Prey was that they had to decloak when they fired. What if, given the Stealth Bomber, they could fire while cloaked? That became an important element."

Nimoy returned to the studio and pitched the idea: a peace overture between the Federation and the Klingon Empire triggers a hostile reaction from those on both sides who had invested the most in the existing state of belligerence. The studio was hooked. This time there was no hokey science-fiction concept, no search for God, just Klingon battle cruisers and starships slugging it out in the stars...for peace.

The man who had once declared "I Am Not Spock," and whose character had been killed off in hopes of luring him back into the fold for one final film in *The Wrath of Khan*, had now assumed a paternal, nurturing role over the series. Nimoy had shepherded *Trek* for half a decade and now recruited *Star Trek II* savior Nicholas Meyer to co-write and direct the film. Hiring Meyer was an inspired choice. Not only did the veteran *Trek* helmer work and write fast, but bringing him onboard would help avoid any problems with Nimoy's co-star and fellow director, William Shatner, who was itching to get behind the camera again and whose ire would surely been raised had Nimoy attempted to direct his third *Trek* film.

"I think Bill had a good time directing *Star Trek V* and we stumbled," admitted Ralph Winter. "I'm sure Bill feels hurt by the results of that, but he's a big guy. He knows what happened and he's got his head held high and he's fine."

Shatner admitted to a degree of disappointment over not captaining from

the director's chair of what could be the Enterprise's final voyage. "I felt a sense of loss that I couldn't be the problem solver," he said. "I would have loved to have been immersed in those very same problems and bring to bear what I had learned on the previous film. But on the other hand there was a sense of tremendous relief, as I was only too aware of the pressures on Nick Meyer both from a production point of view and a political view from the studio and, as time would get short, the anxiety that was involved in trying to get it done on time. I was very sensitized to the things he needed to accomplish."

Shatner is quick to point out that he was very pleased with the film's storyline. "It's a really good idea," he said. "It's a classic *Star Trek* idea in that the important issue of the day is incorporated into the story of *Star Trek*, and by doing so—and because we put it into the future—we're able to comment on it as though it has nothing to do with today, yet it makes a commentary."

About Shatner's demotion from director's chair to captain's chair, writer Flinn laughed, "It's amazing what three million dollars will do. In *All About Eve* there's a marvelous line where George Sanders says 'It's about time the piano realizes it has not written the concerto.' You deal with star actors in every film and every television show."

"Nick is real smart," said Ralph Winter. "He's such a good writer. He's really committed to his work and he works very hard and pushes everybody and the envelope. Leading the troops, he challenged everyone to put out their best and we had a good time doing it. He's terrific and he does things that seem a little unorthodox. He brings a class and sophistication to the material that is great and I think that was his contribution to *Star Trek II* and *IV*. He's done it again."

Going to the beach in Cape Cod, Leonard Nimoy shared the premise credited to him, Rosenthal and Konner. with the vacationing Meyer, who had co-written *Star Trek IV*, but rejected overtures to helm *Star Trek III* and *V* in years past. This time Meyer was hooked, partially because the film he was in post-production on, MGM's *Company Business*, shared a similar glasnotinspired theme, but had been "butchered" by the studio, according to Meyer.

"*Star Trek* in many ways tends to reflect what's going on in the real world," said Meyer. "At its best, *Star Trek* appears to function as pop allegory-pop metaphor, taking current events and issues—ecology, war and racism, for example—and objectifying them for us to contemplate in a science fiction setting. The world it presents may make no sense as either science or fiction, but it is well and truly sufficient for laying out human questions. Removed from our immediate neighborhoods, it is refreshing and even intriguing to consider Earth matters from the distance of a few light years. Like the best science fiction, *Star Trek* does not show us other worlds so meaningfully as it showed us our own—for better or for worse, in sickness and health. In truth, *Star Trek* doesn't even pretend to show us other worlds, only humanity refracted in what is supposed to be a high-tech mirror.

"Leonard said to me, 'Let's make a movie about the wall coming down in outer space.' His statement just spoke to me," Meyer admitted. "What I wanted to do with it, was to widen the world of *Star Trek* before closing out the series, if that's indeed what's happening. The thing I've learned from these movies is that your only chance of succeeding is not to repeat yourself, not to try the same exact thing. I didn't want to go mano-a-mano because I had done that with *II*; I didn't want to make a comedy because I felt *IV* was the most broadly comedic of any of them. So I thought, 'I want to make an ensemble piece and I want it to be a political thriller.' Like everybody else, I was fascinated by the events of 1989 on. I had been in Berlin working on another film and I had seen the wall coming down. God, what are the possibilities? What are the potentials for greatness or disaster? Who would have thought it? It's a bright spot, but it's filled with the potential for real disaster, and this is the theme of the movie, because change is *real* scary. In this film, the intention is certainly to deal with what people do when they are confronted with the prospect of radical change. There are some people who are capable of embrac-

ing it, and some who have a lot of trouble with it."

It was in May of 1990 that Mancuso had first called Nimoy to his office to recruit him to have a new *Star Trek* film featuring the "classic" cast ready for the show's 25th anniversary. By October of that year, Flinn and Meyer were completing their first draft script based on the Konner and Rosenthal story.

"Nick was involved with *Company Business* in London and wasn't going to be able to write the screenplay in time to get the film into production for the release date that would coincide with the 25th anniversary," recalled Flinn. "So he told Paramount that the only way he could do it is if he could co-write the script with me, and that's how it came about. He was kind enough to trust me, and while he was in London we communicated via computer. When we turned in our first draft in December of last year, the studio greenlighted it."

The screenplay evolved constantly, not least of all to reflect the myriad of comments from Nimoy, Shatner and Gene Roddenberry who, according to Nimoy, was very much involved in a creative consultant capacity.

"I'm a Roddenberry disciple," said Nimoy, who was reportedly one of the stumbling blocks in the release of Roddenberry's book celebrating 25 years of *Star Trek*. "He was very much involved. I went to him for regular meetings on this script. Everytime we had a draft, I met with him and we discussed it. He was very intrigued with the idea that we would be exploring the relationship with the Klingons. He was concerned in this particular story about the prejudice question, because it's an interesting issue. Sometimes when you show people showing a prejudice, even though your intention is to show that they're wrong, there are going to be people who identify with them. Here you've got a couple of guys saying, 'What do you think of the smell? Only the top of the line models can talk.' Gene was concerned about that stuff. He said, 'I don't feel good about Enterprise crew talking that way.' We pointed out, 'These are bad people who are racists and who turn out to be assassins.' 'I'm just uncomfortable with a couple of guys walking around in

Federation uniforms talking that way about another race.' And I understood it. It's a danger. By and large, he was quite taken with the idea of a Klingon detente. It was his idea to put a Klingon in the Federation on *The Next Generation*, and this was the beginning of that link."

Co-writer Dennis Martin Flinn, noted, "When *Star Trek* relies on science-fiction, it's a big failure. Maybe that's part of why nobody likes *Star Trek I* and *V* very much. Gene Roddenberry originally called *Star Trek* "*Wagon Train* to the stars" because westerns served the purpose in our society of being morality tales about good guys versus bad guys and, in many cases, in those thousands of westerns it was irrelevant that the setting was the Old West. What was important and great in a movie like *Shane*, for instance, was the story of the individual in society, and *Star Trek* is best when it's a morality play. That's what Gene called the original episodes, so when Leonard came up with the idea that the Klingons could stand in for the Russians and we could deal with the end of the Cold War, we were home free in terms of fundamentals that we knew worked."

Distilling the action/adventure plot was even more attractive to Flinn, who relied on familiar cinematic conventions to drive his metaphoric storyline.

"The idea sprung up from what would happen if someone attempted to assassinate Gorbachev," said Flinn. "In our story, Kirk might be blamed for that. Then comes something that I grew up on in movies, which is 'I've got to get out of here so I can clear my name.' I thought that's a good way to go and it worked for forty years in westerns and detective stories."

Despite his articulate appraisal, Flinn was not a *Star Trek* fan. Like some of the series' most important guiding hands, including Harve Bennett, Nicholas Meyer and *Next Generation* auteurs Rick Berman and Michael Piller, he was unindoctrinated in *Trek* lore before joining the production.

"The first thing I did," Flinn detailed, "was sit down and in two days watch all the films and some of the episodes. Since I wasn't a Trekkie, nothing was risky for me. There was an attitude on my part that if somebody in the first draft says Klingons don't eat with their left hand, they eat with their right, I'll just change it. That gave me a certain amount of freedom. I didn't worship those characters, so I was able to see them in a rather fresh light. The same was true with Nick who, having done *II* and *IV*, knew a great deal more about it than me, but nevertheless is not constrained. He's willing to add to the lore."

Ironically, while the original series prided itself on its progressive social commentary couched in the guise of science-fiction during the liberal '60s ("A Taste of Armageddon," "Dagger of the Mind" and, most infamously, in its pro-Vietnam "A Private Little War," in which the Klingons stood in for the North Vietnamese), *Trek VI* must rely on the same tried and true tradition in today's conservative climate where the entertainment conglomerates shun politics in favor of inoffensive drivel.

"The movie studios are in for the money and the less people they can antagonize the better," concurred Flinn. "One of the new presidents of production at Paramount said when he started that, 'We want to make films that appeal to everyone,' and said this very straight-forwardly like it was a marvelous ambition. He had absolutely no awareness of the detail of what he was saying. Art is grounded in personal prejudices and conflict. It's grounded in the specificity of culture, and to try and make a film that appeals to everybody all over the world is ludicrous. It's like saying we're going to make a film about grass growing, because there are so few things that everybody can agree on. You virtually can't have language in film anymore, only scenes of Arnold Schwarzenegger shooting people. That's clear. That's not in English, so the Cambodian distribution company has no problem with that. All conflict and opinionated writings and relevance to real life has been reduced in favor of fantasies in which two robots attempt to kill each other. In lieu of the fact we need more sequels, they don't ever really do it."

Flinn offered that had *Star Trek VI*'s story been pitched as a contemporary allegory, the studio would never have greenlighted the production. "Science-fiction allows you to do that," he said. "You can hide it from the execu-

tives; they don't get it. Nobody would touch it. The studios would say the military industrial complex goes to see movies and they would come up with a reason not to make a movie that exposes this. That's the kind of advantage science-fiction offers. Issues have gone to television, but they're the exception and not the rule. Our advertisers don't want you to insult anyone, they don't want you to insult serial killers. They may be watching."

Both Meyer and Flinn were not afraid to wield their pen to take the 25 year old characters in new directions. In addition to Spock's attachment to his Vulcan counterpart, Valeris, Kirk, who had always represented the best qualities of 1960's America in the finest Kennedy-esque tradition, was set-up as a bigoted right wing zealot, prejudiced against a very evil empire for having slain his son in *Star Trek III*.

"In the script there's a wonderful line," said William Shatner. "'In space, all warriors are cold warriors.' Both sides have come to define themselves by their antagonism. 'What will I be without my enemy?' The best *Star Trek* stories have their genesis in real life. For this story, you just have to pick up the daily newspaper."

"There are three kinds of people in the universe of *Star Trek VI*," Flinn pointed out. "The people who wanted peace, the people who did not want peace for their own self interest, and then there were the people, like Kirk, who had lived a certain way for 25 years vis a vis with the Klingons, but were intelligent enough to say what does the future have to offer? Maybe this isn't wrong. I think we were lucky to be able to see Kirk as a man who, if he was rigid at all, at least recognized his own rigidity. That in itself was flexible and not rigid. And of course it allowed us to create a character that, in essence, was a spokesman for the uncertainties and the whole idea of the undiscovered country. The future, being scary, got nailed down because we had a character that could say that."

Nicholas Meyer opined, "I think the heroic thing about Kirk and the rest of the crew is their effort to acknowledge, to confront and ultimately try to overcome their prejudice. If a man leaps into a rag-

ing torrent to save a drowning child, he performs a heroic act. If the same man leaps into the same pond to save the same child, and does so with a ball and chain attached to his leg, he must be accounted not less heroic, but more heroic still because he overcomes a handicap. And that's what heroism and drama is about. I think Kirk is more of a hero for being a human being and not less because he's super human, which I never believed."

"The portrayal of Kirk," added William Shatner, "attempts to show a man who has spent a lifetime imbued with the idea that his mission in life is to subdue, subvert and make the enemy submit to his nation's or his Federation's view. That's his whole training and that is the military training. He learns differently and that is the classic dilemma that *Star Trek* has sought to present in its most successful shows."

It was the central dichotomy in Kirk's character, and in the film, that Cliff Eidelman attempted to capture in his score for the movie. "It gave me a theme for the opening," said Eidelman. "It's Kirk taking control one last time and as he looks out into the stars, he has that spark again....one last time. It's his one last spark into space, but there's an unresolved note, because it's very important that he doesn't trust the Klingons and he doesn't want to go on this trip even though the spark is there that overtook him."

Nimoy, too, felt that the script's underlying theme was effective. "Spock experienced prejudice growing up half-Vulcan and half-human," stated Nimoy. "In *Star Trek VI*, Spock becomes an emissary against prejudice and discovers, during the course of the story, his own prejudices."

Despite the strength of its script, *Trek VI* was far from a sure thing. Once the word got out that *Star Trek VI* was indeed underway, while the fans rejoiced the cast became the butt of a many jokes. "The talk shows were making fun of us for weeks," remembered Flinn. "David Letterman was doing the search for geritol—so it was risky already. Two of the actors are 71 years old, but, hell, they're healthy."

With the realization that the previous film had been a commercial and critical disappointment, the producers of *Star Trek VI* sought to make the new film as different from its predecessor as possible.

Ralph Winter elaborated, "*Star Trek IV* reached out to an audience that had never seen a *Star Trek* picture before. We increased our audience 30-40% and *Star Trek V* didn't do that. Everybody started out to make a good movie, a lot of people read that script and thought it was going to be great, but we stumbled. Has that affected our thinking about this picture? Yes, it has. We have a different composer, a different look. We're doing everything we can to give this film a fresh look."

According to a member of the new film's production team, "They got ILM on the project very fast because they didn't want the problem that they had the last time and Lucas can deliver fast."

"We went away from the visual effects on *Star Trek V* because we thought we were going to get something new and different from another guy, which didn't happen," Winter said. "We went back to what we know is proven and the stuff that ILM did is spectacular. We were the benefactors of technology from *T2*. The look of the picture, the cameraman, the set dresser, the designer, everything about this film is trying to stretch and be something the other films haven't. I was a key member of *Star Trek V*, and when someone talks about it, it hurts. You didn't like it? Fine. We're trying to fix it. We wanted to make a film that the fans are going to like for the 25th anniversary. We looked at the areas of the picture where we could make it distinctive and different and not just the fifth sequel to a motion picture. Where we could do it and not spend a tremendous amount of money, we did."

Trek VI writer Denny Martin Flinn was also conscious of the previous excursions' missteps and history in crafting his first draft of the film's script. "I was most definitely cognizant of what worked and what didn't. Part of working on sequels is adding to something that already exists and what exists works real well, so don't fuck it up. That's a tremendous responsibility. With *Star Trek I* the studio said if it hadn't cost us $45 million, we would have made more money. It bombed critically too and it was Harve

Bennett who came along and got back to what had driven the episodes, which is a bit of an action/adventure with a strong guest star. *I* was a bore and *V* also suffers terribly from something that is a dangerous formula in film. If you spend two hours telling people wait until you see what's around this corner, you had better have something around that corner to show them whether it's a monster or a concept of God or whatever the hell it is. *Star Trek I* and *V* turned the corner and never showed anything at all. They were big letdowns. Even when you have a terrific film paced up till then, like James Cameron's *The Abyss,* you still feel this terrible letdown when what's around that corner turns out to be silly, confusing or non-existent. The more linear action films like *II, III, IV* and, hopefully, *VI* avoid that problem."

Added director Nicholas Meyer, "A lot of people said *Star Trek II* was such a terrific movie and had a lot of unkind things to say about *Star Trek I,* but I don't think they realize that *Star Trek II* wouldn't have been so good if someone hadn't gone boldly where no one had gone before and showed us, in effect, what not to do when it was really important. It's damn hard work to make those movies and I'm not going to look down my nose at any of them."

However, even with a suitable script, having a major feature film ready in less than a year was a difficult challenge. With the studio vacillating for months over the future of *Star Trek*, now it was up to the assembled team of director Meyer, executive producer Nimoy, and producers Winter and Steven Charles Jaffe to have a film ready by the end of 1991.

"We got a go on February 13th and we had to have it in theatres by December 13th," said Winter. "That's really a short amount of time and money for the expectation level. The fans don't think about how much the budget was, they just want to know why the picture wasn't good, if it wasn't good."

Problems resulting from the tight shooting schedule typified the production from its inception. Recalled Nicholas Meyer, "I told them it would take 55 days. They said you have 51 and I yelled and screamed and they finally

gave me 53...and I came in at 55."

But the tight production schedule was not the only daunting obstacle. With the recession cutting into box-office receipts and the failure of a crop of big-budget action movies in the summer of 1990, all the major film studios were preaching fiscal prudence when it came to their pictures. *Star Trek* was no exception. With box-office for most of the films in the series averaging in the $70-80 million range, Paramount balked when they were handed the budget for the latest Enterprise mission. The studio halted pre-production in order to cut its inflated budget, threatening to discontinue work on the film unless extensive production costs could be severely curtailed.

"This picture almost didn't get made," Winter explained. "It almost died a number of times. It's being made for less money than the last one and It's quite a feat. The above the line [cast and other non-technical related expenses] is substantial with the number of stars we have, so the money I have available to make this picture is a lot less than you have to make *Alien 3* or *Terminator 2*."

"This movie was actually cancelled at one point," said co-producer Steven Jaffe. "We were at a budgetary impasse and everyone resigned themselves to the fact that it was not going to happen. I went home and was very, very upset about it, because this meant a lot to me for personal and professional reasons. I just couldn't go to sleep. I grew up watching *Star Trek* on television, and doing this movie was a private honor. So I couldn't give up that easily. I said I cannot let this movie die, and I came up with a sort of radical idea that said maybe we can't afford to use ILM, because if it means making the movie with some other visual effects companies that haven't achieved the same reputation or not making the movie, then that's the risk I've got to take. I called Nick, Leonard and Ralph and I [told them my plan]. I spoke to Gary Luchesi and John Goldwyn, who were executives under Frank Mancuso, and said, 'Here's my idea, what do you think?' and they said, 'Well, it's interesting.' In about three hours they called back and said we want to hear your plan. Ralph and I said this is what we're going to do, and in the long run we used ILM and other vendors. But this is one of the jobs a producer has to be prepared to accept: compromise, because there's so many reasons a movie company will say no to making a movie and so few reasons why they will say yes. You're constantly asking yourself how important is this to me. A lot of us took pay cuts and people say, 'You took a pay cut on *Star Trek*, that's Hollywood, not personal.' But it meant a lot to us and the more we got involved with it, the more we were emotionally involved and I'm very happy to say I had a big part in making sure the movie got made. It was all teamwork."

Rejecting the nearly $40 million price-tag for the film, Paramount had put *Star Trek VI* into turnaround in early 1991, hitting the brakes on a project which was screeching toward production at warp speed. "Bill and Leonard made concessions to get this picture made because they wanted to make it, we all did," Winter said. "Everyone made concessions and, frankly, Nick and Steven and I deferred a significant portion of our salaries to get this picture made, because we believed the story was worthwhile."

"They deferred part of their salaries," concurred Walter Koenig. "That's not the same as taking points. This money is guaranteed, I hasten to add. The sixth movie was let's cash in on the 25th anniversary, maybe there's still some tread left on this tire. But it's true the studios were backing down from big-budget films. Paramount had just gotten burned with *Godfather III*."

Said Steven Jaffe, "One of the ways that Nick and I have worked together as producer and director in the past is that I have directed second unit on every movie we've done together from *Time After Time* to *The Day After*, where I was hired exclusively as a second unit director. On *Star Trek* the pressures we were under to do this project were greater and for less money than the others. It's a sensitive subject to me because it's something that comes up every single movie, and we've prided ourselves in the past on bringing in all of our movies on budget and on schedule or under, beginning with *Time After Time*. It's kind of disturbing when you have an enormous amount of pressure put on you as though

you weren't going to try and do it that way."

Scrambling to reduce the film's inflated budget, set-pieces were cut from the film and instead of building all-new Enterprise interiors, it was decided that redressed sets from *Star Trek: The Next Generation* would stand-in for the Enterprise 1701-A. "Those sets were built for *Star Trek: The Motion Picture* in 1978 and I've used them on every one of these pictures," said Winter. "We were fortunate to schedule the sets as soon as they wrapped for the season and we were in there ripping out walls and changing lights. As soon as we were done, we had to repaint, slap it back together and recarpet them. They were used for hallways, transporter rooms and stuff like that."

The bridge, however, was rebuilt from Herman Zimmerman's production designs on the fifth film. "We rebuilt it from the ground up," explained Winter. "On this one we kept the platforms and some of the wider forms and then we rebuilt everything else, we tied it together this time. We try to keep it as similar as possible because we are cognizant of the rules of the *Star Trek* universe and the laws we have set up, but each director brings a new perspective to it. I think the new bridge is very close to the one you saw in *V*. You really didn't see much of it in *Star Trek IV*, there's only one shot aboard the Enterprise. If you looked at what was on *Star Trek: The Motion Picture* and *II* and *III*, that shifted around a lot and the lighting and graphics have changed drastically. We also went on a lot of locations around town. We shot a briefing room scene at a place a block away from the studio, which was perfect rather than build it, and we shot the peace conference at the end out in Simi Valley. If it was easier and cheaper to find an existing location and dress it rather than build it, that's what we did."

■ "The Gang's All Here"

In order to meet Paramount's demands for a pared down budget, the producers were forced to drop the film's proposed opening scene which re-introduced the cast. This was done to save

nearly one million dollars.

"The budget caused us to lose several sequences," said Flinn. "I think they would have been very beneficial to the film. When you're in pre-production, sometimes what you substitute is better, so who's really to ever know? But my original vision of the film, which certainly would have been twice as much money, was an epic action/adventure and it became a kind of detective story action/adventure. The word epic would not be considered applicable. Money always impacts on art."

Noted Meyer, "I loved [the round-up] and didn't want to lose it, but we just couldn't afford it. The movie was made under a very, very tight budget. The thing that *II* and *VI* have in common is that they're the only two in the series that cost less than their predecessors. I run a very tight ship. We wouldn't have gotten the movie made. I don't think the studio was willing to spend that kind of money. They were very disappointed with the revenues of *Star Trek V*, which was a very expensive movie. I don't think it lost money, but I don't think it made the kind of money they wanted. On average, these movies cost 41% more than their predecessors. That's a huge leap, my God."

Of budget-oriented story changes, Mark Rosenthal added, "We discussed the fact that the Klingons are this aggressive race. Originally they supposedly had this reptilian background. In regards to this whole thing about Kirk and his search to uncover the conspiracy behind the assassination....we originally came upon more primitive Klingon tribes who had an almost religious representation for the Klingons the way that they do for the United States in *Dances With Wolves*. They would be much more primitive and violent. We were going to do a whole thing on the anthropology of the Klingons, but all of that was dropped because it would have been too expensive."

Low-budget *Star Trek* was nothing new. Partially attributable to its origins as a television series, but more so to the disaster of the high-priced *Star Trek: The Motion Picture*, which had forever doomed *Trek* to being considered by the studio bargain-basement science-fiction.

"The history is the first picture

cost $45 million or more, the second one cost 13 and the third cost 16," explained Winter. "The fourth cost 21 and the last one cost $33 million. [*II, III* and *IV*] were almost made for the price of the first and the box-office generated somewhere between $70-80 million domestically."

"*Star Trek: The Motion Picture* was the last show there was literally a money tree and the studio said we don't care what you spend, just get it done by this date," added a member of the new film's production team.

Acknowledging the realities of filmmaking and of *Star Trek*, Flinn feels that *Trek* is less prone to suffer from the last-minute budget slashing than many other science-fiction films. For *Trek*, in which *Star Trek: The Motion Picture* is considered the worst of the lot, bigger is not necessarily better. "Money always impacts on art," he said. "Our budget is low for a science-fiction film. But it's hard to call *Star Trek* science-fiction. We weren't trying to do *Terminator, Star Wars* or *2,001*, so maybe *Star Trek* is better off when it comes more from drama and less from the invention of more scenes with aliens and things. In fact, I found that because *Star Trek* grows out of a television series, there has always been an attitude of low-budget: here's an alien planet and there's a foam rubber rock, and there's a red cyclorama in the background. The fans have not only put up with that, but embraced it. It's as if they're saying, 'We don't need you're high-tech jazz to tell a morality play.' Although *Star Trek* has grown enormously technically in 25 years, it is still fundamentally story driven and not special effects driven, even though we do have some marvelous effects in this picture. Maybe it's smarter to do *Star Trek* with a smaller budget and force writers and directors not to rely on fancy pyrotechnics."

Leonard Nimoy, Nicholas Meyer, Ralph Winter and Steven Jaffe labored over their budget projections to trim the proverbial fat and, in order to meet Paramount's demands, were reluctantly forced to delete the film's projected opening scenes in which the retired crew of the Enterprise were recruited for one final mission.

"What I had done originally was to give every one of the seven princi-

pal actors an entrance," said Flinn. "The scenes demonstrated who those people were and what they did when they weren't on the Enterprise. They were either retired or rotated to R&R and it added some humanity and humor to the characters. I called it the roundup. It would have been a very effective sequence and we held onto it until the very last minute, but Paramount was saying we're going to discontinue pre-production unless you cut another million dollars out of the budget."

After the film's opening in which the Klingon moon Praxis is destroyed and Sulu, who has been promoted to Captain of the Excelsior, informs the Federation, the retired crew of the Enterprise is recruited for one final mission by a mysterious Federation envoy with a glowing hand. In the first scene, the envoy arrives at Kirk's home during a rainy and foggy San Francisco evening where Kirk is making love to Carol Marcus—with whom he has apparently reconciled. "This sailor is in port for good," promises Kirk. "Take a look at my retirement pay if you don't believe me. I can hardly afford to cross the street." But when there's a knock at the door, Kirk is stunned to find that he has been called back to duty. As Kirk leaves with the envoy, Carol pleads, "But he's retired....you're retired!", losing Kirk once again to a mission. Getting into a car with the alien, they are propelled through the skyline of San Francisco ala *Back to the Future Part II*. They find McCoy inebriated at an upscale medical dinner, where the doctors are lamenting over a patient who actually had the gaul to request a housecall, and McCoy is disgusted. Looking over the files on the car's computer display, Kirk is surprised to find that Sulu is registered as "Still Active." Even more disturbing is Spock's status being "Classified."

The next stop is at a hangar bay where Professor Montgomery Scott is lecturing to a group of college students in front of the Bird Of Prey fished out of San Francisco Bay from *Star Trek IV*. He is attempting to explain the cloaking device, which they have not yet deciphered, and asks for help from his students. "Since Klingons don't defect, we'll take what we can get," he says of

the vessel which was captained by the Enterprise crew to Earth.

Chekov is found in a chess club where he has just lost to an alien. Kirk asks how he is. "Bored," Chekov answers. "Then I'm your fairy godfather," replies Kirk, who admonishes Chekov, "Never play chess with a full Betazoid." "I was robbed," answers Chekov.

Uhura is recruited at a Federation radio station, where she hosts a call-in show in which a colonist on Mars is bemoaning her oversized girth as Uhura is whisked away—much to her relief. The assembled team with the Federation emissary then proceed to Starfleet Command where the film resumes in which they are briefed on their mission to escort the Klingon Chancellor Gorkon (David Warner) to the peace conference.

"The whole story started earlier and we just had to drop 15 pages," Flinn said. "Maybe what I'm thinking of would have been rambling and slow and dropped in editing anyway, but there was a kind of 'The Over The Hill Gang' rides again attitude and a slower development up to the early stages."

"It would have been a fun round up," said producer Ralph Winter. "But there's no sour grapes with us because that ship has sailed. We all work within constraints and unless you have an unlimited budget, which few pictures have, you've got constraints and it was a very tough choice to make. At that time, it felt that it was the only thing to do. They're only going to spend a certain amount to make this picture and something has got to go overboard. I'm not a fan of the philosophy that to save 10% you make every scene 10% less. It's better to make the scenes you have 100% and throw out a scene that gives you the opportunity to make the rest of the film 100%."

Director Nicholas Meyer misses the round-up as well, but is not bitter at its loss. "I think every director in the world would say, 'Yeah, I could've used more,' and I'm no exception," he pointed out. "I came here to make the movie on a certain assumption and when I got here, my assumption was wrong by certain millions of dollars. I didn't have it, and that's the real world. You have to play the game. I think ultimately people may say how come we didn't do this or that, but that's nit-picking."

Also cut from the script were scenes involving the discovery of clues during a scouting expedition to a Klingon planet, which pointed to the conspirators plotting to sabotage the peace treaty. Rather than discover the evidence themselves, the Enterprise crew puzzled the mystery out onboard. Also suffering from the budget cuts was the money available for casting. The role of Klingon Chancellor Gorkon, for which City Slicker Jack (*Batman, Shane*) Palance had been considered an early contender, went to Meyer and *Trek* film alumnus David Warner, who had played the Federation emissary on Nimbus III in *Star Trek V.* "Palance was an early choice," admitted Winter. "But David Warner does a great job for us. He's a good actor and he fit the role. Mark Lenard played a couple of different roles for the television show and he did a good job and we brought him back."

Other changes were made to the Konner-Rosenthal story, not all of which were due to budget.

"In the movie," noted Mark Rosenthal, "there's this relationship between Spock and Valeris. We said, 'Look, Spock was already killed in one movie, so we can't do that. If this is going to be the last movie, let's do something really shocking. Let's break the mold a little bit.' We really talked about this being their last mission and stated that very clearly, so people don't think they're being jerked around again. In fact, I remember in the first meeting with Leonard we sat and watched the Robert Bligh tape about old warriors. Bligh is an American poet who for the past couple of years has started the men's groups that go out into the woods to find the real man within them. His position is that there are no positive male guardian figures, and one of his theories is that the old warrior in tribal society has to teach the young warriors how to do things. We kind of watched that tape and said, 'These guys are old warriors now, let's really make it that they're at the end of their career.' I very much wanted to have Kirk fall in love with Saavik, a Vulcan, so that they would produce a child who would be

like Spock, who had a human mother and Vulcan father. I thought it would be a wonderful way to bring the characters and their relationships to a close. Obviously they've changed that to Spock falling in love. Frankly, I don't feel it's satisfying. I think Trekkies would have loved it, and it would have provided more of a sense of closure.

"We also wanted to do this thing where while [Kirk and McCoy were] in prison, some of the characters they had met over the 25 years would be there, which we felt really would have tied up the entire series," added Rosenthal. "If you look at the second movie, which Nick directed, he dropped in all of those references from *Moby Dick* and *A Tale of Two Cities*, but this whole thing with Shakespeare [in *VI*], I think, got a bit carried away. We had a literary reference from a wonderful poem called 'The Idle King,' and it was about Ulysses and the end of his life, where he and his crew are very old and they decide to go off on one last voyage. It was very clearly a voyage to death. You know, old men rowing the boat again. So we had this bit where Kirk mentions it to Spock. Then Kirk is turned over to Sulu who turns him over to the Klingons, only it turns out that the President of the Federation arranged it all secretly so that Kirk *lets* himself get arrested. Ours had a little more twist and turns. I think that ours was a lot more textured. [But] all of the beats of the story were worked out in the script. Then Nick came in with Denny. I think there was a lot of budgetary simplification."

With the budget trimmed to a manageable $26 million, Paramount greenlit the picture on February 13th, 1991 with a mandate that the film be ready for release by the end of the year. The cameras starting rolling on April 16, 1991 but before then, the production team had to round out the supporting cast.

■ "Wanted: Master Thespians"

Once Flinn and Meyer fulfilled their first qualification for good *Star Trek,* creating a solid action/adventure story with a message, the second hurdle awaited and that was finding a strong guest

cast. With the assist of casting director Mary Jo Slater, they loaded the last *Trek* with a cast of all the Hollywood heavyweights they could afford.

"Nick wanted an all-star ensemble cast and in addition to the seven stars that have been in *Star Trek,* he wanted to populate it with stars on every player that wasn't a regular, even if you couldn't recognize them," said producer Steven Jaffe. "What's important to Nick, especially with the aliens, is that he wanted them to be very articulate and great actors that could project through the make-up. I think that's a very smart way of making it not just a really good *Star Trek* movie, but a good movie in general. It's very hard for an actor with a couple of pounds of make-up on his face to project through there. A great actor like Chris Plummer has the range and power to blast through it. You feel a personality and not just like you're looking at a guy with a mask on. To that degree, we achieved our goals. There were some people that we wanted that we couldn't afford. In the long run it may have worked out for the best, because I think David Warner is extraordinary in the movie, which would have been totally different from Jack Palance. I was also happy to work with him again, [as] the last time we worked together was on *Time After Time.* Kim Cattrall is extraordinary. We were very happy she wanted to be in the movie."

On being able to achieve the casting for the film he did, Meyer said, "I hunted them down and twisted arms and I said, 'Read the script.' When people read the script, then they wanted to do it. That was a good sign. Christopher Plummer's last day of the movie I felt myself going into a deep depression, and going over to have a cry in the corner of the soundstage. I was so upset when he left. First of all, he's great. Secondly, he's a really terrific guy. We were having fun and it was such a thrill to work with him. David Warner's an old friend of mine. I'd use him everytime I make a movie if I had my way. I think Kim Cattrall is the most underrated actress of her generation. I'm always surprised to find out that she was in this movie or that movie, and then I realize she's so good that she sort of disappears into the role. I loved working with her. I think she's a great actress and a real beauty too."

For Cattrall, who was initially wary of taking the role of Valeris, *Star Trek VI* was an exciting experience made even more intriguing by the constantly evolving script. Time pressures forced the film into production before Meyer could finish his revisions.

"Things changed dramatically," said the actress. "The final scene Leonard and I had together on the page was written as one thing, but [in] he and I doing it, it took on a life of it's own. It's an exciting scene to experience because not until the last moment did either of us know what was going to happen. You've never really seen Vulcans mind meld. The only other instance that Leonard could recall was when he was brought back to life and there was a mind meld. There is such an infusion of two people's chemistry and energy caught between incredible pain and pleasure. It's the closest thing to a sexually heightened experienced that you would get in a *Star Trek* movie."

"I'm used to opening new plays and having rewrites thrown at me," Cattrall continued. "To me, the test of a good writer and director is to challenge the piece. If it's just sort of the masturbation of trying to make something out of what you're not too sure about, then I feel manipulated as well. But what we all wanted was for the best possible story for all of the characters and the audience, because people are waiting for a really good *Star Trek* movie. It was wonderful, the script itself kept evolving. It was like a living thing. I don't think things written in cement or paved in concrete are the best. I think it's such a collaborative art form, that the more people who have a good point of view and want to help the project, the better."

Said Flinn, "*Star Trek* is known for great guest stars. I think [having] a regular cast helps enormously, because what people want more than anything in movies, and maybe in all art, is something old and something new. When the audience is comfortable they're happy, but at the same time that doesn't allow for any originality. So in *Star Trek II* you have Ricardo Montalban. Here we have Christopher Plummer, and you have the

David Warner, seen here as Jack the Ripper in Nicholas Meyer's *Time After Time*, portrayed Klingon Chancellor Gorkon in *The Undiscovered Country* (photo copyright ©1994 Warner Bros.)

best of both worlds. Even in the episodes, whether it was Joan Collins or Teri Garr, they would always meet some alien out there who, on a pure entertainment level, would provide something new so that you could tune in not just for your favorite characters, but the weekly surprise as well. We definitely have that with Christopher Plummer, who is such a marvelous actor."

"The thing that I can say *Star Trek VI* has going for it that none of the other films had, is the preponderance of quality guest performers," admitted Walter Koenig. "We have some really strong people. Kim was wonderful. There's a mind meld scene that the first time a mind meld is really sexy. It's very sensual. Rosanna DeSoto, Chris Plummer, Brock Peters, David Warner are all great."

"I've worked with Christopher Plummer and he's just a fabulous actor," added Jimmy Doohan. "I saw him at Stratford doing Cyrano in Canada, and he just wiped the floor with every other Cyrano in the business. He's just sensational. Thank God, we had a great sup-

porting cast because that's what this movie called for."

Decades before, Shatner had understudied for Plummer in *Henry V* in Canada, and now the two were squaring off among the stars in *Star Trek VI*. Unlike *Star Trek II* where Khan and Kirk never met, Kirk got to spar Shakespeare with General Chang face to face. "Mary, Queen of Scotts and Elizabeth the First never met and playwrights have been putting them together ever since," reflected Meyer. "Did they [Kirk and Khan] really never meet? They should have met."

Flinn was at first worried that Meyer's propensity for injecting classical quotations may have been overdone until he saw what Plummer was able to do with the polished prose. "Once we got this guy, Nick said, 'This guy can really do this stuff,' and kept adding more and more," said Flinn. "Whether it's pretentious or not, I think it depends on how it's used. It's a case of writing for the actor or getting the right actor for the role, which is a very grey line sometimes. Nick did polishes and rewrites right up until the night the scenes were shot. I don't quite agree with using too much of that sort of thing, but once you get Chris Plummer, suddenly it's working. In *Star Trek II*, he put the book in Shatner's hands and the bifocals and he made a marvelous statement that, no matter how information is delivered to us in the 23rd century, great literature will still exist and I thought that was a marvelous statement. In terms of literary allusions, I can only say to you that Nick is very, very well read with an education that is certainly classically oriented. I happen to have appreciated that for some time, and kind of went with the flow when I began working on the script myself."

One of the surprises that the film's casting offered was Christian Slater as a member of the Excelsior crew, serving under Captain Sulu. Noted George Takei, "I have a new puppy and it's the cutest thing. Its tail wags, it just bounces up and down. Well, that was Christian Slater. He was so happy. He lobbied to get on the set because he was a *Trek* fan from a child. My childhood dream was to swashbuckle in Sherwood Forest. He did that, but his dream was to wear a Starfleet uniform. He was like my puppy, bouncing up and down, dashing down the corridor, climbing up a ladder and saying, 'This is where Scotty did so and so.' He was literally a 21-year-old kid in his fantasy land."

Offered producer Ralph Winter about the film's casting, "Nick wanted to go for a classy approach. He wanted to go with actors who were going to make a contribution and really wanted to work with us. Despite not having the budget of some of the enormous pictures, we didn't want to be deterred by that. We wanted to find people who liked the material and would treat it as if it was the biggest picture ever made. We went for the best actors in each role. We were not looking for someone to say, 'Okay, I'll do it,' but people who got excited about the material, who were *Star Trek* fans and would love to be in the picture. That's what attracted us to Kim Cattrall, Christopher Plummer, Rosanna DeSoto and Kurtwood Smith. In other places, we went for a specific look, and also a good actor—Iman."

As for the comely chameloid, writer Flinn envisioned a somewhat dif-

ferent approach to the last woman to stir Kirk's loins. "The person I had in mind was as different as night and day from Iman," said Flinn. "I had Sigourney Weaver in mind, but I'm not sure we didn't come up with a better choice. I didn't imagine that we could ever afford her, but I just saw the character as a big, ballsy space pirate; a female version of the dark side of Han Solo. She turns out to be rather villainous, but a kind of swashbuckling female space pirate, and I thought of Sigourney."

Equally taxing was finding a place for each of the supporting players who demanded their share of screen time. Not surprisingly, in a cast that has been lauded and extolled for nearly 25 years with a nearly religious fervor, tempers and egos have periodically flared and often festered. One of the unique challenges of crafting a *Star Trek* film is providing the ensemble with their share of the action to appease both the actors and their respective cheering sections.

"You've got a picture with seven stars and you want to give everybody a meaningful role," noted Ralph Winter. "That is the challenge of doing something like this as opposed to doing James Bond or Indiana Jones, where it's clear there's only one hero with a lot of supporting characters. You've got a team of seven people that have to be given something meaningful to do. Nick [Meyer] has done a great job of weaving that together. We know who the core audience is and we've got to satisfy them, but beyond that it's got to be fun, it's got to be entertaining and capture your imagination."

One could hardly imagine Bernard Lee clamoring for a larger role as M in the James Bond film series, just as one would have found it equally outrageous if Denholm Elliot had held out for expanding the role of Marcus Brody in the Indiana Jones trilogy. But when George Takei expresses dissatisfaction with his navigating chores as Sulu, people take notice.

"Accommodating them is part of the assignment," Dennis Martin Flinn stated. "If you hate it, don't take the assignment. We had to make sure both Leonard and Shatner were satisfied and they both had notes from the first draft. In

this one circumstance, the actors probably have a leg to stand on. In any original film or work of art, the play's the thing and if somebody says my part isn't big enough, that's just ego talking. What a writer or a director tries to do is tell the story as effectively as possible, but maybe in *Star Trek* part of it is the story and you're adding to the 25 years of lore of these people. The audience wants to know what happened to Uhura and Sulu and we made a conscious effort to promote Sulu, maybe partially because he's been complaining about being a navigator all his life and certain things fell into place..and maybe others didn't."

"It's a terrific picture for everybody," Jimmy Doohan remarked. "George finally got to be somebody on his own ship and Leonard had a lot to do with that."

In *Star Trek II*, Chekov was given a larger role as a member of Captain Terrell's crew. In *Star Trek V* it was Uhura whose nude dance captured the attention of a desert scouting party. Spoiled by *Star Trek IV*, the entire cast got into the action as the reconnaissance parties looked for whales in '80s America. For Koenig, these opportunities to work away from his William Shatner were a godsend.

"*Star Trek II* was a delight from start to finish and one of the greatest delights was working with Ricardo Montalban and Paul Winfield, and not being on the Enterprise having to be judged by our leading man," said Koenig. "It was great not having scenes reblocked by our leading man, which I found very oppressive. I was working with actors who give as well as take. Totally professional. There's no question Ricardo has a strong ego and that's great. He's very colorful. He's really very flamboyant. Working with him was a pure delight. He was always there for your close-up and always very giving. I remember Nick [Meyer] saying something to him about his performance needing fine tuning, and I thought, 'Oh shit, here it comes,' and he said, 'Ah, you're right.' It was beautiful. That's the way every theatrical experience should be. With us, unfortunately it wasn't. The two weeks I worked with Bill as the leading actor wasn't as much fun."

For Shatner, the supporting

cast's concerns are understandable. "Certain people and certain characters lose sight of the overall larger issues and are totally involved in their own world," said Shatner. "That's good for an actor, because he takes care of his own business and traditionally actors are totally self-involved. There's no reason for them to see where does this scene fit in and where does the character fit in. When the actor who came in during the last five minutes of Tennessee Williams' play *Streetcar Named Desire* who plays the doctor who has the last five lines of the play, when asked what the play was about answered, 'It's a play about a doctor who comes in,' that's okay. That syndrome has always been part of an actor's make-up."

Jimmy Doohan blames Shatner for the diminished role of the regular ensemble in their original show as well as the subsequent features—including the deletion of the revelation that Peter Preston, the dead ensign in *The Wrath of Khan*, was Scotty's nephew. Director Meyer, who re-inserted the scene for the ABC television broadcast, disputes this assertion, pointing out that it was a studio decision to tighten up the film.

"Was it the studio or Bill Shatner?" Doohan asked rhetorically. "Bill doesn't like anyone to do good acting around him. I can remember the complaining about that when we were doing the series. The scripts would come in with De having major parts and somebody talked them out of it and parts where I was favored during the second year were all cut out. I'd end up with six lines. De is very diplomatic and won't say anything bad about Bill, but he snickers behind his back."

In discussing Nimoy and Shatner, Kelley admitted, "They are obviously the two stars and I came up in between them. I used to enjoy standing back and watching them. I've done that before with Kirk Douglas and Burt Lancaster. I've never been an aggressive actor. I think one of the secrets of actors performing well is not to be selfish. The better the actor, the better you get. Some people are not that way at all. [But] we all got along wonderfully well. We have a lot of fun together. Bill can have a very funny sense of humor, particularly on a set. Like

all of us, when he wants something, he'll let you know he wants something."

Shatner, who along with co-star Nimoy, has been the principal beneficiary of *Trek*'s success, having segued into other roles successfully as well as that of a popular science fiction writer, is not surprised to be the butt of criticism and is diplomatic in responding to the criticism. "If the original concept of the show was still in effect and the series was still going today, the situation would be exactly the same," he said. "There are people whose names and parts are above the title and people who aren't. That's the nature of the business and that's the way these stories are told."

"I think he's difficult, he's the epitome of the star in many of the negative ways," said Koenig. "He's totally preoccupied with himself and his career and his work on the show. But he's not a vicious man. He's not out to hurt anybody. In fact, part of the problem is he's not even aware he's hurting people because of his preoccupation with himself. I don't want to give the wrong impression. I want it understood that I respond to the working relationship, not the personality of the man. He can be congenial and enormously seductive. It's very difficult to dislike him if he decides he wants you to like him. He has incredible charm, in fact I have to keep slapping myself. I think he's bright and can be creative. I don't think he's a storyteller, but it's important to understand that whatever frustration and resentment I feel is solely based on the working relationship."

As for the criticism he has received on the convention circuit and in the press from not only Doohan and Koenig but other members of the ensemble, Shatner is puzzled. "It's coming from a couple of people," he said. "I don't understand that. I'm not even aware of it, quite frankly. Occasionally I'll hear something from an ardent fan of mine who'll say so and so said this about you, and it bewilders me because I have had no trouble with them. Nothing certainly bad, nothing particularly good either. We have done our job and gone on and I have never had bad words with anyone. I don't know what vitriol is spilling out. The people who I see a lot of—Leonard, DeForest and the people in management

and the directors—I've heard nothing bad from."

Ralph Winter, who had initially expressed trepidation over working with Shatner on *Star Trek V*, has nothing but praise for the actor turned director. "It went a lot smoother than I thought. I had a great time with Bill. He was terrific and he was a lot of fun."

Kim Cattrall also was positive about her dealings with Shatner. "He's sort of a technical shark," she said. "He can technically do almost anything as an actor. He was a gentleman with me and it doesn't matter how I feel about him personally. We're both Canadians and I had a professional relationship. I never told him that when I was first starting out as an actress I was a day-player in a series of commercials he was doing. I don't think anybody does better what he does. He is Captain Kirk and he's amazing in what he does. I can't say I'm the same kind of actor he is. His technical expertise is like somebody doing a skill extremely well and you know that's what he's going to do. I never had any problems with him or his outcrys. I found him respectful, he runs his lines a lot, over and over and over again, which is kind of annoying, but everybody has their own way of working."

 ## "The Human Adventure is Just Concluding"

In order to envision the broad canvas that the film's script encompassed, with locales ranging from the decks of the U.S.S. Enterprise to the Khitomer Outpost to a peace conference on the fringes of the Neutral Zone to a Klingon penal colony, the Trek crew took their show on the road.

"The bridge scenes are the hardest," stated Nicholas Meyer. "I hate that set. It's very confining. It's 360-degrees and it's been done to death. I don't feel that my best work has been done there. My mind just goes numb and I'm grateful less of the film takes place on the bridge [than previously]. I think we made the ships feel more intense in a lot of ways by doing things different with the sets. We found if we made some of the sets smaller—the corridors of the Enterprise shrank, for example—they get more intense."

"*Star Trek II* was done all on a soundstage," Winter said. "*Star Trek III* was done mostly on soundstages, except for two days. I think when we get outside we broaden the scope of the picture. We did that very well in *Star Trek IV,* maximizing the locations. Eight days in San Francisco looked like half the picture was shot there, but it was also the largest logistical nightmare because of the amount of crew we took on location and controlling the crowds in downtown San Francisco."

For the fifth film, Shatner and company shot at Yosemite National Park for Kirk's mountain climbing expedition, and in the desert at Trona Peaks which substituted for the alien vistas of Nimbus III and the planet at the center of the galaxy. On *VI,* the temperature was considerably lower.

"Alaska was very challenging," Winter said. "When we went to Alaska, we took a smaller team and they flew up to the middle of nowhere. You could only get to the places we shot by helicopter or snowcab and the shots we photographed, humans don't get to see very often. The only way to get that is to be there in these harsh, extreme environments with aliens in make-up and stunt doubles. One of the guys who played an alien was so big he took up three seats in the helicopter. Applying make-up in sub-zero temperature had the normal people who live in Alaska saying 'You are nuts, why are you doing this?'"

"I respect Ralph enormously and we had a great working relationship because we were able to, not necessarily divide up the work, but share the burden of the work and there was a lot of burden to bear, mainly stemming from the fact that we didn't have as much money or time as we would have liked," offered Jaffe. "Working with another producer that you like and respect is a rare pleasure, and there would be other times where we would just discuss things together and say how do we solve this problem efficiently and creatively? It also allowed me opportunity to do a couple of complicated second unit directing

sequences.

"I had the task of starting shooting on this movie. I went off to Alaska to direct two and half days of very intense second unit on a glacier, which normally you should have had a week and a half to two weeks minimum. But I realized all bets were off here, and we just had to do the best we could. I went up with Hiro Narita, our first unit director of photography, and did some intense filming in an ice cave on top of a glacier with stunt doubles for Bill Shatner and DeForest Kelley, and it was very satisfying. A friend of mine who edited *Ghost,* Walter Murch, had a wonderful quote. He said, 'Fun is the past tense of shit.' Now I can look back and say about the 2 1/2 days it was great, it was a lot of fun. But we were getting up at 4:00 in the morning, driving an hour, flying an hour in a helicopter and it was like 10 degrees. We had one stunt man in about three and half hours of very heavy make-up, and we had to get out on the glacier, which is an organic location that changes. So whatever I had planned in my one day of pre-production scouting in certain instances, went out the window because the glacier moved. It was a real challenge. You have a crew there of thirty people and four helicopters, and they're all looking at you. You say what do I do?, and I'm thinking this isn't what it was like three weeks ago. It all worked out, it was really stimulating. Nick and Leonard liked the footage, and everyone was pleased and so it was a nice challenge to start the ball rolling and also to have it merge so well with Nick's work. I've directed second unit on a number of films that I've produced, and it's very hard, if not impossible, to tell what's first unit and what's second unit. I'm really proud of that because with Nick it's really easy, we have a shorthand and think in the same terms cinematically. He'll just have to say a few words and I'll know exactly what he wants. It makes it easier for me when I'm that far away and you're presented with choices that you hadn't expected, to say I know what to do for the movie, I know what to do for Nick."

Despite the budget constraints, Winter agreed the Alaska excursion was a trip worth making. "You do it for the camera so it looks like you're really

there, and it adds to the scope and size and reality of the picture," he said. "The audience wants to escape, they want to feel that they're on this harsh and unreal ice planet. The big screen and the wide picture contribute to that, and it's hard to duplicate that on a soundstage. You end up spending so much time and money to build or duplicate that on a soundstage, that you might as well be on location. If you took the real cast up there, the logistical problems are accentuated. You have to be more careful with the people who are not used to that harsh environment than stunt people who are prepared for it."

For Meyer though, Alaska was a missed opportunity. "I would have liked to have gone, but there wasn't the money."

Principal photography began April 16, 1991 at the subterranean dilithium mines of the "alien's graveyard" Rura Penthe. The interior of this Klingon prison camp was actually shot on an exterior location in Griffith Park's legendary Bronson Canyon, which is still recognizable as the Batcave from another TV show that became a cornerstone of '60s pop culture. In this context, it is perhaps even more appropriate to point out that Bronson Cave was also a favorite location for the Flash Gordon serials.

"Theoretically," began cinematographer Hiro Narita, "the Klingon prison was supposed to be an underground mine, a large underground cave with a few tunnels. It would've been too expensive to build it on a soundstage, so we had to deal with this fairly large interior/exterior set during our first week of shooting. They had a very high wall built which was supposed to look as if it were partially rock and partially ice, and halfway up the wall there was a ledge where the guards could walk and check the prisoners. Most of the scenes take place in this large area, which resembles an underground prison yard. We had to work at night to give it the feeling of being an interior, but we didn't tarp the set because we figured even if you saw the black sky, you'd think it was the roof of the mine.

"We were able to dress the actual tunnels to look like mine shafts, but the problem was that we couldn't drill any holes to attach our lights. There was no place to hide really big lights, so we had to devise some practical lights that looked like they could actually be in the shaft. We hid the lights behind whatever rocks protruded every few feet, and the art department also built a series of support beams behind which we could also hide lights. We ended up using lights that looked like industrial mining lights, so I didn't mind seeing them in some of the shots. The miners had battery operated lights built into their face masks. We also smoked the set, which created some problems in the case of the mineshaft because it was open at both ends. We had to block the ends to contain the smoke. Keeping the smoky atmosphere consistent from shot to shot was tricky. I noticed a slight difference in the density of the smoke from angle to angle, but I hope no one else will. The overall effect is very dark and creepy."

Alterations in the caves were made by production designer Herman Zimmerman, who fashioned an elaborate set to extend out from the caves, allowing the night sky to act as the roof of the underground colony. Among other films that have set up shop at the Bronson Caves have been *The Searchers, Ten Tall Men, Julius Ceasar, Something of Value* and *The Last Days of Pompeii.* Needless to say, these sequences presented Zimmerman with his biggest challenge on the film.

"Rura Penthe is an ice planet where you can't survive on the surface for very long," he explained, "and yet Kirk and McCoy have to traverse a great deal of this ice country. Before that can occur, they have to fight an alien in a kind of icebowl—a natural depression they climb into to get out of the wind. That set, more than anything, had to match the location. I went to Alaska on a survey and I couldn't believe how beautiful the glaciers were. They're made out of very translucent ice with a bluish cast and a great clarity and purity so you can see deep into them. Trying to surface-paint our foam set to give it that kind of depth was a real challenge. We wanted to coat the set in resin, which would've given us a tremendous amount of believability, but we couldn't afford it. Fortunately, with Hiro's help, we came up with a technique

that matched very well."

For the production's second week of shooting, the crew moved to Stage 15 on the Paramount lot, the studio's largest, to shoot the surface of Rura Penthe, which would later be edited with the location footage shot in Alaska by Jaffe. The filmmakers shot for three days in a constant deluge of fake snow.

"Some of the physical aspects of the film were tough," admitted William Shatner. "Shooting at night is always tough and shooting at night for a long period of time is tough. And shooting at home rather than on location is even tougher in that the house continues on the day schedule and we start working at six in the evening. The snow scenes were particularly tough, not because it was cold but because it was warm. We did it on the set and the plastic used was particularly odious and I had to roll around in it a lot. We were coughing it up for weeks afterward."

Shooting on nearby Stage 5 where the bridges of the Enterprise and the Klingon Bird of Prey were housed, were also the scenes aboard the Excelsior, in which Captain Sulu first discovers the destruction of Praxis and later rushes to the aid of his former ship, the Enterprise.

Week three of the production occurred on stage 9, site of the Enterprise transporter room and other interiors including corridors and the engineering room, all redressed from the *The Next Generation.* Upon completing work on the Bird of Prey sequences on Stage 5, Steven Charles Jaffe once again donned his director's cap to shoot second unit footage and, before blowing the sets up for dramatic emphasis in the film, he shot one of the production's most pivotal sequences involving the assassination of Chancellor Gorkon by Federation officers in gravity boots, who beam aboard the disabled Klingon ship.

"It was an enormous challenge," said Jaffe. "This was the sort of thing you could take a month on or longer if you were doing it the normal Spielberg way. We didn't have that luxury and I [viewed] at least a hundred video tapes from NASA on weightlessness. I was trying to define in my mind what makes weightlessness....obviously other than floating. What body language sells it and what

objects float and what it does to take the audience's eye from the physical restraints that you're under, like wires and the fact that the set isn't floating. I had to do a real cram course in weightlessness and it got even more intimidating. The more I watched these videos, the more I realized, God I'm into a corner and I don't know how I painted myself here, and what do I do to get out of here? Ralph was extremely helpful to me and I would take off my hat as the other producer and turn to Ralph and say, "Here's what I'm thinking of doing,' and it was great. It was fun to wear both caps and to turn to someone you really trusted.

"We also had a wonderful crew from ILM headed by Scott Farrar, and they understood that we didn't always have the luxury to do things the way they would like to have it done. There's one shot that I did where two people are floating in a corridor and they got shot by phasers. I wanted them shot back the way a shotgun blast would, and given that they're weightless, they could go on forever. Added to this, there was Klingon blood we wanted to see floating to really make it a dynamic shot. We turned one of the sets on its end so that instead of being a thirty foot corridor on the ground, it was suddenly a thirty foot corridor standing straight up in the air. I hung these two stuntmen on wires, put the camera on the ground and shot up at them so your orientation is completely different. When you see the scene projected, it's very hard to see how we did it.

"Added to that, ILM did a wonderful job with the CG blood. I had two elements that were very critical there. I had the stuntmen and the objects they were holding, and the question was what do we do with objects so they don't look hokey. One of them was a big clunky, Klingon lantern. The normal way to do it [so] you don't run any risk of that object looking hokey, is you shoot the object as a separate element against a blue screen. I didn't have the time or the money, and I did some video tests with the object on a wire and letting it go when they got shot, and it did a really interesting thing. It spun and the light pattern continued along the wall as it retracted where the stuntmen had gone, and we thought you'll never get this kind of interactive

One of the assassins who takes the life of Chancellor Gorkon and threatens universal peace.

light if you do it as a bluescreen element; if you went the expensive way. So there were a number of benefits to the budgetary restraints. I wouldn't want to give any studio executives the idea that you should never give them what they want, because they'll never be created, but in this case it helped."

"We did one blowaway arm on General Stex, and we had to make a casting of his arm and design a rig that blows off because he has his arm blown off," said special effects make-up artist and designer Richard Snell. "Interestingly, we did not have to rig it for blood. We ended up not making any blood rigs for the stump that gets phasered off and goes blasting away. They're in zero gravity and the blood would float in the air in globules, [which] was an optical effect that ILM took care of."

Recalling the shooting of that scene, cinematographer Hiro Narita detailed, "We had to remove the ceilings from the sets for many of these shots, but fortunately, most of the sets we used in this sequence were built for the film. Part of it took place in the transporter room, which is a set we borrowed from *The*

Next Generation and painted differently. For some shots where we didn't have to see the actors' entire bodies, we'd place them on a teeter-totter arrangement which looked almost like a small camera crane, then counterweighted the opposite end and moved it slightly to create a floating feeling. We augmented the wire-and-counter-balanced crane work with slow-motion photography, which helped create the illusion of weightlessness; we shot this sequence at about 40 frames per second to slow down the actors' body movements just slightly."

Unfortunately, Narita found that his suggestions on how to hide the wire-work were not always heeded by the film's production designer. "I knew that the plainer the wall, the more noticeable the wires would appear against it, so I suggested that by darkening the wall and adding a pattern to it, we could create enough visual confusion that the camera might not see the wires. Sometimes they followed my suggestions and sometimes they didn't. In any case, it's basically a matter of having ILM remove the wires optically using computer graphics."

ILM, for their part, was asked to create a substance with which every effects man is familiar—blood. The order was not for the human variety, but for the Pepto-Bismol-pink blood of the Klingon race, spurting from wounds in zero gravity. Scott Farrar and Jay Riddle were forced to wrestle with one of *Star Trek*'s unspoken rules, conveying carnage without invoking an "R" rating. The imagery they created is both beautiful and shocking—blood doesn't ooze in zero gravity, but spurts in streams of of pink pearls—and while the audience is stunned by the violence, it is not appalled by the gore.

"We found the imagery needed to be a little stylized," Farrar explained. "We wanted to be on the cutting edge, but not gory—this is *Star Trek*, not a Peckinpah film! Still, we wanted the sequence to have some violence and excitement, unlike anything you've seen in the films before, which are usually kind of mild-mannered. This is definitely a step beyond, and a lot of people were worried about taking that step, but I think it worked out just fine."

Farrar and Riddle modeled the movements of the Klingon blood after

footage of space shuttle astronauts pouring various liquids in a weightless environment. They also experimented by squirting liquids and soap bubbles into water to see how the force caused these substances to react, then filmed these tests at high speed. "We used techniques we developed on *Terminator 2* and *The Abyss* for creating reflective, liquid-like blood," said Riddle. "We created some new software and updated other software, which we call 'blobby.' Blobbies are just a way of creating irregular, undulating shapes by using simple spheres as our computer models. The interesting thing about blobbies is you can start out with something that appears to be one object and pull it apart. In order to create a blob of blood, we placed five or six spheres in a little cluster, then used the software to blend those spheres together to make an object with a smooth liquid surface. The clusters gave us an idea of how these things were going to move and what size they'd be so we could lock down our animation. Then we took those animated spheres and ran them through the blobby program to create our smooth surface. In order to show blood spurting from the Klingons' chest wounds, we first created a bunch of spheres coming out of the wound, and then ran that through the blobby program to create a stream of blood with pieces breaking off from it and floating away, which made it look more like a liquid."

"Interaction with objects in the scene is something we're always striving for," Riddle added, "so we rendered the reflections of the flashing emergency lights in the Klingon ship into our animated blood and cast shadows from our CG blood onto the assassins, shadows which obviously didn't exist in the original photography. We added those shadows by making a match model of the assassins, which means that we created an object in the computer to simulate the shape and movement of the assassins' bodies as they walk. We used our CG blood to cast shadows onto that matched model, then we later composited those shadows onto the assassins."

A great deal of the sequence's effectiveness resulted from the preliminary effort of Art Director Nilo Rodis, who was using cutting-edge technology

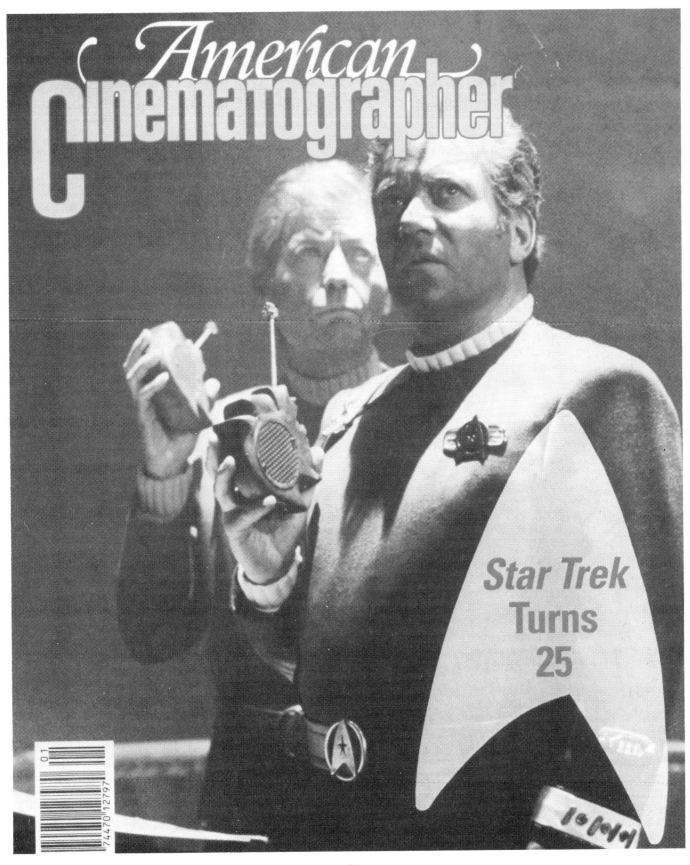

American

Cinematographer

Star Trek
Turns
25

to recreate the film's storyboards on video. "This was especially necessary in the case of the assassination sequence, because the set was supposedly turned upside down," Rodis said. "When we first visualized the scene on paper, there was no set, but once they started building the set, we actually shot that sequence on video, complete with actors. We printed the shots out right from the video screen, cropped them to the Panavision format and replaced the original hand-drawn storyboards. That way, when Stephen Jaffe and the second unit shot the scene, they already knew the basic parameters of the storytelling Nick had agreed on."

Rodis is the first to admit that hand-drawn storyboards often cheat in terms of the dramatic perspective and lighting, and many of them are too complex to ever be filming in a single shot. "I cheat like hell," he laughed. "My medium is paper, and my job is to draw you into the drama, so if I need to put an impossible perspective on the ceiling, I'll do that to dramatize the point. Nick always understood that. Visualization gets you to believe in a mood or a concept, but the longer you stay in that medium, the more unreal it gets, so shooting video storyboards and printing them out on paper became more real. I learned that the sooner I replace the original concept illustration with something more real, the sooner I understand what kinds of problems the crew will have. By dong it this way, we were able to adjust the original idea to work under real-world constraints."

In the completed film, the assassination scene is one of the most spectacular sequences in the movie and has continually elicited astonished reactions from the audience.

DeForest Kelley's strongest memory of the film concerns the moments that follow Gorkon's assassination, when McCoy and Kirk beam over to the Klingon ship and the good doctor attempts to revive the Chancellor. This is seemingly the actor's most physical medical scene in the show's 25 year history.

"Yes it was," Kelley concurred. "When I read the script, I knew it was going to be a difficult scene to do. It's the first time I've ever asked a director to go

to the set before we got on it to look at the situation and know exactly what's going to go on before we get into it. It's also interesting to me—and appealing to me—that [McCoy] lost him; that all the modern instruments didn't mean a damn thing and he goes back to the old fashioned way to try and bring this man around long enough to say something, and the complete frustration and then the horrible feeling when he loses him. I felt it was a very important scene.

"We almost had a tragic acident on that," he continued. "There was a huge lamp up above, a huge round black light. We spent two days on that scene. When I was trying to bring David [Warner] around, this light exploded and the glass just missed my neck and dropped so close to David's head, it was just a miracle that neither one of us was seriously injured. They put another one in right away and we did it again. Later, my fist hit it and it busted my knuckles. Blood started to come out of my knuckles. I saw this blood when my hand came down and I forgot about pulling the punch, and I hit David so hard on the chest that his eyes just popped open. I *really* brought him around."

Moving to stage 8, director Nicholas Meyer shot the memorable state dinner in which the Enterprise crew dines with the Klingon delegation led by Gorkon. There everyone espouses their true feelings about the upcoming peace talks assisted with a healthy dose of Romulan ale. On Stage 14, which housed the Klingon courtroom, Kirk and McCoy are put on trial for killing Gorkon and are defended by a familiar face, Colonel Worf played by *Next Generation*'s Michael Dorn.

"The funny thing is that I heard about it through the grapevine and just rumblings. It wasn't anything definite," said Dorn. "What solidified the whole thing was Nick Meyer was on the set with Herman Zimmerman, the former production designer from our show and the movie, and he just happened to walk by. We were introduced and he said 'I wrote a part for you on the show,' and that was it. It wasn't like I was privvy to the genesis of it because you hear so many things. The answer that they gave me was that the story lent itself to Worf

being in there and they wanted to have a thread between the old and the new."

Another daunting logistical nightmare was the film's finale, the peace conference at Camp Khitomer with its myriad aliens requiring hundreds of prosthetic appliances, action and stunts. "We went on location in Simi Valley and I have never been on a picture where we had 50-60 make-up people," Winter said. "We had more power and lights for the make-up trailers than we did for the shooting of the picture. We ran a 24 hour operation for four days out in Simi Valley that was incredible to plan and pull off, and we started planning for that in March. Several hundred extras and aliens and people and things is staggering logistics and we called in a lot of favors. A lot of people worked really hard and I think that it's on the screen."

The climactic scene in which the Enterprise crew rushes to prevent another assassination, this time that of the Federation President played by genre veteran Kurtwood Smith (*Robocop*), was actually shot at the Brandeis-Bardin Institute, a synagogue in Simi Valley. In it, the temple was redressed to serve as the Federation conference hall and the exterior was given life by the artists at Matte World, who supplemented ILM's work on the production. The scene brought together representatives from all over the galaxy and it included over 150 extras, 50 make-up artists and myriad additional costumes. According to producer Ralph Winter, over 325 lunches were served every day.

Said Klingon make-up designer and artist Richard Snell, "We had a runner that was running back and forth between our shop and location on a daily basis. We had our make-up room set up and I would have a runner go out there with boxes of all the different designs and on a daily basis we'd find out what the shooting schedule was. They threw a lot of loops at us. We'd be shooting one day and the director would say I'd like to see a couple of these designs tomorrow, and if that wasn't what was originally contracted for I'd say we'll have to run a couple of more foam runs for that particular design. I'd make a frantic call back to the shop, saying we need a couple more of these.

What do we have in stock that's seamed, painted, ready to go? So we were delivering prosthetics painted with a base coat of pax paint, seamed and ready to be dropped on the head so there would be a minimum of fumbling by the make-up artists. Once we hand it over to the make-up people, we don't have as much control as we wanted to get it as ready to go as possible."

Filming concluded on the Paramount lot alternating between Stages 5, 8 and 9, completing all principal scenes within the confines of the Enterprise as well as at the President's office at Federation headquarters, now based in Paris, France.

With the completion of principal photography, champagne corks were popped and tears ran freely as everyone among the cast and crew realized that this may very well be the final chapter in the logbook of the Enterprise 1701-A. What had begun 25 years before at Desilu Studios had now come to a close.

"I started my career at Paramount and it looks like after these 25 years I'm going to end it here," said De Forest Kelley, whose memorable portrayals of Dr. Leonard "Bones" McCoy may now be over.

As the cast and crew went home that night, one knew that the *Star Trek* saga was not over because even as the actors walked off the lot, craftspeople were busy repainting and recarpeting the hallways and decks of Stages 8 and 9 for the 24th century as principal photography neared for *Star Trek: The Next Generation*'s fifth season premiere, "Redemption." Suddenly, it was 75 years later, and the Enterprise was setting sail yet again.

■ "Somebody's Got to Shoot the Future"

For cinematographer Hiro Narita, working on *The Undiscovered Country* was an entirely different experience than shooting his last project, *The Rocketeer*, where he had the time and money to create that lavish period fantasy. Not so on *Star Trek VI*, where both time and money were rare commodities indeed.

Narita's involvement in the project began with a phone call from Steven Jaffe, who has been a friend since hiring the cinematographer to shoot some footage of the Golden Gate Bridge for *Who'll Stop the Rain?* fifteen years ago. Having shot both *The Rocketeer* and *Honey, I Shrunk the Kids*, he was somewhat concerned that most producers would look at his reel and see a man who could shoot special effects extravaganzas and nothing else, despite the fact that *The Rocketeer* was a period fantasy and *Honey, I Shrunk the Kids* was really a contemporary comedy with science-fiction overtones. "Even today," he said, "I'll get questions like, 'Do you think you can light a woman?' Before, when I did *Never Cry Wolf*, the only scripts I received dealt with animals. Now that I've dealt with giant scorpions, Spock and the Rocketeer, some producers cannot translate that into other stuff. I don't want to be typecast."

Narita's fears were somewhat assuaged when he learned that the film was going to be directed by Nicholas Meyer, with whom he'd wanted to work since he saw *Time After Time*. "I read the script for *Star Trek VI*—rather reluctantly—and I liked the story," he recalled. "So I decided to meet Nick. I was very open about not having seen the show or many of the movies; I saw the very first one, and I must've seen *II* on television, and that's it. I told him I didn't have enough knowledge to launch on the project, but he liked the fact that I wasn't a Trekkie and didn't have a lot of preconceived notions."

In spite of Narita's best efforts to talk his way out of the job, Meyer quickly saw that he could bring a freshness to the project; a willingness to establish his own unique look, things a fan of the old TV or current film series might be afraid to do. "Nick was looking for something stylistically new," he said. "I don't know if there was any continuity of style from the television series through *Star Trek V*. I've seen enough of the TV series to know that there was a certain simplicity that became a style, but I wasn't sure if there was a consistent style to the movies. I'm sure they unconsciously tried to maintain a certain look, none of which I needed to worry about. I wanted to establish a look based on this story and that was the reason I looked forward to making the film. I always felt the actors would supply the continuity, so changes in the images were not going to shock the audience."

Each of the films in the series has been shot by a different cinematographer hoping to change the look of the all-too-familiar Enterprise bridge, corridors and transporter rooms. Narita's aspirations were no less grandiose, and he and Meyer had discussed the look they hoped to achieve prior to filming: "Nick showed me two films, *Alien* and *Outland*. He liked that kind of look, which depended heavily on art direction and color, and he wanted the spaceships in this film to have a submarine feel."

The task sounded simple: just build sets that would accommodate the new ideas, as Meyer did when he revamped the entire look of the film series for *Star Trek II*. However, Paramount's conservative fiscal caveat made a huge dent in Narita's plans. "Since the ship has been taken out of storage and made to function for this mission, I thought it should have a patched-up, heavier, more claustrophobic look as compared to the open, well decorated set we had to work with, but that was beyond my control," Narita said. "I knew the production designer, Herman Zimmerman, was brought in because he's done other *Star Treks*, and because he knew how to deal with existing sets and so on, but I felt he wanted to be very faithful to the look that had already been established. So I decided to challenge myself to see what I could do within all these limitations. The challenge on my part was to create something new, or at least slightly different, partially using existing sets. In some cases, I succeeded in making it very different, in others I didn't, maybe partially through lack of imagination on my part. Sometimes I was overwhelmed by how little I could do."

Narita very quickly found he was straitjacketed most by the look of the Enterprise bridge built for *Star Trek V*, which featured the black instrument panels its director, William Shatner, had demanded. "I wanted to approach it differently in terms of lighting, but all of the existing practical lights were beyond my control. They changed the color a little bit and some of the graphics, but structurally it was the same. I felt that to create the shafts of light necessary to convey the submarine quality Nick wanted, we needed a certain kind of value and tonality in the background walls, which was difficult to achieve using an existing set," Narita explained.

"I lit as spottily as possible. I didn't want to use too much smoke on the Enterprise, because I didn't want it to end up looking too much like the Klingon starship. For that reason, I decided to keep the look of the Enterprise pretty clean, but with a little more contrasty lighting. To make things even more complicated, we were forced to use the Enterprise bridge to double for that of Sulu's command, the Excelsior. In that case, we just changed the colors on the set. To save money, we also used a repainted corridor set from the *Next Generation* series."

Another leftover from *Star Trek V* was the Klingon Bird of Prey bridge set, which Narita found far more to his taste. "The Klingon interior had a dark background and the same rusty red tone as in the earlier films, so by adding a little bit of smoke, I found it very easy to create those shafts of light Nick wanted. The set had more texture to it in general, and I was able to create some dramatic lighting on the Klingons using a bottom light shooting up through the grating in the floor."

Shooting aboard the Klingon vessel proved more challenging photographically than shooting on the Enterprise, primarily due to an exciting assassination sequence with a bloody zero-gravity aftermath. "I wouldn't say we had a lot of elaborate camera movement on the Klingon ship," Narita cautioned, "but we did have more cuts per scene to create tension and drama. For example, we spent three days shooting the assassination scene and our second units show a lot of pickups as well."

While Narita was accustomed to combining practical and optical effects, he was frustrated by the need to light a scene for principal photography, then relight it to accommodate special effects. "The scene has to look the same, even though we might be multiplying the

amount of light. It's not an easy thing to do. A scene might be lit with a couple thousand watts to begin with, and then, all of a sudden, I'm dealing with 5Ks; how do I keep a similar look? If the color temperature's different, how do I make that footage match as closely to the original as possible? It's never the same and I can only recreate it halfway decently on set. I know eventually we can change it with the timing, but then everything else changes. There were many shots like that, which made things tough. Fortunately, ILM was actually able to readjust the contrast and sometimes burn in areas that were too bright, which was literally like printing a series of stills."

Those familiar with the technical history of the *Star Trek* films will no doubt be surprised to learn that there wasn't a single blue screen shot to be found in *Star Trek VI*. Instead, black screen was used outside the windows of the Enterprise, where space effects would later be added by ILM. "It only became tricky when people passed in front of the screen," Narita related. "In that case, the fore and background people had to be in reasonably sharp focus, and that meant we needed a lot of light. That was very time-consuming, so we tried to avoid overlapping actors with the screen."

In addition to maintaining the status quo with the look of the Klingon ships and the Enterprise, Narita learned that many of the actors from the TV series preferred to appear unaltered by the passage of time. Unfortunately, the crew of the Enterprise are not the same people they were when *Star Trek* took its maiden voyage in 1966. Meyer stepped in when necessary to smooth things out. "The actors wanted to look great," Narita candidly pointed out, "but I lit them in the way the story required. I was constantly concerned about their appearance, but at the same time, my belief was that if a character was lit the same way throughout the film, no matter how good his performance might be, [the lighting] might not help the actor or the picture. William Shatner felt he looked best in certain lighting situations and sometimes I took his suggestions. I'm not sure how understanding he was, but he accepted it."

Narita was fair in his decision to light for the drama, extending this

approach to include those who wore heavy prosthetic makeup as well. "Those actors may not look too attractive either," he smiled. "As we went along, we tried to adjust the coloration on some of the characters slightly. Sometimes in a warm ambient, the Klingons looked too red, so the makeup people had to adjust it or I'd adjust my lighting here and there. On *Star Trek*, I found working with the makeup was much easier than on *The Rocketeer*, where Lothar had to be believable as a real person. At least for this film, they didn't have to look human."

Due to the budget restrictions, in lieu of building sets the production tried to make use of some existing locations in and around Los Angeles. "We shot a peace conference scene at Brandeis University in Simi Valley," Narita remembered. "There was a gigantic circular auditorium which the art department redecorated a bit to make it look like a conference room. Similarly, we shot a briefing scene in an auditorium of a Presbyterian church off Gower in Hollywood. It was just a nice space and we kept the background as dark as possible—only the conference table and the podium were lit—so you'll never know it was a church when you see the film. We also made these triangular shaped lighting supports, which we rented from some rock video people, part of the set. The director didn't mind that look so long as we never saw the lights themselves."

While he did have to contend with some existing locations and sets for the Klingon Bird of Prey and Enterprise interiors, Narita is quick to point out that the *Star Trek VI* did boast some unique sets that were completely unlike anything previously seen in the film series. Foremost among these was a Klingon courtroom built on Paramount's Hollywood lot, used expressly for the sequence in which Kirk and McCoy are tried for the murder of Chancellor Gorkon. To make the courtroom set appear larger, he created a hot spot at its center, where the accused sit beneath a brilliant light which radiates outward before falling off dramatically at the outer edges of the frame; the Klingons in the audience appear as mere silhouettes in seats, thus hinting at greater numbers beyond. To further enhance this illusion, the trial sequence begins with a bird's-eye-view matte painting of the courtroom.

"This was in the most exciting sequences in terms of both the storytelling and the visuals, so I tried to achieve more for less," Narita explained. "Theoretically, we wanted to create the feeling that this arena was many stories high, but we didn't really have any space. The courtroom set was circular, and in this instance we didn't have to conform to any traditional style or look. The center area was at ground level and measured maybe 40 feet by 40 feet; then it gradually widened as it went up to form an amphitheater that was about 80 x 80, with lots of Klingons sitting in these angled rows of seats.

"I was able to create a fairly moody lighting in that scene," he added. "We wanted to make it as dramatic as possible. To create the strong shaft of light in the center of the courtroom above Kirk and Bones, we used an HMI malipso light aimed straight down through a piece of safety glass—just in case something were to happen to the lightbulb. The HMI was blue daylight and I didn't try to correct it, I kept it blue. I let the set be two to three stops overexposed in the center, and everything else was lit very dimly with a warm amber 103 gel. The judge was an albino Klingon, so he had a very pale face and white hair that was almost hidden under a large black hooded cape. Nick wanted this white face only to become visible occasionally, so I aimed a little spotlight at him from above so you only see the judge's nose and forehead when he leans forward into the light. That was the kind of thing I really enjoyed on this film."

Because of the tight schedule and relatively large size of the courtroom set, Narita used a timesaving technique he'd employed for *The Rocketeer*'s South Seas Club sequence. "I used electronic dimmers on the lights for certain shots so I could control the lighting during the shot or change the intensity, though you certainly wouldn't notice the lighting change. It was useful whenever we changed the camera angle."

A highlight of the production was the on-location sojourn to Alaska, where filming of the exterior of a Klingon prison planet took place, particularly the

montage in which Kirk and McCoy escape with an alien. The snowy terrain was familiar to Narita, whose fine work in similarly inclement landscapes can be seen in Carroll Ballard's nature adventure, *Never Cry Wolf*.

"Alaska was the only remote location we used for *Star Trek VI*," Narita recalled. "The exterior was shot on a glacier with the so-called second unit and photo doubles of Kirk and McCoy. I've never seen a glacier like this one: the ice was at least 200 feet thick and the landscape it created was really unearthly, a really unexpected sight. We brought no lighting equipment with us; we were so far away from civilization that everything had to be helicoptered in. We couldn't hand-carry anything between setups. We had to use the helicopter to move equipment because we were afraid we might fall though the ice. Since we had the helicopter with us, we did some aerial shots as well. All told, we shot for three days and we could've used more. The only concern on the director's part was to see if we could make it look even more otherworldly. The sky was still blue, so he wanted to make is a purplish color, which is a job for ILM."

As our heroes make their escape, they are caught in an otherworldly snowstorm, a sequence which Narita found to be one of the more difficult to execute. "It wasn't easy to create a believable blizzard," he admitted. "The sequence was supposed to be an exterior, but we filmed it all on a soundstage. We used two types of plastic snow and mixed together, one with very large flakes and another that was very powdery, both of which were supposedly okayed by the board of health. It looked very convincing to me, but it was difficult to control the amount of snow being tossed by hand or blown by airhoses manned by the grips up on the catwalks. Sometimes it drifted completely off-set before it ever came into camera range! I'd never worked with fake snow on this large a scale. To maintain continuity in the amount of snow from shot to shot was extremely difficult."

Narita soon realized that the fake snow had a tendency to get into the equipment. "For safety's sake," he noted, "we decided not to change magazines on

the set. We had to take the whole camera out of the stage because we were afraid the fake snow might get into the film. Even weeks later, people were still finding snow in their socks."

Narita worked with a different crew this time because the people he normally works with were unavailable. "My assistant was Rob Morey, whom I always like to hire first," he said. "Rob is like having insurance, I know what he can do so when I hire the operator, I tell them they already have an assistant. No one has ever been unhappy." In addition to gaffer Ronnie Rao and grip Ben Beaird, Narita hired one of the few female camera operators, Kristen Glover, who occasionally manned the B camera on *The Rocketeer*. "I met her when she was an assistant many years ago, and I knew she was one of the best assistants in the business, but I hadn't seen her since she started to operate for Stephen Burum and Caleb Deschanel and occasionally shoot. She showed up when I was prepping *The Rocketeer*, and I decided to give her a chance. She was very good; her background is painting and mine is in graphics."

Even as he's shooting, Narita likes to think of the films he shoots in their completed form. Thus, he can look past imperfections in certain individual images if he can see how they might flow with the rhythm of the film. "I like to think in overall terms," he agreed. "I've talked to Kristen about this many times. What she feels is perfect operating is not necessarily the best thing for the scene. Sometimes she'll say, 'I missed a bit of the action because the framing was slightly off,' but I often remind her that those sort of things can help the realism. Imperfection is not always undesirable. A film is like a dance and each shot has to fit with the rhythm. When the camera's static, your compositions have to be precise, but often what the camera operator thinks is a mistake in a moving shot won't be seen on the screen. I've learned that when you shoot lots of action or movement, oddly enough, some 'mistakes' are much more effective than 'perfectly' operated shots. When everything is too perfect, it may look great when we're watching dailies, but you notice the camerawork and not the content. It's the story, not the camera, who's the star."

Not all the camerawork was deliberately imperfect on the film—due to the relentless schedule, one take was quite often the rule under Myer's direction and compromises were inevitable. "It's a reality of filmmaking," Narita conceded. "If you have to cover four pages a day, what do you do? You can't spend five hours lighting a set, so there's a compromise. I don't mind that kind of limitation—it becomes a certain challenge. Sometimes there's something to be said about the kind of rushed quality that comes with one take—other times it's a shame. After all the preparation, why accept less? It's a judgement call."

The fact that its scale was limited means *Star Trek VI* had to focus on characters. "This film does have a strong story," Narita explained. "It just happens that the characters are Spock, Kirk and McCoy."

And Narita does feel he and Meyer succeeded to some degree in creating a much darker, moodier feel for this film than the others in the series.

"We went for a harder edged look and I would say I wish we'd done more," he said. "I know I could have used this film to push myself artistically even more, but I don't think I did. I think we were fighting the tradition of *Star Trek*-type stories and trying to figure out how far we could push it. *The Rocketeer* was a much more comfortable film because we were approaching it with the idea that we didn't know anything about it; there was no history to be concerned with and we knew we wouldn't offend anybody. Here I wasn't sure how much we could get away with. After all, the actors have done this for 25 years. The director worked on the second one and helped write the fourth one. I didn't want to see the film go completely dark and moody just for the sake of change—there were definitely some moments that shouldn't be that way. I had a very good time working with Nick Meyer, even though he was pushing me quite a bit."

■ "ILM Gets 'A Piece of the Action'"

For the newest *Star Trek* voyage, Paramount reteamed with Industrial Light & Magic, the outfit that put the second, third and fourth films into orbit. While that decision was artistically sound, according to *Star Trek VI* visual effects supervisor Scott Farrar, the film's tight budget required its craftsmen to choose effects carefully.

Farrar knows the *Star Trek* animal pretty well, having begun his career as a camera assistant on *Star Trek: The Motion Picture* before graduating to effects camera operator on *Star Trek II* and *III*. However, neither of those films, nor his experiences as co-supervisor on *Who Framed Roger Rabbit?* and *Back to the Future II* and *III* (with Ken Ralston), quite prepared him for this project.

William George, who acted as Farrar's right-hand man and supervised the film's visual effects art direction along with Mark Moore, explained the challenge: "My opinion is that the *Star Trek* series relies on effects to open the picture up, since they're supposed to span the whole galaxy and take place on all these different planets. The fact is that most of these films are set on a stage with these actors talking to each other, so if you don't have a framework of effects, the films suffer. For this film, our effects are there to tell the story they want to tell— the spaceship goes from here to there— but they also open the film up to show that the crew of the Enterprise [is] really in this vast universe where the story's being told."

In fact, director Nicholas Meyer was determined to use ILM's effects to show the larger universe in which the Enterprise crew functioned—a tall order indeed. George pointed out, "Nilo Rodis, the film's overall art director, was working with Nick Meyer and sending us concepts for effects shots, many of which we used, but they were working strictly from the storytelling point of view. Mark Moore and I were responsible for storyboarding the visual effects sequences and designing the shots, and we were dealing with how to make the film both as good and as inexpensive as possible."

Monetary restrictions may actually have had a positive effect in some instances, forcing the visual effects artists to create shots that were richer and more

fluid, and which revealed more in single shots than a traditional series of images would. Visual effects producer Peter Takeuchi and coordinator Jil-Sheree Bergin were responsible for negotiating with Paramount, eventually helping the studio cut the number of shots from over 100 to 51. Even so, the project was a big one. *Star Trek VI* required the services of virtually the entire ILM facility. Getting a fast start was the only way to ensure the film's completion for its targeted December release date, but lengthy pre-production financial negotiations only succeeded in wasting valuable postproduction time.

"The whole goal in the first place was for us to go ahead and do the spaceship shots before they started the live action principle photography," Farrar shook his head, "but the go-ahead never came through, it just got delayed and delayed."

Luckily, Farrar was able to take advantage of the delays. For *Star Trek V*, the Enterprise and other models had been sent across the country to Bran Ferren's effects facilities in New York. The journey, combined with the fact that these models were over ten years old and had been used on nearly all the feature films, meant they were desperately in need of cosmetic attention when they were returned to ILM. The models, especially the Enterprise, were covered with hairline cracks, and their complex paint schemes were damaged. George and model shop supervisor Lawrence Tan used this period to make slight changes to some of the ships as they were refurbishing them.

"We changed the bridge area on the Excelsior model," George said, "because on this show, the bridge is actually very small—it's the Enterprise bridge redressed. The Excelsior was originally built for *Star Trek III*, where it had a cavernous bridge, and the model had a big bubble on top which I felt was always out of scale. We replaced it with a smaller bridge area which helped the overall scale of the model."

Another model that was unexpectedly hauled out of drydock for a final bon voyage was the Klingon battlecruiser, unseen since it was destroyed by V'ger at the beginning of *Star Trek: The*

Motion Picture. "That model needed to be repainted anyway, so I proposed that we make it look very distinct from those in the first film," explained George, "especially since it was one of the few models we could alter to look new for this show. We did some research into military costuming, and came up with the concept that when these ships return victorious from battle, the Klingons build some sort of epaulet onto their wings or paint a new stripe on. We painted the model brown and red with gold highlights, then added golden etched brass epaulets to it, based on some of the helmet designs we'd seen. It contrasts nicely with the Enterprise, which is very smooth and monochromatic and cool, while this Klingon ship is very regal and ostentatious and warm."

Visual effects supervisor Farrar developed new and unusual angles from which to film the familiar models. First he and George reacquainted themselves with the other films in the series. "There were times when we thought, 'Oh, boy, we've come up with a shot that's never been done,' then we screened the films and realized, 'Oh, gee, they did that shot already' or 'I did that shot already!'," Farrar laughed. "Bill is a Trekkie and he was really excited about working on this, so we spent a lot of time designing the angles from the get-go. I wanted to shoot the ships from below as much as possible, unless there was a story point that prohibited it, and Nick Meyer always wanted to maintain a nautical feel—the starships were big galleons, big ships, almost seagoing vessels."

Not only does the dynamic miniature photography convey Meyer's intention perfectly, the models themselves have never looked better. Farrar credits this in part to his mentor, Ken Ralston, who supervised effects for numbers two, three and four. "I learned a great deal from Ken," Farrar pointed out. "Pat Sweeney and Peter Daulton were Ken's motion control people on *Back to the Future II* and *III*, and they found that to get shadowing and texture into the chromed miniature DeLorean, it was better to shoot the key and film passes separately, so they could control how dark or how bright the model was. We picked up on that for the starships and shot separate

passes for each one."

On ILM's motion control stages, Peter Daulton handled the numerous shots of the Enterprise, while Pat Sweeney shot all of the other ships, including the Klingon battlecruiser and Bird of Prey, the spacedock, the Excelsior and various astral bodies. "As it turned out," Sweeney said, "Peter Daulton and I had almost the same number of shots—the Enterprise is the featured model, the one everybody wants to see, so naturally it's in every other shot."

The *Star Trek* models have a more massive and heavy feeling, partly achieved by speeding up the movements of the models. "We allowed the ships to travel faster than on previous *Trek* shows to exhibit their immense power," said Sweeney. "Shooting the key and fill lighting as separate passes also played a big part. We were able to combine those separate passes in post, and manipulate the contrast ratio to make the ships look brighter or more mysterious. I think it's some of the better looking stuff we've shot."

Despite the breakneck schedule, Daulton and Sweeney did their utmost to create more interesting flight paths for their spaceships. "We were concerned about getting everything done on time," Sweeney admitted, "but that's not very satisfying. A lot of the moves were boarded as straight lines, so Peter and I added some extra twists to give them a little more life. Bill George also redesigned a lot of shots from the original boards. When you put this much time and effort into something, you want it to turn out as well as possible."

Sweeney and Daulton compose the images for and, in a sense, direct their motion control sequences. "What makes doing effects a lot of fun is that it's the closest thing to being a director," Sweeney pointed out. "On stage, the cinematographer is the art director, the modelmaker and the cameraman—we have to do all those things at the same time. I'm on a stage with a limited crew and it's a lot of fun because we have to figure out all the problems. Over the years, time has become more compressed. There's less money to do the shots, so we have to find ways to do the same amount of work better in less time. That means the effects

supervisor and art director are swamped with ten things at once, so a lot more of the creativity in the actual shooting is on our shoulders. The supervisors count on us to come up with whatever it takes to make the shot work."

The film's climactic space battle over planet Khitomer involved constant and complex interaction between Daulton's Enterprise and Sweeney's Klingon Bird of Prey. In a scenario somewhat reminiscent of *The Hunt for Red October*, the Enterprise is locked in a life-or-death struggle with an invisible opponent. Again, Farrar's approach to the shot design for this sequence had a decidedly nautical feel. "When the Bird of Prey is running around taking pot shots at the Enterprise, we wanted it to seem like a submarine," he recalled. "It's kind of cheating—it's down low, shooting at these vessels that are up high. I never really thought of it in terms of *Red October*. Even though the Enterprise is trying to locate a ship that it can't see, that's an important story point but it's not the focus of the movie like it is in *Red October*. Of course there are similarities—whether you're under the sea or in outer space, it's always a tense situation when your heroes have to make judgement calls about an enemy they can't see."

The sequence features crosscutting between the ships and action on the Enterprise, the Excelsior, the Bird of Prey and the planet Khitomer. Keeping the audience oriented was challenging, especially considering that the studio had budgeted for a minimum of establishing shots. "The question came up every time they cut: 'Do we have to show the ship or the place?'—and if so, that meant another effects shot," Farrar said. "We felt that by restructuring the story slightly, and by cutting differently, they didn't have to spend money on shots that showed us what we already knew—that the Enterprise was flying in this direction—when what we'd really like to do is show the bad guys making a maneuver. Still, a number of establishing effects shots were added after a rough cut was deemed confusing."

"Throughout the whole Khitomer battle sequence, the Enterprise is being pursued by the new, improved version of the Klingon Bird of Prey, which can cloak itself and fire at the same time," added art director William George. "The Enterprise is a sitting duck. When Scott and I were in the very early design phases, trying to come up with ideas to make the battle a little bit different, he asked me, 'What have you always wanted to see happen on the Enterprise?' and my answer was, 'I've always wanted to see a photon torpedo go right through the ship. There's one place on the primary hull where it's really thin.' We designed that shot and they accepted it. We wanted to make sure that it didn't look as much like an explosion as a shot-gun blast, because the photon torpedo's actually pushing through the ship. We built a huge eight-foot diameter dish with a replaceable breakaway section made of very fragile plaster, then hung the model upside-down. On the side away from the camera were fingers of metal that were dressed as the damaged ship. When a pin was pulled, a spring pushed them right through the thin plaster skin, which cracked since it's supposed to be ceramic tile."

The Klingon Bird of Prey, with its improved cloak of invisibility, can only be glimpsed for an instant as it fires photon torpedoes. This meant cinematographer Sweeney and optical supervisor Bradley Kuehn had to create a whole new effects vocabulary in order to reveal the ship when it fires. Extremely harsh lighting was used to highlight individual sections of the Bird of Prey and allow the rest of the model to remain cloaked in shadows. Kuehn was later able to link Sweeney's shots in optical to create the illusion that as the torpedo explodes from the ship's nose, it illuminates the nose section, neck and wings for an instant.

"That shot's actually made up of five or six Bird of Prey elements which we faded up in sequences as the torpedo blasts away from the ship," Kuhen said. "Other than the harshness of the lighting, Pat shot the ship normally and we reddened it in optical. These shots, which last maybe a second on screen, had to be shot four times for the composite. Each time, it took us more than two hours because of all the passes—six passes on the Bird of Prey, four or so interactive

light passes on the torpedo coming out of the tube and another five passes for the torpedo element."

These miniature effects, as sophisticated as they've become, still employ virtually the same technology that was used on the original TV series 25 years ago. The effects that set *Star Trek VI* apart from its video origins were created and composited inside a computer. Three distinct and unique computer graphics sequences were supervised by the aptly named Jay Riddle, who has puzzled out the web of computer data to create memorable images that seem very real. Riddle was aided by the talented crew that gave us the water tentacle in *The Abyss* and the shape-shifting T-1000 of *Terminator 2*. *Star Trek VI* offered some of the greatest challenges yet faced by the relatively fledgling department.

Probably the simplest of the computer graphics sequences are the "morphs"—in this case, the transformations of an alien being into various other characters, including Captain Kirk. These effects, accomplished through computer averaging, took from three to six weeks to complete. "This was pretty much the same technology we developed for *Willow* and used on *T2*," Riddle said, "which allows us to do nice transitions between two different photographic models. This time, John Berton attempted to do some things we hadn't done before in a morph, like moving the camera and letting characters talk as they were transforming, so a lot of care had to be taken in the plate photography to make sure the two characters lined up."

In order to move up a bit on the morph evolutionary ladder, Farrar, Riddle and animator Jim Berton worked together to create a perfect blend when the shape-shifting creature, played by Iman, metamorphoses into Captain Kirk, played by William Shatner—in mid-sentence. "Fortunately, I had lots of experience with voice playback on the *Back to the Future* series," said Farrar, who supervised the on-set plate photography for the morph sequences. "We used prerecorded video playback with sound sync that was broadcast over a loudspeaker so the actors could hear it and match their delivery to the playback. In this case, William Shatner not only had to listen to Iman's

dialogue and segue into it, he had to be looking the right way to match her eyeline and deliver the dialogue just like she did so they can roll right together in post."

Getting Shatner and Iman's lips to sync up was the difficulty Riddle faced when the footage came in to ILM's computer graphics department. Despite Farrar's best efforts, Riddle found that there were many discrepancies in the way Shatner and Iman pronounced words. "We had trouble just getting their lips to line up," Riddle said, "because even though they were saying the same thing, their mouths weren't doing the same things. We were able to match their mouth movements and blend them together, but once we got into it, we realized that just because the morph itself looks seamless doesn't mean the shot's successful—there are a lot of other things to consider and certain transitions may look silly. We wanted to make the actors look good so we had to learn to time things so that we didn't get any unexpected laughs. In the end, we just made certain features change shape more slowly or at different times, and that worked out really well. We also introduced a slight camera move after we'd done the morph, which takes it out of being this real static looking effects shot."

Farrar believes the best morphs involve extreme change in skin color and features that expand or contract dramatically. He was able to test the outer limits of those parameters when transforming an alien brute into a little girl, an effect made even more challenging by the addition of a live camera move in the original plate photography. "That was the trickiest one," admitted Farrar. "Using our VistaGlide motion control system, we created a push-in, tilt-down and move-back that had to be duplicated for both characters. This meant they had to hit their marks exactly. The little girl had some business towards the tail end of the shot that was somewhat unpredictable, so we had to gear the whole move around her and shoot her part, the 'B part,' first. The actor who played the beast had to watch her playback on a monitor that matched 50% of her image to 50% of his live image from the taking camera. Then he'd have to settle in and match his eye level to hers before she completed her business. The morph itself was pretty extreme: the alien brute had a huge mane of red hair, the girl's was blonde, their clothing was completely different, and this vascular face he's got transforms into her nice pale skin. To me, that's the ticket."

"The fact that they were so different in size and there was a camera move made things difficult," Riddle added. "Scott tried to match the movements of the two actors as much as possible, but the more people move around, the less things line up, so we had problems in getting certain features synced up. We attempted to make the transition between the two look organic; we didn't have it all start and finish at the same time or it would've looked like a big dissolve," Riddle added. "We worked on having the face start before the hair did, so we were able to see the little girl's features coming on even as the brute was shrinking down in size."

One of the greatest challenges for ILM was creating the galactic explosion that nearly destroys the Federation starship Excelsior in the opening moments of the film. It was an audacious move on Farrar's part to use the untried combination of computer-generated effects and a miniature spaceship for the first shot, especially when the film can rise or fall on its opening sequence.

"It's an uncharted course," Farrar conceded. "We're dealing with a lot of interactive work involving film elements of the Excelsior being jostled around by computer graphic elements. Each of them requires a lot of individual animation. We pre-boarded that whole sequence, which begins when a Klingon moon explodes, sending a shockwave through space that hits the Excelsior. The ship gets thrown around and barely makes it out without being destroyed, before we're back to the sea of calm again. When we first discussed this sequence, Nick Meyer made references to different films, such as *The Poseidon Adventure*. We used imagery like the immense tidal wave hitting the boat in that film to establish the scale of our galactic explosion."

Despite all the preliminary discussions, Farrar and Riddle found it difficult to create the proper sense of scale in deep space. "You can't see how big an explosion is when it occurs in deep space, because there's no reference like a man or house to tell you how big this thing is," Riddle explained. "Our animators, Joe Leterri, Alex Seiden and Eric Enderton, worked a lot with the animation to convey size and to give the right speed to these objects as they spread out. We studied examples of explosions in nature and man-made examples like nuclear bombs. Even those aren't big enough! We had to extrapolate a bit because it had to look bigger than any explosion you've ever seen before."

"We had to come up with a concept that would work through a whole sequence from all kinds of different vantage points," Farrar elaborated. "It's tricky to try to keep it from looking like a CG-derived element, or what my art director Bill George calls 'Space Art,' and still give it an organic quality."

Riddle's task was complicated by the fact that this particular form of computer graphics is unlike anything ILM has tried before. While the water tentacle in *The Abyss* was a close blend of animation and modelling, and the *T2*'s shape-shifting T-1000, with his reflective chrome surface, combined lighting and modelling, *Star Trek VI*'s opening sequence involved a complex mixture of rendering and animation. "After the art department gave us their illustration of what the explosion should look like, we created a program that could render the image of the explosion, which was very time-consuming," Riddle recalled. "We could tell from the initial drawing what 'geometry'—simple geometric forms—the computer would use to create this effect. In computer terms, the explosion consisted of some very simple objects—little curved discs, a flat disc and some spheres—that were expanding outward. We worked with those objects to see if the shot needed to be more complicated, with a more irregular shape. We found that the violence of the explosion could be defined more simply by assigning the proper colors and textures, rather than by changing the shape of our relatively simple CG model. The tricky stuff was getting the textures and the turbulent organic explosion after-effects going. When it was done, we'd created a three-dimensional CG explosion which was an expanding spherical plasma ball, filled with all kinds of interesting detail, from which two or three sets of rings appear and fly by us."

A number of the shots from this opening sequence were composited in the CG computer, which created some problems for optical supervisor Bradley Kuehn. Normally, the explosion footage would be delivered to optical, where the spaceship would be composited over it, but in this case the explosion had to be added behind the space-ship in the realm of computer graphics. After pre-compositing the various bluescreen Excelsior elements, Kuehn delivered the footage to computer graphics, where the starship was then scanned into the CG computer for compositing on video with the computer-generated explosion effect.

"This was kind of a learn-as-we-went situation," Kuehn admitted. "The first time we gave them our Excelsior shots, we tried to comp as many of our elements as possible, but we found we were limiting them a bit and making more work for them to do. For example, they had to find special ways to separate some of the elements we'd just put together for them in order to add the interactive light coming off the explosion elements. I think *Star Trek VI* was a simple enough movie that we were able to keep many of the shots moving through optical, but I think marrying digitized model shots to background CG is definitely where the future of optical compositing is headed."

And what of the future of the film series. This is the end, right? Well, no one's saying for sure, but if *Star Trek VI* is indeed the last hurrah for the old crew, at least it's infused the series with new life by taking a number of chances—more violence and a broader universe in which to play—thanks to ILM's effects and Nicholas Meyer's vision.

"The *Star Trek* films have always been rooted in the TV series," visual effects supervisor Scott Farrar opined, "and therefore everybody's been hesitant to depart too much from the style that first developed in the series. Should you go to a location? Maybe not, because the use of exteriors that are built as interior sets is part of the established look, and maybe you don't want to depart from that because it might spoil the idea of what *Star Trek* is. But in this case, we went on location, we shot a lot of footage outdoors and we took some chances and that really added a lot to the picture."

■ "Designing the Future"

In the sometimes bizarre and occasionally Byzantine realm of *Star Trek* film production, the unusual is commonplace. So it is quite natural that Nilo Rodis began his art direction duties as early as four months before the film's production designer, Herman Zimmerman, came on board. Both Rodis and Zimmerman are veterans of the film series: Rodis served as art director on *Star Trek III* and *IV* and as art director and costume designer on *V*; Zimmerman was production designer on the last film and for the first two seasons of *Star Trek: The Next Generation*.

Rodis, whose background prior to working on the series was as an art director for ILM, says that beginning work on a film prior to the production designer only sounds backward. "I've worked with Ralph Winter in the past, and he typically brings me in to read the screenplay to establish the look of the movie with broad strokes, using very little detail. On *Star Trek V*, I was fortunate to come in almost a full year before Herman, and on *VI*, I came in about four months before he did, and I began visualizing the movie for the writer and director, working on its storyboarding and preproduction art. I never did any tight art direction until preproduction, which is how I worked when I was at ILM, so I just carried that over."

Since director/writer Nicholas Meyer was in London at the time, Rodis would draw up his concept sketches, mail them to Paramount, who would FAX the drawings to Meyer. Meyer would then call Rodis the following morning to discuss the drawings. "Working with Nick was a lot of fun," he said. "He's an unbelievably generous director—he really will not tell you how to shoot the sequence or what camera angle to use,

he would just turn me loose and then ask me why I set it up that way, and if he agreed, that was it. Sometimes we'd become a slave to our original design and other times, we'd just use it as a backbone to set the basic ideas that we had. Then I'd try visualizing the scene differently, and sometimes, quite by mistake, innocently enough, it would start something else.

"A good art director," Rodis continued, "should see himself as a bridge between the director and the producer. Sometimes I would listen to the constraints of time and money, and sometimes I would listen to the director's flights of fancy and 'Do it this way regardless of cost.' It's pure art in the beginning because there's absolutely no constraints, especially in the way it's structured since I work at home. I would just sit there in my room and daydream about this movie and break it down into sequences—no storyboards—just ideas of what things might look like."

Rodis recalls that it was fun experimenting with Nick Meyer and Herman Zimmerman with grandiose ideas that both of them knew would never make it on-screen, but which might lead to other ideas that could improve the overall film tremendously. "I try to understand the director's vision first and then get to the essence of that vision," Rodis explained. "Nick is a very practical director and had a tremendous sense of concept versus reality. It became my job to trudge through the agreed concept to find a practical and economical way of fleshing out the sequence. Through careful storyboarding, you can actually shoot an entire battle in less shots by judiciously picking the right moments—but before you can pick out which shots can be dropped, you have to understand how the entire sequence works, so you have to go through it. Design is the same way: sometimes, the first approach seems like it could be very expensive, but it's not once we go through the process of fleshing out the essence of what the director's trying to say; other times, we have to explore the idea to the limit and then back off."

While Rodis acknowledges that the line that distinguishes the art director from the production designer is very

fuzzy on a *Star Trek* film, he suggests that it was his job to come up with fanciful ideas and Zimmerman's task to make them work practically. "Once Herman came on board, the broad design of the movie was complete, and we were into tight details," Rodis said. "At that point, Herman, like most production designers, had to deal with the real-world problems of the budget, while the earlier ideas might not have taken into account how low the ceiling was or how wide the stage would be. Now it was Herman's difficult job to take my fanciful ideas and make them work in the real world. Once we were into preproduction, even though I was still primarily working freehanded, I tried to keep an eye on the dimensions so that the set designers who tightened my drawings up could actually hang measurements on them. Herman is a very hands-on designer, it was fun following him around."

You might think the first thing a studio would want to do if they were engaged in making a series of features is to get the same design team together for each film—but you'd be wrong. Remember, this is *Star Trek*, where zero gravity anxiety is a way of life. "I'm the first production designer to work on two of the movies," Herman Zimmerman marvelled. "Sometimes people lose sight of the fact that continuity is very important in a series, and it's also important to have an integrated, consistent look from the sets to the costumes. Producer Ralph Winter was the one who insisted that they hire me to do *VI* since I'd done *V*. He thought that having Nilo with his experience on *IV* had helped me tremendously on *V*, and figured that having us both on *VI* would make everybody's job easier. Nilo is my dear friend and I can't even say he's my right arm—sometimes I'm more an extension of him than the other way around. Nilo is so valuable because of his conceptual abilities in showing the director what we have in mind. I can ask Nilo for a sketch and twenty minutes later he'll come in with a rough asking me what I think of it."

Timing was vital, according to Zimmerman, because by the time he came on, "We didn't have time to do anything but working drawings." Zimmerman did take the time, however, to build a model of every set. "I wanted Nick to have the opportunity to see what each set was going to look like in three dimensions before we built anything. A director can't walk around in a sketch, but he can look at a model from a number of different vantage points, remove a wall, make a move in his mind. This technique gives him a better feeling for what he can do, and it's a whole lot cheaper than building the set and having the director come up to you and say, 'Well, I didn't know it was going to look like that!' We made quite a few changes that resulted in better sets, and we threw out quite a few sets we decided we didn't need."

Zimmerman also oversaw the refurbishing of sets, props and costumes from earlier films in the series as a means to keep costs down on the tightly-budgeted film. "The only way a studio can afford a series like *Star Trek*, that varies in the quality of the story and in audience response," he observed, "is to save things and use them again." For example, Zimmerman was able to helm the recreation of the Enterprise bridge for *Star Trek V* and, then, for *VI*, make improvements and add finishing touches he couldn't afford the first time around.

"It was originally designed, in my mind, a little too much like something out of *Flash Gordon*. I wanted to bridge the past and the present and take the series more toward the technology we're familiar with for big blockbuster science fiction films today, while remaining faithful to the science fiction that has been created for the first *Star Trek* TV series."

Zimmerman recycled the corridors of the Enterprise—also leftovers from *Star Trek: The Motion Picture*—which were still standing where they'd been erected originally. "I'd already modified them quite a bit for *Star Trek: The Next Generation*," Zimmerman recalled, "where I made them white and straightened out some K-beams. For *Star Trek VI*, Nick wanted the corridors to look smaller, so we put the K-beams back and we also added overhead pipes in true submarine fashion. We added a lot of lights in the corridors and on the bridge, so our cinematographer, Hiro Narita, could create a dimly lit, 'Red October' look with pools of light and shadow. Nothing is flat, so it's unlike the

evenly lit look of *The Next Generation*—that isn't the way things are in real life. When you see the film, I think you'll feel it has a much grittier, more realistic look than the other features have had."

Putting the original *Star Trek* crew into *Next Generation* settings brought Nick Meyer's philosophy into sharp relief against that of series creator Gene Roddenberry. "Nick Meyer did not like the colors of the *Next Generation* sets, which he felt were too pastel, too much like a modern convenience motel," Zimmerman recalled. "Roddenberry felt that in another three hundred years into the future from the original *Star Trek* series, we wouldn't really have to be cramped in space, so the sets didn't have to feel like submarines and they didn't need to be so utilitarian with everything painted grey. Nick Meyer took exception to that; he felt that military life being what it is, they'll still be using good old battleship grey four or five hundred years from now, so we went back to that with my blessing. Nick thought that even that far into the future, especially since entropy is upon us and everything we do each year costs more and more and we get less and less, spaceships will always feel like submarines in space and that's part of what makes them interesting."

An unforseen problem arose from having to shoot much of the Rura Penthe sequence on stage instead of on location in Alaska as planned. Zimmerman was forced to use the large soundstage he'd intended for the Klingon courtroom for the snow scene exteriors instead. "Even though I still had the next largest stage on the lot at my disposal," he sighed, "it wasn't quite big enough to do the courtroom I'd originally intended, so we had to scale it down somewhat."

Ironically, that ended up working to the film's advantage, for the production was limited to 65 Klingon extras, but had to make it look like there were 3,000. "The smaller set actually helped me to convey the sense of a much larger audience; though we only had three rows of Klingons, we implied that there were many tiers above that, each containing another 50 Klingons. We were also helped by a matte painting, a downshot of the entire courtroom that augmented our real set and which will convince the

audience that all of those Klingons are really there."

Rodis calls the trial sequence "the hardest stuff to design for all of us on *Star Trek VI*. We went through a bunch of designs before settling on a circular Klingon courtroom." Rodis' concern was with the lead-in to the scene in which Spock comments that everything was alright. "Originally, Nick planned to cut immediately to the camera crawling over the top of the building that contained thousands of Klingons, and as it came closer and closer, you would realize that Kirk and McCoy were in the middle of a huge problem.. Then Phil Norwood, who was doing our storyboards at the time, came up with a different idea: after Spock said his line, intimating that Kirk was OK, we would immediately cut to a very tight shot of a blown-out, overlit face, and hear voices shouting, 'Kirk! Kirk! Kirk!' As the camera pulled back, it revealed that Kirk and Bones were alone against thousands of Klingons, leading in to the matte shot of the entire court. Phil Norwood had actually suggested to Nick that he cut the sequence even shorter by going from Spock's face to the Judge's face to Kirk's face, so we never went outside the building to show time passing, zoomed into a window and cut inside. Nick absolutely hates ideas like that anyway! That way, until the camera began pulling back, the audience would keep wondering, 'Where is Kirk?'

"With an entrance like that," Rodis lamented, "I had to do something with the set to maintain dramatic interest. I was afraid that if the audience didn't immediately fear for Kirk and Bones, then the scene wasn't going to work, especially after Spock said, 'They're OK.' That was the design catch—we had to immediately make the audience realize they're not OK, and if we didn't make it seem like they were really in big trouble, we'd fail. The whole idea was to isolate Kirk and Bones in the middle of a very austere, oversized, architecturally clunky place. We went through gyration after gyration as to what that would look like. Eventually, we settled on an idea I think Nick brought up in one of our meetings when he said that the Klingons are kind of like Romans throwing Christians to the lions. I just capitalized on that idea and carried it even further: the court was really nothing but a pit, and the camera and the Klingons were always looking down while Kirk and Bones were always looking up."

This very helpless, submissive position became even more so after Meyer visited the set while under construction. The sequence always began with Kirk and Bones arriving in the courtroom via a subterranean elevator platform, which came to rest at the center of the set. Most of their travel would be filmed impressionistically from the side as light and shadow played on the prisoner's faces, but the last few feet as the platform came to a stop was to be handled practically on the set. "That meant that Herman had to accommodate the last few stages of Kirk and Bones' arrival from undergound," Rodis said, "so he had to make the set about four feet deeper than he intended to make it. One day before the set was finished, we did a walk through and Nick said, 'Forget the floor—this is it!' Even though Herman had built the pit about 10 feet high to accommodate the moving platform, Nick wanted the pit to be even deeper because it was more dramatic that way. This did make it harder for Hiro and Nick to shoot some of the planned two shots, though they eventually succeeded in doing so. Now, as I understand it, we show Kirk and Bones' faces squinting into a light that gets brighter and brighter, then we cut to a side shot that shows them emerging from this hole in the floor and then we reveal the Klingons all around."

Rodis and Zimmerman feel that the film looks about as good as any of the others in the series, which is saying a lot considering that many of them were made for two or three times what the current picture cost. "One of Nick Meyer's favorite expressions is 'Art thrives on restrictions' and indeed we proved that throughout this picture," Zimmerman smiled. "We made the restrictions work for us and succeeded in making a rich fabric of environments that support the action, and which are at the same time inventive and practical."

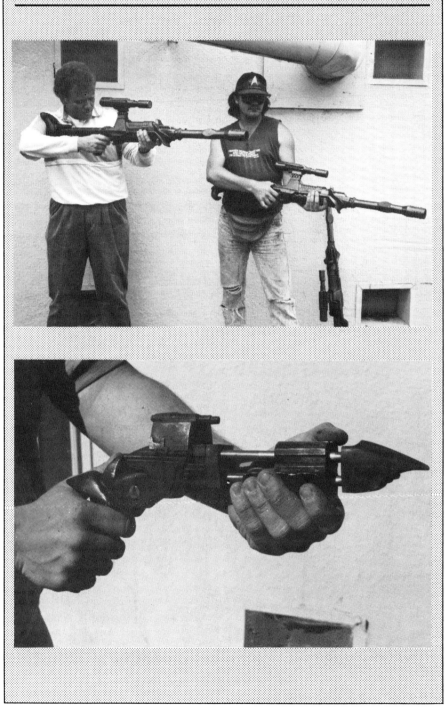

Though not very obvious on a surface level, Star Trek VI: The Undiscovered Country featured a wide variety of props that were utilized during nearly every scene of the film, creating a certain level of reality throughout the proceedings. What follows is a visual guide to some of the more interesting props.

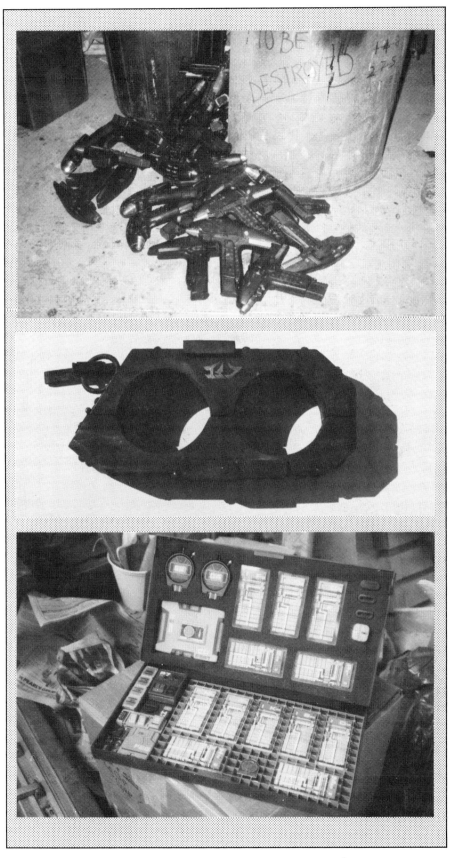

■ "Propping Up A Starship"

Though Greg Jein is probably best known as the builder of the awesome Mothership in Steven Spielberg's *Close Encounters of the Third Kind* and the mammoth miniature street recreations for *1941* and *One From the Heart*, he is also known as a "real grassroots *Star Trek* fan" because of his fascination with the '60s television show. It seems natural that when he's not working for Spielberg, Francis Coppola or George Lucas, Jein has contributed his expertise in model and propmaking to the *Star Trek* films and the *Next Generation* television series—jobs he refuses to admit he enjoys, although his enthusiasm is evident in his work.

After building the 20-foot main section of V'ger for effects supervisor Doug Trumbull on *Star Trek: The Motion Picture*, Jein went on to construct many of the spaceships for the new series. But he didn't have anything further to do with the film series until he was enlisted by Nilo Rodis (whom he met at ILM) to build props for *Star Trek V*, a capacity in which he has continued to serve on *Star Trek VI*.

The first prop of note was a Federation courier's high-tech portmanteau, which Jein refers to as "the *Star Trek* version of the IMF briefcase from *Mission: Impossible*." As in that famed TV series, the courier inserts a coded cassette into a handy futuristic disc drive, the cassette then informing the Enterprise crewmembers of their impending assignment. "The case itself was all plexiglass, which we painted and dressed with *Next Generation* graphics and anything else we had in the shop," Jein said. "The upper interior was lined with grey foam like you'd find in a camera case, while the bottom was made of a hard plastic grid, behind which we placed a holographic material that added a great sense of depth to the case. We wanted the inside to have the feeling of an overstuffed secretary case, so we added lots of gadgets. We made various implements from candy dispensers and other things we had lying around the shop, which were removable in case the actors needed to play with them and had lights in them and so on. We also included one of the recording devices we made for *Star Trek V*—which Scotty wore on his utility belt and Kirk wore on his back—as a kind of personal log. We also added a couple of ordinary stopwatches which we dressed up with lots of graphics. But all of that stuff was essentially eyewash and dressing—the main things in the briefcase were the coded clear plastic chips the officer was supposed to play on the crew's monitors. Unfortunately, I believe they didn't go with our plastic cassettes but used a redressed five inch floppy disc instead so it would insert into an existing disc drive."

The same technology Jein used to make the lucite information chips was also employed for Sulu's Data Counter, a clear plastic clipboard covered with colorful printed circuitry and blinking lights. Its function was to show the new captain of the Excelsior his ship's exact location in relation to the planets of this part of the galaxy. The high-tech graphics, designed by art director Nilo Rodis and graphic designer Michael Okuda, were silkscreened onto the clipboard's clear surface. Jein then mimicked the design with the electrical wiring that ran on the opposite side, directly beneath the pattern so the wires would be hidden from view. A plastic L-shaped housing framed the top and one side, dressed with push buttons and metal grating, actually contained the batteries and circuitry that brought the prop to life.

A portion of Jein's work for the film involved remaking props he'd built for *Star Trek V* that had mysteriously disappeared, a recurring event throughout *Star Trek*'s 25 years of production. In addition to remaking and recycling tricorders, Jein also reused and slightly modified the more macho Federation phasers designed by Nilo Rodis and William Shatner, and originally built by Jein's crew for the fifth film. "We just changed a knob on them," Jein admitted, "and we added one more detail that you'd never notice in the film. On the bottom of each magazine, we built in a registry plate which says what ship the gun is from and what model it is. The ones carried by the crew of the Enterprise are so labelled, while those carried by

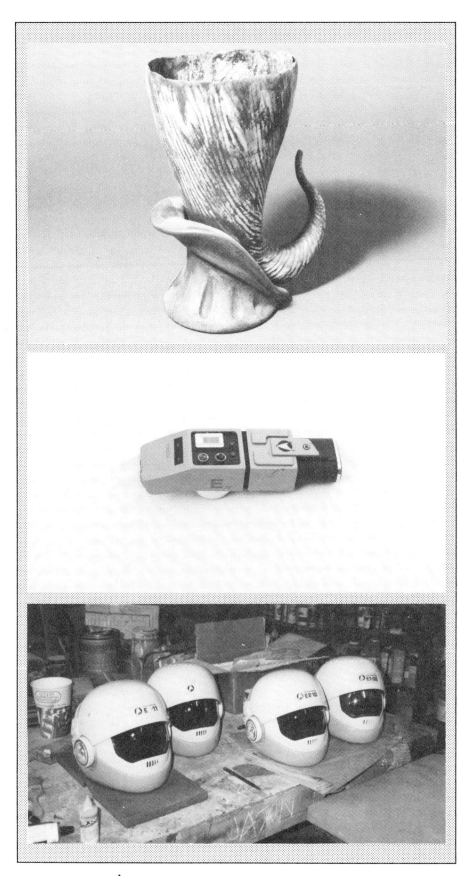

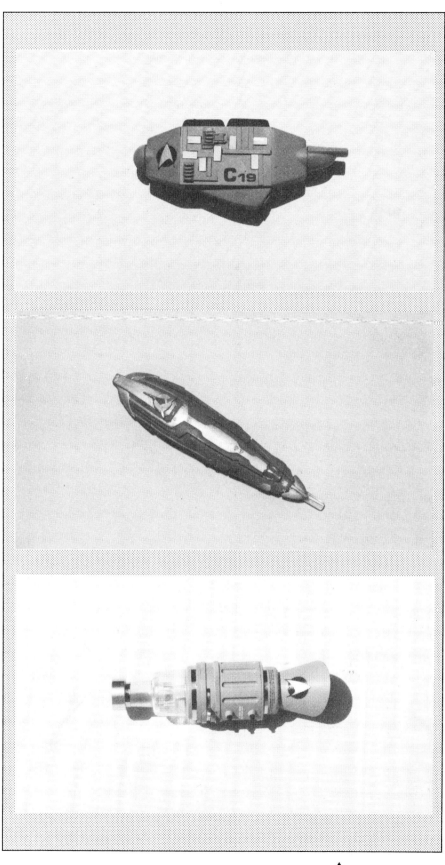

Sulu's men have Excelsior plates."

He also had to remake one of the most famous *Star Trek* gadgets: Uhura's earpiece. "It was all machined aluminum," Jein said. "It's pretty much the same one we made for the last movie, but we tried to improve on the design by having it actually light up when she pushed a button. Unfortunately, the extra electronics made the prop too heavy for Nichelle Nichols to wear in her ear, and the last I heard they tore the battery out to make it lighter, so it didn't light up anymore."

Other props that Jein seems to perennially supply are certain elements of Dr. McCoy's vast array of surgical apparatus. His implements, most of which were made of precision-machined aluminum and turned plexiglass, have a beautiful, alien feel and seem absolutely believable. Four other surgical implements were built for the sequence where Spock and McCoy operate on a photon torpedo. Those instruments also contained electronics, which Snyder made as simple as possible "so the actors could just hit the buttons on them and make different things light up."

Jein couldn't always resist his impulses to insert little in-jokes and homages to the original TV show, as well as to other films and television programs he'd been involved with. "As a tribute to the old days, I put a copy of one of McCoy's hypos from the old series, which actually worked, into his bag."

And where would a reactionary like McCoy keep such tools? Naturally in some sort of pouch that was as far removed from the futuristic *Star Trek* tradition as possible. "When McCoy beamed over to the Klingon ship to treat Gorkon, I thought he should have something to hold his surgical tools," explained Jein, "but not something high-tech because he's anti-high-tech. I found the perfect thing in a military store: a 1940's Swedish medical pouch. All the labels you see on it in the film were already there, but we substituted a Federation pin in place of the one that was most obviously Swedish."

It's been said that Greg's "Jein-ous" is his ability to modify found objects to create fully believable futuristic props. A perfect example of Jein's talents in adapting existing technology to the *Star Trek* universe occurs in the sequence where McCoy operates on Gorkon. According to the script, the good doctor was supposed to watch the dying President's vital signs reading out on a futuristic Klingon mini-viewscreen. Rather than endure the trouble and tremendous expense of building a functioning device from scratch, Jein went to his local electronics store and found the perfect equipment to adapt: a Sony 8mm video monitor. "We just dressed up a store-bought monitor," he revealed. "We repainted it and covered up a lot of the areas where you could normally see the tape rolling around, adding some fake buttons and a ton of graphics to it. When they shot the sequence, they actually played a prerecorded tape of Klingon guts on the viewscreen."

Jein also was able to recycle and reapply various other props he created for *Star Trek V*, finding new and ever more bizarre uses for them which delighted the producers, considering this latest film's tight budget. For example, a device Jein's crew built so Dr. McCoy could extract a bullet from a soldier's leg in *Trek V*, metamorphosed into an evidence gatherer used by Chekov in number six. Chekov used the device, which looks like a cross between a slide loop and a specimen bottle, to check out blood samples left by the assassins in the Enterprise's transporter bay. "He looks through the little eyescoop on the top," said Jein, "and when he sees something he likes, he aims the clear telescopic lense on the front at it, pushes a button and a built-in light flashes. It operates like a 3-D Polaroid mini-transporter, and whatever he photographs is actually transported onto the slide. When he's finished, the little round slide cartridge is ejected from a slot on the side of the grey barrel-shaped main body section. Chekov puts the slide into his evidence container—a little square storage bin with a round hole to store them in—which hooks onto Spock's microscope so he can view them."

Another hand-me-down that appears in Chekov's repertoire this time around is a tool that resembles nothing so much as a Federation cigarette lighter; the top part with the Federation logo

even flips up, but the device is far more ingenious than it appears. "It's actually a mini-welding device," Jein said, "which we made by modifying a commercially available flashlight, so it's thumb-activated. In this film, Chekov uses it to burn through the manacles and shackles on Kirk and McCoy when they beam up from the ice planet."

Jein fabricated a number of interesting helmets, ranging from Enterprise engineering headwear to futuristic hardhats. The pattern for the faceted miner's helmets worn by the inmates of the Rura Penthe penal colony was created at the Oakley manufacturing company (which actually produces sunglasses and thermonuclear protection gear, among other items), using technology that sounds like science fiction even by *Star Trek* standards. "The helmets were designed on a computer," explained Jein, "which then carved the pattern by catalyzing liquid resin. When we got the pattern from Oakley, we could still see all the strata lines on it, so we molded it, cast up a number of copies of the helmet and added working lights and other details."

The insectoid engineering helmets worn by Gorkon's assassins were designed by art director Nilo Rodis. "Richard Miller, who does a lot of ILM's sculpting, came down for a weekend and sculpted a full scale moquette in clay. The lenses were real protective eyewear, like mirrored sunglass lenses, provided by Oakley. Our little fannish touch on the helmets were the graphics we used above the visor area. They read E1 02 and E1 11, meaning engineering section 1, crewpersons number 2 and 11. By coincidence," Jein smiled, "those happen to be the code numbers the *Man From U.N.C.L.E.* series had given their two star agents."

The most innovative and exciting props made for the film were those used by the members of the barbaric Klingon Empire. One of the pieces he was most pleased with was Chancellor Gorkon's bone cane, which was supposed to be a bone from some savage beast he'd once killed. "We carved some bone shapes out of green foam," detailed Jein, "and Nick Meyer approved a design where the handgrip looked like a hip bone and the staff looked like a giant fang. We made four copies, two of which

were strong enough to support David Warner, who played Gorkon, and two of which were light enough to hang on wires for the anti-gravity assassination sequence."

Jein made a number of lightweight floating props for the zero-gravity assassination sequence, including a Klingon clipboard counterpart to Sulu's data counter (also a Jein creation), and a number of small Klingon laptop computers. "The computers were made from the bottom of the Ma saucer I built for *Batteries Not Included*," he admitted. "They have little viewscreens and are open on top so weirdly shaped clear cartridges, like futuristic floppy disks, can be slipped in."

When the action shifted to the Klingon court where Kirk and McCoy are being tried for Gorkon's murder, Jein created the barbaric seven-inch-long tridents the bailiffs carry to keep order in the court. The trident spear tips light up, and for extra nastiness, their handguards are schmitar-shaped.

Another piece of Klingon courtroom paraphernalia destined to be remembered by fans of the series is the albino judge's gavel glove, which resembles a mailed fist clutching a massive cracked steel ball in its metallic pincers. "I carved the ball shape out of green foam, then had one of my crew cast it," Jein explained. "We deviated from the usual Klingon red paint scheme and gave it an aged steel finish." From the moment the piece arrived on set, Jein said, there were problems. "We found that the actor playing the judge had arthritis, so the inside had to be soft and smooth. We had to hollow half of it out and pad it up. Light was supposed to shoot out from the cracks in the metal ball on impact, but the actor got too enthusiastic and the light broke on the second or third take."

To keep Kirk and McCoy at the mercy of their captors, Jein devised a set of asymmetrical Klingon handcuffs designed to pull the captive's wrists uncomfortably close together and remind audiences of old fashioned stocks. "Nick Meyer had the idea that they shouldn't be petite like modern handcuffs, but clunky, with a pillory feel to them," Jein said. "My idea was that once they were on, the guards could flick a little switch that adds artificial gravity to them, so they become heavier and the prisoners can't really raise their hands. When the switch was flicked, there was a little light that went on."

Jein also had fun sculpting a Klingon goblet that appeared to be made from some alien beast's horn mounted on a golden base, and creating what he calls "a Klingon garage-door opener," a V-shaped handheld control that lit up when a button was pushed to operate the main entrance to the Rura Penthe penal colony. When the script called for the warden to carry a nasty-looking scepter trimmed with Tribble fur, Jein made the prop out of metal with large spikes protruding from its back end. To finish it off, and as a sort of in-joke, the rear of the prop sported an aft thruster of a spaceship from the *Buck Rogers* TV show, while the front was detailed with the head of Buckaroo Banzai's pseudopod. One ghoulish prop Jein made was considered too grisly even for Klingons: a Tribble filled with gummy worms and tapioca "guts," which was designed to be ripped open by one of the guards for a snack.

Now if a Klingon were capable of snacking on something that disgusting, you'd think he'd have a phaser that fit into his holster, right? Well, as a matter of fact, ever since the Klingon phasers were redesigned the entire muzzle was cut off to fit into their holsters. That explains why, up until the latest film, no one has ever seen a Klingon draw his phaser. No wonder the Klingon Empire is falling apart. "On this film, Nick Meyer decided he wanted to show the Klingons drawing their phasers out of their holsters, so we had to cut the fronts of the existing pistols and redesign the front muzzle area," Jein smiled, "and now the Klingon phasers actually fit into their holsters."

Jein also got to build a phaser with a slide pump for villainous Klingon Chang. "It was for a sequence where Chang pointed the gun at someone, but he wanted it to have some added menace," he recalled. "We came up with the idea of putting a slide pump on the barrel, so it would be like he was pumping a shotgun and putting it to someone's head. We modified an existing gun, cut the plastic barrel off and replaced it with three metal tubes that fit into the original plastic muz-

zle and added a machined metal slide pump." Jein even went so far as to have a custom holster made for that gun.

Somewhat less exciting on the surface were the briefcases Jein and company built for the Klingon delegates to the Federation peace conference. Constructed from sturdy 1/4" plexiglass so they could be tossed around, painted the standard Klingon oxidized red, covered with decals and graphics from the art department to liven up their exteriors, the briefcases would appear to be quite banal after playing with phasers—and with the exception of one, they were. "Only the hero briefcase opened up," Jein remarked, "the one that contained the assassin's weapon."

Inside that nondescript case was a very organic Klingon assault rifle that Jein designed to break down into the component parts and assemble into a very lethal looking four foot long weapon. "Most of the Klingon stuff I designed had that quasi-organic look," he explained, "because my philosophy is that the Klingons came out of the sea originally and the sea was their basic cultural heritage, so a lot of their props have a biomorphic shape to them. I designed the original rifle on paper, then carved it out of green foam and molded it. Every part of the gun was cast, but some of the original patterns, like the barrel and telescopic site, were molded off a real assault rifle. The hero rifle was supposed to break down into a number of sections, and it took a bit of engineering to make something that snapped together. We looked at a lot of toys to see how they latched together with springs. When some of the parts didn't quite come out right, we had to tear the rifle apart and do it again. Eventually, the rifle consisted of six pieces: a fluid shoulder stock which doubled as a nutcracker, a stock extension [which was basically cast from the Klingon assault rifle stock made for *Trek III* by ILM], the main body section, the magazine handle which fit into the bottom of the body section, the telescopic site which could adjust right or left that fit on top of the main body, and the perforated machine-gun barrel that snapped on the front, which was cast off a real 20mm cannon. In addition to the one we made that broke apart, we also cast up a

few lightweight foam rifles that could be tossed around."

Despite Jein's self-deprecatory warning that he had nothing interesting to say about *Star Trek VI*, it appears he enjoyed creating memorable props and making various homages. "We always try to have fun," he admitted, "and I wanted to bring back some things that I hope the generation of people who grew up watching *Star Trek* will enjoy seeing again."

"This is the End... Or Is It?"

With the idea in mind that *Star Trek VI* would be the classic cast's swan song, co-writer Dennis Martin Flinn devised an ending for the film in which the characters would sign their names to their final log aboard the starship Enterprise, which not only ended the series with an emotional flourish but passed the baton to the next generation, both literally and figuratively. And although the signatures remain in the final cut, several changes were made.

"They reversed the order of the names so Shatner's is last, like an opera," said composer Cliff Eidelman. "It's a minute of signing off, which is real emotional music."

However, the only emotion writer Flinn experiences when he sees the signatures is anger. "They are different than how I conceived them originally," said Flinn. "My original script read the signatures were James T. Kirk, Mr. Spock, etc. What we were doing is offering them a chance to sign the final log. I thought that would be rather touching, especially since it's the last film and all, but it got changed to the actors instead of the characters and I personally dislike it very, very much. One of the actors who's executive producer, who shall go unnamed, likes it since I suppose he'd rather see his own name than his character's name up on the screen. A lot of people have argued both sides and I guess we lost. Frankly, I think no one gives a damn about Leonard Nimoy and William Shatner and those people in any substantive *Star Trek* sense. Those people are Mr. Spock and Kirk and Dr. McCoy, and I don't see any point of the actors signing their name to the log of the U.S.S. Enterprise. I'm upset that other people on the production haven't spoken up more who carry more weight than I do, like the producers who I know damn well agree with me but just did not fight it strongly enough. We're certainly in the majority, but the situation was not easy because I think the director and Leonard are the only two people who wanted that, but nobody wanted to argue except me."

And with the final flourish of Cliff Eidelman's score as the house lights came on in theatres, *Trek* fans were left to wonder if what they had just watched was truly the final mission of the original crew of the starship Enterprise. That question had become an equally hot topic among the members of the *Trek VI* production team prior to the film's release, with rumors running rampant that the ending was changed to be left more open-ended.

"I heard the same thing with *Star Trek II*," said director Nicholas Meyer. "I had nothing to do with bringing Spock back to life and if it had been up to me, my picture would not have ended ambiguously. This movie has only had one ending from the very beginning and that ending has never changed. I remember all the rumors that we filmed multiple endings for *II*. We never did that either. This film was written from the first draft the way it ended. There has never been any studio pressure or suggestion to change that, and I suppose that's because the ending doesn't preclude anything."

Flinn recalled a somewhat different coda for *Trek VI*'s climactic moments. "In rewrites and polishes Nick did the night before shooting, the final, final scene was rewritten. I honestly don't believe this came out of any desire on Nick's part to leave the door open, but out of the story and the metaphorical way that he writes. The nice thing that he wanted to do was a Peter Pan line—I guess he was in an optimistic mood that night—and the way the scene is structured there's no door being slammed, but, of course, you could always finesse that. It's up to the studio—and probably Leonard and Shatner as well."

Like most people both on and off the crew, Flinn, had been under the impression that Paramount had officially

sanctioned *Star Trek VI* as the final chapter of the "classic" cast's voyages, so he was surprised to find then recently installed studio head Brandon Tartikoff mulling *Trek*'s future after an early screening of the film for executives.

"I had always heard that this was the last film," recalled Flinn. "We had a very early screening for the executives [and] they liked it very much. They were all just standing around afterwards and Brandon Tartikoff, who had just literally taken over the studio, and who had virtually nothing to do with the film until that day, said 'Why is this the last film?' Everybody looked at each other saying 'Gee, didn't you tell me this was it?' and then everybody looked at Leonard, who really is the key, and he did not say 'No more from me.' I sort of thought he was saying, 'Well, it's your studio. Make me an offer.'"

"Brandon was very happy with the picture. He said 'You guys have given me an unexpected Christmas present'," agreed Ralph Winter, who added, "I had watched *Star Trek* as a kid and thought it was fun. It was a thrill to be involved with the picture. If you had asked me ten years ago that I would be producing the sixth *Star Trek* film, I'd think you were crazy. It's fun to think that this is really a part of American culture and to become a part of that and to make a contribution to that is fun and rewarding. But the biggest reward is to go to opening night at 8 o'clock and to sit down with an audience that has waited for months, avoided reading the script, wears a costume, brings a phaser and sits there and laughs, cries and has a good time. We do it for ourselves as much as everyone else and if we're entertained, we think everyone else will be. That's the reward.

"For 10 years I've been working on these pictures," continued Winter. "They've always said it's the last one. I'm tired of saying that and being wrong. This is the picture for the 25th anniversary and my feeling is the fans are going to be very pleased. It's a good story and good entertainment and a good mystery of unravelling the story with familiar characters."

And for Jimmy Doohan who will forever be known as Chief Engineer

Montgomery Scott as a result of three years he spent shooting a television show in the late '60s, the possibility of *Star Trek VII* is a relative certainty. "We all know that *Star Trek VI* is going to make a lot of money," he said. "Paramount's not going to let that go. There's going to be a *Star Trek VII*. To me, the last film idea is just a big come-on, come see the last film. The point is the film is going to stand by itself. It doesn't even need the words 'the last.' It'll make money and Paramount will not forget that. The fans just want to see us again and again. They don't care how old we get."

Noted George Takei, Captain Sulu of the Excelsior in *Star Trek VI*, "Maybe I need to recite you the history of the *Star Trek* movies. The first film was titled *Star Trek:* The *Motion Picture*, suggesting that's it, that's the movie. That was released, did mega business and they started talking about the only sequel, because sequels only do a certain percentage of their predecessors. They killed off Spock and you can't imagine doing *Star Trek* without Spock. That was released and made a ton of money and they started talking about a trilogy, which was kind of trendy at that time. But that means three, right? In *Star Trek III* you saw the Enterprise go down in flames, so that was the end. That made two tons of money. Then you start hearing about the last *Star Trek*, number four. Now we've done six and that's what they're telling you again, that this is the last one. Stick around. You'll start hearing about the ultimate, *very* final last movie."

Like Doohan and Takei, Nichelle Nichols is open-minded regarding the reprisal of her role as Commander Uhura in any future films. "This could be the end, but then again, who knows?" she stated rhetorically. "This is a wonderful one to end the series of films with and it wouldn't bother me one way or the other. I loved doing all of the films, each one of them being a miracle to me." Nichols pointed out that there was no great sense of loss on the last day of shooting because, "We never had a last day of shooting. On the supposed last day we went right to a *Good Morning America* interview on stage, we had all of the champagne and food and so forth, then we had a big photographic 'opportunity,' then the next day we had to get back into makeup and have a photo session. So it sort of kept going. I guess the most poignant feeling, for me anyway, was the first day, because going in to *VI* with the understanding that it was definitely the last *Star Trek* film, we were adjusted to that. Then the brass started coming in, the shinier brass from New York started flying in, they heard about the dailies being so good, they started to get excited and whispering began."

Walter "Chekov" Koenig would probably like to ignore those whispers, and leave the 23rd century behind him. "Maybe it's because I feel a certain satisfaction with the way this picture works," he suggested. "There is a sense of closure here. There are certain pragmatic aspects as to why this should be the last film. There are many people, certainly in the media, who feel we've overstayed our welcome to begin with. Each picture seems to emphasize more and more that we're at retirement age—we certainly look like we're at retirement age. When the media brings all that up, it really bothers me. It bothers me because that seems to be the springboard for every comment that comes afterward. To condemn the project or the performers because of their age is very unfair. I see that again and again. Once the statement is made that they all look like the over-the-hill-mob, it seems like there's no room to say anything good or positive. We no longer have Bill thrusting his tongue down some young lady's throat, because that wouldn't work. We've made that concession. We don't get involved in hand-to-hand fighting, because that would perhaps be stretching credibility. But in terms of reflexes, in terms of functioning on the ship, in terms of ideas, I don't think we should be condemned as a group and summarily dismissed as a consequence of the age factor.

"I [also] think the studio feels they have an up-and-coming contender waiting in the wings, *The Next Generation*," he added. "I think they think this is the last picture, not that that stands irrevocable, but their thinking now is along those terms. 'For 25 years you've done a bang-up job. We've made a whole thing about this being the last voyage, let's leave it at that.' There's a cer-

tain amount of wish-fulfillment on my part. I'm ready to let go. I'm not fed up, not oversaturated with *Star Trek*, I'm just ready to let go and see if there's anything else out there. I'd like to be hungry again. With that apprehension, with that need, comes hopefully some inspiration and some creativity."

DeForest Kelley, who is finally taking in Dr. Leonard "Bones" McCoy's medical shingle, considers what he'll miss most. "Just knowing it's not there," he began. "It's been such a big part of my life for 25 years. Nothing has hit me yet. I will think more about it when Tartikoff or somebody else says, 'This is it.' Then you kind of take a breath and say, 'It's not going to be there.' *Star Trek* felt like something that was always going to be there, and it isn't. But I think after the finality of it really hits, then I'll reflect on it and get on with my life."

"The last day of the old series," stated Leonard Nimoy, "when we found out we had been cancelled, I carefully took off my ears, put them in a box and mounted them on a wall in my home. I really thought that was the last time I would wear them. I never thought we would do this again. It looks like I've got another pair of ears to mount on the wall, but this time I'm sure it's the last time. I'm very grateful that it happened. I feel a great sense of accomplishment. Overall, we've done some sincere work. I hope that the general fallout is positive; I think it is. I'm very pleased when I hear that people's lives have been affected positively in one way or the other because of *Star Trek*. In general, I've had very good, positive feelings about it."

Noted William Shatner, "This is definitely the last one, no question about it. The studio says it's the last one, it's written as the last one, the cast accepts it as the last one and it is definitely the last one. I suppose that in its wisdom the studio thinks it's time to call a halt to it and give it a sense of finality. [I'm feeling] great nostalgia, great sadness. I feel a sense of loss. It's a wonderful character and another setting in which to place the character. I love action films with some kind of conflict, so the human conflict is told in action-adventure rather than a sedate tone. A picture should move, and *Star Trek* lends itself to that genre. There

are lots of stories to be told and lots of things to be done in the films still, but unfortunately, for one reason or another—and don't ask me what those reasons are—it's been decided that this is the last film. I leave it with great reluctance and great sorrow."

But as time would prove, Shatner wasn't quite finished with the character just yet.

Star Trek: Generations

Launching The Next Generation On Film

Jean Luc Picard enters the quarters of his first officer, Commander Riker, where his crew is assembled for their weekly poker game. Surprising everyone, the captain asks if he can join them. Staring admiringly around the table, he notes, "I should have done this a long time ago."

So concluded "All Good Things," the series finale of *Star Trek: The Next Generation*, which should have been followed by a poignant wrap party where cast and crew would celebrate one last time before saying their farewells and embarking on the separate paths their careers would take them. Unlike the conclusion of such television powerhouses as *M*A*S*H* or *Cheers*, however, it would only be a matter of days before everyone would regroup to begin production of the feature film, *Star Trek: Generations*. It's a fact that most definitely impacted on the shooting of the show.

"Unfortunately," noted veteran *Trek* director Winrich Kolbe, who also helmed the $26 million *Voyager* pilot, "the movie was there and everybody, especially Patrick Stewart, was involved in the moviemaking process which took away from the attention to that particular show. So the best laid plans of mice and men began to crumble rather early in the shooting and we had to struggle. It's a show that I would never want to do again and would love to do again. I think that's the feeling we all had. I'm very proud of what we did, it's a good looking show and we gave the series a dignified ending, but what a pain in the ass it was to shoot."

Actress Marina Sirtis, who portrays Enterprise counselor Deanna Troi, pointed out that there wasn't a feeling of finality while shooting "All Good Things," although emotions did run high.

"I knew we were doing the movie, but Michael Dorn [Worf] was crying like a baby," she laughed, "and I'm never going to let him live it down because he was the one who kept saying,

Generations: Star Trek creator Gene Roddenberry flanked by two of his "offspring": William Shatner (Captain James T. Kirk) and Patrick Stewart (Captain Jean Luc Picard)(photo copyright ©1994 Albert Ortega)

'I can't wait for this to be over.'

"The day we shot the poker scene," added Sirtis, "was the day that Majel [Barrett] Roddenberry came to the set and she was very, very emotional. She came to my trailer in tears and I was trying to cheer her up by saying, 'Majel, it's not the end. There's *DS9*, *Voyager*, and *Star Trek* will continue.' She said, and I think it's true, that we were the last of Gene's children, and when we're gone, Gene's vision will be gone. Even though *Deep Space Nine* is called *Star Trek*, it's not really based on the precepts that Gene had in mind when he created *Star Trek*."

And now, the children have grown up in the form of *Generations*, the first motion picture based on the syndicated TV series, *Star Trek: The Next Generation*.

Announced in October of 1986, virtually on the 20th anniversary of the original series, *ST: TNG* premiered a year later and introduced audiences to the crew of a new starship Enterprise: Captain Jean Luc Picard (Patrick Stewart), Commander William Riker (Jonathan Frakes), android science officer Data (Brent Spiner), Dr. Beverly Crusher (Gates McFadden), her brilliant son, Wesley (Wil Wheaton); navigator turned chief engineer Geordi La Forge (LeVar Burton), Klingon tactical officer Worf (Michael Dorn), security chief Tasha Yar (Denise Crosby) and ship counsellor Deanna Troi (Marina Sirtis). Of all these characters, only Yar and Wesley would depart, though they ultimately made several guest appearances each.

The series, which took place about 75 years after events of the original show, was initially viewed as an insipid successor to the throne, whose plots were thinly veiled remakes of so-called "Trek Classic" episodes. But the show began to find its own identity in its second season and came in to its own from the third onward. *Star Trek: The Next Generation* remained on the air for seven seasons, and was canceled at the height of its popularity. The culprit? Paramount Pictures, the studio which had decided that they had gone as far as they could with a film franchise featuring the original cast. The time, they reasoned, had come for *Star Trek: The Next Generation* to make the leap to the big screen.

Despite having signed the cast for an eighth season, this decision actually does contain some fiscal sense. Removing the show from the airwaves while still so popular would virtually guarantee box office success. Besides,

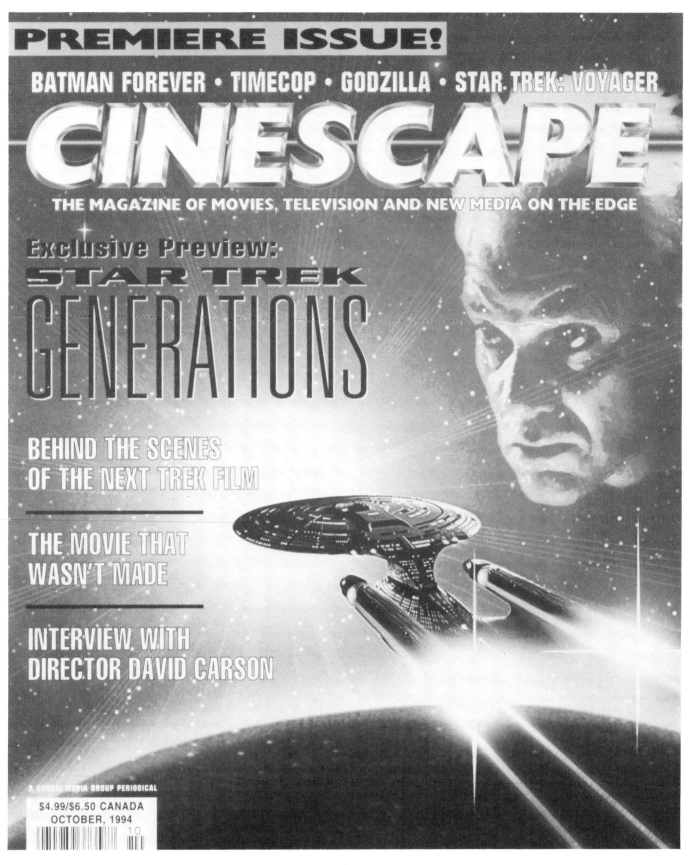

PREMIERE ISSUE!

BATMAN FOREVER • TIMECOP • GODZILLA • STAR TREK: VOYAGER

CINESCAPE

THE MAGAZINE OF MOVIES, TELEVISION AND NEW MEDIA ON THE EDGE

Exclusive Preview:

STAR TREK
GENERATIONS

**BEHIND THE SCENES
OF THE NEXT TREK FILM**

**THE MOVIE THAT
WASN'T MADE**

**INTERVIEW WITH
DIRECTOR DAVID CARSON**

A SENDAI MEDIA GROUP PERIODICAL

$4.99/$6.50 CANADA
OCTOBER, 1994

reruns of the series would undoubtedly air for decades to come and there were two spin-offs to take its place, *Star Trek: Deep Space Nine* and *Star Trek: Voyager.*

Patrick Stewart, for one, was pleased that the show ended when it did, particularly as he was one of the few holdouts who hadn't necessarily committed to season eight. Rumors have it that he was one of the main reasons the studio canceled the series.

"I am flattered by those remarks, that people should think that I have that much power," he smiled. "In fact, Paramount and I had an open arrangement for an eighth season and this time the option was on both sides, which is a little unusual. As it happened, the studio pulled the show. I was never consulted, but I felt their timing was perfect. I liked the idea that we would end the series when we were on top. The very final episode that we did was one of the best that we had done in the whole show. But everyone was pretty much ready to move on. I started to fear that I as an actor might start repeating myself. Days were not as interesting and as exciting as they had been and I was look for fresh fields and pastures new. I wish we had not had to go into the movie quite so quickly as we did. I had four days off between wrapping the series and stepping on board the Lady Washington in Santa Monica Bay. Luckily I did not have to do too much character research before we went."

Like Stewart, Brent Spiner was reluctant to come back for an eighth season, and probably wouldn't have appeared had the series continued. "We had done 178 hours," he pointed out. "One hundred and seventy eight hours of anything is just about enough, I think, and it was a brutal sort of seven years of work. I was glad not to have to get up at 5:00 in the morning anymore. I think we were really almost all ready to stop doing it. Maybe a couple of people would have been interested in doing an eighth, season, but not many of us really. I think we felt, 'Yeah, we have done this now for seven years and with luck, we will get to come back and do it every couple of years.' I'd like to do more movies for the reason that I get to come back together with my friends and have some fun

Star Trek: Generations is produced by Rick Berman, who, along with Michael Piller, co-created the Trek spin-offs, Deep Space Nine and Voyager (photo copyright ©1994 Albert Ortega).

again. It would be like going to summer camp every couple of years."

Generations began when Paramount Pictures approached series executive producer Rick Berman, who had replaced the late Gene Roddenberry as Great Bird of the Galaxy.

"I was asked to do the movie in February of 1993," said Berman. "The plan was I would write two stories with

two separate writers and that I would be involved with selecting which one was the best. One writer for the film was Maurice Hurley, who worked with us before, and the other was the team of Brannon Braga and Ron Moore. We spent the early spring of '93 writing both stories and, by late spring, the studio and I agreed that we wanted to pursue the one with Brannon and Ron. The studio embraced the story very quickly."

One similarity between both scripts is that they featured, in some shape or form, members of the original _Star Trek_ cast which was not, surprisingly, an edict of the studio.

"When I was first asked to do this, I was not asked to do anything with the original characters," emphasized Berman. "They wanted a _Next Generation_ movie. I went to them and said, 'I would like to integrate the characters from the original series, do you have any problem with it?' Sherry Lansing and John Goldwyn, the people I was dealing with in the motion picture division, said great. They said contact Bill and Leonard and see if they have a problem with it and they did not. Then in the script that Ron and Brannon wrote, we developed a story that had all of the characters, originally focusing mostly on the character of Kirk."

◼ A Great Adventure

Maurice Hurley, who had served as a co-executive producer of the series in its early days, and whose greatest contribution was probably the introduction of the cybernetic race, the Borg, describes his screenplay as "a great adventure."

Although ultimately not chosen, it promised quite a ride for fans of the defunct series.

"There was basically a fold in space," Hurley explained, "and an adversary who had been in a battle was blown through it into our universe. It is trying to get home to save its species, but in order to do that — and in order to get home — it has to basically destroy us."

The analogy he draws is to a parent in a schoolyard with his two-year-old child, with the parent on one end and the child on the other. The child is in a dangerous situation, about to die.

"You rush across the schoolyard," he proposed, "stepping on toes, knocking down children, breaking bones, and smashing heads to get to your baby. Then you save your baby and you look back at all the mayhem and chaos and blood that you have caused among all these other two-year-old children. You could have killed one of them, but it

Patrick Sewart and William Shatner together at Creation's "Two Captains" convention. (Photo copyright © 1994 Karen Witkowski)

wouldn't have made a difference to you until after the fact when you looked back and said, 'Oh my God, what did I do? I'm sorry, but I just didn't have a choice.' That's the story. These other people who are here and are about to destroy us are basically saying, 'Sorry, but there's nothing we can do about it. You're all going to have to die.'"

Although the Enterprise is sent out

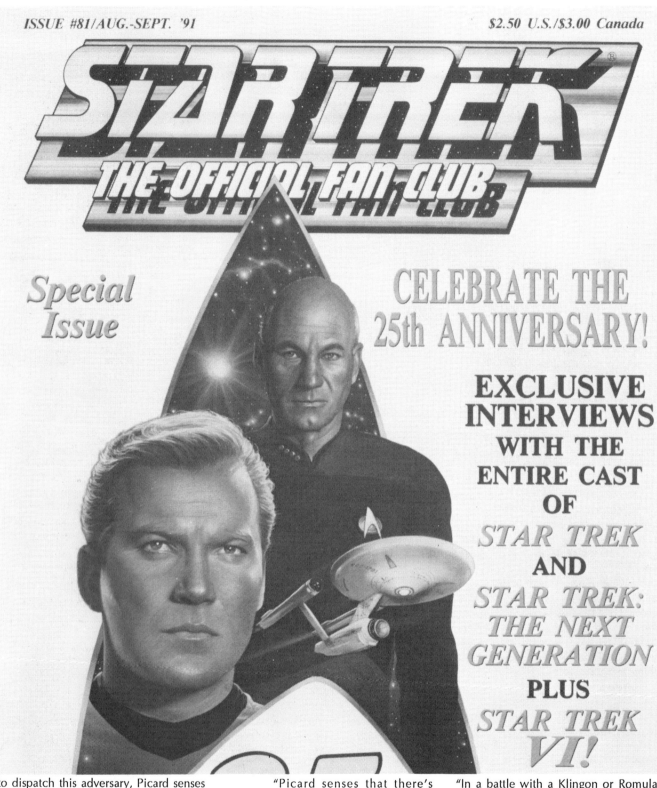

ISSUE #81/AUG.-SEPT. '91

$2.50 U.S./$3.00 Canada

STAR TREK
THE OFFICIAL FAN CLUB

Special Issue

CELEBRATE THE 25th ANNIVERSARY!

EXCLUSIVE INTERVIEWS WITH THE ENTIRE CAST OF *STAR TREK* AND *STAR TREK: THE NEXT GENERATION* PLUS *STAR TREK VI*!

to dispatch this adversary, Picard senses that all is not as it seems with the alien; that the destruction being caused must have a purpose, though it seemingly doesn't.

"Picard senses that there's something else going on here because he finds no subtext for the attack, and all battles have subtext," Hurley pointed out.

"In a battle with a Klingon or Romulan there's a subtext and you can define what that subtext is. Romulans want to kick your ass and in the process of kicking your ass they want you to know how damn smart and superior they are. These people have no subtext and Picard says that's wrong. They have to have one. What is it? That among other things starts him investigating, causing him to veer one way where, on the surface, it seems he should be veering the other way."

Part of Picard's investigation is to go to the holodeck to call up the image of Captain James T. Kirk (the only classic character used in the screenplay), who experienced a similar situation in the original series episode, "The Tholian Web," in which the captain, on board the USS Defiant, is trapped in another dimension.

"It's the only other time on record that it ever happened," Hurley noted, "and the only other person who ever witnessed it was Kirk. So Picard and Kirk have witnessed, separated by time, similar events. Now you want to say, 'Wait a minute, I see it this way, how do you see it? Did it happen to you the same way it happened to me? If it was different, how was it different?' It was Picard's attempt to get an emotional point of view, or another point of view, from the Kirk character that differed from what he was getting from pure facts. For instance, if you describe an event for me and I read it and you say, 'The sky was red and there was a lot of noise,' well, what does that mean to me? What is red? What red are you talking about? What kind of noise? Relate it to something for me.

"If you're dead and all I have is your writings, I have no way of knowing that. If I can go back and talk to you, when you say red you absolutely see a color. So do I. Your color red might be fire engine and mine might be maroon. If I know that, that alters how I view what you're saying. Noise also means something. What's noise to me, what's noise to you? You know what those answers are. The computer would just put down noise, but if the computer regenerated you in terms of a sense of who you are, how you viewed noise is presumably how you would still view it. So I get the subtlety from the personal interview that I don't get off the page. That's all Picard's after.

"But that's not enough," he continued, "so he starts manipulating the image so it basically becomes a couple

of bizarre scenes between Picard and Kirk and it gets confrontational at certain moments. You want to bring back Kirk and not have it get confrontational? Kirk will get confrontational with anyone. In *Star Trek V*, he got confrontational with God! So it became a way to put those two classic characters and two really great actors together, and let them bang on each other."

Despite the fact that Berman has indicated Hurley's script could be filmed as a sequel to the current film, the writer doesn't think it's likely to happen.

"Everything has it's time," said Hurley, "and it's seldom that somebody goes back to the pot. It's a good idea and a good story that Rick Berman and I worked hard on. But that's just the way it is."

■ Warping To The Big Screen

When writing their screenplay, Ron Moore and Brannon Braga, who have subsequently joined the respective staffs of *DS9* and *Voyager*, most definitely had a game plan, beginning with screenings of the first six films in the series.

"We sat down and watched the first six several times," said Moore. "We watched *IV* closely. We watched *The Wrath of Khan* several times because it's my favorite of the six films and I think the best as far as the story level and execution. We just sort of looked for how they handled some things. We didn't really say let's make them like the other ones, but we wanted to get a feel for how *Star Trek* translated to the big screen and what the action sequences were like. For instance, we got very, very used to writing tightly controlled space battles on the series where there are only two exterior shots when a phaser hits and you shake the camera a lot. To break ourselves out of that, we watched the Reliant attack on the Enterprise and how they really milk it."

Added Braga, "Undoubtedly the two best films are *Wrath of Khan* and *The Voyage Home*. *Voyage Home* was laughs. It's the most fun, it's the best movie, I think. But *II* was wonderful because it had a very serious undercurrent, and Khan was a great villain. If

Ron Moore, co-writer of Generations, is basically the man who killed Kirk.

we've done our job, we've captured the best of both worlds. Ron and I both feel that we have captured just the right mix of humor, action and character."

One point that Moore made clear is that writing the film had a different set of requirements than the series did.

"It has to appeal to a different audience, in a sense," he noted. "The studio tells us that we can't assume that everyone going to this movie is familiar with the television show. It couldn't be a story that depended on the TV series and was mired in our back stories. We also didn't want something incredibly technical. We wanted something that was broader and had more action and adventure. We also wanted something with a lot more humor than we normally do on the series. We had a lot more money so we wanted to do things that you couldn't do on the series and yet we wanted to be

Johnathan Frakes with Generations co-writer Brannon Braga.

The Next Generation gathers in the engine room of the Enterprise.
(Photo copyright © 1994 David Strick / Onyx)

able to do things that were big and fun and not like, 'Oh gee, they got loose In the candy store and they really just gorged themselves and it became stupid.' It was a fine line. We had to maintain what the show is about and be true to the series that we worked on for seven years and what it had become — and we had to translate that into a different format and into a different structure."

Concurred Braga, "It was very important to us that this film not be so self-referential to this franchise that the people who aren't familiar with *Star Trek* would be confused. There are embellishments throughout the movie — Farpoint is referred to passingly, as is the Borg, but you've got to be careful on the big screen. This movie's got to have a broader appeal.

"We had a lot of time to do a script," he added. "The biggest challenge was to fill the big screen and to make the action bigger, the humor bigger and to find ways to satisfy the big-screen requirements. We could do things that we could never do on the show in terms of big action sequences. We had to give it an epic feel and we also had to make sure that the film had a broader spectrum because it was our feeling that someone who had never watched this show should be able to enjoy this film in its own right."

Coming up with the actual scenario for the film was not, Braga emphasized, difficult. "It's tough coming up with stories week to week on the series," he said. "The movie was not so tough because we had some spectacular story elements in place at the get go. We knew Kirk was going to be in it and that some of the other original series' characters were going to be in it. We knew that Guinan would be there. We knew what we wanted to do with Data. We had some *major* stuff we wanted to accomplish, so we had great story elements in place. Coming up with the actual space-time Nexus and what the villain is doing was not a struggle. It was a lot of fun. Because it's a movie, you can take big risks with the characters and do more event kind of plotting techniques, because you're not obligated to do an episode the following week. I think what we ended up with was a very funny film with a lot of humor, but a dark film as well. Its theme does deal with death. Picard suffers a terrible personal tragedy, Kirk is facing profound regret in his life. There are some somber moments and ultimately there are some very dark things that happen. I think there are some surprisingly somber sections."

According to Moore, one of the earliest concerns was exactly how the two crews would be brought together, and to what extent.

"The image that Brannon and I were most in love with was the idea of a movie poster for the film showing the Enterprise-D and the Enterprise-A locked in combat, shooting at each other. If you could have a situation where you had the two ships coming to blows, that would be really cool. But it quickly became apparent that finding the motivation for the two to be at such odds and then keeping them both sympathetic and heroic was going to be a real tough sell. It was going to be too much trouble to get to this one cool scene at the end of the film. We knew we didn't want to do a time travel story and we didn't want the original crew to all be ancient like McCoy was in the 24th century, so Rick came up with the idea of a mystery that started in the 23rd century, then picked up 78 years later in the 24th century. We knew that everyone was going to want

the two captains to meet, since they had never met, and that led to a discussion of having them meet somewhere other than the 23rd or 24th centuries, in a place where time had no meaning. That led us to the Nexus."

For Berman, who had been the final arbiter of all things *Trek* since the death of Gene Roddenberry, the idea of having other voices involved in lording over this particular universe was an alien notion.

"The development stages of writing the film and being involved with Ron and Brannon's script was the most delightful part of making the film," said Berman. "It was a very creative time. On the production part of it there were a lot of budgetary battles that had to be fought in the early stages and a lot of people whom I was not used to working with. We also had tremendous problems negotiating with the actors. All the actors wanted to do the movie, but here was a 130-page script with characters they were playing which put them in a very good negotiating position, so the negotiations, which I was never personally involved with, were very traumatic in terms of the pressure that went on between the actors and the studio."

The budget battles didn't stop there. The goal of broadening the television show's high quality into an epic movie framework proved daunting to the

writers, who were charged with taking *Next Gen*'s already high production values and making them even more expansive. The film's early drafts were budgeted at $45 million, a figure at which the studio immediately balked.

"We sort of shot ourselves in the foot to a certain extent because we, on a weekly basis, deliver a series that has almost feature-level production qualities to start with," noted Moore. "You look at the original *Star Trek* series and look at the movies and there is a vast difference. The original series didn't have much money at all, so it was a very cardboard kind of look, but *Next Generation* and *Deep Space Nine* look like mini-motion pictures every single week. So there's a certain logic to the studio saying, 'Here is three or four times that much money, you should be able to give us something that we can put in a theatre and be proud of.' We already had a lot of standing sets, we had a lot of special effects work and we already had a cast. I don't have a sense of getting shafted by them and I don't think Rick does. The first draft came in and they budgeted it at some ridiculous figure and we knew it was absurd. There is always a certain gamesmanship with the budgets, but I don't really feel like I got the short end of things. We had to trim some things back and cut some things, but we do that every week on the series and we're used to it."

Worf (Michael Dorn) looks distrustfully at the cameras.
(Photo copyright © 1994 David Strick / Onyx)

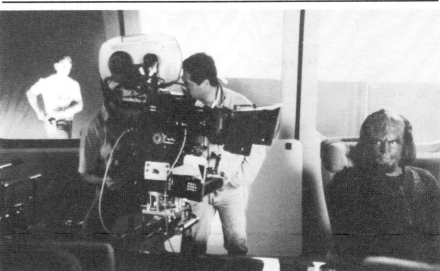

■ Directing The Generations Gap

While Moore and Braga wrote their script, Berman and the studio turned their collective sights toward the director's chair. Initially there had been some talk of hiring a so-called "big screen" director to helm this voyage of the Enterprise, but that plan was abandoned. The point had apparently been driven home by *Star Trek: The Motion Picture*, directed by the highly esteemed Robert Wise, that Academy Awards don't make up for a lack of *Trek* knowledge.

In the case of *Star Trek: Generations*, Berman wisely looked to his own, choosing director David Carson. To his credit, Carson had helmed some of the best episodes of *The Next Generation* (including "Yesterday's Enterprise") as well as the $12 premiere of *Deep Space Nine*, which one would assume served as an appropriate "sample reel" for someone tapped to direct a $26 million feature.

"I think everybody at Paramount was pleased with the pilot of *Deep Space Nine*," offered the English-born Carson, whose other episodic credits include *L.A. Law* and *Alien Nation*, and who had scored as director of many Jeremy Brett Sherlock Holmes dramas in England. "When it was decided that Rick was going to produce the movie, I think everybody thought it would be a good idea if I directed it, keeping up the partnership with him, as it were. It also has to be said that I'm going to be cheaper, which I know had nothing to do with Paramount's decision."

The choice of Carson was an exciting one for many members of the cast.

"David is one of those rare breed who is an actor's director *and* a technical director," enthused Marina Sirtis. "*Star Trek* needs someone like that. We had directors on the series who were very good with the actors and bringing out the motivations, but when it came time to make the show look interesting, they fell flat on their face. Or we had the opposite, where they were moving the camera around and had these great action shots, but when it came time to

EXCLUSIVE MEMOIR
MANDELA: THE PRISON YEARS

TIME

STAR TREK
THE PASSION THAT DRIVES THE ENTERPRISE

William Shatner
and Patrick Stewart

say, 'Why should I be here?', the answer was, 'The camera's there, that's why.' So he's the rare combination of the two. A real joy."

Concurred William Shatner, who hadn't worked with Carson before, "He's an actor's director. He brought an entertainer's intellect to the film; a man who's always looking for the entertainment qualities of the scene."

Brent Spiner noted that Carson's approach on a feature film wasn't very

different than their collaborations on the small screen, with the exception that they had the luxury of more time.

"Generally on the series we were shooting between eight and ten pages a day," he said. "On the feature we were doing between two and three pages a day. That afforded both David and the cast the opportunity to try more and to actually get it right as opposed to just get it. But as a director in general — and I was more aware of it on the film because

in the episodes David has directed, I never had that much to do — I found him really, really bright, prepared and whenever I would be at a loss of where to take something, he had a real clear vision on where it should go. I found him enormously helpful and I admired his sort of digging his heels in because as always happens, I think there are time and monetary constraints that the studio has to be concerned about. But David made his primary concern, I think, to make a good picture and just basically refused to be budged on that notion. He would basically just dig his heels in and say, 'I don't want to just make a movie, I would like to make a very good movie if possible,' and he stuck to that all the way through the final day of shooting."

The choice of Carson also belies the fear that the attitude on *Generations* — as it had been on *ST: TMP* — would be one of making changes for the sake of change simply because the show is being adapted for film.

"Frankly I don't think there's a lot of difference between television and film," offered Carson. "There's all this big noise about how amazing it is and how different movies and TV are, but I think that it's a lot of nonsense. Everyone who's been involved in the series has been doing it for seven years. For example, the guys making the costumes and doing the make-up have been doing it for seven years. How stupid it would be to say, 'Oh, this is a movie, let's get some movie costume and make-up people in here.' I don't think this is a case where one need to change everything, because everything's working very well. You don't need to say, 'This is a movie, we better do this and change it all so nobody recognizes the Enterprise.' You can make modifications to some small things that will delight everybody, but I just think it's a waste of time, money and everything else to make changes for no reason."

He pointed out, however, when you're operating at the speed necessary for television, it's a medium that's far more forgiving than the big screen.

"Things that we do on television, like laser things and beam-ins and beam-outs, have to be treated differently on the large screen because you can see it all so clearly. You can't get away with as much as you can on the little screen. Similarly, in terms of color schemes, like exactly how dark the bridge is and the fact that you can't light it flatly, which is what it basically is on television. It's just a flat, even lighting which the people live in. When you put it up on the big screen, I think you're going to need more contrasts, more light and shades. At the same time, it's much better, it seems to me, to have the people who have been doing the TV series mold themselves to a new concept rather than necessarily bringing in a whole new team. So I think all the prejudice against TV people making features is silly. On the other hand, bringing in feature people to help us to make this look wonderful is probably wise of us."

How daunting, though, was it to go from a maximum television budget of $12 million to a feature film with an ultimate pricetag of about $30 million?

"In a funny way," Carson related, "it isn't daunting. When I was a theater

Avery Brooks, Nana Visitor and Majel Barrett at the premiere of Star Trek: Generations (Photo copyright © 1994 Albert Ortega)

director, I always said if you're any good at your job you ought to be able to take a budget of $500 or a budget of $50 million and do a good job with both. Neither one should faze you. You should simply embrace the limitations of the one and not go crazy with the excesses of the other, and try to just hold on to your creative spark, whatever that is, and be true to it.

"It is very exciting to be doing something on such a large scale for the huge screen," he elaborated, "which you know so many people are going to see because of what it is. At the same time, it has all the same logistical problems and all the other things that have to be solved that are very similar to any other artistic endeavor that involves words, actors and cameras. So I've never found a great difference between the tiny budget of the theater and the larger budget of TV and the enormous budget of the movies. To me, it all comes down to the same thing: how you cut the coat out of the cloth that you're given."

One assumed difference between working on *Generations* and the TV series was the relationship between Carson and Rick Berman, given

the fact that motion pictures are much more a director's medium than a producer's. Carson denied that this was ever a problem.

"When you work on television," Carson detailed, "you are a guest of the production, the producers, the writers and the actors, and you try to serve the production the best that you can within the parameters and guidelines of what everyone is doing on a regular basis. When you do two hour movies or pilots, then the same team structure applies except that you are in on the ground floor and you can work more or less on an even footing with the producers and the writers. Then again, you have to be aware that if you're doing a pilot, as I was with *Deep Space Nine*, all of these people are planning for seven years of work. You're doing two hours of material, but after those two hours it's 'Thank you very much. Good-bye.' Therefore they have to make decisions which affect your two-hour show because they are making their decisions for the future of the series.

"When you come to a movie," he elaborated, "everyone starts with their

delineated roles. In Rick's and my relationship, we had worked closely and happily together on episodes of the series and the pilot of *Deep Space Nine*, but with the parameters that I described. Therefore, when we came to do the film, our roles did not change automatically. What happened was that Rick gave me the space that a film director is normally accorded, which was extremely generous of him because he was working with the same people he had worked on the series with. And he, as producer, is accustomed to having the last word. But he handed me the baton, as it were, to conduct the orchestra and I conducted it. In return for that courtesy, I always worked closely with him in the creation of the whole thing.

"It really was Rick's choice to give me the movie," Carson emphasized, "and it was potentially a big risk for him. I acknowledged that that was a big risk and also acknowledged that I was flattered by his ability to entrust me with it. As far as I was concerned, we were continuing our creative partnership together, going down that path hand in hand, to use an awkward metaphor. The film is not being compromised, but is instead a true creative partnership."

Several problems faced that partnership before shooting even began. Initially, when the first draft script was handed in, it featured an opening sequence that starred the entire original cast. Unfortunately, with the exception of Shatner, James Doohan and Walter Koenig, no one else wanted to be involved, feeling that they had said a more meaningful farewell in the last film, *The Undiscovered Country*.

"*Generations* would have been wonderful if it had been a genuine passing of the torch," said George Takei, whose Mr. Sulu became captain of the Excelsior in *Star Trek VI*. "As it turns out, it's a little prologue, a brief cameo at the beginning. That was not as attractive as I had originally envisioned. For me, *Star Trek VI* was such a glorious experience, that I didn't want to dilute that wonderful after-taste."

Patrick Stewart explained, "It had been an argument of mine....that the film should include as many of the original *Star Trek* members as we could get. For the most part, I was alone in this feel-

DeForest Kelley decided that "The Undiscovered Country" was a better farewell for Bones. (Photo copyright © Albert Ortega)

ing. Most of my colleagues didn't share this point-of-view and felt, since this would be a transitional movie, we should just cut the original cast off. I felt having members of the original cast would provide the opportunity to present something really intense and dramatic. I was thrilled and relieved when offers did go out to the original cast and it saddened me when only three of them were in it. I was particularly saddened that Leonard and De were not in it. I felt they would have made a marvelous contribution. But critical to all this was to have Bill. I felt that having the two captains share screen space was something audiences would enjoy seeing."

Leonard Nimoy might have considered the film if it had been rewritten. "I just didn't buy the script," he explained. "There was a character called Spock who had a dozen lines you could easily assign to anyone else, which they did. I felt they needed to rethink the story, and the response was, 'We don't have time.' So I said, 'Bon voyage — good luck.'"

Rick Berman elaborated on this, noting that the way the story evolved, the only integral character from the original series was Kirk.

"This has nothing to do with Leonard," he said pointedly. "The other [characters] all had relatively minor roles. And in the case of Leonard and De Kelley, they both felt that they had made appropriate good-byes in _Star Trek VI_ and there was no reason to bring the characters back for — I wouldn't call them cameos, but they were only in the first 15 minutes and that was it. In the case of Bill, it was a whole different story. His part has a great deal more depth to it."

Carson clarified one point. "George Takei in a way was in the film," he noted, pointing to early scenes that featured Sulu's daughter. "I thought it was a wonderful way of continuing the generations and speaking about mortality. It was more important for us, I think, to deal with our theme, which is about mortality, the handing on of torches, the passing from generation to generation. To have a child of one of the originals on board the ship actually makes a greater point than producing everybody from the last series. To have the entire old cast makes it become a little bit like all boy's club instead of telling the story. We wanted to have a point. It wasn't a lark

and romp in space."

Nonetheless, Nimoy's departure from the film was a disappointment to Carson.

"You know from the press how Leonard feels," he said. "I think it's unfortunate. I believe at some convention or another — and this is heresy — he tried to explain that if the role wasn't very good, he didn't want to be in it as an actor. The fans' view is, 'What do you mean? We made you. Our loyalty made you what you are and gave you your career. We don't care how big the part is, we just want to see you.' And I understand that point of view. I think it was a pity he wasn't willing to swallow his pride and come along. In the end, though, I think it's a great thing that the issue is not clouded and the film is about the two captains. It's not what Spock is doing, but rather this new relationship between Kirk and Picard. The film is basically about their journey toward each other. That's what makes this movie fun; that's what drives people to see it."

Carson understands the implications of bringing together these two pop-culture legends. "I'm well aware that Kirk and his crew are American icons who

Both James Doohan and Walter Koenig were piped on board as the only original members besides Shatner to join The Next Generation. _(Phot copyright © 1994Albert Ortega)_

Marina Sirtis with husband in hand.   *(Photo copyright © 1994 Albert Ortega)*

I'm very happy with it."

Concurred Jonathan Frakes, "It changed so much and we were really cut out of the other part of the story. Worf and I have the 'B' story now and, originally, we were tied in a little bit to the Nexus story. Now we no longer are. It's like a big Picard episode, with the 'B' story being those on the Away Team. That's what it all comes down to, but, hey, it's a great job. Maybe I'll have more to do in the next movie. I'm not one to complain."

Brannon Braga pointed out that through the course of a season there were 26 hours to explore the various characters, whereas *Generations* would have, at the most, two hours to tell its story.

"We had to choose who this movie was about," said Braga. "The movie's about Picard and Data. To an extent, it's about Kirk. The other characters all have great moments, Dr. Crusher the least of which. But this is just the reality of our time situation. It's not to say if there's another film we won't focus on other characters. We just felt it had to be about Picard because he's our captain and our primary focus. And Data has to be the second most popular character, and we had to tell a story about him. But everyone has a role to play. I can't imagine people are going to be disappointed."

Marina Sirtis doesn't see the ensemble falling into the so-called "gang of four" syndrome of original series cast members, due primarily to the fact that the *Next Generation* cast usually had much more to do than their predecessors.

"I think *Generations* is a transitional movie," she offered, "and consequently had William Shatner and members of the original cast. However, we as a cast always got much more to do on the show than the original gang of four did. They were really supporting actors. On our show, Patrick and Brent were the main characters, but Worf got a hell of a lot, and I got four or five scripts a season based on my character, Gates got storylines, LeVar had much more to do than Jimmy Doohan did as chief engineer. So I don't think we were excluded as much as they were."

Rick Berman was very much aware of the fact that there would be some unhappiness on the part of certain

have achieved a certain mythology in American folk art, if you like. They have a very specific place beyond simply being characters in a TV show. And I am aware of the responsibility of having Kirk and Picard together. It's very tantalizing to have them in the same place, interacting."

Similar problems arose from within, when several members of the ensemble voiced reservations about the screenplay and their relatively minor roles in it. Most notable among the dissenters were Michael Dorn and Marina Sirtis.

"In hindsight, I think it was my own inexperience in filmmaking in Hollywood that messed me up," Sirtis admitted sheepishly. "In England it's very different. There you get a script and you shoot a script. In America, that isn't the way it works. Rewriting is happening up until the day you shoot it. When we were approached about doing the movie, we were reading the first draft. The first draft bore no relation to the final draft. When we finally wrapped the movie, we were all very excited about how good it was.

cast members concerning their seemingly diminished roles.

"This was a movie that had fifteen roles in it that had already been cast before we wrote the movie," he explained, "so you are not dealing with actors who read for a role and get it and are happy just to get it. You have actors who have the role already, who feel they know more about the character than you do, and who undoubtedly feel underpaid and underused. That is something you've got to deal with very sensitively. We have seven characters from *The Next Generation*, Whoopi is eight, three characters from the original series. That is eleven, and a couple of others. You've got like 15 characters, but you can't have fifteen stars in the movie. As this story evolved, we ended up with Kirk and Picard and Data having the three major arcs in this film, and Soran, our guest villain.

"What you try to do is create minor storylines or scenes that the other actors will have that will showcase them to some degree," he added. "It is frustrating for the actors and sometimes those things will be minimized in the cutting room, not because that is the way it was planned, but because when you are pasting the movie in the cutting room and you've got to lose things and shorten things, you end up bringing things down. LeVar had a wonderful scene that was cut dramatically short, not because of LeVar but because of the pasting of the movie. I think if you look at the original *Star Trek* movies, you will see numerous films where a number of the actors had small parts. It is part of the game. When you have an ensemble in any one given movie, it is going to just feature certain people. There were hurt feelings, but what I did is I worked diligently with every one of our actors on their parts, because these people know these characters very well. They played them for over seven years and we worked with them and everybody had notes — especially with Patrick, Brent and Bill — and we made a lot of changes and accommodations. They helped make it better."

One final problem was that there was some hesitancy from William Shatner in regards to reprising his role of Captain James T. Kirk. While the actor

Jonathan Frakes   *(Photo copyright © 1994 Albert Ortega)*

stated that it was the script he was objecting to, *Variety* reported that it had more to do with salary demands. Shatner reportedly wanted $1 million for about three weeks work.

While the situation was obviously resolved, it was just one of many that opened David Carson's eyes about Hollywood posturing.

"Nobody tells the truth about anything," he said pointedly. "If you get sent a script in a series of movies in which you have been the star, and you're

not the star anymore, or you're not on every page, and you suddenly get this script and Paramount makes you an offer you don't like, the last thing you're going to tell anyone is that you like the script. Because if you say that, they know they're going to get you and you're going to get less money. So the first thing any actor with any sense is going to say is, 'I hate the script. What do you think you're doing?' Then the studio will say, 'How about another million?'

"Unfortunately," he continued,

"that's how it works. It's such a lot of bullshit. It works like that because you're forced to work like that; you're forced to posture and position yourself so that you can be in to a good place, which seems to me to be quite absurd. It ought to be a lot of people getting together and saying, 'Hey, why don't we make a movie?' We all get paid enormous amounts of money for doing what we like doing. It just seems odd to me that there should be all this posturing. It isn't necessary."

■ NCC 1701-B

The final draft of *Generations* begins with Kirk continuing his battle with mortality and trying to cope with the aging process. He no longer feels that he's making a difference. In an opening sequence that was cut from the film, he takes a mid-life crisis to new extremes when he space-dives — for wont of a better word — from Earth's atmosphere to a designated area, where he ebulliently greets a waiting duo — the unlikely Scotty and Chekov, rather than Spock and McCoy.

"It *was* a bit of a reach," laughs Shatner, who felt strange shooting a *Star Trek* adventure without Nimoy and DeForest Kelley. "It was very odd. I felt very lonely without my two buddies and I told them that several times."

David Carson explained that the scene was cut for a very specific reason, all tied in to the nuances of the film he was attempting to create.

"Bill was parachuting out of orbital skydiving into a hayfield and landing undignified," recalled Carson, "and Scotty ran along behind him: 'What are you doing? You are too old to be doing this sort of thing,' which is very much like how some of the old movies started. It started with a joke and all of that. I said to Bill, 'The point about this movie is not that you are going off to do deeds of daring for two hours or so, therefore it will be good to have a scene where you are shown as a human being and it is funny and it is sort of interesting. In this movie, the first time you see Captain Kirk, he *is* Captain Kirk. He is a hero."

Kirk, Scotty and Chekov proceed to the christening of the Enterprise-B (an Excelsior class vessel), where a

William Shatner who just portrayed Kirk for the last time. (Photo copyright © 1994 Albert Ortega)

quick press demonstration will have the starship head out to Pluto and back again. Unfortunately, the vessel intercepts a distress call from the transport ship Lakul, one of two transporting El-Aurian refugees to Earth, which is caught in an energy distortion. Enterprise proceeds to the coordinates, where they see the ships ensnared by tendrils of energy. One vessel explodes, taking the lives of 265 people with it. Forty-seven out of the 150 people — including Dr. Tolian Soran (Malcolm McDowell) and Guinan (Whoopi Goldberg) — being transported on the Lakul are saved before that ship is destroyed as well.

Enterprise itself is then caught by one of the tendrils. To free the ship, Kirk proceeds to deck fifteen and the deflector relays so that he can "simulate a torpedo blast using a resonance burst from the main deflector dish" (it's called technobabble, ladies and gentlemen). His efforts are a success and the starship is set free, but not before one final energy blast rips open part of the Enterprise, including deck fifteen. Captain James T. Kirk is gone.

These scenes represent the first time that David Carson had had the opportunity to work with Shatner, and he found himself amazed at the actor's com-

mitment to the character and the character's place in our pop-culture lexicon. "He absolutely gets into shape for it, physically and mentally," said Carson. "He slims down to get ready for the role, he puts on that uniform and he *is* Captain Kirk."

Carson wasn't the only one impressed with Shatner; indeed, some of the actors playing Enterprise-B crewmembers were overwhelmed by his presence.

"All of the supporting players are very good, very professional actors," he noted. "I spent some intensive auditions with them to get the right mix. And yet on the first day, some of [their performances] were quite a bit under where they had been in the auditions. With one in particular, I began to wonder if I had made a mistake, so I called him and said, 'Look, do you have a problem? Are you okay?' He said, 'I'm sorry about today. It was just the situation.' I asked, 'Situation? What are you talking about?' And he said, 'You're English, so you probably don't understand what it means to a 29-year-old American actor to be on the bridge of the Enterprise with Captain Kirk. It is a mind-blowing experience. Even though I'm an actor in a scene, I'm also on a legendary ship with a legendary captain. It's extraordinary. We all felt it.' It really is amazing. They're all 29-to-mid-30s, very experienced actors and not ones who normally feel that kind of stage fright."

Such opening-day jitters helped Carson recognize Kirk's role as a symbol of both progress and the future for millions of people. "I think you have to take great care of the legend and treat it with respect and deference. I think in something like *Star Trek* you can't ignore its roots. You have to assimilate its history and then take it further, improving it by doing it better than it's been done before."

Actor-director Brian Peck, a long-time *Star Trek* fan, was given the opportunity to play Walter Koenig's stand-in thanks to his friendship with the actor's son, Andrew. As such, he was able to make some interesting observations.

"Shatner was downright goofy on the set, in a good way," Peck told journalist Naomi Pfefferman. "This was perhaps, to his mind, one of the last times he would ever play Kirk. He wasn't directing the film and he didn't have to carry the movie like he has in the past. So he was of the mind to have a good time. He did a lot of joking around, and kept suggesting that the film be turned into a musical. He would keep bursting into song and suggesting ways we could do musical numbers. For example, in one scene near the beginning, Captain Harriman says he would be honored if Kirk would give the order to leave space dock. Kirk demurs; Harriman insists, and finally Kirk rises out of his chair and says, 'Take us out.'

"In between takes," added Peck, "Shatner kept saying it would be funny if we took that line as a cue for a big musical number; he'd leap to his feet and start dancing, leaping and singing, 'Take us ouuuuut! Take us out of spaaace dooooock!'"

The Enterprise-B bridge consisted of two levels on the bridge set: the outer ring, and an inner ring you'd step down to, and there's a railing running between them. For the scenes where the starship is rocked by the Energy Ribbon, they'd built the bridge over a mechanical device which would actually shake the set.

"The director would yell, 'Shake!' and they'd turn on this thing," said Peck. "It was *loud*. Don't forget, this was two months after the [January 17th 1994] earthquake, and it felt like a really big aftershock. People were freaking out, saying, 'This feels too much like the real thing!' Anyway, we were rehearsing the scene where the ship gets by the energy field, and the actors had to throw themselves about the set. Kirk was on the upper level, and when the shaking started he was supposed to pitch forward and grab the railing. So the director yelled 'Shake,' and Shatner fell off balance and pitched forward. He grabbed the railing — and it snapped right off in his hands. He plummeted to the bottom level, and there was this momentary gasp, then silence. Everyone was first concerned that he had hurt himself, and second that he'd be very upset. Instead, he leaped to his feet — and started singing the 'Take Her Ouuuuut' musical number. Then he stopped and made a comment, 'Let's fix the railing.'"

Somehow it seems fitting that the set of *Generations*, in all likelihood the last film featuring members of the original series cast, also served as an opportunity for Shatner to mend some fences with Koenig and Doohan, both of whom have been extremely critical of the actor over the years. It was so bad, that Doohan didn't speak to Shatner unless they had dialogue.

"It seemed to me that Shatner was definitely making an effort to be a nice guy," observed Peck. "One day, toward the end of shooting, Shatner started speaking to Doohan, just asking basic questions about what was going on with him. It was during a particularly long lighting set-up, about 45 minutes, when crew people had to do a lot of re-lighting. Normally the actors would have left the set, but Shatner and Doohan and me [standing in for Koenig] just sat there. I got to overhear Shatner and Doohan have a lengthy, in-depth, *friendly* conversation, in which Shatner asked Doohan about his wife, his father, where he grew up as a kid. Eventually Doohan warmed up to the conversation and was very pleasant and told a lot of stories.

"I think I was witnessing William Shatner trying to make amends to Doohan: at one point Doohan even said, 'Bill, you ask really good questions.' Shatner replied, 'Yeah, I'm sorry we

Alan Ruck as Enterprise -D Captain John Harriman. (Photo copyright © Albert Ortega)

never did this before.' They talked more and eventually it was time to do the scene. William Shatner said, 'Well, I'm sorry we have to work, I'd like to talk to you more.'"

For production designer Herman Zimmerman, the Enterprise-B sequences were a pleasure in that they gave him the opportunity to enhance what had come before.

"Enterprise-B," he explained, "is a further improvement on the Enterprise bridge that you saw in *Star Trek V* and *Star Trek VI*. When I did *Star Trek V*, the bridge from the features, which had been used in all the features, was falling apart and needed serious refurbishing. At that point I rebuilt the bridge and made it a little less Buck Rogers. I felt the original design from *Star Trek: The Motion Picture* was a little further away from science fiction as I felt the seriousness of the property itself warranted. So I took the opportunity to make calculated changes, and essentially that's the bridge you see in the feature.

"It's always nice to have the opportunity to work on something like the bridge over a period of time so that you get the opportunity to investigate the things you might have thought were mistakes and make them right. Certainly because the studio does give you a limit

Whoopi Goldberg reprises her roll of Guinan. *(Photo copyright © 1994 Albert Ortega)*

ing effect of the entire *Star Trek* filmic odyssey is the so-called Energy Ribbon, which director David Carson describes as the true villain of the film. "When this thing shows up, you know something bad's going to happen," art director Bill George grinned. "We were charged with really giving the Energy Ribbon personality. We wanted to design something that had an architecture to it, that wasn't just a big glowing thing. An awful lot of thought and research went into it."

Carson was essentially asking ILM to create something out of nothing, which is among the toughest work in effects. Visual Effects Supervisor John Knoll, who was concurrently finishing up *Baby's Day Out* as *Star Trek* was gearing up, had very definite ideas about the look and behavior of the Energy Ribbon. He saw the phenomenon as an actual rip between two different universes, a painful tear filled with volatile energy:

"The image I had in my head was based on a JPL simulation of equipotential magnetic field lines whipping around Uranus. We had already designed the basic ribbon core, which was airfoil-shaped in cross-section as it trails off, but I thought it would be cool to add these magnetic energy tendrils radiating off the core. They were born from the center of the ribbon, and would change polarity as they grew towards front, becoming these fast energy whips lashing at anything in their path. That idea in practice turned out to be a little too smooth and intellectual. The director wanted something that was more unpredictable, so we pushed it towards the electrical direction."

Fortunately, another of Knoll's ILM associates, Co-Visual Effects Supervisor Alex Seiden, had a lot of experience with creating outer space phenomena on a vast scale. Seiden served as a Technical Director on *Trek VI*, which opened with a dramatic planetary explosion followed by a colorful shockwave, an effect he played a key role on. Seiden realized they were literally facing Infinite Diversity in Infinite Combinations in trying to develop the Energy Ribbon, and worked hard to keep the project from hitting too many dead ends as he and Bill George passed various concepts back and forth.

on what you can spend, there are things I didn't do on *V* that I did do on *VI*, and there are things I did on *Star Trek: Generations* that I didn't do on either of those. It's all the same scenery, but used in a fresh way, I hope. I like the Enterprise-B. I think we've made some interesting changes to the Excelsior model that made it a new ship. And we saw the deflector room, which we'd never seen on any of the other ships. All of it really starts the picture off with a bang."

Carson definitely viewed life on the two Enterprises as being very different from each other. "We tried to treat the Enterprise-B and the people in it as if we were dealing with a period piece," he noted. "We were consciously doing a film that was 100 years older than the other one, and we tried to light it differently and use our camera slightly differently. It seems to have worked because people have commented to me that it was slightly more old-fashioned than the Enterprise-D."

Undoubtedly the most demand-

"I actually rendered some things on the computer based on textures Bill painted for me, then I threw them back at him," Seiden recalled. "We painted ideas we liked or mockups of various scenes in Photoshop, then we made hard copies of those, brainstormed ideas about how we would actually do the effect, then showed our concepts to the client. It's fun to create something from scratch, but when supervising work like this, it's always important to rough out the whole thing, then do the details. There's so many paths you can explore, it's easy to get bogged down finessing one little thing while everything else gets lost. In the end we came up with something that had the feel of John's magnetic field, but via a different mechanism."

Another design challenge was creating visual cues that would tell the viewer that the Energy Ribbon was indeed one of the bigger natural phenomena in the universe, according to Bill George: "The scale issue was a bit touchy — in space you don't have any reference. It's not the blast of an atomic bomb but the trees falling over that creates the sense of that bomb's scale and power. So we wanted to show that the Energy Ribbon was way bigger than a starship but we didn't want to see one right next to it because of our experience on *Trek VI*. Director Nicholas Meyer felt the shockwave would look big if we made the starship really small. Unfortunately, that approach just made the ship look really dinky, which inspired one critic to call it the 'SS Plastic Thing'! We decided to add scale by giving the Energy Ribbon a debris field of embers following behind it, the way mud trails behind the current in a clear stream. Alex Seiden programmed a model of this undulating ribbon in the computer, then added the airfoil shape and the tendrils and color variations. We transferred Alex's model to Photoshop, where we painted in a starfield and the debris trail. That enabled us to think the design out, see what's happening in perspective, then add color and detail."

Seiden's design had the menace and unpredictability Carson wanted to see in the Energy Ribbon: the feeling of mass and architecture despite its thinness, and tendrils that look as if they're

about to snap at the closest object. After digital modelling defined the shape of the Energy Ribbon, the methods for animating it had to be established, which was the ultimate step. Since the Energy Ribbon was a natural phenomenon sweeping through the galaxy, Knoll and company relied on nature for their inspiration, programming the rhythmical, cyclical power of an ocean wave into their animation. "There's some procedural (automatic) and some hand-animation in all the energy ribbon shots," Knoll said. "The basic motion of the ribbon was animated by hand, but the undulating movement was created using some terrain-following software. We built the undulation into this big rolling hill sheet and then when we removed the sheet, the ribbon followed that pattern."

Several ILM Technical Directors working with Renderman shaders created the sea of plasma surrounding the Energy Ribbon and debris field particles streaming in its wake.

"Even after we got concept art that nailed down the overall static look of the energy ribbon, it still didn't specify its dynamics," CG Supervisor John Schlag explained. "Given its appearance, how does it animate, how fast do things stream off it, does it roil around like lightning or is it a more gentle curving motion? Three of our technical directors, Henry LaBounta, Joe Alter and Habib Zargarpour, did a lot of work early on to nail down the specific dynamics of the Ribbon's animation. We used particle systems for the plasma and all kinds of both 2-D and 3-D turbulence fields to create something that had enough visual complexity to be seen over and over and still be enjoyable and stay true to the storyline. We added turbulent gaseous plasma we called 'sea foam' because it streamed off the Ribbon as it traveled through space. We made prodigious use of the Renderman shading language to generate fractal clouds to create a more turbulent, lifelike feel."

Generations' script indicated that the Energy Ribbon moved incredibly quickly — the Enterprise-B has to travel at warp speed to catch up to it — a fact Knoll, Schlag and Seiden feared would create some scale problems. "It's really difficult when we're working with a long

scale CG shot, dealing with something that's supposed to be way bigger than we can comprehend," Seiden admitted. "We learned from the T-Rex in *Jurassic Park* that it helped to make it huge enough to break frame. That's an important cue for scale, because something that breaks frame is usually way bigger than you are. In the case of the Energy Ribbon, it's hard to make it appear like it's several planetary diameters in thickness if it fits within the frame; at the same time, it's hard to convey that the Energy Ribbon's far away if it didn't fit."

The problem was compounded by the fact that different CG models were required for the wide, medium and close-up Energy Ribbon effects. "A big scale change involves a different set of trade-offs and priorities," Seiden explained. "Essentially, the two different scales required completely different methods of achieving the result. It's a start from scratch thing. It's really difficult to devise techniques that can work for something when you're supposed to be hundreds of thousands of miles away from it as well as something that works when you're inside of it. Our closeup shots had various planes of turbulent fractal fields coming off it while the long shots didn't have that but other things, like particle systems, did similar things."

Events occurring inside the Energy Ribbon required the most complex visual effects work. When the El-Aurian spacecraft Lakul and her sister ship become trapped within the phenomenon's magnetic field, it's less like being in outer space and more like being inside of something alien, according to Co-Visual Effects Supervisor Seiden: "The Ribbon surrounds you, it's a plasma thing, or a dense electrical storm, so you don't see a lot of deep space in the background. When we had explosions or energy discharges caused by the tendrils flailing, we flashed the entire frame a bit and simulated a fogging of the film. Doubtless in the 23rd or 24th century we'll have much better anti-halation backing on the film, but for some reason they just didn't shoot with that for these shots!"

The shots in which the Enterprise-B tries to stage a rescue of the Lakul within the Energy Ribbon required Knoll and company to make an unheard-

Michael Dorn   **(Photo copyright © 1994 Albert Ortega)**

of decision: did they dare take the Enterprise into the realm of computer graphics? After discussing it with Seiden and CG Supervisor Schlag, Knoll decided the entire effects sequence should be created in CG, including the three starships and the volatile energy tendril that strikes the Enterprise at the climax, blowing Kirk out into space, where he's actually sucked into the Nexus.

"We actually used a recycled explosion element from *The Empire Strikes Back* in there, as well as other CG explosion elements and various sources of exploding CG greeblies or smithereens, some of which John Knoll rendered on his personal computer," Schlag said. "The interaction between the Enterprise and the Energy Ribbon had to be tweaked every day. Using CG allowed us to change the animation of the Enterprise, the Energy Ribbon or the hero tendril that came out and whacked the ship [one last time]."

And as simply as that, a decision that would forever change the future of the Federation was made.

■ Sea Trek

As initially conceived, the first sequence of *Generations* featuring the *TNG* crew would have taken place on the Amargosa Observatory prior to a Romulan attack.

"We opened with two ensigns sitting by a big window," said Ron Moore. "They're sitting there and they're bored, just staring out at the stupid stars they've been studying for a year and they're saying, 'Yeah, join Starfleet. Meet interesting people. Explore the galaxy — and we're here. Nothing ever happens.' Suddenly there's a trembling and the station starts to shake. They look right out the window and there's a Romulan warbird decloaking. The Romulans beam in and start shooting. There's a big shoot-em-up action sequence and one of the ensigns gets thrown against the bulkhead. One Romulan says, 'Where is the trilithium?' and the ensign replies, 'I don't know what you're talking about,' and then he looks over and reacts. The Romulan turns and looks out the window and coming out of the sun is the Enterprise to the rescue. They beam aboard and Worf kicks the shit out of the Romulans, and our introduction of the *Next Generation* crew is as they fight off the Romulan attack."

The scene fell by the wayside after comments offered by *Next Gen* and *Voyager* producer Jeri Taylor dampened the writers' enthusiasm for the sequence. "She said, 'You've just left a big action sequence in the prologue with running and jumping and ships exploding and Kirk getting pulled away. Then there's a fade-to-black and then another action sequence.' It just felt wrong structurally. And it didn't seem like the best way to introduce the *Next Generation* cast."

Instead, we're on the holodeck of the Enterprise-D, where Picard's crew has recreated a 19th century three-mast sailing vessel traveling the ocean. On board, everyone — dressed in full navel uniform — is participating in the promotion of Worf to lieutenant commander, the result of which is his having to walk the plank (apparently when Troi was promoted, she was fed to the lions in ancient Rome). Everyone laughs, with the exception of Data who, attempting to join in while not understanding why, shoves Dr. Crusher overboard. She does *not* appreciate it.

The holodeck program comes to an end when Picard receives a shocking personal communiqué and Riker is informed that the Amargosa observatory is under attack.

Besides using a nautical analogy to *Star Trek*, these sequences represented certain problems.

"It was a week of hell," sighed Marina Sirtis. "It looks cute, but it's not fun if you get seasick, which I do. It did convince me that I'm never going to shoot a movie on a boat again."

Countered Jonathan Frakes, "That was a ball. We were at sea — two miles off the coast of Santa Monica — outside in the sun, and most of what we were doing was action, so there weren't any heavy dialogue things to concern your brain with. I found it wonderful because I like to be on boats. A couple of people in the cast were not thrilled with the heaving of the sea....that's probably the wrong choice of words."

Then there were the usual budget constraints, with Paramount initially reluctant to finance such an expenditure.

"You come to them and say, 'I really want to make this great'," explained David Carson, "and they say, 'You don't have the money, just cut the script.' That scene was a primary candidate to be cut. But I feel that when you're doing a film that's on space ships all the time, you need as much breath as you can get, so we hung on to it in the face of the opposition that said we should reduce the budget. Basically this was indicative of the fact that we had a script that was too big and complex to shoot in 50 days. I think it was only because of the skill of the people involved that got us through it."

Which is not to say that those sequences didn't fall behind schedule. "Boats rock," said Carson matter of factly, "they sway, they don't hold still when you want them to. The sun was constantly moving so you had to constantly turn the ship to get the light right. The ship was also very small so you couldn't have everybody on board all the time. You had to take them off and put them on

Patrick Stewart with Gates McFadden.   *(Photo copyright © 1994 Albert Ortega)*

other boats and then bring the boats up and try and get them together without dropping the actors in the water between. It's quite good fun."

For Herman Zimmerman, it was exciting to use the Enterprise's holodeck in a way that truly represented what that area of the ship was capable of delivering. Also exciting was finding the real ship for those sequences to be shot on.

"It's the Lady Washington out of Seattle, a ship used as a promotion vessel for the city of Seattle," he noted. "It has a

really fine captain and a lot of very energetic young people. We almost didn't get the ship. Very coincidentally it came sailing in to Dana Point Harbor when we were down there looking at another vessel. When we saw this one, we ran right over and said, 'What will it take for us to use your ship?' It turned out to be a very happy accident."

Like Carson, Zimmerman bristled at Paramount's suggestion that the sequence be cut for fiscal reasons. "Nobody wanted to do that because of the obvious tie-ins to Gene's original basing of Starfleet Command on the 19th century English Maritime tradition. It was indeed fortunate we were able to find a ship we could use and schedule it in such a way that we could keep our budgetary constraints in line and include that wonderful production value. Everybody who knew anything about *Star Trek* was delighted to have the opportunity to do this because it was so right on to the way that the *Star Trek* military structure was created. It's a beautiful ship and well photographed. It's not easy to shoot anything on the deck of a rolling ship, and it's pretty exciting stuff. It is the second opening of the movie. It's like we have a long cold opening, then the *real* opening is here on the holodeck."

For Brannon Braga, this scene is dramatically important in that it serves as the impetus for the android Data to install a computer chip that will enable him to experience the full gamut of human emotions.

"When he pushes Crusher into the water, it's an awful moment," said Braga. "No one thinks it's funny and Data realizes he can't even grasp such a basic concept as humor, something so fundamental. Imagine what it's like not being able to laugh with everyone else. It must feel awful. He's the only guy in the room day after day after day who just doesn't get it. Yes, there are more formidable and important emotions to consider in life, but what could be sweeter than laughing? That seemed like a very poignant incident to make him suddenly decide to try it. It's a nice motivating factor."

According to Brent Spiner, the opportunity to play a new and different kind of Data was like "dying and going to heaven."

"I had been sort of euphemistically painting on a very narrow pallet for a long time with kind of muted colors," Spiner explained, "so it was a real opportunity to cut loose. When I first read the script, I was a little concerned about it just because it was so different from the character, even though it represented an evolution. In thinking about it, I finally came to the conclusion that in worse case scenario, they would love me in France."

■ Dr. Soran, I Presume?

When the Enterprise reaches the solar observatory, they see signs of a recent battle and only five of nineteen life forms are being detected. Uncharacteristically, Picard has Riker begin the investigation while he proceeds to his ready room. A somewhat surprised Riker arranges an Away Team which beams over to the observatory where among the survivors is Dr. Soran — seemingly unaged from when he was first seen aboard the Enterprise-B. Everyone beams back to the starship, where Riker fills Picard in, though the captain still seems distant.

"The Amargosa station is a fragile, older station," explained Herman Zimmerman. "It's probably sixty years old when we see it and it's more in line with the original series in terms of design. It's like doing the history of the future. For instance, in the original series they

Malcolm McDowell portrays "Generations" guest villan Dr. Tolian Soran.
(Photo copyright © 1994 Albert Ortega)

used plastic buttons and cubes of clear acrylic that were just glued on to painted surfaces — which we now use keypads for — as controls for various computer elements, and we went back to that inside the observatory. We were trying to pay homage to the original series because we had an excuse to do so."

Later, Soran insists on meeting with Picard and tells him that he must get back to the observatory to continue the experiments being run on the Amargosa Star. He has a window of 12 hours before years of research will be lost. Picard responds that it will not be possible to return him until an investigation of the attack is completed.

Geordi and Data beam back over to the observatory, where they discover indications of trilithium, which, if harnessed properly, could create a weapon more powerful than anti-matter energy. Soran mysteriously appears, knocks Geordi out and is about to fire a phaser at Data, when the android cowers in the corner, begging not to be hurt.

Back on board the Enterprise, Troi meets with Picard, who reluctantly reveals that his brother and nephew (introduced in the fourth season episode "Family") have died in a fire back on Earth. Continuing, the captain relates that his nephew was the closest he's ever been to having a child of his own. But, now, there is no one left to carry on the Picard name. Troi is left to consider this.

"Apparently this is one of the strongest scenes in the film, and I'm very happy about that," said Sirtis.

As was Patrick Stewart. "During the months prior to filming, my attention shifted to the character of Picard and in creating a storyline for the captain which had something more than just the narrative sequences in it. One of the things I was happy with was that, through meetings with the writers and producers, we developed a 'B' story for Picard that is very private, personal and a very intense emotional story that runs parallel to the main action story. For me, that was the most satisfying element of the pre-production on the movie."

Originally, Picard's brother, Robert, died of a heart attack in his vineyard, and there was a moment when Picard says, "I wear this uniform and

there are risks that go along with being a starship captain, which I accept, but Robert walked out to his vineyard one morning and died of a heart attack and his only enemy was time."

"That brought home a certain realization that, 'I can fight Klingons and I can do this and do that, but there is one enemy out there waiting for me that's going to get me eventually. It gets everybody, no matter what kind of job they have.' So that, we liked," said Ron Moore. "But Patrick felt that he was missing the element of continuation of the family line, the tradition and that those mean a lot to some people. Patrick felt that he wanted more of that sense of family and that it's something very important for Picard. Once we heard that, we realized that could give us some interesting beats to play in the Nexus. At the end, Patrick was the one who said, 'And it should be a tragic, horrible death. If the captain is going to react in a way he's never reacted before, this one better really hit him between the eyes. You know, burn him to death.'"

Although one may argue that it's an extreme dramatic development to rip apart Picard's family, David Carson felt that it fit very nicely in to the film's theme of mortality, which began with Kirk's experiences in the past.

"One of the strands of the theme of mortality is, of course, your immortality through your progeny or family," he offered. "You don't have many movies about mortality or death. It's one of the great things that *Star Trek* is able to do; it's able to take an enormously grand theme and play variations on it. Kirk's variation was different, Picard's was different. Soran's is different. But they are all variations on that theme. Everything has to do with death and rebirth, some way or another."

Back on the Enterprise, Riker announces that a quantum implosion within the Amargosa star has resulted in a break down of the star's nuclear fusion, seemingly the result of a solar probe that was launched from the observatory several moments earlier. In four minutes the shock wave will envelope the observatory. When Geordi and Data don't respond to communication efforts, Riker and Worf beam over to rescue them. There they

find Soran, who begins firing a phaser. While ducking, they notice a frightened Data in the corner of the room.

When Soran's communicator signals, he grabs the unconscious Geordi and they are transported away to a Klingon Bird of Prey which has decloaked to retrieve Soran and vanishes again.

Riker, Worf and Data are beamed back to the Enterprise, which achieves warp speed just as the shock wave destroys the observatory.

On the Bird of Prey, we find that Soran is working in conjunction with the female Klingon renegades B'Etor and Lursa, and that they have stolen trilithium from the Romulans. Soran will deliver to them a trilithium weapon once they help him achieve his ultimate goal: the Nexus.

One of the things that David Carson wanted to do to elevate *Generations* above the television series that inspired it, was to enhance the presentation of the Klingons.

"These are Klingon scenes like you ain't ever seen them before," he laughed. "As a group, they're much more animalistic and a more potentially violent bunch of people than they've been before — as you see them as a group running this ship, clustering around and behaving *not* like Enterprise officers. They very much have an animalistic quality to them. They're not subtle, which is why I like them. If you make them all like Worf, you've flattened them out. I always felt that Worf represented a civilized Klingon, but when you get down to the level of a renegade Klingon, they're a pretty rough bunch of people, grunting and snorting and pushing and shoving. Lower depth Klingons."

For Malcolm McDowell, veteran of such genre fare as *A Clockwork Orange, Time After Time, Blue Thunder* and *Tank Girl*, this approach to the Klingons provided him with some enjoyable acting opportunities.

"Soran is fun because he can't stand these filthy pigs, the Klingons," he smiled. "I play it like he's got utter contempt for these barbarians. It's not there overtly, but it's like, 'My God, they stink. When was the last time they cleaned their teeth?' They threw me for a loop and I could barely get my lines out because there was so much hissing, spitting and groin rubbing going on. But the Klingons are fun and their make-up is incredible."

Enterprise: the crew has discovered the connection between Soran and the Duras sisters, while Dr. Crusher comes to the conclusion that Data's emotion chip has been fused in his neural net, which may make his behavior erratic. She can't remove it without dismantling his cerebral conduit, so Data is going to have to cope with his emotions as best he can.

Then, Crusher pulls up a file on Dr. Soran, which details that he is over 300 years old, lost his entire family when the Borg destroyed his world, and escaped with a handful of survivors from the Lakul to the Enterprise-B.

"That was the mission where James Kirk was killed," muses Riker.

They learn that Guinan, also an El-Aurian, was rescued as well, so Picard goes to talk to her. Guinan explains that Soran doesn't care about power or weapons; that all he wants to do is get back to the Nexus. The Nexus, she explains, exists on a different plane than our universe. It's as though joy were a real thing that you could wrap yourself in, and it fills you with complete contentment. Seventy-eight year earlier, she and the others were "pulled away," in the character's words, and every one of them felt as though a part of themselves had been left behind. All they wanted to do was get back, but that became impossible. Guinan did, however, recognize that her time in the Nexus had changed her.

"I knew things about people," she says, "about events....about time....Soran may still be obsessed with getting back. And if he is, he'll do anything to find that doorway again."

Picard asks aloud how destroying a star could help achieve this, then excuses himself. It is Guinan's suggestion that another starship seek out the energy ribbon, because once Picard enters the Nexus he's not going to care about Soran or the Enterprise.

Soran's motivation was an important aspect in the character's creation.

"We tried to craft a more multidimensional villain and a formidable nemesis for Picard that, in a way, had never been done in the series," said Brannon Braga. "In movies you seem to need a bigger villain. Soran is obsessed with time and time running out and time as a predator stalking him. He's desperate to get back to the Nexus and cheat death. Yet he's a villain who's suffered a personal tragedy as well. The Borg killed not only his family, but his entire world. Hopefully there's a sympathetic element to him. Hopefully people will relate to him, perhaps more than anybody. At the same time, you're appalled at what he's doing to get back there, while you can totally understand why he wants to get back to the Nexus. I don't think he's your typical cardboard cut-out bad guy."

Which is precisely what drew Malcolm McDowell to the character. "He's obviously a very strange man and there's a bit of a poet in him as well. Of course he does have his dark side, but I never play villains as if they are villains," said the actor. "I play them as quite normal people doing quite nasty things, although there's a reason for everything. Nobody is just black or white; there's always those gray shaded areas and those are the most fascinating things to play.

"I read the script," he added, "and I didn't really understand a word of it with all that Nexus stuff. I didn't know what the hell they were talking about, but I thought there was a glimmer of a part there. A glimmer of something that could be fun. So they asked for a meeting and I went into a meeting with them, and they asked me to read for it. I said, 'No, I won't.' It was ridiculous. What do they think it is, Shakespeare? So I wouldn't read it, but I had a very good meeting with Rick Berman and David Carson and I got the part."

David Carson considered McDowell a key to the movie, believing that if the villain isn't satisfactorily frightening and powerful in a *Star Trek* vehicle, the story quickly flattens out. "I think McDowell's wonderful — we were very lucky to get him," he said. "Like all the *Star Trek* villains, he has to go up against everybody, so he carries half the movie. He sits at the same level of Picard and Kirk, and he does very well. Malcolm McDowell is especially equipped to be a *Star Trek* villain because he is such an incredibly talented performer, an instinctive actor who can also handle words, which people on *Star Trek* need to be able to do."

Beyond Soran, Carson was intrigued by the basic idea of the Nexus, likening it to a temptation or drug. "It's something that affects you like a drug, therefore it's something that is desirable, not unlike a hallucinogen into which you can sink and be happy within the confines of it. You really need to be able to find the strength to deny it. So for us it has a sort of addictive feel to it. The possibilities of the addiction and from the craving that the addiction can breed comes the behavior of someone like Soran, who is trying desperately to get his fix, no matter what the cost and how many lives it takes."

"*That's* what I played," interjected McDowell. "I enjoyed finding the character, because it really wasn't on the page of the script. I really — in my mind — have this idea that this man was like a drug addict who had to get a fix and wouldn't let anything divert him from that. He was a very concentrated man. I really liked Soran as a character."

Back on the Klingon Bird of Prey, Soran is in the midst of torturing Geordi, attempting to learn what he knows about trilithium and why the Enterprise seems interested in it. Geordi has no useful information, and, as originally shot, Soran racks his body with pain via a device he has attached to Geordi's heart, stopping it for five seconds. When this doesn't gain him results, he increases the stoppage to 30 seconds. The heart-stopping scene was cut although the punchline ("His heart just wasn't in it," Soran tells the Klingons regarding the interrogation of LaForge) remains in the final film.

The torture sequence marked McDowell's first filmed sequence as Soran, and he found that it set up his character's appearance throughout the film. "I don't have that many scenes," he explained, "but the ones I do have count well. LeVar was very good in that torture scene and I love the way that Soran says, 'I'm an El-Aurian, and we're listeners,' except me, because I talk through this bloody scene."

It was also an arduous sequence

to get on film, with director David Carson shooting the scene from a wide variety of angles.

"I don't think there was an angle he didn't get. He covered it every which way and I bent over at one point and said, 'How about sticking a camera up my ass, because it's the only angle you haven't got yet,'" laughed McDowell, who broke the crew up with that one.

Carson explained that the reason this sequence was cut had entirely to do with the overall length of the film. "It said what it needed to say three times in slightly different ways and it said it in the center of the film where you needed to be moving more swiftly than we were able to," he said. "So what we decided to do in the end is not go into a great torture scene with Geordi screaming, but to give the *impression* that this extremely evil man is now going to torture him and make him feel extraordinarily unhappy and uncomfortable, which is what we ended up with. The scene had repeated its theme as interrogation scenes often do. 'Now, I want you to tell me what Captain Picard knows about trilithium.' 'I'm not going to tell you.' 'Well, I want you to tell me.' 'I'm still not going to tell you.' 'Well, I still want you to tell me.' And that's the way it went. One of the tragedies about cutting the end of the scene was that we lost some of the detail of Soran's character."

In the stellar cartography area of the Enterprise, Data and Picard are studying monitors displaying images of the Energy Ribbon. Data details that this anomaly travels through their galaxy once every 39.1 years, and that it will pass through their sector of space in approximately 31 hours. Correlating the effects of the destruction of the Amargosa star, they discover that there has been some alteration of gravitational forces throughout that sector. When Data, who is still suffering from his emotion chip, charts the course of the Energy Ribbon, Picard realizes that Soran is attempting to change its trajectory. The reason Soran doesn't fly a ship into the Ribbon is that every ship that has approached it has been destroyed.

"He can't go to the Ribbon," says Picard, "so he's trying to make the

LeVar Burton with his wife. (Photo copyright © 1994 Albert Ortega)

Ribbon come to him."

Further analysis reveals that Soran will destroy the sun in the Veridian system so that it will alter the course of the Energy Ribbon to envelope the third planet — a Class M world — which will then draw Soran back into the Nexus. To make matters worse, Veridian Four, which will ultimately be destroyed as well, is populated by 230 million beings. Enterprise is put on red alert and the ship heads for the Veridian System at maximum warp.

Of the stellar cartography room, Herman Zimmerman enthused, "I think it's the single most important set in the picture, only because if you don't understand the scene that takes place in that set, you may not get the rest of the picture. That seems kind of important. The Energy Ribbon is a fantastic idea and I tried to make a set that was equally interesting. It's three stories tall, about 300 degrees of really incredible star field graphics, much of it supplied by ILM and also a lot of it done live on set. It's an

The original model of the Starship Enterprise NCC 1701-D introduced to audiences in 1987.

enormous starfield that changes right in front of your eyes, so as the story is unfolding to Picard and Data, it's unfolding to the audience as well."

■ Destroying The Enterprise... Again

The Bird of Prey enters orbit of Veridian Three. Soran prepares to beam down to the surface, giving Lursa and B'Etor an encoded computer chip with the information they need to construct a trilithium weapon. He'll transmit the decryption sequence once he's safely on the planet's surface. At that moment, it's announced that the Enterprise is approaching. Soran tells the Klingons that the Federation ship must be eliminated, and to this end he notes that "it's time we gave Mister La Forge his sight back," while holding Geordi's visor in his hand.

The Klingon ship decloaks, and

Picard communicates with Lursa. He suggests a prisoner exchange: Geordi for him. The Klingons agree, with Geordi coming back to the Enterprise while Picard is beamed down to the planet's surface, *without* weapons or a combadge. He's on a large plateau, ringed with trees and underbrush. A scaffolding has been erected against a rockface, with ladders connecting a complex structure, all leading to a narrow ledge. Soran, protected in a forcefield, verbally taunts Picard. Picard tries to dissuade him from this course of action, but is unable to even when mentioning Soran's wife and children.

Soran points out that the Borg taught him a lesson: if there is one constant in the universe, it's death. "Aren't you beginning to feel time gaining on you?" he, asks. "It's like a predator. It's stalking you....In the end, time is going to hunt you down and make the kill."

When Picard points out that death is a truth of their existence, Soran responds that within the Nexus time has no meaning; the predator has no teeth.

In space, Lursa and B'Etor study the engineering section of Enterprise via an alteration made in Geordi's visor. Discovering the ship's shield operation modulations, they adjust their photon torpedo frequencies to match. The Bird of Prey decloaks and begins firing at the Enterprise, their torpedoes passing through the ship's shields and striking directly into the hull. The volley continues, with a hull breach on levels thirty-one through thirty-five.

Riker and Data devise a plan that by utilizing a low level ionic pulse it will reset the plasma coil of the Bird of Prey, thus causing it to automatically cloak and rendering their shields and weapons momentarily useless. This is put into effect and Enterprise launches torpedoes, which find their target and destroy it. Victory is theirs....temporarily. Geordi informs the bridge that there's a warp core coolant leak which means that in five minutes there will be a warp core breach. Riker orders everyone to evacuate into the saucer section, which will then be separated from the ship.

Separation is complete with only ten seconds to spare, but before the saucer section can move to a safe distance the Enterprise explodes, the force of the explosion knocking the saucer section into the planet's atmosphere.

The saucer section enters the atmosphere of Veridian Three, and plows its way through a dense rain forest, tearing up the jungle as it travels. When it finally comes to a stop, the saucer section is split open.

Needless to say, the destruction of the Enterprise raised the ire of more than a few Trekkers, as did the original Enterprise's demise in *Star Trek III: The Search for Spock.*

"But look at that crash sequence," proclaimed Brannon Braga. "It's great. It's something we always wanted to do on the series, but didn't because saucer separation was very expensive and elaborate. But we always wanted to crash that sucker! Come on, we've been with that same starship for seven years. Let's get a new one!"

Ron Moore added that the genesis of the Enterprise's destruction began in a story called "All Good Things," which had nothing to do with the series finale of the same name. "It was a story that was going to be the cliffhanger for the sixth season," he said. "Brannon and I had come up with a story where Starfleet recalls the Enterprise home and is going to split the crew up. The Enterprise was going to become the Queen Mary, basically, and on the way home, the characters all decide what they're going to do with their lives, and in the course of returning home there is a big battle and the saucer separates from the battle section, which explodes and the saucer crashes on the planet's surface. The producers hated that story for the cliffhanger and we tossed it aside, but when we were doing the movie, this crash of the saucer was one of the first things Brannon and I came to Rick with. It's a statement that we're going in a different direction with the features and that we're going to take risks and be bold. It's not just going to be another episode thrown up on the big screen."

David Carson stood completely behind the decision to destroy the Enterprise, particularly in this manner.

"I think it's interesting that you have a battle where you have a winner and a loser, but as a by-product of winning, you find that your ship is in trouble. So, no sooner do you have a chance to celebrate your victory than your ship hits the rocks, as it were. You generally believe, I think, like all the good guys, that the Enterprise is going to make it. Well, we have a small problem in the warp core, we evacuate the ship, do the separation sequence and the damn thing blows up, and off we go back on the rollercoaster again.

"The action sequences inside the ship are very, very exciting," he continued. "You have battle scenes and suddenly you've got a disaster movie like *The Towering Inferno,* with all these people being moved out of the ship and scurrying into different areas. It's sort of like getting ready for an earthquake. You know it's going to happen and everyone's preparing for it. And everything's getting worse and then the crash happens and it just goes on and on. It should, I hope, be a very frightening and terrifying sequence that takes you just beyond the battle and puts everybody into a *major* jeopardy situation. I think that will be real exciting."

Added Herman Zimmerman, "The shattered bridge was very interesting from the point of view of the people who have worked on the show for all these years. The Enterprise never looked so good, but it was for only about three days when we started tearing it apart. It's very ironic that I got a chance to do things I didn't get a chance to do when I first built the bridge [seven years ago]. I beefed up the ceiling, put in some other computer terminals, changed the colors to more realistic — for the big screen — colors, and I raised the captain's seat up six inches, giving him a little bit more commanding presence and getting Worf, in particular, closer to Picard. As soon as everybody saw it, they said, 'Oh God, this is so nice,' and then we started destroying it. And it is now gone. It's history. We have the Voyager set sitting in that location now."

The saucer crash sequence started, like every effects sequence for *Generations,* at art director Bill George's

drawing board, where he and John Knoll drafted every conceivable effects approach. Mark Moore later refined those concepts, which were presented to *Star Trek: Generations'* producers for approval. Some of the shots that were not approved included a lengthy boom-up shot in outer space at the start of the sequence where we would see the saucer separate from the secondary hull, due to pacing considerations; and a shot of the saucer flying over the trees, whose leaves blow off in its wake, for budgetary reasons.

George also put a lot of energy into designing the climactic crash of the Enterprise D saucer section onto Veridian 3, along with Knoll and storyboard artist Mark Moore. "John and I sketched out ideas - I'd do them on paper, he'd do them in the computer - and then we had storyboard and concept artist Mark Moore refine that," George recalled. "One thing I felt was my responsibility as art director was to define how big the saucer was so we were all on the same page. I figured out the size of the ship as listed in the Tech manual, then I did a drawing of the saucer over the Golden Gate Bridge. I also researched the height of trees in the rain forest, which is 150' max, and on Veridian Three I figured maybe they're a little taller. Then I did this drawing showing the scale relationship between the saucer and the trees - I figured the Enterprise bridge would be almost even with the top of the trees."

As George worked on the crash, he began to realize that *Generations'* director David Carson envisioned having lots of cutaways to the Enterprise Bridge, which was making the sequence much longer and certain folks at ILM nervous - but not George: "I also worked on *Alive!,* where they had this lengthy crash sequence, and I remember watching the cut sequence and thinking, 'This crash is taking forever - it's ridiculous!' But you know what - it worked just fine. So I realized when working on this project that the sequence could be a minute and a half long and it *would* work. David Carson wanted to cut away to the inside of the saucer then cut back outside. What worked best was when the ship hit something and we cut inside as the crew reacted to the hit, so David asked us to design some shots where the ship was glancing off things on the planet's surface."

After evaluating George's concept art and Carson's approach to the sequence, Visual Effects Supervisor John Knoll and his ILM associates decided the best way to film the crash was to build a 40' x 80' landscape miniature of a Viridian 3 forest, then smash a 12' diameter model of the Enterprise-D saucer into it following re-entry. "Originally I wanted to build a 24' saucer, but that was unwieldy and too expensive," Knoll admitted. "The set we built had a little bit of a slope in the back, but was mostly flat, with a long slot running through the middle of the 'forest', and coming up through the slot was a big post that the saucer sat on. The slot worked almost like a zip-lock bag - two pieces of rubber came together and the flanges would open as the post passed by and close behind it. Most of the shots were done by getting the slot covered up and dressed with all this foliage and stuff so you wouldn't see there was a line running up the middle of the set. The entire thing was elevated 10' off the ground. Under the set was a little cart that carried two guys back and forth on a track below the slot. It was kind of amazing that the mechanism that raised, lowered and tilted the saucer was actually controlled by two guys, in radio contact with the camera crew, 'flying' the saucer from the cart under the set.

"The cart was driven by a big endless cable that went around a couple of pulleys, which was connected to a big pickup truck we rented that drove back and forth. When the saucer 'flew' over the middle of the set, it was going about 15 miles per hour for most shots. We had the post at maximum extension at the back of the set and it would drop down as it crashed. The nice thing about using a pickup truck is it's real well-known technology, so if we wanted it to go faster, we just stepped on the gas and the speedometer was right there. That was probably one of the more unusual uses for that rental truck!"

There's a certain childlike giddiness one senses in ILM's effects artists when they actually get to crash, blow up or otherwise wreak destruction on one of their creations — it seems to bring out that part that probably enjoyed such

things as a kid, the part they wanted to recapture when they got into effects work. "It was a whole lot of fun!" Knoll laughed as his Co-Visual Effects Supervisor, Alex Seiden, chimed in: "When you spend a lot of time around here doing CG, to be able to get out and blow some stuff up is really cool!"

Knoll's partner in crime was veteran Effects Cinematographer Kim Marks, who filmed the saucer crash non-motion controlled using high-speed cameras running at 240 frames per second on most of the shots to create the proper sense of scale and mass. Sometimes effects are done with mirrors: in order to get the camera low enough for some of the low-angle shots Carson wanted, Marks had to shoot into a mirror because otherwise the saucer would've crashed into the camera. As it was, at the end of each shot, the saucer would invariably smash right through one of the 2'x4' mirrors, raining broken glass and dirt from the slot on the 'saucer pilots' under the set. Fortunately, they were under a large shield that covered the car, wearing glasses and helmets to protect them from the avalanche.

Although the saucer and the set were both shot in-camera, there was some compositing work required to finesse the shots. "Since it was shot outside on our backlot, we needed to do a little cleanup and remove some telephone lines in the background," Seiden explained. "We sometimes added new sky, or had our digital matte department extend the set, or enhance it with foreground elements of trees shot on our stage. Those enhancements turned our raw, exciting but flawed plates into really great shots."

Like many of the effects artists who worked on *Star Trek: Generations*, because of some kinship they felt to the *Star Trek* series, Seiden was also able to fulfill one of his childhood fantasies in a scene that took place after the crash, when Federation rescuers stood atop the Enterprise D's saucer. "The Enterprise was basically a Photoshop matte painting using photographic elements of the saucer and the set pasted together, but the Starfleet officers matted onto the saucer were a bunch of us shot against bluescreen outside, marching around and

picking stuff up" he grinned, "and I was one of those guys. So I got to be in a *Star Trek* movie, which was a longstanding dream of mine."

Meanwhile, Back In The Nexus

One potential highlight of the film's action set pieces was to have been a confrontation between the crew of the Enterprise and Lursa and B'Etor on Veridian Three.

"The whole gag here was the set-up," said Ron Moore. "We crash in the jungle and we know that Soran is going to put out that star pretty soon — and when he does, the shock wave is going to destroy this planet."

As a result, the Enterprise crew is able to salvage one surviving shuttlecraft, which they plan to use to evacuate the children. Said Moore, "So they are getting the shuttle ready to go, and they are leading kids out across the destroyed hull of the Enterprise to walk around to the shuttle bay when all of the sudden these laser blasts come out of the jungle and pin them down. They go, 'What the hell, who's out there?' It turns out that Lursa and B'Etor have survived with a few of their men and got off the Bird of Prey in an escape pod before it exploded. Now they're trapped on the surface and know the shockwave is coming and they want the shuttlecraft. There is a standoff and they won't listen to reason. There is a mediation that takes place in Ten Forward, which has been completely trashed."

Subsequently, in the ops lounge during a briefing, Troi tells Riker that she senses sexual tension from the two Klingon sisters. Noted Moore, "And Worf says, "Yes, that's been my experience as well. The more excitement, the more danger that's going on, the more sexually energized these women tend to get.' And they all kind of start seeing where this is going and Beverly says, 'You're not suggesting that somebody sleep with them, are you?'"

In a scene which would assuredly have been a tour de force for

Brent Spiner, Data under the influence of his emotion chip, imitates a suave Valentino and returns to Lursa and B'Etor, still waiting in Ten Forward. When he returns, Moore laughed, "his uniform is torn and his hair is mussed and he's limping and he says, 'I believe I've opened negotiations,' and then his arm falls off. Rick Berman thought that was going to be the biggest laugh in the entire picture, and I thought it was a scream. Afterwards, the girls are a little more amenable to reaching some kind of a compromise.

"It was fun stuff," he added with a sigh, "but the script was 140 pages and at some point it had to go. David Carson said, 'Cut it all,' and we said, 'But it's got our favorite stuff.' When we took a hard look at it, we realized he was right."

As filmed, while the Enterprise is in the midst of its death throes, Picard has discovered that the forcefield separating him from Soran has a small opening within some a pile of rocks not protected by the field. He begins digging his way in from underneath and barely avoids a disruptor blast from Soran. The attack stops, however, when Soran sees the Energy Ribbon coming into view. He begins climbing the scaffolding to the awaiting ledge, when Picard, who has made it inside the field, catches up. The two men begin to fight, with Picard being knocked down a few levels of the scaffolding. Soran runs to the probe launcher and fires, the probe heading toward the sun. Picard has failed!

The sun darkens and collapses, with night instantly forming on the planet. The Energy Ribbon begins its new course, taking Picard and Soran in its wake. The planet explodes from the shockwave a minute later.

Within the Nexus, Picard finds himself in a living room at Christmas time with a wife and children — his children — clamoring for his attention. Picard suddenly has everything he has ever wanted: a family he could call his own. He's removed from this euphoria when he looks at an ornament that features a star which blinks out, its light expanding outward in its glass sphere. Although it's the way the ornament is designed, it reminds Picard of exactly why he's there.

Brent Spiner looking more human.   *(Photo copyright © 1994 Albert Ortega)*

He's stunned to suddenly find Guinan standing next to him. She explains that she is on the Enterprise but also here, and that he should consider this Guinan an "echo" of the one he left behind. She details that when Enterprise-B beamed them off the Lakul, they had been partially in the Nexus, so everyone left a bit of themselves behind.

Since time has no meaning in the Nexus, Picard wants to go back to the mountaintop on Veridian Three to stop Soran before he can destroy the star. He'll need help, but Guinan can't go with him. She suggests someone who can.

"It happened in a cabin near Mount Whitney in a town called Lone Pine, California," said Rick Berman of the following scene, "and it was terrific. Everybody had chills going up and down their backs."

Picard meets Captain James T. Kirk, who is living out the life he has always wanted. He's residing in a rustic home, his dog Butler is with him, and he's living with a woman, Antonia — the one he let get away many years ago.

Picard tries to convince him to leave the Nexus, but Kirk refuses, determined to make things "different this time." Moments later he's riding a horse on his uncle's farm, spurring the animal on and making a dangerous leap over a ravine. This jump, however, has a disturbing effect and he realizes why: the numerous times he made that leap in the past, it was scary as hell. But this time it wasn't. "Because....it's not real," muses Kirk.

At that moment, he's back to being the Kirk we've always known, telling Picard to not let them ever promote or transfer him. "Don't let anything take you off the bridge of that ship," he says, "because while you're there, you can *make a difference.*"

Of this scene, David Carson enthused, "Each character discovers why it is they are where they are as they go through their scenes, more specifically Kirk, who discovers what's happening. Which actually makes the themes interesting from the audience's point of view because it pulls you along a storyline that the character is discovering within himself. You see what the temptation is and why he doesn't want to go anywhere. So it's quite an interesting and seductive thing to do to an audience at that stage of the movie."

Patrick Stewart gleefully recalled one particular exchange between Picard and Kirk in which Picard states, "You are a Starfleet officer. You have a duty!"

Laughed Stewart, "I'm told that the cinema audiences cheer when Kirk says, 'Don't you talk to me like that. I was out saving the galaxy when you're grandfather was still in diapers.' It's a funny line and, of course, it reverberates in a multitude of different ways, too, because it's not only Kirk speaking to Picard but it is the actor Bill Shatner speaking to Patrick Stewart. I thought that was charming."

Herman Zimmerman noted that there had been some discussion of tinting the Nexus sequences. "Like in *The Wizard of Oz*, when you're in Kansas it's black and white, and when you're in Oz it becomes color. But we decided that was a convention we didn't need to follow for this picture because you move around so

fast in the Nexus. We decided, instead, to do some optical transitions and background music that would make it obviously a place that's different from normal reality. It's a tough concept in some ways to make the audience understand."

Using the unique properties of the Nexus, Picard and Kirk are deposited on the Veridian Three mountaintop, working together to stop Soran from achieving his goal, and only able to do so after Kirk makes the ultimate sacrifice, plummeting to his death after doing all that he can to save the 230 million inhabitants of Veridian Four.

■ You're Dead, Jim

For William Shatner, those closing sequences of his involvement in *Star Trek* bring a variety of emotions to mind. On the one hand there was the interaction between he, Stewart and McDowell ("I've always admired Malcolm," said Shatner. "To have the opportunity to play opposite him and Patrick Stewart was to take on part of the Royal Academy class."), as well as the fact that he has played a character through nearly every stage of his adult life

"I don't know whether it's ever been done," he noted. "There was definitely a conscious effort along the way to take the aging into consideration as well as the changes in psychology. While it's extraordinary to play a character over 30 years, it hasn't been thirty years for me. It's been intermittent. After three years of making the series ten years go by and then there was a movie we shot for a couple of months, and then it disappears for another two or three years. It is very intermittent although the *Star Trek* comet trails the people in it. But to have people think of the character as an entity and to mourn the death as though it was a real person, that's a wonderful feeling."

Then of course there was the character's death scene, which probably required more preparation for Shatner than any other piece of film he has ever shot.

"You can only play, you can only perform, you can only read the lines as a result of your own experiences," Shatner explained. "I can't read a laugh line or a line of love the way you would

because I don't have your experience of it, I only have my own. So, my coloring of a line is based on my experience. As a result, playing the death scene required me to look at what I would feel like if I were to die, and we all avoid looking at our own death. We all wear rose-colored glasses, not on life so much but on the absolute certainty that you are going to die. For all intents and purposes, your life is meaningless because you have lived and died and who remembers? So, all those thoughts that we avoid completely and only in the most stressful moments do we think of, and then avoid thinking about them again until the next stressful moment, I had to think about because I wanted to play the death of the character as honestly as I could. I required myself to look at what I would feel like if I was to die and how I would like to die and what it was like to die. That's what I played.

"It was odd and it grew to be more and more odd and stranger as the time to shoot it approached," he added. "But I believe you die the way you live. Captain Kirk lived pretty much the way I wanted him to live. He was a distillation of all that I would like to be: heroic and romantic, forceful in battle and gentle in love, wise and profound. The ideal soldier/philosopher.".

For Brannon Braga, it was a very "strange" moment when he and Ron Moore wrote the words "Kirk dies."

"I know it sounds corny and pretentious," he reflected, "but when we wrote that line, sitting in a condo in Mauii, we kind of sat there for a moment, a little shell-shocked. Ron especially, because he had been a big Kirk fan most of his life. So it was weird. We knew this was imaginary, yet this moment would be meaningful to a lot of people."

Added Moore, "When we got to *the* scene, I was walking, pacing the room, talking, and Bran was at the computer. We were discussing it, on a roll, and then I said the line, 'Kirk dies.' It just sort of hit me. I had to sit down for a minute. There were tears in my eyes. 'Wow, I just killed a childhood hero.' I'll always remember that moment."

Those final moments of battle were exciting to Malcolm McDowell, who also thought it was funny to be watching what was going on from the inside. "There was this actor who had been performing this part for 30 years, there was the usurper of the crown and there's the guy, me, in the middle who's about to kill him," laughed McDowell. "It was kind of weird. Of course, he refused to die. It took him days and days and days to die. He didn't want to go. The scene seemed to go on forever and I can understand why after 30 years.

"For his book [*Star Trek Movie Memories*], Shatner interviewed me and asked, 'What's it like to kill Captain Kirk?' I said, 'Well, I think half the country is going to applaud me and the other half is going to want to kill me.' And he said, 'Which half is going to applaud you?' and I said, 'That's the half that's so sick of you after 30 years that they want to strangle you.' He took it in good sport."

When Leonard Nimoy killed Spock in *Star Trek II*, his death was a slow, emotionally drawn out one. Kirk, on the other hand, parts with the words to Picard, "It's been fun."

"I think it's really simple and doesn't get maudlin or too meaningful," said David Carson. "He's been meaningful about how important it is to make a difference and the bad boy in him, the naughty school boy, is twinkling because the odds are against them, it sounds like fun. It sort of has an irony to it. An enjoyment of life that's important for the Kirk character, and rather than quoting Shakespeare, Peter Pan or something pretentious, like the other movies have given him to do, I think to make it very simple and moving is the best way to approach it."

At the film's conclusion, Picard, having buried Kirk, is picked up by an Enterprise shuttlecraft and brought back to the remains of the starship, where survivors are being transported aboard the recently arrived USS Farragut.

As Picard arrives at the crash site, Data and Troi are searching through rubble, seeking a life form picked up by Troi's tricorder. From within the debris, Data removes his cat, Spot, and actually begins to cry. He believes his emotion program is malfunctioning again, but Troi responds that it's working perfectly.

Searching through what's left of the ready room, Picard and Riker find the captain's family photo album. Riker looks around, disappointed that the ship is

gone, having hoped to one day sit in its center seat. "Somehow," says Picard, "I doubt this will be the last ship to carry the name Enterprise."

The final moment with Data crying, was significant to Brannon Braga because it signified the fact that the Data storyline had become more prominent and meaningful than either he or Ron Moore had anticipated.

"I think a lot of people relate to Data's arc in a very basic way," he said, "though it supplies more than anything the comic relief in the movie. It's also a very poignant storyline, a very touching one, and having seen it on film, it turned out even better than we could have hoped. I think the Data story will perhaps be more popular than the rest of the movie, which wasn't exactly what we expected."

Brent Spiner saw the character's arc in *Generations* as merely the beginning of a new path for Data to follow. "If I had my way about it," he mused, "which I hardly ever have, to me it seems that the character went from being child-like and naive in the series to being a different kind of child in this one because of the newness of the emotions and the inability to control them and know exactly how to handle them. He was a child with emotion and I think the obvious place to take the character is into gradual maturity — an emotional maturity and that can only mean romance, can't it? What I would hope would happen would be a deepening of emotion and the subtleties of emotion and how to deal with them."

In terms of Picard's rather laid back response to the ruined Enterprise, David Carson felt that it was an appropriate one.

"Picard, you have to remember, has died once, gone to heaven and come back," pointed out Carson. "He's now the Picard that you've known. To see Picard moved as he is by the deaths of his brother and nephew is a totally new thing for everybody. We won't have seen Patrick act like that before. I think he should be restored to understanding at the end of the movie, and I don't think we should wander around the ship with Patrick as he says, 'Oh my God, what happened?' He is more philosophical about it. His thing at that point is to deal

William Shatner
(Photo copyright © 1994 Albert Ortega)

with mortality, not only on his own level but from the point of view of the ship as well. That's why the last line is so important. He goes on, continues and evolves."

Considering the entire film, Brannon Braga attempted to sum up his and Ron Moore's dramatic intention.

"We wanted to explore mortality," said Braga. "We didn't want to be religious the way *Star Trek V* was. It didn't really hit us until late in the process that it might be similar. In that film, Kirk met God. One could construe that Soran is searching for paradise/God. I really don't like to think of it that way, because that's not the kind of science fiction we do. The Nexus is a space-time phenomenon that has, certainly, very mysterious properties to it, but we wanted to keep it grounded in believability.

"What this film is absolutely about is time," he continued. "It's about Picard, a man obsessed with what the future holds and his impending death and the death of his family line; a man obsessed with the past, Kirk. What he did or didn't accomplish in his life and was it right? And a Nexus in space-time that gives both men the ability to cheat death and live in any time that they want forever. Ultimately they realize that it's not real. Why would you *want* to cheat death? It's a part of life. Cheating death in a sense is like cheating life. It's not real. Picard has a line in the movie where he says, 'What we leave behind is not as important as how we lived.' So it's really about how these different characters come to terms with their particular personal dilemmas."

■ Trek Rumors

Throughout its production, *Star Trek: Generations* was plagued by a variety of rumors which gradually had the effect of creating a negative buzz of intergalactic proportions.

"We lived with rumors for years with the television show because *Star Trek* is so popular and it means so much to so many people," said Rick Berman. "They are so passionate about it, yet you get gossip and you get rumors. But it wasn't until we made a movie that the rumors were getting printed in national magazines. There were stories printed about the test screenings that we had that were totally false — just made up by somebody. Not even somebody misinterpreting something. I was just envisioning 16-year-old disgruntled kids who for some reason didn't get an autograph or something like that, sitting down on the Internet at 3:00 in the morning and typing out some kind of a story. And the next day it is in a national newspaper.

"It's kind of scary," he continued, "but we have had a love/hate rela-

tionship with *Entertainment Weekly*. They do incredible things — very, very favorable things and then they will write an article that very often takes these things and base them on totally incorrect hearsay. The greatest thing is we traced this. You have a 15-year-old who writes something on the Internet and the next day it is in a tabloid. But then *Entertainment Weekly* will have read it in the tabloid and then all of a sudden a major newspaper will say that we read it in *Entertainment Weekly* and all of a sudden you have read something in five different sources that was all totally uncorroborated nonsense that was just some disgruntled person making something up. That was frustrating for us, but there has been a lot more good publicity that we have had than bad."

One of the strongest tabloid stories claimed Patrick Stewart and William Shatner absolutely hated each other. Shatner, in particular, gets his ire up when he reads these stories, all of which he brands falsehoods.

"They're so mean-spirited," said Shatner, "that they would prefer to tell a lie, a total fantasy about two people disliking each other than to tell the truth about something as equally interesting, that two people *did* like each other. It seems to me that the audience would like to hear that the two actors playing the parts had an instant liking and respect, and here are the games that they played, and the laughs they had. Why wouldn't that be just as interesting as the fantasy of us fighting on the set, which is ludicrous? It is such an instance of what the tabloids do, and we, in the eye of the public, are besieged by those kinds of lies. People read it and think that it's probably true."

Admitted Patrick Stewart, "Bill has a bit of a brutal reputation that precedes him, particularly in his relationship with his colleagues and I was uneasy about that. Also there were stories that Bill had made certain negative remarks about our show in the early days, with him not being very supportive — I've got to take that up with him one of these days. But when we finally sat down together [after the ShoWest Convention], we flew from Las Vegas to Los Angeles in Paramount's private jet. Just the two of us alone up in the sky for an hour and it was perfect

because it gave us the opportunity to sit down and talk. We didn't talk about career. We certainly didn't talk about *Star Trek*. We talked about very personal things and it was the foundation to help us to work so well together when the movie began. He has become a good friend."

Shatner had first met Stewart a couple of years ago in New York City when they shared a stage at Creation's "Two Captains" convention.

"I didn't really get to know him that first time," Shatner admitted, "but I got to know him much better as the schedule went on while we were filming, and I learned to appreciate the man and the actor. He's a wonderful actor, a first class man and I'm looking forward to the fact that we'll be good friends for the rest of our lives."

Malcolm McDowell also had a bit of trepidation beginning production, not knowing exactly what to expect from Shatner. "I've heard mixed things about working with him," he related, "but actually he was extremely nice and we couldn't have had a better time."

Finally, more rumors were circulated about the reshooting of the film's climax between Patrick Stewart, William Shatner and Malcolm McDowell. A variety of publications, most notably *Entertainment Weekly*, indicated that a screening of the film on September 13, 1994 went disastrously; that the audience hated it. Executive producer Rick Berman countered this by stating to *EW*, "It's a tiny little piece of the film that we're going back to fix."

Berman was obviously downplaying the mega-hype of the mainstream press. His "tiny little piece of the film" was actually the entire ending sequence when Picard and Kirk use the Nexus to go back in time to stop Soran. To achieve this, and to enhance some of the film's special effects, Paramount okayed an additional $4 million to the budget.

The reason for all this is simple: the audience apparently enjoyed the movie but felt that it was anti-climactic, given all that had come before.

"The press doesn't know what they're talking about," proclaimed Malcolm McDowell. "The screening went extremely well, but, in fact, even when we were shooting the end of the film we always felt it was rather anti-climactic, which is what the audience intimated. They were rather silent and quiet. People *should* have wanted to cheer when I got killed and they didn't. Remember in *Blue Thunder* when I got killed? Everyone cheered. Kirk's death happened too quickly."

Rick Berman disagreed, noting, "I don't think that we knew it was anticlimactic. We knew that we had less time to shoot the ending than we wanted. This was at the very end of the shoot and we were running out of time — that's what the movie's about, right? And we didn't have the time to do it properly. When we came back and screened the film for a test audience, we had a wonderful reception to the movie, but the test audience — and more importantly, all of us — saw the six and a half minutes involving Picard, Kirk and Soran, and felt that it was not as exciting as it could be and we were blessed in that Paramount said to us, 'If you want to go back an redo it, go back and redo it.' So, there was a part of us that kept moaning about the fact that we would have to go back to that dreadful mountain in Nevada, but we did. We went back and reshot that six and a half minutes and made it better.

"We were talking about the press and gossip," he elaborated. "I read incredible things. I read that we had terrible reports, which was completely incorrect. It was one of the highest testings — first testings — that Paramount had ever done. I read we were doing the reshoot to alter Kirk's fate, to make his fate more ambiguous. Totally incorrect things that somebody just makes up and all of a sudden the next day you read about it on the front page of the entertainment section. We went back because there was this six and a half minute segment that we wanted to punch up and make a little bit more exciting. So, it ended up working out for the best. *Clear and Present Danger* is a very big movie — it is one of the top grossing movies of the year. They went back to Mexico to reshoot a bunch of scenes. You don't read about it in the paper, though, because it's a normal process."

David Carson explained that the interesting thing about the film's two endings was that the same basic ideas

Patrick Stewart   *(Photo copyright © 1994 Albert Ortega)*

used in the first version are in the second version as well.

"In other words," he said, "that Captain Kirk gives his life for 230 million people; that he dies trying to save the universe and dies with Captain Picard. He uses his strength and his ability to leap into battle with a smile on his lips and all that sort of thing to physically attack and deal with Soran who, as we have seen already in the film, Picard can't deal with — he's head-butted down a ravine. So when he comes back, he

needs Kirk's physical skills and his ability to deal with things physically while Picard goes and deals with the launcher, and that is basically the first ending.

"When we put it together," Carson pointed out, "we discovered that, much as with the torture scene, the huge climax of the Enterprise crashing has people thrown around inside the ship. We developed that into an enormous climax and we developed the Klingon battle into this huge, noisy battle and we found also that we had to go with the moodiness at the end of the scene. We have this extraordinary scene where Picard discovers that his family is burned to death and he cries. We had moving scenes of highs and lows coming up, so the simplicity of this ending was also governed by this 50-day schedule that we had to deal with. So we had to make some simplicity work on our side, but to make a long story short, when we got to the end and discovered that we had these huge calamities in our ending, which were satisfactory and good and true and simple, it wasn't satisfying enough. It didn't go that whole way to satisfy. So, we went as the filmmakers to Sherry Lansing and said we are very anxious about the ending. We would like to do some more. We know from *Casablanca* that endings have been reshot, so it is nothing new. I thought that perhaps with a bit of luck they would let me have the actors and bits of metal and we could get on a building on top of Paramount somewhere and do it, and I would get a day to shoot it if I was lucky. I thought I could change it enough to make it more powerful and stronger, but when Sherry saw the film, she said, 'This is a wonderful film. Let's go for the ending. Let's go and expand it and get the guys together more.' So, what we did was instead of having Kirk nose-to-nose constantly to Soran, which is how the first one was, we put him in a different sort of physical danger, which was the bridge and the danger created by Soran. We just expanded the ending, but we didn't throw one ending away and rewrite it."

Production designer Herman Zimmerman added, "What the audience *won't* see is Captain Kirk being dispatched by Soran in a rather ignominious way. Shot in the back with a disruptor is not a good way to go. Now Kirk has to sacrifice his life intentionally as any tragic figure would. It brings him up to the level of a Prometheus or Agamemnon — the willing accomplice in sealing his own fate."

Zimmerman went on to explain exactly how the "wrong" ending was shot in the first place. "The studio wanted to make the picture for a budget and the writers wrote to that budget, rather than writing the thing that in their hearts they would have preferred to do," he

said. "When the studio saw what they commissioned, they felt it was worth re-examining it. We have the two captains finally meeting each other and it would be a shame to give it short shrift, which the original script did. They decided to go for it and make a more exciting ending and give Kirk and Picard more heroic things to do. And I think they've accomplished that. The new ending is different in detail but not in substance. We still have to have a moment for Captain Kirk's last heroic gesture, and we still have these two guys dispatch Soran and foil his plot to get back to the Nexus."

William Shatner explained that when he was told that a reshoot would be necessary, his reaction mirrored Stewart's and McDowell's: "Was it my performance?"

"Somehow," Shatner shrugged, "everybody lost sight of the fact that I was being shot in the back and the whole ending kind of slipped away. They wanted more and they were going to change the shot in the back, but the dialogue remained the same. So, yes, I had to go back and die again, but by that time I had worked out the performance, so I didn't need to look at it with the clarity of what's it like to die and what am I going to be like when I die and how frightened I am of dying and what would Captain Kirk do when he crosses the threshold? I had already done that, so the second time I knew the performance."

David Carson didn't find the shooting of Kirk's death scene — either one of them — to be particularly difficult.

"The challenging thing about it is not that he dies, but *how* he dies and the expectations of everybody who has been with him in his various mythical exploits over the last 30 years. The hero dies and he has to die correctly. That was the most challenging thing to work out. I think, for example, part of the mythology has been when Kirk dies, he dies alone. Now, because our story is about the handing of the torch, obviously when he dies he passes the torch in many ways. His mortality, which is what the film is about, comes into the new generation, the next generation. So, he had to die with Picard and one of the differences we made between the ending that we created to start with and then the change that was

made, was that I tried to create this barrier around Kirk so that Picard could not get at him and he couldn't touch him. He was under all this incredible amount of metal which was tangled. So, I started in a way where you see Picard coming down and you see him see this thing in a distance, and then you see him for a long time looking through the metal and see what the damage is and he doesn't see Kirk. And we reveal Kirk right at the end when Picard comes to look at him and you see the distance between them; the two men are incredibly well separated. So, we tried to be truthful to those things and yet looked at our own needs. I think the performance that Bill gave, and that we worked on for that week, was a very delicate and moving one."

"The new ending," Zimmerman added to the scenario, "has much more interaction between Kirk and Picard. You see that they like each other, they're friends, and when Kirk does make a heroic gesture that ends in his death, it's that much more poignant that these two friends, having barely gotten to know and respect each other, have parted so soon."

Patrick Stewart was also pleased that the ending was being reshot in order to enhance the film. "At the moment when Bill says, 'It sounds like fun' and we gallop out of the Nexus and arrive at the planet, basically I said, 'Okay, Captain, you go this way and I'll go that way,' and we split up. Whereas that's not what everyone wanted to see. The fans wanted to see the two captains shoulder-to-shoulder. That was the whole purpose of bringing them together and that's not how it was. So the reshoot was a very sensible action. I think it could have been even more of that buddy quality in the last part of the movie."

Paramount, which would have cut their losses by simply dropping the film into release if they thought that it's chances were slim (i.e. *Star Trek V: The Final Frontier*), decided to invest more for a greater return. It's exactly the same scenario that surrounded the studio's *Fatal Attraction*, the revised ending of which is often credited for the film's worldwide box office success.

Being given the opportunity to do the reshoot was rather surprising to the production, but indicative of the studio's shifting attitude throughout production.

"Even though I complain about the size of the budget and the length of the shooting schedule, we have managed to go to town in a grand way in much of it," David Carson said. "The studio sort of started out saying, 'Well, it's *only Star Trek*,' and we didn't subscribe to that. We thought we would push the envelope and try to get as much as we could. When they [Paramount] started to see what we were doing, they started saying, 'Wow, we have a great action movie coming out. Not only a great action movie, but it's got emotion, humor and it's going to be a great movie. Get ready, everybody,' and they started turning attention our way." Which ultimately led to the financing of the reshoot.

■ Generations: The Aftermath

Star Trek: Generations opened in America on November 18th, 1994 to generally mixed reviews.

On the positive side, *Newsweek* noted, "This time out the Powers That Beam have found solid footing with *Star Trek: Generations*.... The film serves up lots of familiar faces and shtik, big-bang special effects, new hardware and character development and an ageless theme. For Trek devotees, it's a supernova of unpredictable sci-fi thrills." *Time*, which made the film its November 28th cover story, enthused, "The new film [is] a smashingly entertaining mix of outer-space adventure and spaced-out metaphysics." *Newsday*, which gave the film three out of four stars, stated, "As bombastic and self-involved as any 'Star Trek' movie, this may be the best by virtue of balance: thoughtful storyline, grandiose special effects and Patrick Stewart. Add a star if you've already been beamed aboard."

USA Today was less enthusiastic, awarding two and a half stars out of four. Wrote reviewer Susan Wloszczyna, "Bottom line: The highly awaited time-travel teaming of Picard and Kirk....isn't quite the clash of the follicle-impaired titans that it's meant to be....[There's] too much technochat about plasma cores. Not enough plot core." The New York

Daily News stated, "'Generations' is full of wizardly special effects — including a stunning but ultralong crash sequence that gets repeated for good measure — but quickly becomes uninvolving. The screenplay could use one of those emotion chips from Data's skull." Michael Medved of *The New York Post* savaged the film more than most, noting, "This bloated bomb turns 'Star Trek' into 'Star Drek.' It's the seventh motion picture in this profitable series and by far the worst — even less satisfying than 'Star Trek V: The Final Frontier,' the previous runt of the litter....Unfortunately, the lavish sets and dazzling explosions only provide distractions in the midst of the plodding plot, which culminates in an old-fashioned fistfight involving three superannuated actors (Shatner, Stewart and McDowell) whose stodgily choreographed fisticuffs resemble the bare-knuckle brawls in Grade B westerns of 60 years ago."

Yet despite these diverse reactions, the most important "review" has come in at the box office. *Generations* had the best *Star Trek* opening weekend of them all, pulling in over $23 million. By the end of its second week of release, its grossed had amassed to $50 million, a week's throw from the film actually turning a profit. Naturally this leads to the distinct possibility/probability that an eighth film will be produced. Already questions are circulating, with *Entertainment Tonight* reporting that the film will not feature any members of the original cast, focusing exclusively on *The Next Generation*. This point made sense to William Shatner, who finds it highly unlikely he would be asked to return, although he does understand the audience's skepticism regarding that point.

"I understand the nature of your question, having fooled you a couple of times before," he said, referring to Spock's death at the end of *The Wrath of Khan* and the destruction of the Enterprise in *The Search for Spock*, both of which were ultimately resurrected. "Not fooled you, but people said, 'Well, the movie made money, maybe we better bring you back to life' and stuff like that. We certainly meant it at the time, but in this case there is a whole different cast and they want their time and place in the

sun. It would be impossible to bring the two casts together. We are separated by time and I've never liked the science-fiction game of time travel. It seems to me to pull the plug on any tension, besides which it stretches the imagination. It's hard to imagine it being at all possible, so from those points of view I have never liked the idea of time travel."

When pressed as to whether or not he would swear that there is no possible way he will bring Kirk back, Berman replied, "No, I will not." Interestingly, the Maurice Hurley screenplay written as a potential *Star Trek VII*, and which Berman has indicated could be the follow-up to *Generations*, has Picard recreate Kirk on the holodeck to converse with him regarding a crisis the Enterprise is facing. So one never knows, do one?

As far as the appeal of *Star Trek: Generations* for the moviegoing audience, the film's production designer, Herman Zimmerman noted, "This script is an examination of all our lives. It's an examination of our situation as human beings. That's why I think Gene Roddenberry would like this movie. It's an examination of us facing our mortality. No other animal except the human species understands that he's a finite creature and is going to die some day."

The same, apparently, can't be said of this franchise, which keeps trekking along, growing stronger as it does so. As they said 15 years ago, and as they are undoubtedly saying now as the Enterprise-D continues to boldly go, the human adventure is just beginning.

■ Appendix A

ILM Beams Up Star Trek Effects

by Ron Magid

Like many imaginative kids growing up in the '60s, Bill George loved *Star Trek*. Living in a small Northern California town of 2300 people, he never dreamed he'd actually be able to contribute to the *Star Trek* legend. But through his own unique talents and various twists of fate, George has had an ever-larger role in the almost thirty-year saga of the starship Enterprise and her extended space family, having worked on five of the seven films.

George began his special effects career as a modelmaker working under master builder Greg Jein on *Star Trek: The Motion Picture* in 1979. After contributing some remarkable models to the sci-fi classic *Blade Runner*, George headed north to Industrial Light & Magic where he built many of the miniatures used in *Star Trek II*. After working alongside art director Nilo Rodis-Jamero designing "tons and tons of new spaceships" for *Star Trek III*, George was unavailable for *IV* and we all know what became of *V*. When George at last returned to the Federation for *Star Trek VI*, it was as full-fledged Visual Effects Art Director on that classic, a post he readily assumed again for the seventh installment, *Star Trek Generations*.

But there was one more "coincidence" if you will: during his modelmaking days at ILM, George worked on the 6' miniature Enterprise-D for the *Next Generation* pilot, the same model he restored and shot for *Generations*. Ironically, while he was building that model seven years ago, he was less than thrilled with the design. "I have to admit, when I first saw the *Next Generation* Enterprise, I didn't like it much, but it has definitely grown on me. I view most of the Star Trek ships as Art Deco, they're very simple shapes put together, but I think the Next Generation ship is more Art Nouveau. Quite frankly, it was a very difficult model to build because of that. It's definitely the next stage, and it's more organic."

Because of his modelling background, it was George's responsibility, and one of his greatest pleasures, to renovate the 6' Enterprise D, which had languished in a crate since the TV show's second season, as well as retrofitting the *Trek* features' Excelsior class Enterprise-B to make it look like its design was actually moving in the direction of the Enterprise-D.

"The art department down in L.A. designed these little wings on the side of the Enterprise-B's secondary hull and also added some details to the engines that took it in that direction," George said, "and we built them here in the modelshop. I think the design looks a lot more balanced. It's actually a design refinement."

Meanwhile, the big job of prepping *Next Generation*'s Enterprise-D for its up-close and personal big screen debut was getting underway. "There's some things I've always wanted to do to that Enterprise," George laughed, "but Rick Berman, the producer, just wanted us to give it a facelift. I always wanted to change the paint job, because we didn't have a lot of time to paint it when we built the model back in 1987, and the green and blue color scheme didn't read on television. The 6' model had been sitting in the closet and it was pretty beat up. We stripped off all the paint and decals, bonded all the dents and scrapes where the motion control camera had run into it. We took the color more toward a battleship grey, and also, per *Generation*'s visual effects supervisor, John Knoll, added some glossy areas because he liked the tiled look of the original movie Enterprise. When there's raking light across it, you can see that panelled look and it's really beautiful. We also modified the lifeboats, these little brownish squares on top of the saucer, which are a really interesting feature but never really showed up before. We added lines around them and little numbers to accentuate them more. The new paintjob ended up selling a lot of what I wanted. It just spruced it up and made it really purdy. It was like taking your car to the bodyshop."

Except this wasn't any ordinary vehicle; it was the starship Enterprise, an icon. And therein lay the first of *Star Trek*

Generation's many effects challenges: how to photograph a craft audiences have seen from every conceivable angle and make it seem fresh.

"During one of our meetings, Rick Berman said, 'People have watched our show for seven years and they've fallen in love with the Enterprise and when they see it on the big screen, we want them to fall in love with it all over again.'" George said. "He was charging us to come up with shots that were really dynamic. One of the difficulties and challenges was that *Next Generation*'s effects were really high quality, so our work really had to excel. Fortunately, we were shooting in a screen format very different than television, so the shots could be composed and balanced more dynamically."

Berman needn't have worried. Visual Effects Supervisor John Knoll worked with George to devise optimum shots of the Enterprise-D to do the obvious shots better than they'd been done in the past. A simple description in the script like, "The Enterprise orbits Veridian 3," gave George and other *Trek* fans working on the show at ILM the chance to create a classic movie moment with the TV icon. "I always get a lump in my throat when I see that shot because it's the classic orbiting the planet shot: We're looking at the Enterprise from underneath as it arcs majestically past the planet and there's a little bit of a lensflare as it passes in front of the sun. You wouldn't actually see the ship arcing around the planet, but we cheated. I think that's really the most beautiful shot of the Enterprise."

They also didn't shirk when it came to alien vessels, designing a spectacular rescue by the Klingon Bird of Prey, using the familiar model built for *Trek III*. "There's a shot John Knoll designed where the Bird of Prey comes in and beams some people off this solar observatory at the last minute, then gets out of there before it's destroyed," George said admiringly. "The Klingon ship just slides in almost like it's skidding, and it's decloaking as it's spinning and screeching to a halt near the observatory. It's really beautiful."

But perhaps the greatest design challenge was the Energy Ribbon, a group effort between Visual Effects Supervisor Knoll, Co-Visual Effects Supervisor Alex Seiden and George. After much trial and error, they arrived at an undulating ribbon surrounded by a plasma energy field, which was to be animated using computer graphics (CG).

"We made reference to the opening planetary explosion sequence from *Trek VI* a lot," George says. "Fortunately, Alex Seiden did an awful lot of those shots, so it was great working with somebody who'd solved a similar problem before. Approaching these effects are like battles, and after we've been through a few battles with people and we've been successful, it's a bonding experience. Alex is quite brilliant and I'm feeling more comfortable with working with computer graphics. Doing computer graphics requires more than just knowing how to run the equipment; you need an understanding of art, balance of nature and have to be able to translate that knowledge through your fingers into the computer. It's not just the machine, it's the operator."

In fact, *Generations* afforded George his first chance to design and build a new alien spacecraft — the Lakul — entirely in the computer. "It was actually based on a truck we designed for *Back to the Future* that John Knoll liked," George revealed. "I really enjoyed building the Lakul with Rob Coleman, who was our CG modeller. Designing the basic shape went pretty smoothly, it was a bit brick-shaped but we added some pontoons to it and that helped. But detailing it became a bit frustrating because I couldn't get my hands on it. Rather than trying to communicate which things should be changed, it was easier for me to make a quickie model with greebels the traditional way and set it on Rob's desk. I'd come back two hours later and his CG model would be perfect. I'm encouraged that computers haven't completely taken over. It's becoming obvious that the old and new tools work best together."

George also put a lot of energy into designing the climactic crash of the Enterprise-D saucer section onto Veridian 3, along with Knoll and storyboard artist Mark Moore. "John and I sketched out ideas — I'd do them on paper, he'd do

them in the computer — and then we had storyboard and concept artist Mark Moore refine that," George recalled. "One thing I felt was my responsibility as art director was to define how big the saucer was so we were all on the same page. I figured out the size of the ship as listed in the Tech manual, then I did a drawing of the saucer over the Golden Gate Bridge. I also researched the height of trees in the rainforest, which is 150' max, and on Veridian 3 I figured maybe they're a little taller. Then I did this drawing showing the scale relationship between the saucer and the trees — I figured the Enterprise bridge would be almost even with the top of the trees."

Despite the trials and tribulations of his professional involvement with *Star Trek* for the past fifteen years, George still fondly recalls discovering the book that changed his life: *The Making of Star Trek*, by Gene Roddenberry and Stephen Whitfield. The eager ten-year-old poured overy every page, studying the various design sketches for the Enterprise and other classic *Trek* ships, never dreaming that one day a whole new generation of fans would be ogling his designs in much the same way. As his copy became more and more dogeared from use, George fixated on one design that had never been realized in three-dimensions, the Intrepid, whose most distinguishing feature was its huge spherical primary hull. The modelmaker in him vowed to build it, and he thought it might make a nice addition to the final season of *Star Trek: The Next Generation*. He contacted his friend, Mike Okuda, who was one of *Next Generation*'s art directors and designers. "He said, 'We have a problem in that we don't have a ship contemporary to the Enterprise-D that the average viewer can look at and know it's a different ship,'" George remembered. "I took that to heart and I thought I'd really like to design a ship contemporary to the D that had a spherical primary hull like the Intrepid, so I sent a sketch I did to Mike to see if he'd use it if I built it. He said, 'I can't say yes, but we might,' so, working on the weekends, I ended up building this thing around the time we started working on *Generations*. Producer Peter Lauritson ended up renting it from me and using it

for the final episode of *Next Generation*; it became the Pasteur. So that was really thrilling to see that used, and I was really proud that it was the spherical primary hull that harkened back to that really early design."

Talking with Bill George in his office at ILM, one gets the impression that he's one of the happiest guys on this planet, having grown up with *Star Trek* and now getting to expand it as it moves into the next generation and beyond. "I feel really lucky. Certainly I'm not into it as much as I was when I was a kid, but somtimes it makes me think that when I grew up in a small town and dreaming about being on the *Star Trek* sets, I never realized that ultimately I would have a big part in designing spaceships and things that millions of children could be playing with. When I was a kid I was so into that stuff, so to see them make toys and models based on my designs is just....wow."

■ Appendix B

Star Trek Generations' Motion Control And CG Model Work

by Ron Magid

The remarkable effects for the classic '60s *Star Trek* TV series were state-of-the-art for their day, magnificent imagery that weekly pushed the limits of what audiences could expect from that square invader that had taken over their living rooms. Effects pioneers like Linwood Dunn, whose credits include shooting the famed RKO Radio logo, compositing King Kong's timeless imagery and creating the Dunn Optical Printer, the workhorse of special effects creation since the '30s, brought his formidable talents to the fledgling sci-fi television series. In fact, the Enterprise's famed numerical designation, 1701, was Dunn's street address! Since *Star Trek* preceded *Star Wars'* computerized motion control revolution by over a decade, virtually all of the show's effects involved locked off matte paintings and miniature shots, a failing that was ultimately remedied through six motion pictures that took the Enterprise to the limits of motion control technology. Now, for this seventh installment in the *Star Trek* filmic series,. a new generation of artists have truly taken effects where no one has gone before, as the classic *Trek* Enterprise-B and the *Next Generation*'s Enterprise-D enter the digital realm.

But there was more to the decision than just concern for the traditions of *Star Trek*. Knowing what each of the *Trek* films has made in the past, Paramount believes this enables them to predict what *Trek* films will gross in the future. Consequently, before a script is even written, every item needed to make the film is tightly budgeted, including visual effects.

"Of course, *Generations'* screenwriters did exactly what you'd expect them to do," said Visual Effects Supervisor John Knoll. "They went way beyond the bounds of television and did something much more cinematic, so the script was jammed full of really cool, expensive effects. Then we went through

this incredibly painful process of story-boarding the effects, without minding the budget, to best serve the script. Even after we figured ways to execute the expensive shots more cheaply, it was still more than they wanted to spend. That's when we really started hacking into it, which was the most painful part: we had all the storyboards up on the wall, the bare minimum number of shots to tell the story, there's nothing left to cut and we still had to cut stuff out. Fortunately, we found some sneaky ways to keep a couple of effects in there, like combining shots, but it was tough."

Under the circumstances, ILM had anticipated using traditional motion control spaceship miniature effects primarily, and in fact, many of *Star Trek Generation*'s space shots, including the climactic space battle over Veridian 3, were handled that way. Model Supervisor John Goodson refurbished the *Next Generation*'s 6' Enterprise-D model and retrofit the Enterprise-B, a redress of the Excelsior model originally built for *Star Trek III*. Knoll supervised almost a complete re-build of the spacedock miniature unused since *Star Trek: The Motion Picture* (it was shown in stock shots in *Star Trek II*). The model required a major refit since it was built to house Enterprise-A, but this time Enterprise-B was going in there; Knoll removed the Spacedock's middle row of lights, which gave it a more pleasing Panavision shape that fit much better into the anamorphic frame.

Knoll also uncrated the Klingon Bird of Prey originally built for *Trek III* and last seen in *Trek VI* for a climactic space battle with the *Next Generation*'s Enterprise-D. Although the battle was handled primarily using motion control, the budget didn't allow for breakaway models and pyro explosions, so the impacts were done with CG and traditional compositing tricks, including flashes of light, the CG equivalent of the old burning steel wool trick on "charred" areas and flying CG debris.

Even the weaponry of *Star Trek* made the blazing transition into computer graphics. "The Bird of Prey's disrupters, those short little energy bolts, were hand-animated by Don Butler," Knoll said. "The Enterprise's phasers were done more or less the same way,

but with a little more complexity — we had some animation flashing through the beams. But the effect I was most excited about doing in CG was the photon torpedoes. I liked them best in *Star Trek: The Motion Picture*, where they had these big, bright, impressive shards of light like they really had a lot of power, but they were hard to shoot. Apogee, John Dykstra's former effects house, created the effect by shining a laser beam through a clear crystal that they shot in smoke, which looked beautiful but was really tedious to do. I was unhappy with the way the photon torpedoes looked on the last couple of shows, where it was always done using some kind of animation effect. So on this film, we decided to digitally simulate our photon torpedoes using computer graphics, and since the look was wide open, I opted to go back to the look of the first film. I actually just digitized some pieces out of *Star Trek: The Motion Picture* and used those as reference, then I wrote a simulator program that generated a photon torpedo that looked like the ones in *Star Trek: The Motion Picture*, and we could animate it going from any point to any point."

At the climax of the battle over Veridian 3, the Enterprise-D attacks the weak spot in the Bird of Prey, blasting it out of the stars. Figuring there's no way to improve on perfection, Knoll conserved his budget by re-using the climactic destruction of the Bird of Prey from the end of *Star Trek VI*. Ironically, that effect is so flawless, it served as the reference for another of *Generations'* explosions, this one in CG: the demise of the Lakul in the Energy Ribbon.

"Replicating the dynamic of an exploding spaceship in the computer was something that took us a while to nail down," said CG Supervisor John Schlag. "We worked long and hard on an explosion for the Lakul by combining CG data and digitized real world pyro elements (recycled from *Empire Strikes Back*) and layering a lot of stuff into the shot, but it didn't have the realistic feeling we wanted. When we analyzed the exploding Bird of Prey that was done pyro for *Trek VI*, we noticed that the big pieces of the Bird of Prey moved much more slowly while the small pieces blew by in a couple of frames. When we added that sense of momentum to our dynamic simulation, right away it was much improved. Then Barbara Nellis, our Technical Director for this shot, converted the CG Lakul model from Softimage into another format, where she blew it all to pieces, then brought that back into our own software. Henry LaBounta wrote some additional software to munge the ship pieces into blown up shapes as opposed to perfect model pieces. It really was a big payoff."

ILM decided to build the Lakul and its sister ship using computer graphics in the first place so the alien vessel could move freely through the CG Energy Ribbon model, and to control the interactive light, among other effects nightmares. Those proved to be good arguments for digitizing the Enterprise-B as it entered the intergalactic phenomenon as well.

"All the shots of the Enterprise-B in the Ribbon were done with computer graphics," Knoll confirmed. "The decision was made to do that so we could have particles streaming around the Enterprise as though they're deflected by the shields, and do effects with tighter interaction than we could've gotten away with using motion control."

The Enterprise-B was first and foremost a motion control miniature. The big question was: would the CG and motion control models cut together seamlessly? To make sure they did, photographs of the actual Enterprise-B motion control miniature were used as templates to create the computer wireframe schematic — sort of a three-dimensional blueprint of the starship minus its skin — that was used to animate the flight of the CG Federation ship through its shots. "To render the 'skin' of the Enterprise-B, we actually took a bunch of flatly lit detail photographs of the ship with a real long lens from directly above and below, from both sides, and from front and back," Knoll explained. "Since the geometry of the CG Enterprise-D matched the photographs of the motion control model, when we laid the texture maps that were derived from those same photos over that geometry, it matched the motion control model exactly!"

Once the Enterprise-B was digitized, animating it in the CG realm enabled ILM to create totally convincing images of the Federation starship entering the Energy Ribbon, interacting with the CG Lakul and becoming hopelessly trapped after the Lakul's destruction.

"When the Enterprise is getting dragged sideways into the Ribbon," Knoll said, "we were able to convey the sense of this huge wind blowing past it using particle systems and shaders on CG sheets perpendicular to the camera. The intent was to create an Energy Ribbon atmosphere with a lot of directional motion between the 'camera' and the ship. It looks like a giant storm in space."

But the CG Enterprise-B wasn't only reserved for long shots of the Energy Ribbon; in fact, one of the most dramatic shots of the starship occurs as the camera follows the Enterprise closing in on the Ribbon.

"It's a medium shot with the Energy Ribbon in the distance and the CG Enterprise B-filling the right side of frame," Schlag sighed. "All three of our technical directors had their mitts on it at some point. Not only is there a factor of two change in the scale of the Energy Ribbon as we pull into it, but since we're riding so close behind the Enterprise, we had to do a lot of work to make it hold up. There's a lot of detail on that ship, but rather than going hogwild and fixing every little detail, we just started the shots and fixed the problems as they came up. Scott Frankel did the texture work on it and Ben Snow did a lot of the sweatwork to fix up the Enterprise and make it look really good at close range. By the time we were done with it, it was pretty much ready for prime time, at least for medium shots."

Knoll himself built the CG model of the Enterprise-D on his home computer, then used the model in some half-dozen shots, according to CG Supervisor John Schlag, who noted that *Star Trek: Generations* was the easiest film he'd ever recruited talent for at ILM: "After finishing *Forrest Gump*, which was a really difficult show with a huge number of composites we all worked many Saturdays on, I ran screaming into the hills for two weeks, then came back and immediately signed onto *Star Trek*. The thing that made me do it, aside from the interesting collection of shots, was it gave me a chance to be a part of the whole *Trek* thing, which for better or worse is a

significant contribution to American culture. In fact, that's been a significant factor for many of the people on this show. If you think about it, Industrial Light & Magic is practically an entire company filled with *Trek* geeks, and people who do special effects don't do it for the money anyway, they do it because they really like what they're doing."

One of those *Trek* Geeks, not surprisingly, is Visual Effects Supervisor John Knoll, who saw in *Star Trek: Generations* the opportunity to bring his career full circle. Turns out that even though ILM only handled effects on *Star Trek: The Next Generation's* pilot episode, Knoll did the motion control programming on the Warpdrive stretch effect.

"So I did the two shots of the Enterprise-D going into warp drive on the feature," he grinned sheepishly. "The original effect was done using motion control and slitscan, which was really the only thing that was practical at the time. The problem with the slitscan approach, which involved projecting a slit of light onto the model from front to back, was we couldn't have rimlight, all the light had to come directly from the side, and we couldn't do slitscan on a light pass. If you analyze the warp drive stretch in the TV show, you'll notice the portholes go off as soon as the stretch starts! It worked fine for what the TV show intended to do, but today it just barely holds up, even on television. When we were faced with doing the same thing for the feature, I figured since the technology now exists to do this the right way, we should use computer graphics. That way the ship could stretch out, its blinkers could keep going and the lighting wouldn't change. Admittedly, back in 1987, we couldn't really do a completely realistic CG Enterprise that looked as good as the motion control model, but I think we achieved that this time. Basically, we took a CG model of the Enterprise-D and just snapped it into warp drive. It's easy enough."

■ Appendix C

Star Guests

Each of the STAR TREK films have introduced new characters to the proceedings, and with few exceptions most of them were done away with in one way or another. What follows are the brief commentaries of some of those guest stars.

STAR TREK II: THE WRATH OF KHAN
RICARDO MONTALBAN
KHAN NOONIAN SINGH

Ricardo Montalban first portrayed Eugenic superman Khan Noonian Singh during Star Trek's *first season in the episode "Space Seed." Some fifteen years later, producer Harve Bennett came up with the idea of resurrecting the character in* Star Trek II *much to the delight of audiences and Montalban himself.*

In those days, there wasn't the dearth of material that we have today on television. Some shows were quite special, and certainly *Star Trek* was one of them. I was quite familiar with it. As an actor, I thought it would be great fun to do it. Khan was not the run of the mill sort of portrayal. It had to have a different dimension. That attracted me very much. And when they sent me the script, I thought it was a fascinating character and I loved doing it.

Khan was a character that was bigger than life. He had to be played that way. He was extremely powerful both mentally and physically, with an enormous amount of pride. But he was not totally villainous. He had some good qualities. I saw a nobility in the man that, unfortunately, was overridden by ambition and a thirst for power. I saw that in the character and played it accordingly. It was very well received at the time, and I was delighted.

Then I forgot about it. You go on to the next thing, the next and the next. I did so many things and finally ended up on *Fantasy Island*. There I was and, lo and behold, they called me again to play this character. I got the script and began reading the role. It was an interesting character, again.

At the time I was so immersed in the character of *Fantasy Island*, that when I started to articulate the words of Khan for myself, I didn't sound like the character to me. I sounded like Mr. Roarke, and I was very concerned about it. Then I asked Harve Bennett to send me a tape of the old show that I did. I ran it two or three times. When I first saw it, I didn't even remember what I did. On the third viewing, a strange thing happened to me and I started reliving the moment, and the mental process that I had arrived at at that time began to work in me and I associated myself with that character more and more. Finally, I took the script, found one of the scenes and did it to myself, and I did feel then that Roarke had disappeared and that indeed I was into this character.

Now this character presented a different problem. The original character was in total control of the situation. Guided simply by his overriding ambition. The new character, however, was now obsessed. He was a man obsessed with vengeance for the death of his wife, for which he blamed Kirk. If he was bigger than life before, I felt he really had to become bigger than life almost to the point of becoming ludicrous to be effective. If I didn't play it fully and totally obsessed with this, then I think the character would be little and insignificant and uninteresting. The danger was in going overboard. Very often, an actor will play things safely and it works. You can play safe, you can underact, put the lid on and it works beautifully. In this case, I thought if I did that it would be very dull. I had to be, if not deranged, then very close to it. I had to find a tone of really going right to the razor's edge before the character becomes a caricature.

I don't think the lack of a face-to-face moment between Kirk and Khan was a drawback. Actually, that was an element that was interesting. It was difficult as an actor, but that separation of the two ships gave it a really poignant touch to the scenes. The fact that being so strong, there was such pressure knowing that he can't get his hands on Kirk. I didn't mind that. I minded as an actor. I wish William Shatner and I had somehow been able to respond to each other at the time. The actual situation, though,

I thought was a plus. I think we left the audience wanting them to get together, and we don't.

I get fan mail from Japan because of this role. It's amazing. These people are quite remarkable. I'm delighted to have been part of this phenomenon.

KIRSTIE ALLEY
LIEUTENANT SAAVIK

One of the more interesting guest stars to join the regular Star Trek *crew was Kirstie Alley as the half-Vulcan, half-Romulan Lieutenant Saavik (though all references to her Romulan heritage were dropped in the final film). Alley, who would go on to great fame in films and the NBC television series* Cheers, *was asked by Nicholas Meyer to reprise the role in* Star Trek VI: The Undiscovered Country, *but she turned him down, probably because, according to her, the producers offered her less money for* Star Trek III *than she had gotten for* Khan, *and then replaced her with Robin Curtis.*

I liked the *Star Trek* TV series. In fact, I've been rehearsing Spock for some years now. I would pretend that I was his daughter. Every week, every episode, I'd sit there thinking, 'I should play Spock's daughter.' I mean, I could arch my eyebrows as good as Leonard Nimoy. Get 'em waaay up there. Whenever I'd watch the show I'd write dialogue for myself so I could actually take part in the story. When Leonard said a line, I'd respond. So when I was told about the part, I was very excited. I went in and acted like Spock, then Nick Meyer said, "Boy, you have him down. Did you know that?"

I admit I didn't know if [the fans] would like a female Vulcan. It was a little difficult because when Mr. Spock is unemotional, it works because he's a man. When a woman is unemotional, she's a bitch.

We really had to work on it so that she could be sensitive and let the Romulan part of her come out a little bit. That's why the tears near the end. I was very sad. I would have cried standing at the end of that, even if I wasn't supposed to. It was very touching.

MERRITT BUTRICK
DR. DAVID MARCUS

The late Merritt Butrick had the distinction of portraying the son of James T. Kirk in The Wrath of Khan, *a role he subsequently reprised in* The Search for Spock. *Before his passing his co-starred in the TV series* Square Pegs *and even guest starred in the "Symbiosis" episode of* Star Trek: The Next Generation.

I was raised on *Star Trek*. It was kind of odd to play the role I played. It's like I was born at the right time. When we first read the script, at Nicholas' house, it was.if you closed your eyes, like you were *inside* the TV and looking out. Very strange feeling. They were voices we were all familiar with.

[In the film] there used to be quite a communication going on about [being Kirk's illegitimate son] between Saavik and I, which has been eliminated from the film, so we won't dwell on it. The standard joke was that I, not Kirk, was a "dumb bastard." When the first fight I have with Kirk inside the planetoid originally happened, I actually took Kirk to the floor. Then he disarms me, because I'm not really a fighter—I'm a scientist and a scientist shouldn't be able to defend himself against an officer. My first line to him was, "You dumb bastard!" You see, we were still there on the satellite, we could hear the screams, so I think he's murdered my friends. So at the end of the film, Saavik comes to me and says, "So, you turned out to be the dumb bastard!" Quite literally, that was her way of saying "Hello!"

I like fantasy. I suppose I like that unexplainable edge to things. What I liked about the film was that it still held some of the original values, which in my mind are those of the old troopers coming to grips with aging, the new troopers growing up, etc. So it's still about people, not only about space or special effects.

BIBI BESCH
DR. CAROL MARCUS

An old joke about the original television series was that Captain Kirk would get a different woman every week. With The Wrath of Khan, *the audience can finally understand why. Dr. Carol Marcus, it turns out, is the mother of the Admiral's illegitimate son, David and it would seem that he has never been able to love anyone in quite the same way as he does her, so he went from one galactic bed to another. Film and television actress Bibi Besch brought Carol Marcus to life.*

You can't really approach it as doing an SF picture. You have to approach it as an acting assignment and try to make it believable. With doing *Star Trek*, it is a bit like a cartoon, but you can't play it like a cartoon.

[In terms of fitting in] I didn't do it as a counterpoint or contrast to how everybody else was. I brought it down to a very simple human level. I'm a scientist, I was a young scientist when this guy was a young cadet. I tried to make it as human as possible, rather than trying to fit into something that already was because this character hadn't existed before and I didn't really feel that I had to do that.

There was a little bit more about our relationship that didn't end up on the screen. But not much, really. It was sketchy to begin with. Sometimes, I think of my character as just a lot of exposition—a means of getting to the plotline. I would love to do a future *Star Trek* with a little more exploration.

It's difficult to play a woman who has had a relationship with someone that everybody knows. So I tried to make it believable for myself. I fantasized about an early affair and why it turned out the way it did. What kind of people we both became, how I got to be where I was, not just as a scientist but as a woman who wouldn't have told Kirk for all those years that he had a son.

STAR TREK IV: THE VOYAGE HOME
CATHERINE HICKS
DR. GILLIAN TAYLOR

Catherine Hicks, who also co-starred in Francis Ford Coppola's time-travel film Peggy Sue Got Married *and was featured in* Child's Play, *portrayed a 20th Century marine biologist in got mixed up with the Enterprise crew in* Star Trek IV.

I'm really proud of *Star Trek IV*, and that's coming from a non-*Trek* fan. I must have been on another channel as a kid. I've started watching the show since, and I'm getting a crush on Spock. But while we were shooting, I deliberately didn't rent the movies because I thought I would use my total ignorance of Gillian's character. She doesn't know what's going on either.

There aren't that many great roles written, and I liked the way they wrote Gillian. This was a good script with intelligence and structure. Many people who wouldn't put ears on would want to do this *Star Trek* film.

I was in the mood to play an intellect. I was due for my dose. I had played doctors, but not yet in the movies. I'm proud of my mind, I'm well educated. It's not a great mind, but it's a quick one. I also liked Gillian's sarcasm. Also, if I sense a character is a little lonely, then I want to keep her company. It's like, "Don't worry, I'm going to play you. I'll be your friend." I loved Gillian's line, "I have no one here," before she jumps into the transporter beam. I don't know why, it just touches me. It's poignant and sad. At the time, I didn't know it, but seeing the film, I realized that was my favorite line. My favorite moment, even though I'm not playing it, is when William Shatner as Kirk quotes D.H. Lawrence. Something comes across the ages. It's such a surprise that this man knows that—it makes us kindred spirits for one second.

I can understand the appeal of *Star Trek* because I found myself getting attached to these people. It's something about their warmth with each other, it kind of seeps into your heart. It's like a family. You want to see what happens to them. I'm starting to understand why they have this huge following. The *Star Trek* phenomenon couldn't happen to nicer people. Honestly, the cast is all touched with magic. I feel like we were in Oz together, and I'm glad that the magic wand touched them, because they're all good-hearted people.

STAR TREK V: THE FINAL FRONTIER
LAURENCE LUCKINBILL
SYBOK

One of the more surprising revelations of The Final Frontier *is that Mr. Spock has a half-brother named Sybok, who is the one that commandeers the Enterprise on a quest to meet God. Actor Laurence Luckinbill was given the*

task of—believably—portraying Spock's sibling.

Sybok is a very complex character. He's not a villain; quite the contrary, he's a dyed-in-the-wool good guy who basically goes a step too far in trying to make everybody in every galaxy experience God *his* way. To get a real handle on the character, I found myself asking many very basic questions, like what is religious experience and what is ambition?

He is a character who has a hold vision and is consumed with his wants and desires. That enormous drive and ambition is what I focused on in playing Sybok.

[The moment between Spock and Sybok] was your classic confrontation between brothers who had been apart for other than pleasant reasons. To be brothers and yet be at opposite ends of the pole can be a terrible thing.

I believe my character had a definite edge on Leonard's because Sybok, despite being from Spock's family and being a full-blooded Vulcan, was able to be both human and non-human and to basically go off-the-wall. In fact, it was Sybok's basic unpredictability that was the basis of the struggle between our characters. My character in this movie may have had the greater freedom, but I think what we discovered was that Spock's character may have encompassed the greater truth.

I'm not really sure if what happens at this film's end means I survive. At the end, I merge with this alien being who Sybok thinks is God. I don't think anybody is really sure whether Sybok is dead or not, so it's conceivable that I might wash up upon some shore in a future *Star Trek.*

STAR TREK VI: THE UNDISCOVERED COUNTRY
KIM CATTRALL
VALERIS

It had been the intention of writer/director Nicholas Meyer to bring back Lieutenant Saavik for The Undiscovered Country, *but when actress Kirstie Alley refused to reprise the role, the character was rewritten to a full Vulcan named Lieutenant Valeris, a protégé of Spock's who plays an integral role*

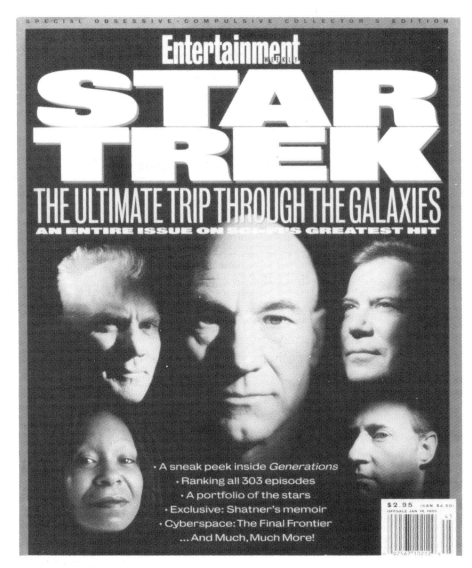

SPECIAL·OBSESSIVE·COMPULSIVE·COLLECTOR'S·EDITION

Entertainment

STAR TREK

THE ULTIMATE TRIP THROUGH THE GALAXIES
AN ENTIRE ISSUE ON SCI-FI'S GREATEST HIT

• A sneak peek inside *Generations*
• Ranking all 303 episodes
• A portfolio of the stars
• Exclusive: Shatner's memoir
• Cyberspace: The Final Frontier
...And Much, Much More!

$2.95 (CAN $4.50)
OFF-SALE JAN 18, 1995

in the film's proceedings.

I took the name Valeris from the Greek god Eris, the god of strife. We dropped the vowel because it sounded more Vulcan and I felt it was very much my own. She's a '90s *Star Trek* woman, she's complete. I don't think she's like the other women in *Star Trek* like in the '60s, where they were mostly beautiful women in great looking, tight outfits with fabulous make-up and hairdos. [They were] more set decoration instead of real motivators in the mechanics of plot.

I wanted a very definite Vulcan woman. I didn't want my hair just sort of swept back in some non-descript way. I wanted a bold look and make it very different from what had come before. I came into Nick after everything was settled and

said I want to have traces of Leonard [Nimoy], so I dyed my hair black and had it done very sort of '60s, and shaved my sideburns. I felt my ears would look much stronger because I have a very feminine face and I wanted to look very strong because I was a warrior.

[In] all the characters you play as an actor, there is some part of me that has to be in there because it's an expression of me. But for this role it was taking on a somewhat obscured view since I could not access the emotions that I could visually access for a character, since I'm playing an alien and I'm not reacting as Kim would react. It's much more separate from me and I had to rely on the right side of the brain much more than the left.

● ● ● ●

THESE WERE THE VOYAGES....

CAPTAINS' LOGS
THE COMPLETE TREK GUIDEBOOK

If you haven't picked up a copy of the indispensable TREK reference book, CAPTAINS' LOGS, you don't have the first — and last — word on the history of the future.

The Original CAPTAINS' LOGS features:

COMPLETE FPISODES GUIDES and OVERVIEWS w / credits and commentary from the actors, writers, producers and executives behind the entire TREK saga, including:

✷ TREK CLASSIC (Seasons 1 - 3, 79 Episodes)

✷ TREK: ANIMATED (Seasons 1 - 2, 22 Episodes)

✷ TREK: THE LOST YEARS
(The Unproduced '70s TREK SERIES)

✷ THE TREK FILMS
(from STAR TREK: THE MOTION PICTURE to THE UNDISCOVERED COUNTRY)

✷ THE NEXT GENERATION
(Seasons1- 5, 126 Episodes)

✷ DEEP SPACE NINE (The Pilot)

£13.99
ISBN 1 85283 899 X

● ● ● ●

WELCOME TO THE EDGE OF THE FINAL FRONTIER...

EXPLORING DEEP SPACE & BEYOND
The First Comprehensive Guide to the New Wave in Science-Fiction Television

This book chronicles the making of television's most important genre shows located on the outskirts of explored space. EXPLORING DEEP SPACE begins by looking at the history of space stations in science fact and fiction, followed by an indepth analysis of the creation of DEEP SPACE NINE.

Also lying on the fringes of the final frontier are Warner Bros'. BABYLON 5, a space station on which the five warring intergalactic federations come together in search of peace; and SPACE RANGERS, an ambitious action / adventure set in the cosmos from the creative team behind BACKDRAFT and ROBIN HOOD:PRINCE OF THIEVES.

Featured in this volume are:

✷ DEEP SPACE creators
Rick Berman and Michael Piller

✷ The cast of DEEP SPACE NINE
including Avery Brooks, Rene Auberjonois and Terry Farrell

✷ BABYLON 5 creator J. Michael Straczynski

✷ SPACE RANGERS creator Pen Densham

£6.99
ISBN 1 85283 571 0

EXPLORING DEEP SPACE

AND BEYOND

By Mark A. Altman and David Ian Solter

BOXTREE

HOW TO ORDER YOUR TREK TITLES FROM BOXTREE

1 85283 899 X	Captains' Logs	£13.99
1 85283 399 8	Captains' Logs Supplemental	£ 9.99
1 85293 340 8	Next Generation Technical Manual	£13.99
1 85283 571 0	Exploring Deep Space and Beyond	£ 6.99
1 85283 388 2	The Deep Space Logbook (First Season)	£ 9.99
1 85283 398 X	The Trek Universal Index	£ 9.99

All these books are available at your local bookshop or can be ordered direct from the publisher. Just tick the titles you want and fill in the form below.

Prices and availability subject to change without notice.

Boxtree Cash Sales, P.O. Box 11, Falmouth, Cornwall TR10 9EN

Please send cheque or postal order for the value of the book and add the following for postage and packing:

U.K. including B.F.P.O. £1.00 for one book, plus 50p for the second book, and 30p for each additional book ordered up to a £3.00 maximum.

Overseas including Eire – £2.00 for the first book, plus £1.00 for the second book, and 50p for each additional book ordered.

OR please debit this amount from my Access/Visa Card (delete as appropriate).

Card Number ☐☐☐☐☐☐☐☐☐☐☐☐☐☐☐☐

Amount £ ....

Expiry Date on Card ....

Signed ....

Name ....

Address ....

....